M

AMERICA BEYOND CAPITALISM

Reclaiming Our Wealth, Our Liberty, and Our Democracy

Gar Alperovitz

WILEY

John Wiley & Sons, Inc.

For Noah
and for his generation

Published by John Wiley & Sons, Inc., Hoboken, New Jersey
Published simultaneously in Canada

For general information about our other products and services, please contact our Customer Care Department within the United States at (800) 762-2974, outside the United States at (317) 572-3993 or fax (317) 572-4002.

Wiley also publishes its books in a variety of electronic formats. Some content that appears in print may not be available in electronic books. For more information about Wiley products, visit our web site at www.wiley.com.

Library of Congress Cataloging-in-Publication Data:

Alperovitz, Gar.
    America beyond capitalism : reclaiming our wealth, our liberty, and our democracy / Gar Alperovitz.
        p. cm.
    Includes index.
    ISBN 0-471-66730-7 (cloth)
1. Democracy–United States. 2. Income distribution–United States. 3. Wealth–United States. I. Title.
    JK1726.A428 2004
    330.973–dc22   2004003617

Printed in the United States of America

10 9 8 7 6 5 4 3 2 1

Contents

Preface

They called it "Black Monday"—the day in 1977 when five thousand workers at the Youngstown Sheet and Tube plant in Ohio were told the mill was going to close. An aggressive group of young steelworkers was dumbfounded. They had put their lives into the mill. Did this really have to happen? Gerald Dickey was the first to have the idea: "There are skills and men here who know how to make steel. Why don't we set this up as a company that we ourselves own—we could do it jointly with the community."

That was the start of a major fight. The religious community, led by the Catholic and Episcopal bishops, put together an ecumenical coalition. I was called in to help (some of the church leaders had read my work). With the support of a couple of creative government officials, we hired top steel industry experts to develop the kind of plan that is now common in successful steel operations.

Then something interesting happened—and we learned two fundamental things, which are at the heart of the following book:

First, the seemingly radical idea of the workers and the community owning and running a giant steel mill was hardly considered radical at all at the grassroots level. Indeed, the vast majority of the community, the local congressional delegation, both senators, and the conservative governor of Ohio, James Rhodes, supported it. The state prepared loan-guarantee and other legislation to back the effort. What made sense to ordinary Americans was far different from what many had thought.

The second lesson was equally important. For complicated reasons, Youngstown never got its mill.[1] However, the struggle to find a new way forward that began on Black Monday continued—and in many parts of Ohio (and elsewhere throughout the United States), worker-owned firms inspired by that initial fight are now commonplace. The second lesson is the lesson of commitment to the long haul.

I am a historian and a political economist. I have been a legislative director in both the U.S. House of Representatives and the U.S. Senate, as well as a high-level policy adviser in the Department of State. I was nominated by leading environmental, consumer, labor, and other national organizations to be a member of the Council of Economic Advisers. I have been a Fellow of Kings College, Cambridge University, of the Institute of Politics at Harvard, and of the Institute for Policy Studies in Washington. I worked with steelworkers in Youngstown and with the Mississippi Freedom Democratic Party and Martin Luther King Jr. at the 1964 Atlantic City Democratic National Convention. I am also a former anti–Vietnam War activist. And I am, lastly and importantly, someone who grew up in a medium-size Midwestern industrial city—Racine, Wisconsin.

I mention these personal facts to underscore several critical aspects of the lessons of Youngstown—and my reasons for writing a book that argues that it is not only necessary but possible to "change the system":

Though I am now a professor with all the usual academic trappings and degrees, I am not primarily an academic. What I have to say about political possibilities is informed, for better or worse, by some rather hardheaded real-world experiences—especially concerning difficult longer-term change. Here are four examples:

First, when I worked in the Senate in the early 1960s it was for Gaylord Nelson—the founder of Earth Day. The idea that environmental issues might one day become important in America seemed far-fetched then. Everyone *knew* this was a nonstarter. I witnessed close at hand the rise from "nowhere" of what once had been called "conservation" to become the "environmental movement." I view current setbacks and political obstacles with a certain historical sense of the possible, and I view long-run change coming "out of nowhere" as always—minimally!—conceivable (whether the powers that be like it or not).

Second, I recall, vividly and personally, the days in 1965 and 1966 when virtually the entire leadership structure of the nation supported the Vietnam War. The president and the Congress (with only a tiny handful of exceptions), most of the press, and most of the corporate and labor leaders all thought the war right (or at least did not oppose it). In 1965 and 1966 even Martin Luther King refused to challenge the Johnson administration directly on the war.[2] I also recall that, contrary to those who said nothing could be done, slowly and steadily a citizens' movement built power and momentum until the war was stopped.

Third, way back when—in my early days in Wisconsin—Senator Joseph McCarthy of our state dominated politics, both nationally and locally. "They shot anything that moved politically," people used to say. Fear dominated every suggestion that progressive ideas might be put forward. Anyone who thought otherwise was obviously foolish. But of course, what came next was the 1960s. Both those who lament and those who cheer the passing of the 1960s era of activism often read history as if things ended in the 1970s. My reading—from the perspective of Wisconsin in the McCarthy-dominated 1950s—is that those who say that nothing can be done because reactionaries control everything simply do not recall or do not know how impossible the world felt *before* the "unexpected" explosions of the 1960s.

Fourth, my personal memories also include the way the civil rights movement developed "out of nowhere"—or so it then seemed—to challenge the oppression that was the

American South. The idea that nothing could be done was also rampant in the pre-1960s South—and there it was enforced not simply by reactionary politicians willing to blacklist anyone who spoke up. It was enforced by deadly terror: blacks—and even some white Americans—were murdered for demanding their basic rights. (As a young Senate aide, I drove through Mississippi with civil rights activist Bob Moses, followed at every turn by armed state troopers; the poor farmers we stayed with kept a shotgun by the door.) Those who tell me the opposition to change, now, is so great that nothing can be done would do well to read just a bit about what it was like before the civil rights movement *was* a movement.[3]

One final recollection—this one not so close at hand but nonetheless vivid in my life experience as well. Most people forget how marginal conservative thinkers and activists were in the 1950s—and even after the Goldwater debacle of 1964. The ideas and politics that currently dominate American reality once were regarded as antique and ridiculous by the mainstream press, political leadership, and most of serious academic thought. Committed conservatives worked in very difficult circumstances to develop their ideas and practices and politics for the long haul—and though I disagree with them, they, too, have demonstrated what can be done against seemingly long odds.

If you think I am recalling these various experiences and old war stories to suggest that even the most daunting political obstacles can often be overcome by those who are serious, you are right. I am, however, no utopian. I think it is entirely possible that, like Rome, the U.S. empire will fail and decay. Or that our domestic and international troubles will lead to violence and the suppression of what remains of American liberties. Indeed, as I shall suggest, at best I think things are likely to get worse before they get better. I note, however, that Chile has survived even Pinochet. Those who view things historically understand that the challenge is always to build to and through even the worst difficulties.

The American Revolution itself stands as a reminder of how the then most powerful empire in the world could be challenged. (The signers of the Declaration of Independence, we do well to recall, did so knowing that if they failed, they would be hung for treason.)

This book argues that the only way for the United States to once again honor its great historic values—above all equality, liberty, and meaningful democracy—is to build forward to achieve what amounts to systemic change. I shall explain what I mean in due course, but here let me note that fundamental change—indeed, radical systemic change—is as common as grass in world history. It may be that history has stopped in the United States circa 2004, but I doubt it. The lessons of Youngstown have been reinforced by the experiences I have cited—above all, that what seems radical is often common sense at the grassroots level and that a commitment to the long haul is the only way to test what might really be possible.

One other lesson is important: serious ideas count. Moreover, people understand and respect serious ideas. Here I again honor committed, thoughtful conservatives (as distinct from right-wing ideologues who use ideas to bludgeon the opposition). Though I disagree with the writings of men like Russell Kirk, Henry C. Simons, and Friedrich A. Hayek, I respect their commitment to developing tough-minded theory—and their understanding that this is critical to the development of a truly meaningful politics.

We often ignore this truth, thinking that what counts is "the message" or "how issues are framed" for public consumption. What ultimately counts is a coherent and powerful understanding of what makes sense, and why—and how what makes sense can be achieved in the real world. By "coherent" I mean rigorous intellectually as well as politically.

Some feel that ordinary Americans are uninterested in ideas or cannot understand them. I disagree. Historically it is not only thoughtful conservatives who have shown that ideas count but, in other eras and other times—whether one agrees or disagrees—Marxists and liberation theologians as well. And Americans at the time of the Revolution. And feminist theorists from Seneca Falls on. The lesson here is that it is time to roll up our sleeves and get serious about the intellectual work that needs to be done if an effort to achieve fundamental change is ever to succeed. We need to ask ourselves the following questions:

If the current political-economic system is no longer able to sustain equality, liberty, and meaningful democracy, what specifically do we want? And why, specifically, should anyone expect what we want to be any better than what we now have? And how, specifically, might what we propose deal with the everyday problems now facing most Americans? And finally, even if we can say what "system" would be better, why, specifically, do we think it might be attainable in the real world?

As I said, I am no utopian. Why in the world should anybody want to support a movement for serious change that does not attempt to give straight and tough answers to such obvious questions? My book, I hope, will help stimulate more tough-minded discussion of such matters.

Although this book is not explicitly about the war in Iraq (or the war on terrorism), I also hope it will help us reach to some of the underlying structural relationships—and issues of democratic decision making—that have allowed the over-militarization of U.S. foreign policy. I have previously written a great deal on foreign policy and military matters.[4] This work attempts to go deeper—to the structural foundations of the system that permit the kinds of policies that so endanger the modern world.

Quite apart from any particular book, I believe there is a real hunger for new thinking among many Americans. Indeed, it would not surprise me—given the growing pain and frustration—if in the coming decades, we were to experience something like the Federalist debates of the founding era—a time of great and historic public rethinking of fundamentals. It may well be that the intellectual (as well as political) debates that antiglobalization activists have helped initiate are the opening guns in such a national dialogue.

The first sections of this work offer an introduction to critical ideas about what it takes to sustain equality, liberty, and democracy—the kind of ideas that in recent years modern political and economic theorists have been developing and refining in their books and articles. (Part I of the book is also an invitation to continue the effort, to go further.) And it is an invitation to plain speech. The great Russian writer Leo Tolstoy is reputed to have warned fellow intellectuals that "if you can't explain it to an ordinary peasant, that is your problem, not theirs."

I might add that this better be the case if we are talking about ideas for a democracy! The Americans I grew up with in Racine, Wisconsin, are damn tough-minded. They can more than handle ideas about how really to achieve equality, liberty, and democracy—if the ideas are presented in ordinary English. They are no different in this respect from millions of others, historically in this nation and around the world, who have decided to get serious about things that count.

The question is not the capacity of citizens to understand. It is not even whether writers and thinkers take the time to explain themselves. What opens people to making the effort is that they are forced to abandon the pose that politics doesn't matter, and that ideas are irrelevant. Two final personal experiences are instructive in this regard—both from the time of the Vietnam War.

The first involved a meeting in Massachusetts and a government official who had been sent out to calm the opposition. This once had been an easy task; the rationale for the Vietnam War went largely unchallenged for many years. What stands out in memory, however, was a housewife at this meeting, challenging the official—and backing him down, step by step—on each point of fact, of law, and of history involved. She had simply decided it was time to get to work and master for herself the politics and the underlying intellectual rationale.

The second was my first experience knocking on doors with a young activist at the time. At the first stop, the person who answered the door hesitated and then said, "I'm against the war, but no one else is on this block." At the second, third, and many more stops, almost the same words were spoken in almost the same way. The reality, of course, was that far more people agreed—and ultimately triumphed—than anyone imagined at the outset or in their own isolation (including our own).

My heroes are the people who fought for civil rights in Mississippi in the 1930s and 1940s—when the struggle that laid the groundwork for what came later was undertaken by individuals whose names few now remember. That was when the real work was done.

Acknowledgments

This book represents years of learning and reflection to which many, many people have contributed. My profound thanks, and my acknowledgment of their contributions, goes to them.

First, to four central figures in my life from the past, long gone: my parents, Emily and Julius Alperovitz, who taught me about the meaning of community in our Midwestern town; and to two teachers, William Appleman Williams and Joan Robinson, who taught me something of how to understand one's own time and place and responsibility in history and with respect to different political-economic systems.

Second, to five younger colleagues who worked hard as friends and assistants to make this book a reality: Alex Campbell, Joe Guinan, Brendan Leary, Preston Quesenberry, and Thad Williamson. Thanks to my editor, Eric Nelson, and to Kimberly Monroe-Hill, who helped give that reality clarity and precision. Special thanks to Jeff Chapman for help with data issues.

Third, to a diverse group of colleagues, friends, research assistants, interns, and students who over the years contributed insights and other important help: Robert Ashford, Dean Baker, Ben Barber, Matt Berres, Angela Blackwell, David Binns, Sam Bowles, Bob Brandwein, Pierre Clavel, David Cohen, Neil Cohen, Ken Conca, Ann Crittenden, Lew Daly, Christian Davenport, Steve Dubb, Lee Ebersole, Steve Elkin, David Ellerman, Jeff Faux, Mark Fraley, Bill Galston, Jordan Gans-Morse, Stephanie Geller, Teresa Ghilarducci,

Laura Gilliam, Christopher Gunn, Leon Howell, Nien-hê Hsieh, David Imbroscio, Christopher Jencks, Carrie Johnson, Michael Jones, Karen Kaufmann, Alexandra Kogl, Dave and Fran Korten, Hany Khalil, Ann Ladd, John Logue, Ying Lou, Christopher Mackin, Jane Mansbridge, Enrique Martinez-Vidal, Claire Morgan, Ian Murray, Dawn Nakano, Katharine Nelson, Bertell Ollman, Avery Ouellette, Ronald Phillips, Jeff Pope, Louis Putterman, Nikhil Raval, Tom Ricker, Jeremy Rifkin, Kristin Rusch, Mary Saville, Adria Scharf, Miranda Scheurs, Juliet Schor, Jerome Segal, Todd Swanstrom, Jennifer Thangevalu, Sanho Tree, Eric Uslaner, Avis Vidal, Marcus Weiss, Jonathan Wilkenfeld, Linda Williams, Edward Wolff, Donn Worgs, and Jordan Yin.

Fourth, to philanthropists and friends in the foundation world who have helped make the sustained effort that went into this work possible: Smith Bagley, Anne Bartley, Hodding Carter III, Tom Cohen, Dayna Cunningham, Michael Edwards, the late W. H. "Ping" and Carol Ferry, Lisa Fuentes, Archibald Gillies, Robert Giloth, Peter Goldmark, Wade Greene, Charlie Halpern, Chet Hewitt, the late David Hunter and Barbara Hunter, the late Jane Lehman, Lance Lindblom, Julia Lopez, David Maurasse, Bernard "B" Rapoport, Jan Philipp Reemtsma, Roger and Vicki Sant, Gail and Jonathan Schorsch, Susan Sechler, Adele Simmons, Ed Skloot, the late Philip Stern, and Cora and Peter Weiss. And, above all, to my friends Patricia Bauman and John Bryant who have been there with encouragement and support through all the difficult, long years. Thanks also to the following institutions that have contributed in one way or another to the work that led to this book: the Arca Foundation, the Bauman Foundation, the Annie E. Casey Foundation, the Nathan Cummings Foundation, the Ford Foundation, the Hamburg Institut für Sozial forschung, the John S. and James L. Knight Foundation, the John D. and Catherine T. MacArthur Foundation, the Bernard and Audre Rapoport Foundation, the Rockefeller Foundation, the Samuel Rubin Foundation, the Summit Foundation, the Surdna Foundation, and the Stern Family Fund.

Fifth, to people close and dear to me—for their sustaining support, love, friendship, and insights: my children, David and Kari, and their partners, Joanna and Jamie. And to four wonderful friends—Ron Goldfarb, Bernd Greiner, Ted Howard, and Marc Raskin—who have been strong and true through both the ups and downs over the years.

Finally, to my wife, Sharon, for all the reasons, and with all my love.

Introduction

How do we detect when a society is in trouble—*real* trouble? What canary in the coal mine signals danger? The real signs of major trouble are to be found not only in huge deficits, unemployment, even terrorism. The time to pay close attention is when people begin to lose belief in things that once mattered profoundly—like the most important values that have given meaning to American history from the time of the Declaration of Independence: *equality, liberty,* and *democracy.*

The long trends are ominous: the beginning point of the following study is the painful truth that there is now massive evidence that for decades Americans have been steadily becoming *less* equal, *less* free, and *less* the masters of their own fate.

The top 1 percent now garners for itself more income each year than the bottom 100 million Americans combined. Even before the war on terrorism produced new threats to civil liberties, the United States (as a conservative judge, Richard Posner, has observed) criminalized "more conduct than most, maybe than any, non-Islamic nations."[1]

And repeated studies have shown the majority of Americans know full well that something challenging and fundamental is going on with "democracy": Four out of five in a recent assessment judged that "[g]overnment leaders say and do anything to get elected, then do whatever they want." Another study found that seven out of ten felt that "people like me have almost no say in the political system."[2]

1

We tend to dismiss such signs of trouble. Most political debate focuses on who wins this or that election or on immediate problems like medical costs, tax cuts, unemployment. Some writers sense that something deeper is at work—that, for instance, with the radical decline of labor unions and the rise of the global corporation, the balance of power between labor and corporations that once kept U.S. politics within a certain range simply no longer operates. (The administration of George W. Bush in significant part reflects this shift in underlying institutional power.)

A few have recognized that we face even more fundamental questions. Thus Kevin Phillips writes of a new American "plutocracy" in which wealth "reach[es] beyond its own realm" to control political power and government at all levels.[3] Robert Kaplan suggests that we are moving in the direction of a regime that could "resemble the oligarchies of ancient Athens and Sparta." He believes: "How and when we vote during the next hundred years may be a minor detail for historians."[4]

But the idea that the American "system" as a whole is in real trouble—that it is heading in a direction that spells the end of its historic values—*that* idea is difficult, indeed all but impossible, for most people to grasp.

It is, however, the first major contention—or rather, observation—at the core of this study. Moreover, as we shall see, though the evidence is rarely confronted, it is a contention that is not at all difficult to support. Indeed, it is obvious to most people when they reflect on the long-developing trends in connection with equality, liberty, and democracy.

If the critical values lose meaning, politics obviously must also ultimately lose moral integrity. Cynicism, apathy, and a sense that the powerful control, no matter what, must grow until, finally, recognition that current political processes are at a dead end quietly becomes endemic. The polls already indicate that beneath a patina of conventional political concern, the basic elements of such an understanding are not far off.

Beyond this, if equality, liberty, and meaningful democracy can truly no longer be sustained by the political and economic arrangements of the current system, this defines the beginning phases of what can only be called a *systemic* crisis—an era of history in which the political-economic system must slowly lose legitimacy because the realities it produces contradict the values it proclaims.

Moreover, if the system itself is at fault, then self-evidently—indeed, *by definition*—a solution would ultimately require the development of a new system.

For most Americans the idea that a "different system" might be possible is something very few have considered. With the collapse of the Soviet Union—and the decline of older, more democratic visions of socialism—what, specifically, would it mean to "change the system"?

Furthermore, the United States today is the most powerful political-economic system in world history. To most Americans, the notion that ways might ultimately be found to transform the institutions at its very core seems utterly utopian and impractical—even if one had an idea of what an alternative system might entail.

The conventional wisdom, of course, leaves us at a dead end. The old ways don't work, but no one even imagines the possibility of systemic change.

Or so it seems.

The fact is, just below the surface level of media attention, theorists, policy makers, and informed citizens have been generating an extraordinary range of new ideas in recent decades. As we shall see, these suggest that traditional economic and political strategies are not the only ways, institutionally, to secure equality, liberty, and democracy.[5]

The appeal of many of these ideas, moreover, reaches across traditional left-right political divisions. They deal in a thoroughgoing way with matters ranging from the local and mundane to the radical and systemic—including: How to build democracy with a small d in each community as a basis, ultimately, of rebuilding Democracy with a big D in the system as a whole. How, as technology advances, to ensure that people have enough free time and security to have real rather than illusory freedom of choice. And how—the ultimate and most important issue—the vast wealth of the nation can be managed so as to directly democratize its benefits.

Even now, as we shall also see, the most interesting new approaches suggest the outlines of a radically different system-wide political-economic model. Furthermore, the quietly intensifying crisis itself is forcing ever greater understanding—and it is producing (and promises continually to produce) ever more refined clarifications of the basic ideas.

That this has begun to occur should not be surprising. In general, when traditional ways no longer work, people are forced to rethink what they have been doing. We often do not stand back from our current moment in history to reflect on the simple fact that this might also be happening here and now, and as time goes on, in our own society.

Even if it were possible to bring together the emerging new thinking to define the outlines of a system that might in principle be able to sustain equality, liberty, and democracy—and do so in ways better than either U.S. capitalism or its traditional socialist rival—could such an exercise ever have meaning in the real world of politics?

It is, of course, theoretically possible that nothing major will ever change in the United States—but it is also highly unlikely. Serious historians understand—indeed, take for granted—that political-economic systems come and go over time, and that the current American system is probably not the be-all and end-all of world development.

To grant the simple possibility that the present system, like others in history, might one day be transformed opens a certain perspective on possibilities both for the coming century and for its opening decades. The tendency of those who think about systemic change is commonly toward abstraction. Words like "revolution" appear often in traditional writing. This, however, is only one way to think about structural change. It is striking that—again, just below the surface of most media concern—there has also been an extraordinary explosion of practical real-world economic and political experimentation in the United States that ties in with (and points in the direction of) some of the main features of the new system-oriented ideas.

Systemic change above all involves questions of how property is owned and controlled—the locus of real power in most political economies. The ownership of wealth in the United States is more concentrated even than income: the richest 1 percent of American households are now estimated to own half of all outstanding stock, financial securities, trust equity, and business equity!*6 At the heart of the new thinking is a different principle—that the ownership of wealth must benefit the vast majority directly. Especially interesting, accordingly, is the evidence assembled in the following pages of long-developing trends that have produced thousands of new worker-owned firms, community-owned enterprises, even state and national examples of alternative ways wealth might be owned to benefit small and large publics.

In Newark, New Jersey, a nonprofit neighborhood corporation employs two thousand people to build and manage housing and help run a supermarket and other businesses that funnel profits back into health care, job creation, education, and other community services. In Glasgow, Kentucky, the city runs a quality cable, telephone, and Internet service at costs far lower than commercial rivals. In Harrisonburg, Virginia, a highly successful company owned by the employees makes and sells cable television testing equipment. In Alabama the state pension fund owns a major interest in many large and small businesses. In Alaska every state resident as a matter of right receives dividends from a fund that invests oil revenues on behalf of the public at large.

---

* This is an overall national figure. The most recently available data register median black financial wealth at a mere 3 percent of non-Hispanic white financial wealth. "Changes in Household Wealth in the 1980s and 1990s in the U.S.," in *International Perspectives on Household Wealth*, ed. Edward N. Wolff (Elgar Publishing Ltd., forthcoming).

The emerging changes in these and hundreds (indeed, thousands) of other related instances involve new institutions—and the process of change is different from that which we commonly understand in connection both with traditional politics and traditional systemic change. Typically, political *reform* involves *policies* that improve or clean up around the edges of existing systems. Typically, *revolution* involves changing the *institutions* at the core of the system, often violently. What is happening in several key areas involves the steady building of a mosaic of entirely different institutions but in a manner that is both peaceful and evolutionary.

Even a very widespread evolutionary build-up of new local and state institutions, of course, would be a far cry from system-wide restructuring. I believe, however, that such developments may have significant implications beyond their immediate impact. Importantly, they are exploring principles of ownership in everyday life that have broader applications at other levels. The deeper question explored in the following pages is whether the emerging political-economic context might open the way to building upon and beyond the new ideas, on the one hand, and upon the emerging trajectory of practical institutional development, on the other.

The election of candidates committed to the key values might—or might not—lead to modest gains in the short term. Given the underlying pressures constraining traditional politics, however, those who have faced the issue squarely know that even when better candidates win office, serious change is unlikely following any currently feasible political strategies.

On the other hand, the social and economic pain that is now hitting Americans at virtually every level is also increasingly confronting diverse groups with ever more severe choices. In case after case, the converging viselike pressure of events is forcing new questions.

Either at some point a new strategic approach will have to be found, or issues of central importance to workers and to ethnic, racial, elderly, gender, family, and other constituencies on both the left and the right are likely to become increasingly and profoundly compromised. The growing pain levels point to the likelihood, ultimately, of a backlash—especially as the pressures the Bush era has unleashed continue to hit home.

Furthermore, the growing national fiscal crisis inevitably forces attention to the extraordinary income and wealth controlled by elites and major corporations. Quite apart from matters of equity, there are very few other places to look for resources. With the decline of traditional twentieth-century progressive strategies, a new and more militant "twenty-first-century populism," which targets those who control the lion's share of the nation's income and wealth, is already beginning to take shape. Far-reaching ethnic and demographic changes—and the coming minority status of non-Hispanic whites—are likely to reinforce the pressures leading to change as the twenty-first century unfolds.

The trajectory that points toward an ever more sharply focused challenge to corporations and elite concentrations of income and wealth, moreover, is beginning to converge, even now, with the developing trajectory of change defining a host of alternative institutions in which wealth ownership benefits the public directly—and in which community-based democratic practice is important.

It is quite possible—even probable—that life in the United States will get worse before it gets better (if it gets better) in the coming decades. We are likely to experience profoundly challenging times. Even in an era focused narrowly on issues of terrorism and war, however, large-order, longer-term change is rarely precluded. There are reasonable possibilities in the coming period of history (as in most periods of history) for much more fundamental change—building to and through the difficulties—than many conventionally hold.

There have been five major political realignments over the course of U.S. history—from before the Civil War to the Progressive era and beyond. Each has occurred in the face of arguments that nothing of great political significance was feasible. Further realignments over the course of the twenty-first century are not only possible but likely. The question is what they might entail and how far-reaching they might ultimately become.[7]

PART I

THE PLURALIST COMMONWEALTH

Equality, Liberty, Democracy

WE OFTEN FORGET THAT IT was once simply assumed the United States would move inevitably in the direction of ever greater equality. A 1963 *American Economic Review* article observed that "most recent studies" of U.S. economic history take for granted that "since the end of the depression the nation's wealth has been redistributed and prosperity has been extended to the vast majority." A respected group of researchers declared, "The United States has arrived at the point where poverty could be abolished easily and simply by a stroke of the pen." The title of an important book by the liberal economist John Kenneth Galbraith proclaimed the "Affluent Society."[1]

Such assumptions now appear strange, indeed, unreal. Statistical studies show growing, not diminishing, inequality. Writers like Galbraith have been forced to a radical reassessment: "Alas, I am not nearly as optimistic now as then. . . . [T]hose who dismiss the pro-affluent movement of these past years as a temporary departure from some socially concerned norm are quite wrong."[2]

9

Compensation of the ten most highly paid CEOs averaged $3.5 million a year in 1981. By 1988 it had jumped to $19.3 million. By 2000 it was $154 million—an increase over this period of 4,300 percent.[3]

In 1948 Nobel laureate Paul Samuelson had attempted to illustrate the extent of inequality in his popular economics textbook with the following example: "If we made . . . an income pyramid out of a child's play blocks with each layer portraying $1,000 of income, the peak would be far higher than the Eiffel Tower, but almost all of us would be within a yard of the ground."[4]

By the closing years of the century, Samuelson found that the Eiffel Tower no longer adequately expressed the orders of magnitude involved. He replaced it with Mount Everest.[5]

Another troubled economist, Lester Thurow, wrote, "No country not experiencing a revolution or a military defeat with a subsequent occupation has probably ever had as rapid or as widespread an increase in inequality as has occurred in the United States in the past two decades."[6]

Consider an even deeper problem: "As American democratic institutions begin their third century," political scientist Robert Putnam observes, "a sense is abroad in the land that our national experiment in self-government is faltering."[7] Quite fundamental forces have also undermined the experience of democracy for millions of Americans—and again what is striking and profoundly worrisome is the trend.

In the 1960s roughly two out of three regularly told pollsters they believed government was run "for the benefit of all." Asked in 1999, "Would you say the government is pretty much run by a few big interests looking out for themselves, or that it is run for the benefit of all the people," a mere 19 percent said that it is run for all. Fully 75 percent now felt that government was run for the benefit of special interests.[8]

Voting—one bottom-line test of democracy—also declined dramatically. In the 1960 presidential election more than three out of five of those eligible voted; only slightly more than half did so in 2000. Less than 40 percent now bother to participate in congressional elections (understandably, since partisan redistricting has made almost 400 of the 435 seats in the House of Representatives all but impossible to contest!).[9]

An angry Republican senator, John McCain, describes the American political system as "an elaborate influence-peddling scheme in which both parties conspire to stay in office by selling the country to the highest bidder."[10]

Another obvious source of the "democratic deficit" is the enormous power of giant corporations. Careful academics, like the former president of the American Political Science Association, Charles Lindblom, put the point this way: "It is the large enterprises that pose obstructions to political democracy. Through their spending and relations with government officials they exercise much more power than do citizens. . . . [This is] a mammoth violation of the political equality deemed necessary for genuine rather than spurious democracy."[11]

Another political scientist, Carl Boggs, is less restrained: "[T]he largest corporations are able to dominate virtually every phase of economic, political, and cultural life; they set the agenda for nearly every dimension of public policy."[12]

Democracy's steady decline, theorist Michael Sandel laments, is ultimately evidenced in "a widespread sense that we are caught in the grip of impersonal structures of power that defy our understanding and control."[13]

Finally, consider the matter of liberty.

At the most obvious level, the war on terrorism has brought extraordinary threats to traditional American liberties. Georgetown University law professor David Cole writes: "Secrecy has become the order of the day. Criminal proceedings are governed by gag orders—themselves secret—preventing defendants or their lawyers from saying anything to the public about their predicament. . . . The Patriot Act authorizes never-disclosed wiretaps and secret searches in criminal investigations without probable cause of a crime, the bedrock constitutional predicate for any search."[14]

Nor is this the worry only of liberals. An angry conservative, William Safire, charges, "Intimidated by terrorists and inflamed by a passion for rough justice, we are letting George W. Bush get away with the replacement of the American rule of law with military kangaroo courts."[15] Safire goes on, "These used to be the Great Unwatched, free people conducting their private lives; now they are under close surveillance by hundreds of hidden cameras. . . . This is not some alarmist Orwellian scenario; it is here, now, financed by $20 billion last year and $15 billion more this year of federal money appropriated out of sheer fear."[16]

Fear of crime also has fueled what the African American columnist, the late Carl Rowan, termed a "wild zeal" to guarantee personal safety and the willingness of many judges to countenance a "retreat from our historic protection of civil liberties and privacy rights." In 2002 one in eight black men age twenty to thirty-four was in prison or jail.[17]

For serious conservatives, liberty inherently requires small government, but here the underlying structural trends are also daunting. Not only is government big, but even when Republicans have been elected there is little evidence that its basic scale can be significantly altered. Indeed, government increased as a share of the economy during each of the first years of the George W. Bush presidency—from 18.6 percent in fiscal year 2001 to an estimated 20.2 percent in fiscal year 2004. "For those who cherish individual liberty and a free society," political economist Robert Higgs observes, "the prospect is deeply disheartening."[18]

Liberty in traditional conservative thought also depends on maintaining the underlying institutions of free-market capitalism—above all the independence, culture, and energy of the entrepreneur. The entrepreneur once did play a central role in the system—but this was more than a hundred years ago. Today roughly 90 percent of working Americans are employees—a very different kind of individual.[19]

A society can continue for a very substantial period along a path characterized by ever greater divergence between the core values and ideals that give it legitimacy and the institutions and practices that create and constitute the everyday realities its citizens experience. Plausibly, a society could continue indefinitely on such a course—though clearly, cynicism and apathy would result, and at some point increasingly serious demands for change most likely would be heard.

It would be surprising, however, if some of its most serious thinkers did not attempt to reassess the relationship between traditional theories and values, on the one hand, and politics, strategies, and underlying institutions, on the other.

Indeed, a steadily developing rethinking is now evident among individuals and groups on all sides of the traditional political divide—left, right, and center.

1

Equality

Beyond Tax-and-Spend

For two decades economists concerned with inequality have debated the precise role global competition, changing technologies, sectoral balances, and other strictly economic factors have played in generating the worsening trends. Whatever the final resolution of the technical debate over how much weight to assign different forces, the important truth, as Barry Bluestone points out, is that none shows "the least sign of weakening."[1]

Accordingly, what is of truly fundamental concern for those who care about equality has been the collapse of the *political*-economic strategies it once was hoped might counter the deepening trends.

And the central question is whether there are any other ways forward, even in theory.

The evolving progressive reassessment begins with a cold appraisal of the reasons traditional approaches no longer work. There is very little doubt about what has happened to undermine liberal redistributive strategies.

First and foremost has been the radical decline of America's labor unions. Always weak in comparison with other advanced nations, peacetime U.S. union membership peaked at 34.7 percent of the labor force in the mid-1950s; it was a mere 12.9 percent in 2003 (8.2 percent in the private sector). The downward trend is all but certain to continue; responsible estimates suggest union membership in the private sector may sink below 5 percent by 2020.[2]

The decline obviously weakens union bargaining power over wages. Far more important, however, is that historically labor's political power has played a central role in the passage of social legislation and redistributive programs. "The political conse-quences of high levels of unionization are . . . straightforward," political scientist Michael Wallerstein observes. "[O]ther things being equal, union movements representing a large share of voters are better able to influence policy."[3] Through-out the Western world, many studies show, greater unioniza-tion has been one of the best predictors of greater equality.[4]

Labor has been the most important countervailing force (partly) offsetting conservative political power throughout much of the twentieth century. As labor has continued to decline, the way has been opened to a series of aggressive cor-porate and other campaigns that have challenged redistributive programs of all kinds—first by the Reagan administration, then by the Gingrich Congress, now by the Bush administration.[5]

The globalization of economic activity also has played a role, and it has increased the already enormous power of the large corporation economically and politically. Globalization brings with it ever expanding opportunities for relocation to other countries—and this adds to corporate leverage and the capacity to threaten departure unless demands are met. Business in turn has used its increased bargaining power to win concessions from labor.[6]

Worldwide competition for investment has added to the pressures, forcing government to reduce business tax rates, shifting more of the burden to low- and moderate-income earners. Globalization thereby also implicitly reduces the capacity of governments to spend on redistributive social programs. In 1945 corporate income taxes amounted to 35.4 percent of federal receipts. By 2003—as labor's political power decreased, as corporate power increased, and as glob-alization proceeded—such taxes had fallen to 7.4 percent of federal receipts. More than three-fifths of U.S. corporations paid no federal taxes at all in each of the years between 1996 and 2000![7]

The post–World War II social, economic, and cultural concentration of suburban political power and the urban exodus of the post-1960s decades have brought additional difficulties. Increasingly the largely white suburban middle class is simply no longer willing to pay for a progressive political agenda it believes will mainly benefit the black and Hispanic poor. At the same time, racial and ethnic divisions have weakened the capacity of the majority to unite behind redistributive measures.

Thomas and Mary Edsall document the radical implications in their book *Chain Reaction:* "Just as race was used, between 1880 and 1964, by the planter-textile-banking elite of the South to rupture class solidarity at the bottom of the income ladder . . . race as a national issue over the past twenty-five years [broke] the Democratic New Deal 'bottom-up' coalition. . . . The fracturing of the Democrats' 'bottom-up' coalition permitted, in turn, those at the top of the 'top-down' conservative coalition to encourage and to nurture . . . what may well have been the most accelerated upwards redistribution of income in the nation's history."[8]

Finally, we may add the rise of the post-1970s Republican South—a change that has added force to each of the key factors and to conservative politics in general. By 1994—for the first time in modern history—Republicans constituted a majority of the Southern delegation in both the Senate and the House of Representatives. The new form of racialized Southern politics, political scientist Augustus B. Cochran III points out, inevitably produced "policies that favor political and economic elites to the disadvantage of the vast majority of average citizens."*[9]

---

* Michael Lind goes further: George W. Bush's Texas "is a toxic by-product of the hierarchical plantation society of the American South, a cruel caste society in which the white, brown, and black majority labor for inadequate rewards while a cultivated but callous oligarchy of rich white families and their hirelings in the professions

Taking the various factors together, in fact, provides only a minimal estimate of the unfavorable prospects for traditional strategies aimed at reversing growing inequality—for several additional reasons.

First, there is very little evidence that inequality-related trends have ever been significantly altered because of progressive political strategies per se—that is, efforts to enact reforms in normal, noncrisis times. Inequality has been significantly reduced in the twentieth century mainly as a result of major crises like the Great Depression (which spurred unusual political and policy change), and in the context of war-related conditions that produced a special policy environment, tight labor markets, and a compressed wage structure (especially World War II but also, in other ways, the boom years of the Cold War, including the Korea and Vietnam wars). Even in the best of times, the capacity of traditional political strategies to achieve major impact on their own in "normal" circumstances has been far weaker than many commonly acknowledge.[10]

Second, a close examination of traditional conventional measures makes it obvious that on its current path, *real* inequality will continue to worsen, no matter what. Most academic discussions of inequality are based on relative assessments. While useful for many purposes, such measures mask important relationships—especially of absolute political-economic power, and of cultural and social differences. If you have $1,000 and I have $50,000 this year, and next year you have $2,000 and I have $100,000, the relative measures widely used in conventional reporting will indicate that there has been no increase in inequality because the ratio of 1-to-50 is unchanged. However, absolute inequality—the real-world difference between us—obviously has gone from $49,000 to $98,000.

---

dominate the economy, politics and the rarefied air of academic and museum culture." Michael Lind, *Made in Texas: George W. Bush and the Southern Takeover of American Politics* (New York: Basic Books, 2003), p. 160.

The *absolute* income gap between the top 5 percent and the bottom 20 percent exploded from $191,800 in 1979 to $419,700 in 2000 (in 2000 dollars).[11]

Contributing to both the relative and absolute trends during much of the final quarter of the twentieth century was the fact that hourly wages of the bottom 60 percent did not rise as fast as inflation—with the result that the real income each person earned, hour by hour, was actually lower in 1995 than in 1973. For very large numbers of Americans, the only reason total family income rose—very modestly—was that people worked longer hours and/or spouses (mainly wives) went to work in increasing numbers.[12]

Put another way: unless they worked more hours or someone else in the family went to work during these years, many would have been better off if the economy had simply stood still at the 1973 level. Economic growth not only did not increase the real pay that an hour of work earned, it brought with it price increases that reduced real income.[13]

We also appear to be reaching a limit of those who can add to family income. The percent of wives working rose from 28.5 percent in 1955 to 42.3 percent in 1973 to 61 percent in 2002. Though spouses will provide a continuing contribution to family income, nothing like the qualitative shift that occurred during the second half of the twentieth century is ever likely to occur again.[14]

Traditional redistributive political strategies which aim to deal with inequality are based on what are sometimes called "after-the-fact" methods. It is accepted that capitalist economic systems as a matter of course produce highly unequal distributions of income. It is hoped that "after the fact"— after the basic income flows have been generated—progressive taxation, combined with various social programs, can alter the underlying patterns.

No one would deny the possibility of some future tax changes, but there has long been little expectation that significant after-the-fact approaches for dealing with inequality can be revived—even before the administration of George W. Bush added to the difficulties. Galbraith's summary judgment of the well-understood realities is trenchant: "The only effective design for diminishing the income inequality inherent in capitalism is the progressive income tax. . . . That taxes should now be used to reduce inequality is, however, clearly outside the realm of comfortable thought."[15]

Another Harvard economist, Richard Freeman, minces few words about the dead end that has been reached: "[C]urrent 'strategies' run the gamut from inadequate to sham."[16]

Some liberals continue to hope against hope that somehow a revival of progressive politics can one day reverse the decaying trend. But clearly, if serious after-the-fact redistributive measures are no longer viable, something much more fundamental is needed.

In recent years those who have confronted the issue squarely have increasingly come to the judgment that if change is ever to occur, an assault must ultimately be made on the underlying relationships that have produced the inequality trends in the first place—especially those involving ownership and control of the nation's wealth.

Freeman, for instance, urges, "If we were to start democratic capitalism with a blank slate, we would naturally divide the ownership of existing physical assets equally among the population. . . . Our main strategy—be we left or right—for fighting income inequality under capitalism, should be to assure a fair initial distribution of physical and human capital themselves." Freeman states the essential principle of such an approach in this way: "Equality of income obtained in the first instance via greater equality in those assets, rather than as an after-the-fact (of earning or luck) state redistribution of income from rich to poor, would enable us to better square the circle of market efficiency and egalitarian aspiration."[17]

Former secretary of labor Robert Reich also urges a similar, wealth-related, shift in focus: "The asset elevator has been lifting America's wealthy to ever-higher vistas, without their moving a muscle (except, perhaps, to speed-dial their brokers). Current tax law is lifting them, and their children, even higher. Hence the case for allowing the rest of America on the elevator, too."[18]

And former chief counsel to the U.S. Senate Finance Committee Jeff Gates holds: "[A]bsent an accompanying ownership-participation element, unbridled free enterprise is destined to throw both the social and economic system badly out of balance."[19]

The emphasis on wealth (rather than simply income) by these writers and others involved in the quietly growing reassessment has brought with it a related emphasis on underlying institutions (rather than simply policies). One specific line of development stresses the possibility that workers might own their own companies, a straightforward idea that if extended and applied across the board implies a political-economic system quite different from both traditional socialism and corporate capitalism.[20]

Radical economists Samuel Bowles and Herbert Gintis also begin their analysis by agreeing that political progressives need to reconsider failing traditional approaches: "[E]galitarian strategies should abandon what has hitherto been an exaggerated emphasis on . . . tax and transfer policies." Not only is this a political dead end, but asset-based redistribution, they urge, "can use markets to discipline economic actors." Indeed, they hold that worker-owned firms ultimately may prove to be "more efficient than the capitalist firm, in the technical sense that the democratic firm uses less of at least one input to produce the same output."[21]

"Workers frequently have access at low cost to information concerning the work activities of fellow workers," Bowles and Gintis point out, "and in the democratic firm each worker as a residual claimant on the income of the firm has an interest in the effort levels of other workers." The ordinary firm must spend a good deal of money monitoring work activity. Quite apart from the equities involved, this is a drain on economic resources.[22]

Jeff Gates, drawing on his experience in the Senate, stresses the political possibilities of worker-ownership strategies: "The political potential in this area became obvious to me when, over the span of a two-week period . . . I was asked to provide speech material for both Republican Senator Jesse Helms and Democratic presidential candidate Jesse Jackson." Gates and others have produced long lists of those endorsing the principle of employee-owned firms ranging from Ronald Reagan and George Will on the right, to Robert Kuttner and Robert Reich on the left.[23]

Worker ownership clearly is not the only wealth or "asset-based" approach that flows from the argument that a new strategic principle beyond after-the-fact taxing and spending is necessary. Another major strategy begins with the observation of Washington University expert Michael Sherraden that the federal government already provides very large indirect tax subsidies to encourage asset ownership by middle- and upper-income Americans. The most obvious of these are the tax deductibility of home-ownership mortgage interest, tax, and other payments; and of savings contributions to Keogh, IRA, and 401(k) plans. In fiscal year 2004, public subsidies of $98 billion were projected to go to home-owners and another $113.8 billion to those who saved through any one of the plans; taxpayer costs for 2004–2008 were estimated to be more than $1 trillion.[24]

Sherraden suggests that if such huge subsidies can be given to middle- and upper-income groups to encourage savings, incentives also should be used to develop asset holding among the poor. He proposes a system of Individual Development Accounts (IDAs) through which the government would directly match the savings of the poor—thus doubling their efforts and allowing low-income individuals to benefit from the ownership of capital: "Instead of focusing welfare policy on income and consumption, as we have done in the past, we should focus more on savings, investment, and asset accumulation. This idea might be summarized by the term *stakeholding*. . . . A stake in the system means, in one form or another, holding assets."[25]

Although not as striking in their institutional implications as worker-ownership ideas, over the decade of the 1990s a stream of related asset-based wealth-holding and wealth-building proposals has expanded on Sherraden's theme— and on the general principle that wealth should benefit much broader groups directly. Most of the specific plans also emphasize the obvious point that any capital investment started early enough and held long enough ultimately will pay off handsomely.

A proposal by former Senator Bob Kerrey of Nebraska, for instance, would establish "KidSave Accounts" to which the government would contribute $1,000 at birth for every child, and $500 per year thereafter for the next five years. The funds would be invested and allowed to grow until the individual reaches age twenty-one—at which time roughly $20,000 would be available for investment in education or for other purposes.[26]

Significantly, the KidSave proposal was cosponsored not only by liberals, but by centrist and conservative senators Joseph Lieberman of Connecticut and John Breaux of Louisiana as well. A related proposal by Robert Kuttner aims to provide each child with a $5,000 capital grant at birth and up to $1,000 a year thereafter until age eighteen. Kuttner estimates that if conservatively invested, such an amount will produce a capital fund of roughly $50,000 per individual at maturity.*[27]

---

* In a related proposal the Clinton administration put forward the idea of Universal Savings Accounts as a supplement to Social Security. In such IDA-like accounts the savings of the poor would be supplemented by up to $1,300 per year. The Blair government in Britain introduced a "baby bond" proposal based on similar asset-based ideas in early 2003. See Robert B. Reich, "To Lift All Boats," *Washington Post,* May 16, 1999, p. B1; Will Hutton, "A Chance for a Robin Hood Budget," *The Observer* (London), April 6, 2003, p. 30.

"Imagine if instead of being promised at birth that you will get a Social Security pension decades in the future . . . you were given a trust fund based on bonds or stocks whose returns would constitute your social transfer," comments Richard Freeman. "The incompetent poor would then be more like the incompetent rich: they would have income from assets that would let them live at some basic level, without depending on income transfers."[28]

Yale professors Bruce Ackerman and Anne Alstott take such wealth-holding ideas a step further by proposing that every individual be given a "capital stake" of $80,000 on reaching adulthood—to be used for any purpose they chose. The Ackerman-Alstott program also adds an important new dimension to asset-based strategic thinking: They urge that the program be initially financed by a 2 percent wealth tax, thus linking the principle of broadening wealth ownership to much larger publics, on the one hand, to a strategy that challenges the extreme concentration of existing wealth ownership in the hands of tiny elites, on the other.[29]

Several writers have pushed the basic principles underlying wealth-holding proposals forward to their logical—and much more far-reaching—system-wide institutional conclusions. Yale economist John Roemer, for instance, proposes a very radical long-term strategy he calls "coupon socialism," which in theory would ultimately totally "change the system" and pass on the benefits of *all* major stock ownership to the citizenry at large.

Under the Roemer proposal, taxation would first transfer ownership of capital to the government. Every adult would then receive an equal endowment of voucher-like coupons—nontransferable dollars—which could only be used to purchase stock through a new form of mutual fund. The resulting profits would be distributed to such investors—that is, to all adults—thereby ultimately providing an income stream from the now widely distributed ownership of capital.[30]

An important feature of Roemer's approach is that although the ownership of wealth would be revolutionized, the management and functioning of firms would not be disturbed. Since individuals could choose where to invest their coupons, competition for the funds they represent would continue to discipline market behavior.

A similar, equally radical, long-term system-wide asset-changing proposal is that of political scientist Leland Stauber. In this approach, too, the management and competitive situation of firms is not altered, and mechanisms of market discipline are maintained. Instead of individuals benefiting directly from the change in asset ownership, however, municipalities—as representatives of the public—are the ultimate recipients of dividends from the ownership of capital.[31]

A midrange position that also develops the full institution-changing logic of wealth-holding ideas is that of the Nobel laureate British economist, the late James Meade. Under Meade's approach, taxation of large-scale wealth produces funds to be used, first, to pay off the national debt, and second to accumulate surplus public capital. The surplus, in turn, is invested in corporate stock by investment trusts and other private financial institutions. The "beneficial ownership" of roughly half the nation's capital in this proposal is ultimately passed on to the public in the form of a "social dividend," distributed "free of tax to every citizen . . . which depends solely upon the age of the citizen, a distinction being drawn between the payment to a child or to an adult of working age or to a pensioner."*[32]

---

* Progressive taxation recoups some of the income flowing to the well-to-do. A second strategy offered by Meade involves new forms of enterprise characterized by labor-capital partnerships that also implicitly change the beneficiary ownership of wealth—an idea echoed in Martin Weitzman's 1984 book, *The Share Economy*, which advocates changing the labor contract from a wage (dollars per hour) to a share of revenues (each worker would receive two-thirds of company revenue per worker). Martin L. Weitzman, *The Share Economy* (Cambridge, Mass.: Harvard University Press, 1984), pp. 3–5.

If Roemer, Stauber, and Meade come to their system-wide extensions of asset-based, wealth-holding concepts from the left, others have come to related ideas from a very different direction: Norman Kurland, Robert Ashford, and Stewart Speiser have picked up on the earlier writings of corporate lawyer and investment banker, the late Louis Kelso, to urge far-reaching programs of "universal capitalism" that draw heavily on Kelso's 1958 *The Capitalist Manifesto* (written with philosopher Mortimer Adler).

Kelso realized from his professional experience that one of the main—and strikingly obvious!—reasons his rich clients were able to multiply their ownership of stocks and bonds was that their existing wealth provided them with collateral that allowed them to borrow money for further investment. They could also hire experts to manage that investment. If the poor had access to collateral and experts, Kelso reasoned, why could they not also make money by investing borrowed funds?

Drawing on the precedent of federal programs that insure home mortgages, Kelso proposed that a new Capital Diffusion Insurance Corporation be established to guarantee loans so as to allow individuals to buy a diversified and professionally managed portfolio of stocks. The portfolio would remain in escrow until dividends repaid the loan, at which time the individual would take full ownership, thereby gaining a "second income" with the help of the government-backed or collateralized ownership of capital.[33]

Although Kelso's proposal would also ultimately result in a major system-changing buildup of wealth among the citizenry, unlike Roemer, Stauber, and Meade, he did not propose taxing away or expropriating existing wealth. Instead, a steady shift in ownership would be slowly accomplished as *new* wealth is created in the normal processes of economic development over long stretches of time.

The key principle involved in all variations on the Kelso approach is that ultimately the stock pays for itself out of the dividends it earns. Speiser puts it this way: "This is a method of acquiring new capital that has been used for centuries by wealthy people and profitable companies. *They simply let it pay for itself.* New factories opened by major successful corporations pay for themselves out of their own output. . . . This is the key to capital accumulation, and it is all based on *long-term* credit, which is not available to the little guy now but is always available to the large corporation or the wealthy person in our society."[34]

William Greider, an important progressive writer, now also urges the essentials of a Kelso-type strategy: "The central mechanism for democratizing ownership . . . is reform of the credit system—enabling people without any wealth of their own to borrow the funds to buy shares of capital ownership, loans that will be paid back by future earnings from the very income-producing assets they have acquired."[35]

Few of those concerned with equality would abandon traditional redistributive strategies entirely (especially those that might still yield some benefits to people at the bottom of the system). The emerging shift, however, points to a longer-term system-wide principle—namely, that ultimately movement toward greater equality requires that the ownership of capital be altered. This in turn requires new institutions.

Clearly, the longer-term system-wide wealth-changing proposals are beyond the range of current political feasibility. But just as clearly, growing disillusionment with traditional after-the-fact policy ideas has set the stage for a much deeper and ongoing reassessment. If the old ways no longer work, is there any other option? New proposals to broaden the ownership of wealth are increasingly commonplace—and given the growing discontent, appear all but certain to continue to grow in number and refinement.

Two obvious questions are: first, whether—even if over very long stretches of time—the emerging principle can ever be significantly embodied in practical institutions; and second, whether it can receive any degree of substantial political backing against the huge odds and interests that stand in the way of major change.

We shall return to these matters in Parts II and IV—and to the question of whether there is any other way to give meaning to values based upon, or even remotely related to, the idea of equality in the new century.

2

Liberty

Money, Time, and Real Freedom of Choice

As we have seen, two distinct trends have produced growing concern that the political-economic system no longer appears able to sustain a culture of liberty. The first and most obvious involves restrictions on individual liberties in response to terrorism and war, and in response to crime. The second, and more fundamental, relates to foundational issues involving the underlying structures and institutions of the political-economic system as a whole.

Our primary interest at this point is with foundational problems—the bedrock questions at the very heart of the system.

It is essential to understand the deep-seated nature of the problem confronting those concerned with liberty—even, in the first instance, when approached from the perspective of the traditional (conservative) assumptions prominent in contemporary discourse. That a dead end has been reached, with virtually no way back to traditional approaches, is painfully obvious to sophisticated thinkers. Indeed, in this respect, thoughtful conservatives are in as much of a quandary as thoughtful liberals concerned with equality; the system-wide nature of the problems they face is no different.

Traditional conservative approaches to liberty depend, foundationally, upon two important institutional judgments: first, that "big government" must be reduced; second, that a free-market capitalist economy must be protected and sustained, both because it is held that free markets are essential to liberty in general, and because it is held that they nurture the spirit of entrepreneurship and a culture of free individualism.[1]

That "big government" is anathema to individual liberty is *the* fundamental structural argument of traditional theory. Ultimately, a reduction in government's reach, scale, and function is the premise of all secondary arguments—the necessary condition that allows the citizenry to build a society capable of nurturing and sustaining liberty against its many challenges. All power corrupts, it is held—even (perhaps especially) benevolent power.[2]

Despite President Bill Clinton's assurance that the era of big government is over, the reality is that government in the United States *is* big—far bigger than most realize. Rhetoric aside, the central fact is that conservatives have simply been unable to alter the fundamental patterns and orders of magnitude.

Government grew from roughly 7 percent of the economy in 1902 to roughly 31 percent in 2003. By a more comprehensive measure, the current figure is at least 36 to 37 percent, and some recent estimates of the impact of regulatory and other indirect activity add an additional 8 percent, bringing the total to 44 to 45 percent of the economy. (Milton Friedman believes the actual number is closer to 50 percent.)[3]

"I will do many things for my country," columnist George Will lamented during the Reagan years, "but I will not pretend that the careers of, say, Ronald Reagan and Franklin Roosevelt involve serious philosophical differences."*

Richard Nixon left office with a government more expansive than that left by Eisenhower; that of Reagan was larger than that of Nixon; government at the end the first Bush presidency was larger than that of Reagan. And even before

---

* Near the end of Reagan's presidency, William Buckley observed, "No, [Ronald Reagan] has not reversed the great trends of the century that have given more and more responsibility to government, less and less to society." William F. Buckley Jr., "Musical Monuments," *Washington Post*, January 6, 1987, p. A21.

a major military buildup expanded the federal budget, there was little statistical evidence that George W. Bush would be able to more than marginally alter government's overall scope and scale.[4] Indeed, not only did government increase as a share of the economy during his first years in office but, much to the dismay of many conservatives, Bush successfully pushed through $400 billion in new prescription drug spending in 2003 and continued to support it in 2004 despite raising the projected cost to $530 billion.[5]

It is not that conservatives have not tried—and still continue to try. A broad range of strategies have been attempted—including selective budget cutting, balanced-budget laws, tax reduction designed to "starve government," even attempts to amend the Constitution. Just as traditional liberal strategies may have slowed the trend of growing inequality (but failed to reverse the trend beyond temporary moments), so, too, the conservative approaches that have so angered liberals have altered priorities and cut back important programs, thereby helping slow the growth of government. What they have *not* done is significantly reduce the general scope and scale of government.[6]

A cottage industry of political scientists has probed the institutional, constituency-based, organizational, and other reasons that government has grown, and why its core structures have been so unyielding. One group of scholars has argued that government grows because citizens oppose government in general, but want specific programs of interest to them in particular. Another group of theories derives from the work of the late economist Mancur Olson and from related work by Anthony Downs, James Buchanan, and Gordon Tullock. These emphasize that special interests have large incentives to secure government benefits—and also have the power to organize to gain their objectives. Even though greater numbers in the public may pay the costs, it is difficult and expensive to organize them since few individuals have enough incentive to participate effectively.[7]

Still another theory is that of political economist Robert Higgs, who argues that a series of crises—World War I, the Great Depression, World War II—have been exploited in ways that not only expand government but lead to a "ratcheting" upward of government's scope and scale. Once expanded in the context of crisis, constituencies develop around programs and make it impossible to reverse the now upwardly "ratcheted" new levels.[8]

Whatever theory or theories in the end prove to offer the most accurate explanation, the bottom line is that there are powerful reasons why very little structural or trend change has occurred—even when conservatives have been elected to office. When the smokescreen of rhetoric attacking big government is pierced, we can understand why the chief architect of the so-called Reagan Revolution, Budget Bureau Director David Stockman, left office convinced that real change was "impossible." Or why the conservative economist Milton Friedman might lament, "We have been, despite some successes, mostly on the losing side."[9]

Similar problems confront the argument that individual liberty also depends, foundationally, on maintaining the underlying institutions of free-market capitalism—especially the independence and energy of the entrepreneur. Although it is also held that a thoroughgoing entrepreneurial economy is required to disperse power and nurture a culture of liberty, giant corporations now control such key industries as energy, telecommunications, steel, autos, home appliances, many food products, and so on. Simply by way of illustration:

General Electric, Whirlpool, and Maytag sell 80 percent of all ovens and 85 percent of all dryers; Procter & Gamble, Unilever, Colgate-Palmolive, and Dial account for 83 percent of bar soap sold in the United States. Three companies dominate 60 to 66 percent of the cable television, online job recruitment, and college textbook markets. Two companies control 75 percent of the soft drink market.[10]

Globally a mere three hundred multinational corporations account for an estimated 25 percent of productive assets. "The sales of General Motors and Ford," Noreena Hertz of Cambridge University observes, "are greater than the GDP of the whole of sub-Saharan Africa; the assets of IBM, BP and General Electric outstrip the economic capabilities of most small nations; and Wal-Mart, the U.S. supermarket retailer, has higher revenues than most Central and Eastern European states including Poland, the Czech Republic, Ukraine, Hungary, Romania and Slovakia."[11]

Nor, as traditional theory assumes, do such firms avoid government. Richard Nixon's secretary of the Treasury, the late William Simon, recalled how during his "tenure at Treasury I watched with incredulity as businessmen ran to the government in every crisis, whining for handouts or protection from the very competition that has made this system so productive." Simon went on to bitterly observe: "I saw Texas ranchers, hit by drought, demanding government-guaranteed loans; giant milk cooperatives lobbying for higher price supports; major airlines fighting deregulation to preserve their monopoly status; giant companies like Lockheed seeking federal assistance to rescue them from sheer inefficiency; bankers, like David Rockefeller, demanding government bailouts to protect them from their ill-conceived investments; network executives, like William Paley of CBS, fighting to preserve regulatory restrictions and to block the emergence of competitive cable and pay TV."

And, he added, "always, such gentlemen proclaimed their devotion to free enterprise and their opposition to the arbitrary intervention into our economic life by the state. Except, of course, for their own case, which was always unique and which was justified by their immense concern for the public interest."[12]

Traditional conservatives, like the founder of the University of Chicago free-market school of economics, Henry C. Simons, begged fellow conservatives to recognize that "[t]urned loose with inordinate powers, corporations have vastly overorganized most industries." Indeed, this highly respected conservative (and Milton Friedman's revered teacher) held that "America might now be better off if the corporate form had never been invented or never made available to private enterprise."[13]

Another leading conservative, Friedrich A. Hayek, years ago urged that "if we continue on the path we have been treading [toward what he termed the 'monopolistic organization of industry' closely allied with government], it will lead us to totalitarianism."[14]

The traditional response to the reality of corporate power has been an antitrust effort to break up giant firms. But few any longer believe the kind of economy that undergirds the traditional theory can be restored by such means. An occasional antitrust battle has been won, but in the more than one hundred years since the Sherman Anti-Trust Act was enacted, there have been only a handful of successful challenges to major corporations. Commonly, even when large corporations have lost legal battles—as in the recent Microsoft case—they have been able to hire top legal teams and use delaying tactics until a new administration comes to power or until technological advantage has given them de facto control of the economic landscape of concern.[15]

Even in the few cases where antitrust has succeeded, the understanding of traditional conservatism that corporate power threatens values of liberty and democracy has all but disappeared. In the modern era antitrust discussions are narrowly focused on technical economic matters and complex (and debatable) measurements of the potential impact on consumers. William Safire is one of the few to stress what was once self-evident to fellow conservatives: "With the round-heeled Michael Powell steering the Federal Communications Commission toward terminal fecklessness; with the redoubtable Joel Klein succeeded at Justice's antitrust division by an assortment of wimps; and with appeals courts approving the concentration of media power as if nothing had changed since President Taft's day, the checks and balances made possible by diverse competition are being eradicated.

"The longtime anti-business coloration of liberals reduces their ability to take on the convergence con," Safire observes. Accordingly, "It is for conservatives to ask ourselves: Since when is bigness goodness?"[16]

The power implications of the giant corporation are one thing. Equally important is the indirect cultural and human impact of the historic shift away from entrepreneurial capitalism. "Dependence," Thomas Jefferson urged, "begets subservience and venality, suffocates the germ of virtue." Jefferson held that only under conditions of widespread small-scale individual property ownership could a people "safely and advantageously reserve to themselves a wholesome control over their public affairs."[17]

A hundred years later Woodrow Wilson warned that if America's children in the future were to "open their eyes in a country where they must be employees or nothing . . . then they will see an America as the founders of this Republic would have wept to think of." Louis Brandeis asked, "Can any man be really free who is constantly in danger of becoming dependent for mere subsistence upon somebody and something else than his own exertion and conduct?"[18]

That a nation in which nine out of ten people are *employees* is radically different, culturally, from a nation of *entrepreneurs*—and that the problems this raises for liberty must also be confronted—is something very few conservatives have even been willing to discuss in recent years. They have mainly looked away from what was once a central element in their philosophical stance—perhaps because the implications are so difficult to accept.[19]

For these many reasons, viewed in broadest historical perspective (and whether one agrees or disagrees with them), such traditional theories of liberty increasingly appear as walking intellectual corpses—ideas that for better or worse no longer have much structural relationship to the living realities of the modern political-economic world. Philosophical conservatives have developed wonderfully coherent abstract theories based on assumed first premises—but the premises commonly sidestep the hard problems defined by the long, unyielding, real-world structures and trends. (None of this, of course, has prevented politicians from continuing to hammer away at traditional ideological themes to rally support for favored policies.)

If, even from within the perspective of traditional conservatism, what have been understood as the institutional foundations of liberty no longer seem achievable in the real world, are there *any* strategic approaches that might one day come to terms with the underlying foundational issues?

One modern line of attack stems from the work of the late Robert Nisbet, a highly regarded conservative sociologist. Broadly speaking, traditional theories involve an implicit balance of power conception. On the one hand, liberty can be enhanced by weakening the state; on the other, it can be enhanced by protecting or bolstering the position of the individual (by, for instance, encouraging an entrepreneurial economy). A critical—indeed, absolutely essential—way to support the individual, Nisbet held, is to nurture the kinds of "intermediate institutions" that stand between the lone individual and the state, thereby providing both social support and a buffer against centralized power.[20]

The rise of fascism before and during World War II, Nisbet contended, demonstrated that isolated individuals were psychologically and politically vulnerable to the appeals of powerful leaders like Hitler: "Only in their social interdependence are men given to resist the tyranny that always threatens to arise out of any political government, democratic or other." A decline in the importance of churches, unions, and various local and neighborhood civic associations had been disastrous. Planning an all-out effort to nurture the conditions that support such institutions, Nisbet urged, was therefore required to protect individuals against the claims of centralized power.[21]

Peter Berger, William Schambra, and several other writers have offered variations on this basic theme in recent years. The concept of "mediating structures," Berger urges, is "politically promising. *It cuts across the ideological divides . . .*" and offers ways to transcend the dangers of a world characterized by the "'liquid molecules' of individuals caught in a chaotic private world, and the leveling tyranny of the totalitarian state."[22]

The argument intersects with the similar but slightly different argument that democracy (not liberty) requires nurturing local citizen associations. And in both cases—as Nisbet's general contention suggests and we shall further explore—the argument leads to the question of how the local context in which individuals and associations flourish or fail can be made secure (see Chapter 3).

A very different strategy aimed at bolstering the individual side of the state-individual balance has been offered by the well-known management consultant Peter Drucker— one of the very few who have been willing to confront the implications of the trend that has transformed entrepreneurs into employees.

Drucker suggests that the only way to establish the kind of stability and security once theoretically offered by individual entrepreneurial property is through government policies that achieve the "evolution of jobs into a kind of property." This requires that there be no "'expropriation [of the job] without compensation,' and that employers take responsibility to anticipate redundancies, retraining employees . . . and finding and placing them in new jobs." What is needed is "redundancy planning rather than unemployment compensation."[23]

A similar, even more sharply focused extension of the argument that jobs must be made secure—even a matter of right!—was included in early drafts of the Humphrey-Hawkins Full Employment Act. And, of course, the idea that real liberty requires job security is at the heart of most academic-freedom arguments urged in defense of tenure arrangements common among college professors: without a secure place to stand, it is very difficult to achieve the independence that liberty urges as a central value.[24]

Finally, such arguments and strategies, of course, also speak to the concern urged by scholars like Edward Luttwak that economic insecurities generated by "turbo-capitalism" are ultimately responsible for a liberty-destroying culture that "vents its anger and resentment by punishing, restricting and prohibiting all that can be punished, restricted and prohibited."[25]

Traditional conservative premises also, of course, have long been challenged on their own terms. Political theorist Alan Ryan points out that there "have been many societies in which private property was taken seriously and political liberty was almost wholly absent." After all, he and others note, all the fascist systems we know of were built upon and grew out of what previously had been free-market capitalist foundations.[26]

Again, in a recent book Stephen Holmes and Cass Sunstein stress that without effective and indeed costly government programs, Americans "would enjoy few or none of their constitutionally guaranteed individual rights. Personal liberty, as Americans value and experience it, presupposes social cooperation managed by government officials. The private realm we rightly prize is sustained, indeed created, by public action."*[27]

For the most part, liberals who have confronted the deeper foundational issues have focused on how the conditions that define the real-world situation facing the individual can be

---

* Holmes and Sunstein challenge the position of conservatives who "cling instinctively to a cost-blind approach to the protection of the so-called negative rights of property and contract." To stare hard at the public costs of maintaining property rights, they urge, shatters "the libertarian fiction that individuals who exercise their rights, in the classic or eighteenth-century sense, are just going about their own business, immaculately independent of the government and the taxpaying community." *The Cost of Rights: Why Liberty Depends on Taxes* (New York: W.W. Norton, 1999), p. 29.

altered so as to increase freedom of action and the power to choose. One major line of thought emphasizes questions of time.

Individual liberty obviously can never be fully realized if men and women must work devastatingly long hours simply to feed and shelter their families. Only if individuals have time that they can dispose of freely as they see fit can liberty be truly meaningful.

Walter Lippman held that free time was "the substance of liberty, the material of free will." John Maynard Keynes looked forward to an era ("much sooner perhaps than we are all of us aware of") when a reduction of working hours would confront man "with his real, his permanent problem—how to use his freedom." Herbert Marcuse judged that "the reduction of the working day to a point where the mere quantum of labor time no longer arrests human development is the first prerequisite for freedom."*[28]

The reality, however, is that the political-economic trend that reduced the workweek from more than seventy hours at the end of the nineteenth century to roughly forty hours today has been essentially stalled for almost fifty years. Such writers as economist Juliet Schor, historian Benjamin Hunnicutt, and philosopher Jerome Segal have suggested that the productivity gains offered by modern technological development offer radically new possibilities for the expansion of free time as a foundation for individual liberty and freedom of choice. They also have begun to propose strategies to encourage a resumption of the previously downward-moving trend over the course of the twenty-first century.[29]

One commonly urged approach would strengthen and revise current forty-hour-a-week laws limiting full-time work and regulating overtime pay.[30] Segal proposes that public

* And, of course, Karl Marx believed that the "realm of freedom really begins only where labor determined by necessity and external expediency ends. . . . The reduction of the working day is the basic prerequisite." Karl Marx, *Capital*, Volume III, trans. David Fernbach (London: Penguin, 1991), pp. 958–959.

LIBERTY   39

policy should aim ultimately to reduce the workweek to twenty-five hours—and that the additional money needed to maintain basic needs be provided by an expanded form of the Earned Income Tax Credit, which currently provides a wage supplement for low-income working families.[31]

Other answers to the underlying question have been proposed by such political theorists as Bill Jordon, Philippe Van Parijs, and Yale law professor Anne Alstott. All have argued in general that a publicly guaranteed floor-level amount of income (beyond mere subsistence) is essential if liberty is to have meaning in the modern era. Van Parijs, whose work has been at the center of discussion here and in Europe, holds: "If we are serious about pursuing real-freedom-for-all . . . what we have to go for is the highest *unconditional* income for all consistent with security and self-ownership."[32]

Significantly, the conservative Nobel laureate, James Buchanan, also urges a "demogrant" form of basic income given equally to all (and financed by a flat tax). For many years Milton Friedman has also consistently urged the importance of a "negative" income tax involving cash supplements to low-paid workers—the underlying principle of which has been enacted on a bipartisan basis in the form of the Earned Income Tax Credit.[33]

Historian Eric Foner reminds us that during the early years of the Republic, the central focus of debate was not simply "liberty" but "equal liberty"—an idea that also reaches beyond legal and constitutional protections to consider the capacities and real-world conditions of the vast majority. "Even a conservative like John Adams, who distrusted the era's democratic pretensions," Foner observes, believed this required enabling "every member of society" to acquire land. Alexis de Tocqueville put it this way: "[N]othing struck me more forcibly than the general equality of condition among the people." Tocqueville went on to stress, "[T]he more I advanced in the study of American society, the more I perceived that this equality of condition is the fundamental fact from which all others seem to be derived and the central point at which all my observations constantly terminated."[34]

A final group of theorists has returned to the question of "equality of condition" in the search for strategies to nurture liberty by bolstering the position and capacities of the individual. Most have also built upon John Dewey's argument that "effective freedom" is radically different from the "highly formal and limited concept of liberty." It requires "effective power to do specific things." Thus Georgetown University professor and *Washington Post* columnist E. J. Dionne states, "To be the master of one's own fate—a fair definition of liberty—means not simply being free from overt coercion (though that is a precondition); it also involves being given the means to overcome various external forces that impinge on freedom of choice and self-sufficiency. It means being free *to* set one's course."[35]

Similarly, Alan Ryan observes that most people understand that freedom "involves the expansion of our options—" and that "'[f]reedom of choice' implies a wide range of options." The full implications of the argument have been developed by Nobel laureate Amartya Sen in work outlining the "capabilities" and "outcomes" needed to make freedom real. "Capability is . . . the substantive freedom to achieve alternative functioning combinations (or, less formally put, the freedom to achieve various lifestyles)."[36]

All arguments that focus on the importance of "equality of liberty," of course, bring with them a series of proposals for improving the education, health, and economic conditions of those whose capacities for choice are limited by the way in which economic and other resources are currently allocated.

Broadly speaking, emerging modern theories of liberty converge on three central propositions:

First, liberty requires institutional and structural support for individual economic security to replace that which at least in theory was once provided by entrepreneurial property. Second, it requires support for the community-wide conditions needed to nurture the intermediate associations and civil society organizations that are essential to sustaining a culture supportive of liberty. Third, it requires greater amounts of equitably distributed free time (without which little real freedom of choice is possible) and support for individual development (without which the capacities needed to exercise real freedom must inevitably be limited).

It is noteworthy that the last of these important conditions inherently depends upon some form of resource redistribution, a reality that returns us to the principal conclusion of Chapter 1 in connection with equality—namely, that this in turn ultimately requires new approaches to the ownership of wealth. The first and second—establishing conditions in which local community associations can flourish and in which job security can be maintained—require additional political-economic strategies. Many of these intersect with evolving new approaches aimed at rebuilding the local foundations of system-wide democracy.

3

Democracy

From the Ground Up

WHAT OF THE CENTRAL question of democracy itself? Many have noted the trends of failing belief, the radical decline in voting, the massive role of money and corporate influence in lobbying, media, and elections—and in general, the large numbers who surveys show feel that "our national experiment in self-government is faltering." That millions of Americans believe "people like me have almost no say in the political system" has been a wake-up call for many on the left, right, and center.[1]

Several lines of reassessment have become increasingly important as the crisis has deepened. The first, directed to foundational "grassroots" community issues, has come into ever more sharply defined focus in recent years.

The work of Harvard political scientist Robert Putnam kicked off a major debate on one aspect of the problem.

Putnam probed well beneath such surface-level issues as the fall-off in voting to focus instead on local citizen associations, networks, formal and informal clubs, neighborhood groups, unions, and the like. Large numbers of Americans, he suggested, were now both actually and metaphorically "bowling alone" rather than in association with others. Putnam suggested that a decline in associational activity, in turn, had produced a decline in trust and "social capital"— foundational requirements of democracy in general. His response was straightforward: the nation should develop as many ways as possible to encourage local involvement—the only way, he held, Americans could hope to renew the basis of democracy throughout the larger system.[2]

Quite apart from Putnam's studies, general analysis, and recommendations (many of which were challenged by scholars), of particular interest was the explosive reaction to his argument—and the reorientation of strategic concern it represented. The outpouring of interest his first rather academic article on the subject produced revealed that Putnam had struck a powerful nerve. "Seldom has a thesis moved so quickly from scholarly obscurity to conventional wisdom," observed former White House aide and political scientist William Galston.[3]

Especially important was what was *not* at the center of attention: Putnam and many who responded to him did not focus on national parties, national interest groups, national lobbying, national campaign finance laws, or national political phenomena in general. What he and they focused on was the "micro" level of citizen groups and citizen involvement. *Here,* at the very local level, was now the place to begin to look for democratic renewal.

The heart of the larger foundational argument—and this is a critical emphasis—might be put thus: Is it possible to have Democracy with a Big D in the system as a whole if you do not have real democracy with a small d at the level where people live, work, and raise families *in their local communities?* If the answer is no, then a necessary if not sufficient condition of rebuilding democracy in general is to get to work locally.

Putnam essentially put into modern form Tocqueville's contention that in "democratic countries knowledge of how to combine is the mother of all other forms of knowledge." There is also clearly a close connection between Nisbet-style "intermediate association" arguments for liberty and neo-Tocquevillian associational arguments for democracy.[4]

But Tocqueville, in fact, had gone beyond "associations" to take up the deeper question of how—and whether—

democratic practice is reflected not only in civil society, but in actual local government. "Municipal institutions," he stressed, "constitute the strength of free nations. Town meetings are to liberty what primary schools are to science; they bring it within the people's reach, they teach men how to use and enjoy it."

John Stuart Mill similarly held that direct experience with local governance was essential to "the peculiar training of a citizen, the practical part of the political education of a free people." Mill pointed out that "we do not learn to read or write, to ride or swim, by being merely told how to do it, but by doing it, so it is only by practicing popular government on a limited scale, that the people will ever learn how to exercise it on a larger."[5]

Understood in this broader framework, Putnam's thesis is only one of a group of arguments that focus primary attention on what goes on in local communities. Indeed, an important and expanding group of theorists have picked up on the more demanding "small d" Tocqueville-Mill argument that an authentic experience of participation in local government decision making is essential if democracy is to be meaningful. A forceful statement of the more fundamental judgment is that of political scientist Stephen Elkin, a theorist who stresses that citizens must experience the actual use of power: "Civic associations cannot do [this] job: The element of authority is missing." Again, "for citizens to have any concern for the public interest . . . they must have the experience of grappling with its elements. For any significant number of citizens this can happen only through local political life."[6]

Other democratic theorists who urge reinvigorating democracy through a renewal of local governing institutions include Jane Mansbridge, Michael Sandel, and Benjamin Barber. Mansbridge argues that citizens are "most likely to come to understand their real interests in a small democracy, like a town or workplace, where members make a conscious effort to choose democratic procedures appropriate to the various issues that arise." In his study, *Democracy's Discontent,* Sandel holds that it is important to recover the meaning of the "republican tradition" in American political life—a tradition that "taught that to be free is to share in governing a political community that controls its own fate. Self-government . . . requires political communities that control their destinies, and citizens who identify sufficiently with those communities to think and act with a view to the common good."[7]

Barber's treatise on *Strong Democracy* emphasizes the importance of different forms of knowledge to different degrees of democratic practice: "[K]nowing your rights and knowing the law are concomitants," he suggests, "of minimalist or weak democratic politics." Something far more powerful is needed—and this requires a very different understanding of how knowledge is acquired. "In the strong democratic perspective, knowledge and the quest for knowledge tend to follow rather than to precede political engagement: give people some significant power and they will quickly appreciate the need for knowledge, but foist knowledge on them without giving them responsibility and they will display only indifference." It follows that "only direct political participation—activity that is explicitly public" can achieve real civic education in a democracy.[8]

The necessity of an authentic experience of government has, of course, also been stressed over the years by numerous conservative theorists—and they, too, have consistently urged the importance of direct local involvement. Hayek speaks for many: "Nowhere has democracy ever worked well without a great measure of local self-government, providing a school of political training for the people at large . . . where responsibility can be learned and practiced in affairs with which most people are familiar, where it is the awareness of one's neighbor rather than some theoretical knowledge of the needs of other people which guides action."[9]

The basic community-oriented emphasis can also be found in a line of arguments urging decentralization of government *within* large cities so as to increase opportunities for genuine participation. Early in the postwar era, philosopher Hannah Arendt (drawing on a Jeffersonian idea) suggested that "ward republics" be established at the neighborhood level. "It is futile," urban theorist Jane Jacobs similarly urges, "to expect that citizens will act with responsibility, verve and experience on big, city-wide issues when self-government has been rendered all but impossible on localized issues, which are often of the most direct importance to people." Jacobs, too, proposed transferring a number of municipal decisions to the level of neighborhood districts.[10]

There are also converging themes of community self-determination in the work of important black theorists: political scientist Phillip Thompson, for instance, draws on the earlier work of W. E. B. Du Bois to argue, "Mass incarceration of black male youth, extensive state 'therapeutic' management of poor African American communities . . . make it clear that African American communities are in need of strong independent civic institutions capable of providing their own civic voice and social order in the face of extensive external corporate and governmental control."*[11]

The argument that nurturing democracy with a small d is necessary if big-D Democracy in the system as a whole is ever to be renewed brings into sharp relief some of the real-world conditions required to make this meaningful. A central

---

* A number of specific proposals to undergird local organizations, neighborhood efforts, and broader public participation have been offered by different writers. In connection with their "associative democracy" approach, Joshua Cohen and Joel Rogers have proposed devolution of certain public functions and financial assistance to citizen groups so that among other things they can become "more supportive of the range of egalitarian-democratic norms." Jeremy Rifkin suggests public payment of a "social wage" for community-serving work in—and tax deductions for time contributed to—legally certified tax-exempt, nonprofit organizations. Samuel Bowles and Herbert Gintis have urged limited tax credits (rather than deductions) for contributions to nonprofit organizations. Joshua Cohen and Joel Rogers, "Secondary Associations and Democratic Governance," *Politics & Society,* vol. 20, no. 4 (December 1992), p. 425; Jeremy Rifkin, *The End of Work* (New York: G. P. Putnam's Sons, 1995), pp. 256–259; and Samuel Bowles and Herbert Gintis, "From the I.R.S. to the P.T.A.," *New York Times,* April 19, 1995, p. A23.

question concerns the economic underpinnings of local democracy. It is obvious, for instance, that active citizen participation in local community efforts is all but impossible if the economic rug is regularly pulled out from under them. What, precisely, is "the community" when citizens are forced to move in and out of specific geographic localities because of volatile local economic conditions? Who has any real stake in long-term decisions?

That a substantial degree of economic stability is one of the critical preconditions of local involvement is documented in several important studies. A recent analysis of the 2000 election by the U.S. Census Bureau demonstrates that "citizens who had lived in the same home for five or more years had a voting rate of 72 percent . . . "—much higher than rates for individuals who had lived at their residences for a shorter time. Again, Sidney Verba, Kay Schlozman, and Henry Brady have shown that "years in community" is a positive predictor of both national and local-level civic involvement, with the effect nearly twice as strong for local involvement. Another detailed survey of nearly thirty thousand Americans undertaken in 2000 similarly shows that years lived in one's community and the expectation of staying in one's community are correlated with increased civic participation.[12]

A related issue involves the power relationships that set the terms of reference for municipal government. Numerous scholarly studies have demonstrated that local government decision making commonly is heavily dominated by the local business community. Commonly, too, the thrust of decisions favorable to business groups radically constrains all other choices. The use of scarce resources to develop downtown areas, and especially to attract or retain major corporations, inevitably absorbs funds that might alternatively be used to help low- and moderate-income neighborhood housing, schools, and community services.

The issue is not simply one of distribution. *City Limits,* an aptly titled study by Harvard political scientist Paul Peterson, demonstrates that as a result of the underlying relationships, policy choices are often "limited to those few which can plausibly be shown to be conducive to the community's economic prosperity." Partly this is because businessowners have more money, hence usually more political influence. But quite apart from such considerations, local political leaders feel they must promote economic development, and they accordingly feel they need the help of the business community.[13]

The "democracy with a small d" question is whether there can be any meaningful democratic *decision making* when allocations to achieve business priorities implicitly preempt alternative choices. If not—if most choices are radically hemmed in from the start by the need to be responsive to business—what is there to decide? And if there is little to decide, what is the meaning of democracy? And how, precisely, might the situation be altered, given the power of business interests in the system?

The conclusion—though not always brought into clear focus by theorists concerned with democracy and civil society—is inescapable: if the local foundations of democracy are to be meaningfully rebuilt, this also requires an approach to achieving greater local economic stability that does not rely so heavily on traditional business-oriented strategies. If municipalities are to be "delivered from their present economic bondage," political scientist David Imbroscio observes, they must find ways "to promote economic vitality in their jurisdictions via the implementation of 'alternative' economic development strategies based on something other than capturing footloose investment."[14]

To the extent local economies can be made more stable, the economic environment in which local entrepreneurial businesses may flourish also obviously improves; hence, one of the foundational institutions of traditional conservative theories of liberty can also thereby be strengthened.

How to do this becomes the key question. One method is obvious: as many have noted, cities anchored by universities, state capitals, and other major public facilities commonly enjoy greater economic stability. Economist Ann Markusen also points to many community-stabilizing policies that have been used to deal with dislocations associated with the Department of Defense base closings and related experience. Many experts—for instance, city planning professor Arthur C. Nelson, and sociologists John R. Logan and Harvey L. Molotch—have proposed a range of "development-from-below" strategies. These include diverse education and training programs, and loan, tax, procurement, and other policies to encourage business retention, entrepreneurship, and neighborhood capital accumulation.[15]

A more fundamental structural approach intersects with the asset-based strategies considered in Chapter 1. An important feature of worker-owned firms is that they not only change the ownership of wealth but also are far more anchored in local communities by virtue of the simple fact that worker-owners live in the community. "The only real way a community can regain control over its economic future is to rebuild from the ground up," urges Michael Shuman, the author of *Going Local.* Over the long haul, he adds, this can only be done by supporting the development of noncorporate "community-friendly" enterprises that have many integral links to the locality.[16]

Real community democracy, in short, requires real community economic health—and the kinds of institutions that can sustain it. But this is obviously only one element in a comprehensive approach.

4

Democracy

Inequality and Giant Corporations

A SECOND LINE OF ATTACK on what many now call the "democratic deficit" zeroes in on the multiple ways the organization of the larger economy impacts democratic life.

One form of the question focuses on the challenge economic inequality poses to democratic practice—and the degree to which different institutions do or do not foster equality. "[I]f income, wealth, and economic position are also political resources, and if they are distributed unequally, then how can citizens be political equals?" asks political scientist Robert Dahl. "And if citizens cannot be political equals, how is democracy to exist?"[1]

The superior ability of the rich to participate politically is not limited to buying influence via donations and lobbyists (and television ads); they also have superior education, more time, more developed skills, greater personal security, and far greater access and experience in managing politics and government. A recent study found that 81 percent of individuals who donate at least $200 to congressional campaigns make over $100,000 per year; 46 percent make at least $250,000. Those among the bottom fifth vote less, attempt to speak to or influence public officials less, participate in organized groups less, and indeed, are only one-tenth as likely to make any form of campaign contribution as those in the top decile.[2]

Michael Lind's formulation of the antidemocratic result is succinct: "From its fortified command post in the large organizations of the private sector, protected by the concentric moats of alumni preference, college tuition, professional licensing and pro-managerial state laws, the white overclass dominates U.S. politics."[3]

If meaningful democracy requires greater equality among the citizenry, and if, as we have seen, existing economic arrangements simply do not permit "after-the-fact" strategies to significantly alter inequality, what then? Either nothing can be done, or clearly a rather different long-term arrangement of economic institutions is necessary, at least in principle. Strikingly, the emerging theory—beginning now from the question of democracy—converges with the emerging theory illuminated by Chapter 1's examination of the problem of equality on its own terms. (And, as we have seen, the logic that flows from such considerations points ultimately in the direction of asset-based strategies and alternative wealth-holding institutions.)

The same question—though rarely stated openly—is also implicit in discussions of campaign finance reform. There is not much disagreement about the extraordinary importance of money in modern political campaigning. The Center for Responsive Politics estimates total spending for and by congressional candidates, presidential candidates, and the parties in 1999 to 2000 at over $2.5 billion—plus roughly another $200 million dollars for "issue" advocacy campaigns.[*4]

"Only those who have accumulated lots of money are free to play in this version of democracy," observes William Greider. "Only those with a strong, immediate financial stake in the political outcomes can afford to invest."[5]

A "soft-money" campaign finance bill was approved by Congress in 2002. Sophisticated Washington insiders recognized immediately, however, that even if the law was not

---

* As of this writing, the 2004 Bush presidential campaign had built a campaign fund in excess of $200 million, breaking all previous records. See Thomas B. Edsall, Sarah Cohen, and James V. Grimaldi, "Pioneers Fill War Chest, Then Capitalize," *Washington Post*, May 16, 2004, p. A1.

reversed by the Supreme Court,* big contributors could easily find alternatives to channel money to special-interest
front groups and to exert influence in other ways. Trying to
get money out of politics, Senator Mitch McConnell comments, is "like putting a rock on Jell-O. You can squeeze it
down, but it just goes in other directions." (This reality has
not escaped the average voter: a 2002 Gallup poll found that
two-thirds of respondents believe that "no matter what new
laws are passed, special interests will always find a way to
maintain their power in Washington.")[6]

The deeper issue is thus profoundly challenging: even the
most far-reaching reforms are unlikely to succeed, it appears,
given the underlying pattern of inequality.

Put another way: until the foundational question of
whether some other way to reduce inequality is confronted
and resolved, it is unlikely that the *democratic* question of
how to curb the influence of money in politics can be effectively dealt with. And given the failure of traditional
approaches, for better or worse this again brings the problem
of democratic renewal back to asset-based strategies and new
institutional approaches to altering wealth ownership.

Intimately related to economic inequality is the matter of
time—in this case as it concerns democracy as well as liberty. From Aristotle on, it has been obvious that democracy
becomes meaningless if people do not have time to participate. Barber, concerned that a third of the workforce works
more than forty-five hours a week, emphasizes that democracy requires "time to be educated into civil society, time to
participate in deliberation, time to serve on juries, occupy
municipal magistracies, volunteer for civic activities." Various ways to reduce the workweek, as we have seen, have
begun to be put forward. However, most of these in turn
require some way to distribute income more equitably—

---

* In a decision handed down on December 10, 2003, *McConnell v. Federal Election
Commission,* the Court approved many but not all of the provisions of the law.

hence, also wealth—so that time itself can be more equitably distributed.*[7]

The implications different economic arrangements have for democratic practice are also obvious in connection with the political influence of large corporations. As we have noted, Thomas Jefferson, Louis Brandeis, and such theorists as Henry C. Simons (along with many traditional conservatives), to say nothing of Karl Marx, all held large corporations to be incompatible in various ways with democratic practice. Although their alternative systemic solutions—entrepreneurial and smaller-scale capitalism, on the one hand, socialism, on the other—no longer appear viable, the underlying question has not gone away.

We are here at the very heart of the system problem. The key question: Is there any way to achieve democratic control in the face of the self-evident power of giant enterprises? Are there *any* viable longer-term alternatives?

A host of studies have documented some of the most obvious realities. The large corporation regularly

1. Influences legislation and agenda setting through lobbying
2. Influences regulatory behavior through direct and indirect pressure
3. Influences elections via large-scale campaign contributions
4. Influences public attitudes through massive media campaigns
5. Influences local government choices through all of the above—and adds the implicit or explicit threat of withdrawing its plants, equipment, and jobs from specific locations

---

* Inequality is also related to trust and to social capital, Putnam's main concern. Studies by Eric Uslaner and his associates indicate that inequality is the strongest single predictor of trust across nations. It follows that from this perspective as well—that is, if trust and social capital are to be reconstituted as a basis of democratic renewal—there is no way to avoid the question of how to deal with inequality. See Eric M. Uslaner, "Producing and Consuming Trust," *Political Science Quarterly*, vol. 115, no. 4 (2000–2001), pp. 569–590, cited material on pp. 588–589.

6. Influences choices at all levels by virtue of the simple fact that in the absence of an alternative, the economy as a whole depends on the viability and success of its most important economic actor—a reality that commonly forces citizen and politician alike to respond to corporate demands.[8]

One of the main "countervailing" forces checking the political powers of the corporation has been organized labor. With the steady decline of labor union membership, however, there has also been a weakening of labor's direct and indirect capacity to constrain corporate influence. Corporations now commonly account for three out of every four political donations in congressional elections—outnumbering labor contributions almost 14 to 1.[9]

Robert Kaplan is blunt: "[T]he influence that corporations wield over government and the economy is so vast and obvious that the point needs no elaboration. . . . Democratic governance, at the federal, state, and local levels, goes on. But its ability to affect our lives is limited."[10]

A former president of the American Political Science Association, Charles Lindblom, concludes his prizewinning book *Politics and Markets* with this judgment: "The large private corporation fits oddly into democratic theory and vision. Indeed, it does not fit."[11]

The classic twentieth-century strategies aimed at making corporations more accountable centered, first, on antitrust efforts; second, on various forms of public regulation. Such strategies do not attempt to move beyond the corporation as an institution; they essentially hope to use publically backed efforts to constrain its activities. With antitrust now of marginal importance both economically and in terms of its original "democratic power" applications, regulation is the main remaining traditional alternative.

But it is also increasingly clear that the effectiveness of regulatory strategies is extremely limited in many areas, and

under attack in several others. During the final decades of
the twentieth century, deregulation occurred in connection
with trucking, airlines, railroads, telecommunications,
energy transmission, and large sectors of the financial services and banking industry. Corporations also have been able
to develop powerful lobbying and other tactics to influence
federal agencies and commissions established to oversee
their functioning. Although the Enron, WorldCom, and other
scandals forced its hand in certain areas, the administration
of George W. Bush has been particularly aggressive in challenging traditional regulatory strategies.[12]

In its first years in office the administration froze and ultimately weakened regulations covering workplace ergonomic
rules, medical privacy standards, preferences for union labor
in federal contracts, and rules covering the disqualification of
companies with prior workplace, environmental, and other
compliance records from new government contracts. The
Bush administration has also attempted to weaken appliance
efficiency standards for items such as air conditioners and
refrigerators, abandoned a campaign pledge to limit carbon
dioxide emissions, and quickly settled the Microsoft antitrust
case. It weakened protections for wetlands, eased mining
laws, and simply sidestepped the Kyoto accord on global
warming. In June 2003 Bush's Federal Communications
Commission appointees relaxed media ownership rules permitting a single corporation to own mutiple major outlets in
one city (allowing, in the biggest cities, one company to
directly control three television stations, eight radio stations,
and a newspaper).[13]

Scholarly analyses have illuminated the foundational logic
that commonly reduces the impact of traditional regulatory
strategies. One large body of research provides detailed studies of the systematic and regular processes through which
"iron triangles" of corporate and other pressures hedge in
and co-opt regulatory systems—allowing just enough reform to buy off critics without seriously challenging basic

corporate priorities. Quite regularly, political scientist Marver Bernstein observes, "faced with the organized opposition . . . a commission finds its survival as a regulating body dependent heavily on its facility in reaching a *modus operandi* with the regulated groups."[14]

Nobel laureate George Stigler demonstrated early on that regulation often is actually sought by leading firms in an industry as a way to maintain dominance. Even when it is thrust upon the industry, regulation commonly "is designed and operated primarily for its benefit." The result is what another respected conservative, James Q. Wilson, calls "a government of cartels and clients." (Ralph Nader characterizes the same implicit collusion as "corporate socialism, a condition of federal statecraft wherein public agencies control much of the private economy on behalf of a designated corporate clientele.")[15]

As the comments of conservatives like Stigler and Wilson suggest, these are not simply liberal or academic concerns. Nor do they relate only to the policies of the Bush administration. We have noted the experience of William Simon, Richard Nixon's secretary of the Treasury—and his "incredulity as businessmen ran to the government in every crisis, whining for handouts or protection." David Stockman, the architect of the so-called Reagan Revolution, came to the conclusion that the political power of "strong clients" like Boeing, Lockheed, General Electric, and Westinghouse was simply overwhelming. They "know how to make themselves heard. The problem is, unorganized groups can't play in this game."[16]

The "Chicago school" conservative economist Henry C. Simons analyzed the underlying logic of power and came to the conclusion that "regulatory strategies" involved the worst of all solutions. Even public ownership was better, he felt— even from the perspective of free-market economic theory. At least it provided for public disclosure of information and open oversight. The state, Simons proposed, "should face the necessity of actually taking over, owning, and managing directly . . .

industries in which it is impossible to maintain effectively competitive conditions." Likely candidates included railroads, "utilities, oil extraction, life insurance, etc." For similar reasons Simons suggested that it might make sense for metropolitan governments to "acquire much or most of the land in their areas."[17]

Although the problem of "regulatory capture" is real, it does not follow that there is no role for regulatory strategies in a longer-term foundational approach. Many gains have been achieved in connection with the environment and other matters.[18] A central question is, under what conditions can regulation be made to work effectively and efficiently? Part of the answer clearly involves the extent to which an engaged citizenry has the experience, time, and money to force regulatory agencies to hold corporations to publicly determined standards.

But this in turn brings the question back, again, to issues of citizen democratic experience, on the one hand, and inequality, on the other. Both also drive the question back, once more, to the institutional foundations—particularly economic—that are required to nurture a truly democratic citizenry (see Chapters 1 and 3).

At this stage of the reassessment process, no fully comprehensive proposal has as yet been put forward that even in theory fully confronts the challenge to democratic practice presented by the power of the large corporation. Various thinkers have, however, begun to offer a number of suggestions that move in the direction of a comprehensive approach that might one day plausibly be combined with other emerging ideas to produce an integrated strategy. (See below and Chapter 6.) These proposed partial solutions center on the legal status of the corporation; the role of public and quasi-public "stakeholders"; the degree to which the corporation can be democratized from within; and the leverage that public or quasi-public ownership of corporate stock can confer.

The large for-profit corporation is a creation of society. It has no independent right to exist absent a public charter that spells out its rights and obligations. For much of the nineteenth century, significant scale corporations in the main were authorized only to undertake specific public or quasi-public projects—for example, the construction of waterways and canals. Large, independent, limited-liability corporations evolved slowly, gaining real economic purchase only after the Civil War.[19]

A number of writers have urged replacing or supplementing current state chartering of corporations with federal chartering to avoid states "racing to the bottom" to set minimum chartering requirements (a reform also urged by Henry C. Simons years earlier). Senate Minority Leader Tom Daschle and former House Minority Leader Richard Gephardt, among others, have proposed related legislation to establish "R corporations" that would receive preferential tax treatment if they agreed to a stipulated code of conduct. Sociologist Charles Derber has proposed that corporate charters define an explicit public purpose and include social, environmental, and accountability requirements.[20]

More fundamentally, Rabbi Michael Lerner, the editor of *Tikkun,* suggests a "Social Responsibility Amendment" to the U.S. Constitution that would require each corporation to renew its charter every twenty years. If a corporation could not prove that it serves the common good, its charter would be revoked and its assets distributed to another community group that could better meet important social goals.[21]

A second line of strategy centers on proposals by another group of analysts that employee, community, and other stakeholders be granted seats on corporate boards so they can directly represent their interests. Ralph Estes of the Stakeholder Alliance suggests that corporations also be required to provide the Securities and Exchange Commission with an extensive array of information on social and environmental performance—and that such information be made available to workers, to consumers, to suppliers, and to the communities corporations serve through mandated "Corporate Reports." In addition, "stakeholder councils" with limited powers would be established to provide oversight for the enterprise.[22]

The challenge confronting proposals to redefine the legal status of the corporation is obviously similar to that facing regulatory strategies. Although changes in citizen capacities might one day alter the underlying relationships, currently the corporation clearly has sufficient independence to avoid or severely limit the proposed constraints. Similarly, while stakeholder representation also offers the possibility of greater accountability, it has done little so far to alter the fundamental power relationships in U.S. companies where it has been tried, or in countries such as Germany where a related approach—"codetermination"—has been attempted.* Indeed, many observers feel that unless bolstered by much more fundamental reforms, such participation can all too easily lead to the "co-optation" of labor representatives and other stakeholders.[23]

The third line of proposed strategies emphasizes internal corporate democratization: Columbia University professor Seymour Melman theorizes that workplace democracy might ultimately "encompass every major aspect of activity necessary to production, and thereby construct an alternative to the hierarchical systems of both business and government—an alternative to state capitalism." A comprehensive system of self-governing employee-owned enterprises, Robert Dahl holds, "would tend to . . . give all citizens a more nearly equal stake in maintaining political equality and democratic institutions in the government of the state." David Ellerman, the former adviser to the chief economist of the World Bank, proposes that all corporations be restructured as partnerships, with all workers included as partners with ownership and governance rights.[24]

---

* Several U.S. corporations currently have labor representatives on their boards—including Daimler-Chrysler, Bureau of National Affairs, and United Airlines.

The thrust of such democratization proposals is in line with a trend among sophisticated corporate managers that emphasizes the efficiency gains greater employee empowerment can produce.[25] It is also in line with the developing thrust of worker-ownership proposals for small- and medium-size locally based firms. However, there are obvious limits to this approach as well. Critically, most of the ideas for *internal* democratization simply do not confront the *external* political and power dynamics of the very large-scale firms that are of central concern. Even democratized corporations have reasons to exercise their inherent political power when their particular interests are at stake.

A final line of developing strategies involves significantly greater institutional change. This focuses on the large blocks of stock held by public and private pension funds.

In the 1970s Peter Drucker coined the phrase "pension fund socialism" to underscore the potential leverage that large-scale capital accumulations might give major pension funds. A few years later the activist-writers Jeremy Rifkin and Randy Barber suggested that pension funds be required to finance a Midwest regional "rust-belt" reinvestment plan centered on worker and community-based firms; a more recent treatise by sociologist Robin Blackburn has offered detailed analyses and recommendations for a comprehensive long-term strategy. Blackburn and others also have urged unions and public authorities to shift their current pension investment priorities to achieve other public goals—and a number have invested successfully in housing, on the one hand, and businesses that provide jobs in certain states, on the other (see below and Chapter 10).[26]

The broader corporate-accountability and democracy possibilities that an extension of public pension fund strategies might ultimately offer is suggested by recent developments in California. CalPERS (California Public Employees' Retirement System), the state employee pension fund, is the second-largest U.S. pension fund and third-largest in the world. It has long used its financial power to encourage corporate governance reforms, recently divesting itself of tobacco stock and rejecting investments in companies fleeing the country for offshore tax relief. CalPERS' leadership also helped organize a national coalition of state treasurers who oversee combined portfolios of more than a trillion dollars to force investment banks to reassess conflicts of interest.

Beyond this, CalPERS requires companies seeking investment support to follow a specified code of conduct in their international investment practices: firms from emerging-market nations are judged according to their governments' records on human rights, labor rights, corruption, and investor protections. "Show me a company locating offshore in Bermuda or polluting the environment and I'll show you a company that's going to screw its shareholders," declares California treasurer Phil Angelides. "Transparency, democracy, labor rights, these are all issues that should be part of fund managers' due diligence."[27]

Though the financial interests of the public pension fund as shareholder can sometimes be in tension with other issues of public and employee concern, the evolving experience of CalPERS and other pension funds suggests that a growing body of "democratic accountability" experience vis-à-vis the corporation is steadily being developed by such efforts.[28]

There are also some obvious structural parallels—and potential connections to be made—between the new strategies and some of the strategies emerging in connection with equality:

In Chapter 1 we reviewed wealth-related proposals by Roemer, Meade, and Kelso that involve large-scale publicly backed stock ownership aimed at producing a supplemental income stream for citizens. Those of Roemer and Meade also require some form of public authority—very similar to the agencies that manage public pension funds—to oversee the investment of stock on behalf of the citizenry.

The developing trajectory of public pension fund practice, on the one hand, and the proposed publicly backed income-producing strategies, on the other—taken together—point logically in the direction of a system-wide wealth-ownership approach that, at least in theory, might one day offer ways to achieve both greater democratic accountability and greater equality.

Standing back from the steadily evolving reassessment process, the historically interesting questions are the pace at which each of the emerging strategies for dealing with the power of the corporation might continue to develop and be refined—and whether key aspects of each might be integrated with other emerging approaches to one day achieve a fully comprehensive democracy-enhancing approach.*[29] We shall return to these questions shortly.

---

* See Chapter 7. CalPERS and several other public pension funds also allocate a share of investment to economic development within the borders of the state—a strategy that can in turn be used to help achieve community economic stability goals related to the support of local democratic experience.

5

Democracy

Is a Continent Too Large?

O NE FINAL IMPORTANT cross-cutting democracy issue began to surface, very quietly and initially very marginally, as the reassessment process continued to develop momentum. This involved what should have been an obvious question to those interested in equality, liberty, and democracy all along: namely, is it really feasible—in systemic and foundational terms—to sustain such values in a very large-scale, centrally governed continental system that spans almost three thousand miles and includes almost 300 million people? And if not, how might a democratic nation ultimately be conceived?

Reflection on the impact of very large scale on democracy can be traced back to the Greeks, and later especially to Montesquieu, who held that democracy could flourish only in small nations. The judgment that very large scale is inimical to democracy was also taken very seriously by the founding fathers. Indeed, at a time when the United States hardly extended beyond the Appalachian mountains, John Adams worried: "What would Aristotle and Plato have said, if anyone had talked to them, of a federative republic of thirteen states, inhabiting a country of five hundred leagues in extent?" Similarly—again, at a time when the nation numbered a mere 4 million people—even James Madison (who challenged the traditional argument that democracy was possible only in small nations) believed that a very large (rather than a "mean"-scale) republic could easily become a de facto tyranny because elites at the center would be able to divide and conquer diverse groups dispersed throughout the system.* Few people imagined democracy in a continent.[1]

One can also isolate important and difficult aspects of the question of scale in the larger complex of issues that in the nineteenth century culminated in the Civil War.[2] For our purposes, however, it is sufficient to recall that a sophisticated theoretical debate over scale problems began to develop in academic and political centers during the early years of the twentieth century, continuing up to and through the 1920s and 1930s.

The traditional response to the argument that democracy is difficult if not impossible in very large scale units has been to propose decentralization to the states. The point of departure for the more sophisticated debate is recognition that many states are simply too small to manage important economic issues, or for instance (in the 1930s as well as in modern times) a number of important ecological matters. Logically, if a continental national system is too large and many states are too small, the obvious answer must be something in-between—the unit of scale we call a "region."

Historian Frederick Jackson Turner put it this way: "There is a sense in which sectionalism is inevitable and desirable"—going on to observe: "As soon as we cease to be dominated by the political map, divided into rectangular states . . . groups of states and geographic provinces, rather than individual states, press upon the historian's attention."[3]

---

* "*Divide et impera,* the reprobated axiom of tyranny, is under certain qualifications, the only policy by which a republic can be administered on just principles. It must be observed however that this doctrine can only hold within a sphere of a mean extent. As in too small a sphere oppressive combinations may be too easily formed agst. the weaker party; so in too extensive a one, a defensive concert may be rendered too difficult against the oppression of those entrusted with the administration." James Madison to Thomas Jefferson, October 24, 1787, in *The Papers of James Madison,* vol. 10, ed. William T. Hutchinson et al. (Chicago: University of Chicago Press, 1977), pp. 207–215.

A leading conservative theorist who urged the same logic during the 1930s was Harvard political scientist William Yandell Elliot: "Regional commonwealths would be capable of furnishing units of real government, adequate laboratories of social experiment, and areas suited to economic, not-too-cumbersome administration."[4]

"The libertarian argument against 'too much government,'" Henry C. Simons held, "relates mainly to national governments, not to provincial or local units—and to great powers rather than to small nations." Simons believed a "break-up" of the United States "desirable" (though he did not think it politically feasible). The alternative, he urged, required taking seriously a process of "steady decentralization."[5]

Another Harvard professor and president of the American Political Science Association, William Bennett Munro, did not mince words about the issues and logic that he believed needed to be confronted: "Most Americans do not realize what an imperial area they possess," he said, adding, "Many important issues and problems . . . are problems too big for any single state, yet not big enough for the nation as a whole . . . They belong by right to regional governments."[*][6]

The then innovative experiment with regionalism, environmental management, and public ownership—the Tennessee Valley Authority—was related to the early twentieth-century

---

* Lewis Mumford and others associated with the regional planning movement also urged decentralization. However, they rarely confronted larger constitutional questions aimed at restructuring the continental political economy as a whole. See Mark Luccarelli, *Lewis Mumford and the Ecological Region: The Politics of Planning* (New York: The Guilford Press, 1995). Similarly, Howard Odum and other writers concerned with Southern regionalist sociology and culture during the 1930s rarely posed constitutional political-economic questions. See Howard W. Odum and Harry Estill Moore, *American Regionalism: A Cultural-Historical Approach to National Integration* (Gloucester, Mass.: Peter Smith, 1966); Harry Estill Moore, *What Is Regionalism?* (Chapel Hill: University of North Carolina Press, 1937); Michael Steiner and Clarence Mondale, *Region and Regionalism in the United States: A Source Book for the Humanities and Social Sciences* (New York: Garland Publishing, 1988); and Robert L. Dorman, *Revolt of the Provinces: The Regionalist Movement in America, 1920–1945* (Chapel Hill: University of North Carolina Press, 1993).

regional rethinking movement, as were proposals by Franklin Delano Roosevelt for similar regional authorities throughout the country. Even though President Harry Truman continued to offer such ideas (in connection, for instance, with the Columbia River), the regionalist movement was cut short by a combination of anti–New Deal politics and the advent of World War II and the era of the Cold War.[7]

The underlying issue of scale, however, is plainly still with us. Moreover, the extraordinary cost of modern campaigning in large areas has added to the advantages that scale gives to wealthy elites and corporations, thereby further undermining democratic possibilities. Money talks louder when expensive television ads are the only way to reach large numbers. During the election of 2000 an estimated $1 billion was spent on television alone. A total of more than $50 million was spent by George Bush, Al Gore, and their backers in only two states (Pennsylvania and Florida) where the outcome was expected to be close.[8]

We rarely pause to consider the truly huge size of the American system. The fact is, the United States is extreme in scale. Germany could fit within the borders of Montana alone; France is smaller than Texas. Leaving aside the two nations with large empty land masses (Canada and Australia), the United States is larger geographically than all the other advanced industrial (OECD) countries taken together—that is, Austria, Belgium, the Czech Republic, Denmark, Finland, France, Germany, Greece, Hungary, Iceland, Ireland, Italy, Japan, Korea, Luxembourg, Mexico, the Netherlands, New Zealand, Norway, Poland, Portugal, the Slovak Republic, Spain, Sweden, Switzerland, Turkey, and the United Kingdom.[9]

Moreover, population growth alone is likely to raise ever more challenging questions as time goes on. Census Bureau "middle series" projections suggest the United States will add another 120-million-person nation to its population by midcentury—for a total of approximately 400 million; and then will add another 170 million, to roughly double the current population to 570 million by century's end. There are reasons to believe these may well be conservative estimates, but even if they are discounted considerably, the population of the United States will become extraordinarily large by any measure as time goes on (see Chapter 14).

What is of interest now are a series of discrete indications that the question of scale has begun to resurface in diverse quarters—in part as a resumption of the trend that was interrupted by World War II and the Cold War, in part in response to emerging considerations and global developments.

A 1973 book, *Size and Democracy*, by Robert A. Dahl and Edward R. Tufte, opened the modern discussion by offering a detailed assessment of the then available studies. A variety of questions had to be confronted by those concerned with democracy, it concluded, as "the inexorable thrust of population growth makes a small country large and a large country gigantic."[10]

Daniel Bell subsequently joined in, arguing that the "nation-state is becoming too small for the big problems of life, and too big for the small problems of life." Bell went on, "[T]he flow of power to a national political center means that the national center becomes increasingly unresponsive to the variety and diversity of local needs. . . . In short, there is a mismatch of scale."[11]

George F. Kennan took the argument a step further: "We are, if territory and population be looked at together, one of the great countries of the world—a monster country. . . . And there is a real question as to whether bigness in a body politic is not an evil in itself, quite aside from the policies pursued in its name." Kennan proposed long-term regional devolution which, "while retaining certain of the rudiments of a federal government," might yield a "dozen constituent republics, absorbing not only the powers of the existing states but a considerable part of those of the present federal establishment."[12]

The radical historian, the late William Appleman Williams, suggested a strategy embodying socialist principles: "[T]he issue is not whether to decentralize the economy and the politics of the country, but rather how to do so. The solution here revolves about the regional elements that make up the existing whole." And the modern conservative regionalist, Donald Livingston, asked in 2002: "What value is there in continuing to prop up a union of this monstrous size?" He went on: "[T]here are ample resources in the American federal tradition to justify states' and local communities' recalling, out of their own sovereignty, powers they have allowed the central government to usurp."[13]

The titles of several general works are themselves illustrative of the modern trend: *Downsizing the USA*, by Thomas H. Naylor and William H. Willimon; *The Nine Nations of North America*, by Joel Garreau; and Robert Goodman's *The Last Entrepreneurs: America's Regional Wars for Jobs and Dollars.*[14]

A converging trend of environmental thinking is also significant. Much of the work of the Environmental Protection Agency is already organized along regional lines, and as Harvard analyst Mary Graham observes, "Many environmental problems are inherently regional in scope, rather than national or local." Among the interesting proposals here are suggestions by Kirkpatrick Sale that emphasize small "bio-regions" and work on "eco-regions" by World Wildlife Fund experts in the Conservation Science Program.[15] A fully developed long-term ecological vision in which many "regions within the United States could become relatively self-sufficient" has been put forward by Herman Daly and John Cobb. "[T]he nation-state is already too large and too remote from ordinary people for effective participation to be possible."[16]

The various developing arguments have also received indirect support from research on the achievements of smaller-scale nations—some roughly equivalent to U.S. regions. The Scandinavian nations and such countries as Austria and the Netherlands, for instance, have demonstrated that smaller scale has commonly helped—rather than hindered—their capacity to deal with major economic, social, and environmental problems. In general, equality has been greater and unemployment rates lower than in most larger European countries. Moreover, although such nations are far more involved in trade than larger nations, for the most part they have found more effective ways to manage the dislocations and other challenges brought about by economic globalization.*[17]

In a related development, political scientist Michael Wallerstein has demonstrated how the United States's very large scale and huge labor force have made union organizing both difficult and expensive. This in turn has tended to limit union size, thereby both weakening collective bargaining and undercutting one of the primary organizational foundations of progressive political-economic strategies in general.[18]

The modern reemergence of regionalist ideas is no accident. Although the primary thrust of the argument concerns what it takes to achieve democratic accountability and participation, the American discussion is part and parcel of a worldwide trend that is already producing different forms of regional devolution in nations as diverse as Britain and Canada, on the one hand, and China and the former Soviet Union, on the other (see 165–166).

A global perspective, in fact, suggests that the quietly emerging—and seemingly unusual—American arguments are only the beginning of something that is all but certain to grow in force and sophistication as time goes on.

---

* In 2000 unemployment in the European Union averaged 8.4 percent—while that of Austria was 3.6 percent, Denmark 4.6 percent, Luxembourg 1.9 percent, the Netherlands 3.3 percent, and Norway 3.5 percent. *OECD in Figures: Statistics on the Member Countries* (Paris: OECD, 2002), pp. 20–21. Norway, Iceland, Sweden, the Netherlands, and Belgium also all ranked higher than France, Germany, Italy, and Britain—and the United States—in a 2003 United Nations composite index that included standard of living, social and economic equality, access to knowledge, personal security, human and labor rights, and environmental sustainability indicators. United Nations Development Programme, *Human Development Report 2003* (New York: Oxford University Press, 2003), pp. 237–239, www.undp.org/hdr2003 (accessed 07/10/03).

6

The Pluralist Commonwealth

INCREASING NUMBERS OF Americans concerned with equality, liberty, and democracy have begun to despair that traditional strategies to achieve the nation's most fundamental values simply no longer work. If corporate capitalism (to say nothing of the socialist model) appears unable to sustain equality, liberty, and democracy, is there any conceivable, logically coherent way forward?

It is possible to bring together critical elements of the evolving foundational thinking, and project and extend others, to define the underlying structural building blocks of a political-economic system "model" that is different in fundamental ways from both traditional capitalism and socialism.

The schematic model flowing from the various considerations emphasizes the systematic development of a robust vision of community democracy as the necessary foundation for a renewal of democracy in general. It prioritizes a variety of strategies to undergird local economies and thereby establish conditions favorable to nurturing local civil society associations and to increasing local government's power to make meaningful decisions.

Partly to achieve such local democracy objectives—but for much larger reasons as well—the model also projects the development over time of new ownership institutions, including locally anchored worker-owned and other community-benefiting firms, on the one hand, and various national wealth-holding, asset-based strategies, on the other. These ultimately would take the place of current elite and corporate ownership of the preponderance of large-scale capital.

At the national level a major new institution—call it a "Public Trust"—would be projected to oversee the investment of stock on behalf of the public, as state and other pension boards commonly do today. Variations include allowing the proceeds to flow to individuals, to states, to municipalities, to the federal treasury—or perhaps to fund such basic public services as education or medical care for the elderly.

Over time a fundamental shift in the ownership of wealth would slowly move the nation as a whole toward greater equality directly—through, for instance, worker-owned enterprises; and also indirectly—through a flow of funds from the larger asset-based strategies and investment on behalf of the public. (Capital would likely be assembled both by the taxation of elite income and wealth and by Kelso-type loan-guarantee strategies to finance the broadened ownership of new investments.)

Over the long arc of the twenty-first century and beyond, the flow of funds from such sources would also be allocated to help finance a reduction in the workweek so as to permit greater amounts of free time, thereby bolstering both individual liberty and democratic participation. In addition, the traditional entrepreneurial foundations of liberty are strengthened in the model by the strategies that stabilize the local economy (as, of course, is individual job security as well).

Finally, the emerging model implicitly moves in the direction of, and ultimately projects, a radical long-term devolution of the national system to some form of regional reorganization and decentralization—a strategic move important not only to democracy and liberty, but to the successful democratic management of ecological and other issues as well.

The overall system model defined by the critical structural elements might be termed a "Pluralist Commonwealth"— "Pluralist" to emphasize the priority given to democratic

diversity and individual liberty; "Commonwealth" to underscore the centrality of new public and quasi-public wealth-
holding institutions that take on ever greater power on behalf
of the community of the nation as a whole as the twenty-first
century unfolds.[1]

Although at this stage of development the model is obviously
general in form, certain features of the Pluralist Commonwealth's political-economic architecture are striking. Of particular interest is that its basic elements, taken together, offer
an integrated approach to dealing with a number of the fundamental power problems presented by large-scale economic
enterprise in any system—capitalist, socialist, or other.

First, over time the model steadfastly attempts to nurture
and rebuild democratic experience by supporting various
mechanisms to make democratic practice real in the lives of
citizens. The development of a meaningful democratic culture is foundational: a guiding judgment is that without
attention to nurturing the conditions needed to support an
active and engaged citizenry, very little can be done either in
theory or in practice to achieve larger democratic goals.

Second, the model opens a steadily expanding wedge of
time for individuals to participate in democracy. This is one
of the Pluralist Commonwealth's most important elements.
Without time to participate, authentic democratic processes
to constrain economic actors (be they private or public), and
to monitor a revitalized public sector, are simply not possible.

Third, the model's financial mechanisms also aim to
translate technological gains into greater equality—thereby
offering long-term possibilities for equality of democratic
participation in general and for challenging and containing
the power of large-scale enterprise in particular.

Fourth, as in the case of modern public pension fund
management, the change in ownership legitimizes the public's inherent right to ensure that major firms are made
accountable to larger concerns—even as competitive practices are encouraged through a variety of well-established

techniques.* New ownership forms also inherently facilitate accountability measures requiring greater openness and transparency in enterprise management and governance.

Fifth, the longer-range Pluralist Commonwealth vision ultimately and over the long haul also reduces the scale of public institutions that hold firms to account. Though it is increasingly difficult to achieve effective "vertical" political associations across a continent, regional scale units (as, for instance, now in certain states) offer important strategic possibilities for greater political control of corporate practices.

Neither traditional socialism nor traditional capitalism deals well with the power problems presented by large-scale enterprise. Significant economic actors in the socialist state are commonly unaccountable either to market forces or to the public; they are power systems within a power system.[2] The modern for-profit corporation is for the most part unaccountable to the public—and contrary to traditional theory, in most cases unaccountable to its shareholders as well. As the Enron and other scandals have shown (and many scholarly studies demonstrate) managers and top executives largely run the system, dominating boards and annual meetings alike. Rarely are successful challenges to their power successful, even by major shareholders.[3]

The Pluralist Commonwealth structurally tethers large-scale firms at the top by lodging stock ownership in a Public Trust entity accountable to (and open to scrutiny by) the public—and it steadily expands four major vectors of activity and structure (robust community democracy, steadily increasing free time, greater citizen equality, regional decentralization) that over the long haul offer expanding opportunities for democratic control from the bottom. Additional

---

* Typically public pension funds hire contending teams of investment managers, discarding losers and rewarding winners in a disciplined process of internal competition. "This is not financial rocket science," observe financial experts Alicia Munnell and R. Kent Weaver in a related discussion. ("How to Privatize Social Security," *Washington Post*, July 9, 2001, p. A17.)

elements of the model include new public chartering requirements, the addition of specific stakeholders to corporate boards, and the democratization of corporate structures from within.

That the emerging system model leaves numerous questions unresolved is obvious. On the other hand, the Pluralist Commonwealth clearly defines a series of strategic propositions around which debate is already beginning to form. As research, dialogue, and further development continue over time, specific issues are likely to be increasingly clarified and answers found to the most important unresolved questions. Driving the process is the fact that traditional solutions simply no longer even attempt to offer theoretically plausible responses to many critical questions.

It is commonly held that free-enterprise capitalism is the most efficient of all systems—certainly more efficient than traditional socialism—and that other possibilities must inevitably also be inefficient. Even at this stage of its development, however, there are reasons to believe the Pluralist Commonwealth could equal or possibly surpass the efficiency of real-world capitalism.

First, although some of the wastes and inefficiencies of capitalism are occasionally highlighted in the media, we are beginning to grasp just how vast these may be. The electricity crisis in California in 2000 and 2001 cost the state tens of billions of dollars. A conservative estimate is that over $10 billion was directly attributable to market manipulations by private firms. Corporate scandals in 2001 to 2003 cost New York State alone an estimated $13 billion.[4] The Enron scandal cost workers and pension holders $1 billion. The savings and loan bailout in the first Bush administration cost taxpayers $125 billion in direct costs, plus an estimated additional $275 billion in subsequent years for interest and increased service of the national debt. Lobbying by the oil, pharmaceutical, insurance, television, banking, and other industries regularly generates further billions of dollars of questionable federal subsidies. This is to say nothing of numerous widely publicized scandals and bankruptcies that have illuminated many other obvious and well-known, but commonly ignored, costs routinely associated with current economic practices.[5]

Second, various quasi-public and public firms (e.g., worker-owned firms, municipal electric utilities) have been shown to be at least as efficient as traditional corporations—and in many instances, more efficient. Public pension management strategies of the kind that would likely be used in the proposed public asset management systems have also been demonstrated to commonly be as efficient or more efficient than those of private pensions.[6]

Third, salaries paid to public managers in comparable positions are far lower. For instance, William J. McDonough, then the president of the Federal Reserve Bank of New York, received $297,500 in 2001, while William Harrison, the CEO of J.P. Morgan Chase, took home more than $21 million. Top executives managing large state-run pension investments (e.g., CalPERS) received compensation of less than $450,000 in 2001—while William Foley, the chairman and CEO of Fidelity National Financial, garnered more than $13 million. Compensation for top executives in the Tennessee Valley Authority is regularly much less than compensation for executives managing major private electric utilities.[7]

Fourth, it is clear that additional strategies to achieve economic efficiency are already being developed—and are likely to continue to be developed. Kelso, Roemer, Meade, and Stauber all have suggested ways to combine the public's interest in important economic activity with strategies to ensure the independence of strictly business decisions and the use of market discipline—and additional variations and refinements are likely to be put forward as time goes on. Investment managers who oversee endowments for universities and other public institutions have also developed strategies that can be drawn upon to balance longer-term growth objectives with the need to ensure against cyclical fund-flow downturns.

Critics of public involvement in economic matters commonly implicitly compare new approaches with the efficiency properties of a competitive but exceedingly abstract and rarefied free-market model. The result is a self-serving "heads-I-win, tails-you-lose" economic argument: traditional political-economic practices are evaluated "as if" they were (or should be) purely efficient free-market operations, ignoring what everyone knows to be the actual dynamics of corporate political-economic behavior. Meanwhile, alternatives involving proposed public strategies are evaluated "as if" they must inherently involve grave political-economic market distortions—ignoring studies that demonstrate the measured efficiencies of a wide range of available alternative practices.

The truth is, various forms of manipulating the market are central to the operation of the current corporate-dominated political-economic system, not peripheral to it. They come with the territory—as everyone knows full well when they shift their gaze away from abstract theory to the real world of oil company lobbying, drug company political payoffs, Microsoft anticompetitive maneuvering, Enron corruption, and Andersen accounting complicity.

The Pluralist Commonwealth model breaks the logic of the traditional argument—first, by challenging the utopian idea that most firms keep away from government in the current system; second, by developing various strategies that allow for both competition and increased citizen accountability; and third, by structurally changing ownership patterns in ways that achieve greater transparency so that when the inevitable problems, public or private, arise, they can be openly debated and corrected. Finally, of course, the model's shift to new ownership forms inherently recaptures for broader public use excessive funds that might possibly be garnered through corporate political maneuvering.

We may add that to the extent the political-economic system defined by the Pluralist Commonwealth is able to achieve greater equality through the overarching wealth-holding changes it contemplates, it would likely also achieve much greater efficiencies in the development and use of human resources. Leaving aside the morality of the implicit choices of the present system, countless studies demonstrate that we currently throw away literally millions of productive people whose contribution to the economy could be enormous. To cite only one instance, recent research reveals that minority and other low-income students with high test scores are five times as likely not to attend college than high-income students with comparable scores. A mind, as the saying goes, is a terrible thing to waste—as are the contributions that might be made by so many Americans whose potential skills and capacities are left behind by the current system.[8]

PART II

THE DEMOCRATIZATION
OF WEALTH

A THEORETICAL MODEL IS A beginning point for serious discussion. The obvious question is whether there are any reasons to believe that the various elements of the Pluralist Commonwealth—separately and taken together—might ever build to significant scale and power.

At the very heart of the Pluralist Commonwealth is the principle that ownership of the nation's wealth must ultimately be shifted, institutionally, to benefit the vast majority. Are strategies based upon this fundamental principle technically feasible? Can they be politically viable?

Although theorists who urge wealth-oriented strategies occasionally cite illustrations from real-world experience (like the well-known Mondragon worker cooperatives in Spain), practical applications have not been at the center of the debate. Furthermore, even when one or another writer has pointed to current developments, it has commonly been within a narrow frame of reference and, even more commonly, viewed in static terms.

The fact is, literally thousands of on-the-ground efforts that illuminate how wealth-holding principles can work in practice have developed in communities throughout the nation over the last several decades. The range of practical activity—and the growing trend—have rarely been appreciated even by experts working on such matters. Specialists in narrowly defined sectors are aware of developments in their own field of expertise, but because of what is sometimes termed the "silo" effect, they often do not know of experiences in other areas.

Important political-economic forces have produced—and are likely to continue to produce—the conditions and unusual political alliances that have generated the new institutional developments and related policy activity. Moreover, opportunities for much broader political support appear all but certain to develop as the efforts gain momentum and as external political-economic conditions narrow the choices facing different groups.

The key question is not whether practical ways to implement wealth-owning principles are viable, but how rapidly they may move to substantial scale as the century progresses.

And whether the emerging efforts might one day establish foundations for a broader institution-shaping politics, and—as the external environment continues to change—perhaps thereafter of more fundamental system-wide political-economic restructuring in the direction of the Pluralist Commonwealth.

7

A Direct Stake in Economic Life

Worker-Owned Firms

THAT INDIVIDUALS WORK harder, better, and with greater enthusiasm when they have a direct interest in the outcome is self-evident to most people. The obvious question is: why aren't large numbers of businesses organized on this principle?

The answer is: in fact, thousands and thousands of them are. Indeed, more Americans now work in firms that are partly or wholly owned by the employees than are members of unions in the private sector![1]

The Appleton company, a world leader in speciality paper production in Appleton, Wisconsin, became employee-owned when the company was put up for sale by Arjo Wiggins Appleton, the multinational corporation that owned it—and the 2,500 employees decided they had just as much right to buy it as anyone else. Reflexite, an optics company based in New Avon, Connecticut, became employee-owned in 1985 after 3M made a strong bid for the company and the founding owners, loyal to their workers and the town, preferred to sell to the employees instead.[2] In the case of Science Applications International Corporation, the founder, Dr. J. Robert Beyster, has for more than thirty years simply believed that people "involved in the company should share in its success."[3]

One factor that has contributed to the rise of employee-owned firms is that multinational corporations often must seek the very highest profit they can make on invested capital—whereas workers living in a community are content with substantial profits (rather than the highest possible) since the other benefits of keeping a plant in town outweigh differences in profit rates. (Often, of course, when employees take ownership, the change produces greater efficiency—and greater profits than those which the multinational registered.)

A major boost to employee-ownership came from passage in 1974 (and thereafter) of federal legislation providing special tax benefits to Employee Stock Ownership Plans (ESOPs)—the legal structure that most such firms now utilize. Technically an ESOP involves a trust that receives and holds stock in a given corporation on behalf of its employees.

At the heart of the ESOP idea is the basic financing concept urged by Louis Kelso for broadening the ownership of wealth—namely, if some form of guarantee or collateral can be arranged to provide loans for productive investment, new wealth ownership by diverse groups (in this case employees of a firm) can be developed and paid for by the profits that the investment itself generates (see 25–26).

Although ESOPs based on this principle date from the 1950s, the modern federal legislation gave tax incentives to corporations contributing stock to an employee trust and to retiring owners of businesses who sell their corporations to employees and reinvest the proceeds within a defined time frame.

There are approximately 11,000 ESOPs now operating in communities in all regions of the United States. Asset holdings total more than $400 billion. The National Center for Employee Ownership (NCEO) estimates that total worker holdings (of all forms of stock ownership and stock options) reached approximately $800 billion in 2002—that is, roughly 8 percent of all U.S. corporate stock.[*4]

---

* There are also a smaller number of worker-cooperatives (perhaps two to three hundred) that are commonly organized along one-person, one-vote lines and on the basis of equal shares. Ownership can be structured in a number of other ways as well. An example is the Bureau of National Affairs (BNA) in Washington, D.C., a leading pub-

W. L. Gore, the maker of Gore-Tex apparel, is one of the most impressive modern ESOPs. The company, owned since 1974 by (currently 6,000) worker-owners in forty-five locations around the world, has no bosses or formal titles. To ensure communication and innovation, those working at any one site number no more than 200. Depending on their particular skills, workers may lead one task one week and follow other leaders the next week; teams disband after projects are completed, with team members moving on to other teams. W. L. Gore revenues totaled $1.33 billion in 2003; the firm regularly ranks on the *Fortune* "Best Companies to Work For" list.[5]

Another impressive ESOP, Weston Solutions, Inc., is the second largest environmental firm in the country. Its highly specialized services range from forestry and urban planning to high-hazard nuclear and chemical waste cleanups. The company has helped rehabilitate "sick" (asbestos, lead paint) school buildings from New York and Chicago to Decatur, Alabama. It was the lead information technology contractor in recovery operations after the space shuttle *Columbia* disaster. The company is 100 percent owned by its 1,800 employees. In recognition of its creative structure and its "consistent record of profitability, growth and financial stability," Weston received the *Environmental Business Journal's* top "gold" award for 2003.[6]

ESOP firms are also common in nonspecialized areas: Fetter Printing Company in Louisville, Kentucky, is 100 percent owned by its 200-plus workers. The firm has annual revenues of $17.5 million and was recently ranked as one of the top twenty-five printers in the United States. Fastener Industries

lisher of legal and regulatory information, which has been employee-owned since 1947 through a non-ESOP employee stock purchase plan. Roughly three-quarters of approximately 1,900 employees, along with a number of retirees, elect the board of directors. Annual revenues are over $250 million. BNA has been named to *Fortune*'s list of "100 Best Companies to Work For in America" three times, and has been included in *Working Mother* magazine's list of "100 Best Companies for Working Mothers" nine years running. It won the Employee Ownership 2000 Business Ethics award. BNA, "About BNA," www.bna.com/about (accessed 03/10/03).

in Berea, Ohio, is owned by more than 100 worker-owners. Machinists who have participated in the ESOP since 1980 commonly receive the equivalent of an additional three months' pay in dividends each year and retire with personal shareholding accounts of up to $350,000. Parametrix—100 percent owned by over 350 employees—is an environmental engineering firm headquartered in Sumner, Washington. The company was recently selected as one of the best companies to work for in Washington State—and was named 2001 National ESOP of the Year by the ESOP Association. In Harrisonburg, Virginia, ComSonics—100 percent owned by 160 employees—makes cable television (CATV) test and analysis devices and boasts the largest CATV repair facility in the United States.[7]

A 1998 survey of Washington State firms found that median hourly pay in ESOP firms was 12 percent higher than pay for comparable work in non-ESOP firms. Worker-owners of ESOPs also ended their careers with almost three times the retirement benefits of others with similar jobs. A 1990 study by the National Center for Employee Ownership estimated that an employee making $20,000 a year in a typical ESOP would accumulate $31,000 in stock over ten years—no small feat, considering that median financial wealth was just $11,700 during this period. A 2000 Massachusetts survey found ESOP accounts averaging just under $40,000.*[8]

---

* As these (and other) studies suggest, excessive media coverage sometimes given to failed worker-owned firms badly distorts the general picture of efficiency. Again, the bankruptcy of United Airlines is sometimes mistakenly attributed to the fact that it was significantly owned by employees. Aside from the fact that most airlines have experienced extraordinary difficulties in the wake of September 11, 2001—and that most ESOPs have been organized in (and work best in) small- and medium-size non-publicly traded firms—many worker-ownership experts judge that United's failure to deal with participation and related organizational issues (not its ownership structure) was a major factor in its poor performance. Southwest, which also has significant worker ownership—and a strong participatory culture—is one of the few profitable bright spots in the airline industry. J. Michael Keeling, "Statement Regarding United Airlines," 2003, www.esopassociation.org/media/united_airlines.html (accessed 03/07/03); James Flanigan, "United Is a Poor Model for Employee Ownership," *Los Angeles Times*, December 4, 2002.

It is also clear that ESOPs—and worker ownership in general—have broad political appeal for both practical and philosophical reasons. The ESOP concept has been endorsed by (among others) Ronald Reagan, Ralph Nader, Mario Cuomo, William F. Buckley, William Greider, Jack Kemp, Richard Gephardt, Mikhail Gorbachev, and Coretta Scott King. Both parties backed the tax legislation that now provides over $2 billion in annual support to ESOPs. Other forms of federal help include loan guarantees and the financing of worker-ownership feasibility studies in the event of plant closures or major layoffs.[9]

A number of state programs also provide support for worker ownership. One of the most widely recognized, the Ohio Employee Ownership Center, conducts feasibility studies for potential independent worker buyouts and for transition buyouts from retiring owners. The Michigan Workforce Transition Unit offers employee-ownership efforts feasibility-assessment assistance. Massachusetts funds the quasi-governmental Commonwealth Corporation, which provides technical and financial assistance to firms seeking to establish an ESOP.[10]

The extraordinary growth of ESOPs over the last thirty years has brought with it growing sophistication, the development of expert advisory and technical assistance organizations, a group of advocates and a group of critics, and—what is important—an expanding and diverse constituency interested in next-stage development of the institution.

Critics of ESOPs commonly decry the lack of democratic control offered to workers in most trust arrangements. They point out that unlike such leaders as W. L. Gore, many—indeed, most—ESOPs do not involve real participation; they often function mainly as a tax-favored legal mechanism to help employees accumulate additional assets over time. (It is estimated that only between a quarter and a third of ESOP companies pass through full voting rights to worker shareholders.) Moreover, since ESOPs commonly award stock in proportions related to wage and salary levels, they do little to improve overall compensation ratios and in some cases actually increase internal firm disparities due to compounding effects when stock values increase or dividends are received.*[11]

Several considerations suggest that greater democratic participation and control of ESOPs is likely to develop as time goes on—hence, also open the way for broader support. First, a significant share of ESOP companies (some three thousand, or nearly 30 percent of ESOPs in privately held companies) are already majority-owned by workers. Of these, 40 to 50 percent already pass voting rights through to plan participants. Second, as workers within specific firms steadily accumulate stock they become majority owners as time goes on. Surveys by the National Center for Employee Ownership reveal that the proportion of privately held ESOPs that are majority-owned increased approximately 50 percent during the past decade. Majority-owned firms increased from 38 percent of ESOP association members in 1989 to 68 percent in 2000.[12]

It is conceivable that as more and more ESOPs become majority-owned, workers will ignore the fact that in many firms they have little power. On the other hand, the more likely result—as *Business Week* observed in 1991—is that ultimately workers "who own a significant share of their companies will want a voice in corporate governance." In Ohio (which has been closely studied) a survey completed in the mid-1990s found that 53 percent of majority-owned ESOPs passed through voting rights. It also found that employee ownership was becoming more democratic over time, with three times as many closely held companies passing through full voting rights to ESOP participants as had been the case in a previous 1985–1986 survey.[13]

---

* Since ESOPs in general compensate workers better than non-ESOP firms, however, as the number of ESOPs grows nationally, the overall impact is in the direction of reducing inequality in the economy as a whole. Also, federal law does not offer tax deductions for stock contributions above a certain level, and since turnover among managers is also higher at the top than among blue-collar workers at the bottom, in practice internal compounding effects are commonly reduced.

The third—and perhaps most important—reason to expect change is that several studies demonstrate that greater participation leads to greater productivity and thus greater competitiveness in the marketplace. In general, ESOPs have been found to be as productive or more productive than comparable non-ESOP firms. Annual sales growth, on average, is also greater in ESOP than in non-ESOP firms. When ESOPs are structured to include greater participation, however, the advantages of worker ownership increase substantially. Studies undertaken by the National Center for Employee Ownership, by several teams of economists, and by the U.S. General Accounting Office all confirm that combining worker ownership with employee participation commonly produces greater productivity gains, in some cases over 50 percent.[14]

The number of ESOP-style worker-owned firms increased from 1,600 in 1975 to 4,000 in 1980, to 8,080 in 1990, and as we have noted, to roughly 11,000 in 2003. The number of worker-owners involved rose, correspondingly, from a mere 248,000 in 1975 to 8.8 million in 2003. There is no question that the feasibility and efficiency of wealth owning through worker institutions has been demonstrated, and that the basic concept has substantial potential for future development.[15]

Likely directions for next-stage advances have been outlined in systematic proposals put forward on both the left and the right. During the Clinton administration one expert, Joseph Blasi, developed a comprehensive package that included tax and other benefits, along with substantial support for state-based technical assistance efforts. The Blasi plan also proposed restructuring tax benefits to redress the greater concentration of ownership among higher-paid employees as a result of awarding stock in amounts related to salary and wage level.[16]

One of the most conservative Republican members of Congress, Dana Rohrbacher, has gone further. Rohrbacher has introduced legislation—the Employee Ownership Act of 2001—the goal of which is to have "30 percent of all United

States corporations . . . owned and controlled by employees of the corporations" by 2010. The proposed legislation would define a new entity, the Employee Owned and Controlled Corporation, (which Rohrbacher calls "ESOP-plus-plus"), in which over 50 percent of stock is held by employees, 90 percent of regular employees are enrolled in the plan, and all employees vote their stock on a one-person, one-vote basis. Various tax benefits would encourage adoption of the ESOP-plus-plus form.[17]

The development in the 1970s and 1980s of broad Democratic and Republican political backing for employee-ownership ideas and supportive state and federal policies was in part related to the economic difficulties experienced by many communities during this period. Employee-owned firms not only embody new wealth-owning principles, they help local economies. The law that established New York State's program makes the connection particularly clear: "The general welfare is directly dependent on the economy and plant closures are a problem. The purpose of this Act is to encourage employees of these plants to continue them as employee-owned enterprises, thereby retaining jobs."[18]

The 1990s economic boom tended to obviate such concerns. With the return of increased economic difficulties and the uncertainties created by globalization, supportive efforts are likely to build upon, and expand, the now well-developed and growing foundation of accumulated experience.[19]

Traditional cooperatives also, of course, have long been based on democratic ownership ideas related to the Pluralist Commonwealth vision. It is rarely realized that there are more than 48,000 co-ops operating in the United States—and that 120 million Americans are co-op members. Roughly 10,000 credit unions (with total assets of over $600 billion) supply financial services to 83 million members; 36 million Americans purchase their electricity from rural electric cooperatives; more than a thousand mutual insurance companies (with more than $80 billion in assets) are owned by their policyholders; and approximately 30 percent of farm products are marketed through cooperatives.[20]

Ongoing co-op development is likely to draw upon the experience of successful modern models like Recreational Equipment, Inc.—an outdoor equipment retailer and producer that employs six thousand people, operates sixty stores, and had revenues of $735 million in 2002. Recreational Equipment is owned by its 2 million members, each of whom receives a refund—usually about 10 percent—on purchases at the end of the year. Named one of the "100 Best Companies to Work For in America" by *Fortune* magazine from 1997 to 2002, Recreational Equipment offers employees a substantial profit-sharing plan and has taken part in numerous joint ventures with local environmental groups.[21]

8

Enterprising Cities

Right, Left, and Center

A DECADE AGO DAVID OSBORNE and Ted Gaebler devoted a chapter of their classic book, *Reinventing Government*, to the emergence of new forms of municipal businesses. The chapter's title is indicative both of the trend and of the driving force behind it—"Enterprising Government: Earning Rather Than Spending." As they observed, "[p]ressed hard by the tax revolts of the 1970s and 1980s and the fiscal crisis of the early 1990s, entrepreneurial governments are increasingly . . . searching for nontax revenues."[1]

The trend Osborne and Gaebler spotted has continued to develop—and though few have paid close attention to the emerging experience, an extraordinary range of local municipal efforts embodying Pluralist Commonwealth wealth-related principles now exists. Moreover, the massive Bush-era cutbacks in federal funding now hitting cities and states have dramatically increased pressures to explore such new sources of revenue for public services.

One of the most important areas of activity is real estate. As early as 1970 the city of Boston embarked upon a joint venture with the Rouse Company to develop the Faneuil Hall Marketplace (a downtown retail complex). Boston kept the property under municipal ownership and negotiated a lease agreement that provided the city with a portion of the development's profits in lieu of property taxes. By the mid-1980s Boston was collecting some $2.5 million per year from the

Marketplace. One expert estimates that Boston took in "40 percent more revenue than it would have collected through conventional property tax channels."[2]

Another innovating 1970s city was Hartford, Connecticut, under the leadership of then city council leader Nicholas Carbone. When Hartford's new Civic Center complex was constructed, the city decided to retain title to the land, leasing out the rights for office space, retail establishments, and a hotel to private-sector operators. The city also took over an abandoned department store and leased it to a major airline for office space. As Carbone stressed, a basic goal was to "give the city control over land use [so as to allow it] to realize the increasing value as land prices increased."[3]

Entrepreneurial "participating lease" arrangements for the use of publicly owned property are now common in many parts of the country—including, by way of illustration, New York, San Diego, Los Angeles, and Washington, D.C. Under such leases a developer pays the public landlord both a yearly base rent and an additional amount pegged to project performance (e.g., private profits or gross income). The principle at work is similar to that which private developers commonly use in shopping center leasing: "The more money the developer makes, the higher the rent."[4]

Alhambra, California, earns approximately $1 million a year in rent revenues from a six-acre holding it leases to commercial tenants. (It also requires tenant businesses to reserve a majority of jobs for low- and moderate-income community residents.) Cincinnati; San Antonio; and Louisville, Kentucky, have all acted as partners in commercial developments, reaping a share (e.g., 10 to 15 percent of net cash flow) of revenues from hotels and other ventures. In 2002 Louisville announced plans to build a new downtown hotel on a similar basis. San Diego holds almost seven hundred leases—including Mission Bay Park, SeaWorld, and a variety of retail, agricultural, and commercial sites. Annual revenues are more than $40 million.[5]

Land development is so-called old economy. A fast-growing arena of new activity involves high-tech Internet and related services. In Glasgow, Kentucky, the municipally owned utility offers residents electricity, cable, telephone services, and high-speed Internet access—all at costs lower than private competitors. The city also has access to an intranet that links local government, businesses, libraries, schools, and neighbors. Residents can choose their cable TV provider: the municipality offers a package of eighty digital cable channels for under $15.95 a month (in 2003).[6]

Tacoma, Washington's, broadband network Click! also offers individuals and private companies Internet and cable service, as does Cedar Falls, Iowa. Almost three hundred communities as of this writing were operating networks like those in Glascow, Tacoma, and Cedar Falls.[7]

Municipalities have also been active in the venture capital area, offering start-up investments and retaining stock in businesses that hold promise for the city's economy. In 1987 a survey of 322 cities found that only 32 (9.9 percent) used venture capital investments as an economic development tool. A similar survey roughly a decade later found more than a third of responding city governments reporting venture capital efforts of one kind or another. Working with the New York Power Authority and two private companies, a New York City agency, for instance, put together an initial investment pool of $60 million. All profits and other gains were reinvested, yielding a fund worth $175 million at the end of the first five years of operation.[8]

Municipally owned sports teams are also widespread. Communities that own (or have owned) minor-league baseball teams include Indianapolis; Rochester, New York; Franklin County (Columbus), Ohio; Lucus County (Toledo), Ohio; Harrisburg, Pennsylvania; Lackawanna County (Scranton), Pennsylvania; and Visalia, California.[9]

At the major-league level, the Green Bay Packers football team is owned by a nonprofit corporation rather than a private corporation or wealthy private individual. The particular ownership structure, while not precisely the Pluralist Commonwealth model, does not permit any individual to own more than a small part of the team and makes it all but impossible for the team to be relocated to another city or purchased by outsiders.[10]

Other developing areas include health services and environmental management. Denver Health, an innovative publically accountable enterprise, transformed itself from an insolvent city agency ($39 million in debt in 1991) to a competitive, quasi-public health-care system with positive earnings of over $10 million annually during the 1990s. Among other things, it operates a satellite system of eleven primary care centers and twelve school based clinics that employ some three thousand Denver-area residents.[11]

Hundreds of municipalities generate revenues through landfill gas recovery operations that turn the greenhouse gas methane (a by-product of waste storage) into energy. Riverview, Michigan, one of the largest such recovery operations, illustrates the trend. In the mid-1980s Riverview contracted with DTE Biomass to build a gas recovery facility at its Riverview Land Preserve. More than 4 million cubic feet of methane gas are now recovered daily. In turn, the sale of gas for power production helps produce over forty thousand megawatt hours of electricity per year. Riverview's royalties covered initial costs of the effort in the first two years of operation and now add to the city's cash flows. (Among the many other innovative and successful methane recovery operations are those run by the Illinois Department of Commerce and Community Affairs, the South Carolina Energy Office, Los Angeles County, and Portland, Oregon.)[12]

The basic principle at work in municipally owned real estate development is that appreciation of land should be turned to public advantage. In many communities, Community Land Trusts (CLTs) following this principle also use ownership strategies to help produce stable and affordable housing for low- and moderate-income residents.

A Community Land Trust is a nonprofit corporation established to develop and own housing (or own land leased for housing) especially in neighborhoods undergoing development that is driving prices beyond the reach of low-income residents. One of the earliest and most influential is the Burlington (Vermont) Community Land Trust (BCLT), organized with bipartisan support when an early 1980s economic boom caused housing costs to spiral out of reach for many long-term residents.[13]

Land is owned by BCLT and leased to home-owners. Member-residents devote no more than 30 percent of their income to rents or mortgages. Those benefiting from the resulting low costs sign contracts agreeing that future housing resale prices will not increase beyond a certain percentage, thereby allowing other low- and moderate-income families to continue to benefit from the trust's ongoing efforts.

A recent report by PolicyLink in Oakland, California, observes that CLTs are also reaching out to other groups and constituencies:

> [T]he community land trust in Concord, New Hampshire, is working with the Neighborhood Reinvestment Corporation on an IDA program to help families save for homeownership. North Camden CLT in New Jersey has spear-headed a comprehensive community planning initiative. Durham Community Land Trust in North Carolina provides construction job training for community residents. The Burlington Community Land Trust has been a mainstay of the city's Enterprise Community, cleaning brownfield sites, developing community facilities for various social service organizations, and redeveloping abandoned commercial buildings.[14]

Various groups are also beginning to extend the CLT concept in new directions. In 2001 the Nehemiah Corporation announced a new multimillion urban trust to purchase land and provide below-market leases to community service organizations. (Nehemiah is making its initial land purchases in Atlanta, Baltimore, Charlotte, Indianapolis, and North Camden, New Jersey. A similar approach has been adopted by the New Columbia CLT in Washington, D.C.—which is purchasing land to help support low-income residents who, in turn, are also developing cooperatives.*15

An important related approach utilizes ownership strategies that capitalize on other public investments: when a municipality invests in mass transit development—as, for instance, in connection with new subway construction—land values near transit exits commonly rise. Traditionally, most municipalities have relied on "after-the-fact" taxation of developers and others who build stores, apartments, and other developments to take advantage of the public investment in such areas. In recent years, however, many municipalities have realized that public ownership—as opposed to traditional tax strategies—offers the possibility of greater returns (and other advantages as well).

In Miami for instance, Metro-Dade Transit participates in two large transit-linked joint development ventures. Dadeland South Station includes two office buildings totaling 472,000 square feet, a 305-room luxury Marriott Hotel, 350,000 square feet of retail space, and 3,500 parking spaces, generating annual revenues in excess of $600,000 for Miami-Dade County. Dadeland North Station currently consists of 320,000 square feet of retail space and forty-eight apartments and ultimately will include a mix of hotel, office, and residential development. Total city revenues over the

* Support for Community Land Trust development is also increasing from both private and public sources. The Institute for Community Economics, founded in 1967, operates a Revolving Loan Fund and provides technical assistance to community groups interested in establishing CLTs. Federal support is also available through Community Development Block Grant and HOME Investment Partnerships programs aimed at developing affordable housing. Vermont, Massachusetts, and other states have also provided assistance to CLTs, and such cities as Burlington, Vermont; Portland, Oregon; and San Francisco have demonstrated techniques municipalities can use to help.

term of the lease for the latter (through minimum rent payments and a percentage of gross income) are projected to run between $40 and $100 million.[16]

The Valley Transportation Authority of Santa Clara County, California, has designed its Transit Oriented Development program to encourage mixed-use development within two thousand feet of transit stops. Its Almaden Lake Village Project is expected to generate $266,000 a year for the city through a long-term ground lease with a private developer—and will also offer one in five of the newly developed residential units at below-market cost to low-income households. The Washington Metropolitan Area Transit Authority in Washington, D.C., has established fifty-six revenue-generating joint development projects that earned $14 million in 2002, making it the public authority's largest nonfare box revenue source.[17]

The expanding experience and growing sophistication of such ownership efforts suggest the likelihood of additional applications of Pluralist Commonwealth principles as time goes on—especially given the severity of growing municipal financial problems. As we shall explore further in Chapter 13, such efforts also have implications for long-range population dispersion strategies designed to recapture increased land values brought about as the result of public investment policies that target jobs to smaller towns and rural growth points (see pp. 148–151).

It is often held that public ownership must be inefficient. Studies of municipal electric utilities, however, belie this view. One out of seven Americans (a total of roughly 40 million people) rely on power from the two thousand public utilities currently operating in urban and rural settings. Although the majority of such systems are located in smaller communities, publicly owned systems are also found in large urban areas such as Los Angeles, Long Island, San Antonio, Sacramento, Nashville, Jacksonville, and Memphis.[18]

Residential customers of investor-owned utilities (IOUs) commonly pay electricity rates roughly 20 percent higher than those paid by public power customers. Commercial IOU customers pay rates 11 percent higher. Industry studies suggest that most of public power's price advantage is due to the fact of public ownership itself; locally controlled public utilities often can be especially responsive to customers' needs and do not need to pay dividends to private shareholders. At the same time, public utilities—through payments in lieu of taxes and payments to municipal general funds—contribute substantially more to state and local governments than do private utilities through taxes. During the 2000 California electricity crisis municipally owned utilities were also able to maintain lower costs and provide secure ongoing service.* A number of public utilities have pioneered ways to protect the environment and improve sustainability by promoting conservation and by becoming industry leaders in the use of wind, solar, geothermal, biomass, hydroelectric power, and other renewable sources of energy.[19]

Related both to the new forms of local public ownership and the experience with municipal electric utilities is the question of privatization. Columbia University professor Elliot Sclar's studies suggest that many of the hoped-for gains of contracting public services to private firms have proven to be exaggerated or illusory. Superficial assessments, he notes, often ignore the high costs of monitoring and rewriting contracts to maintain quality control. In addition, often cost savings are simply the result of lower-quality services. Sometimes corruption enters into the picture. It is estimated that difficulties in the privatization of waste collection in New York City, for instance, cost businesses $500 million.[20]

There is evidence, however, that the *threat* of privatization can sometimes improve the efficiency of public enterprise,

---

* A typical residential customer of Sacramento's public utility paid about $70 a month; in Los Angeles, public power might cost $78 a month (May 2002 data). The same customer paid $114.38 to PG&E, $114.17 to SDG&E, or $122.62 to Southern California Edison, the three largest private utilities—40 to 50 percent more. Sacramento Municipal Utility District, "Rate Comparison," www.smud.org/rates/res_comparison.html (May 2002) (accessed 06/12/03).

even when privatization does not, in the end, occur. Stephen Goldsmith, a former Republican mayor of Indianapolis—subsequently a high-level adviser in the Bush administration and as of this writing the chairman of the Corporation for National Service—ran for election on a platform of widespread privatization. After taking office as mayor, Goldsmith became convinced that "competition—not privatization per se—provided the key to improving city services and reducing costs." Public employees were allowed to bid on city contracts, and to redesign their offices and operations in the process. Public employees won a majority of the first sixty contracts put out to bid, with estimated savings of $135 million in the program's first three years.[21]

Sclar's assessment is that much of Goldsmith's achievement was also related to his administration's "ability to exhibit a genuine willingness to take the unit's employees seriously. Goldsmith, in effect, officially sanctioned [them] to go ahead with changes that the employees had wanted for more than a decade."[22]

The result—a creative integration of the (local) public ownership and democratization principles of the Pluralist Commonwealth vision—defines an obvious area for development and refinement as the fiscal crisis continues to force further change.

9

Building Community

Neighborhoods and Nonprofits with a Mission

THE BEDFORD-STUYVESANT neighborhood in Brooklyn, New York, was hit hard. Redlining by banks, blockbusting by real estate speculators, and extortionate rents devastated low-income housing. Between 1940 and 1960 "Bed-Stuy" went from three-quarters white to almost 85 percent African American and Latino. Nearly 30 percent of families lived on less than $3,000 a year. Infant mortality was the highest in the nation.[1]

Was there anything that could be done? Especially given that public funds available were inevitably minimal compared to the scale of need?

Some things were obvious. First, local residents themselves would have to take the lead. Second, if public support was not going to do the job, some other source of funding would have to be found. Third, anyone who expected a quick fix was naive. The only way forward was to think long-term—and to start organizing now to solve immediate problems, step-by-step, in a manner that also laid foundations for an approach that might ultimately build to a new answer.

But this required a new institutional form—one that combined the community-serving mission of a nonprofit organization with the wealth-building and ownership capacities of an economic enterprise.

The neighborhood-based Community Development Corporation (CDC) grew out of such circumstances—a hybrid self-help entity that operates at both the community-building level and the economic level, and that exhibits micro-level applications of Pluralist Commonwealth principles. The Bedford-Stuyvesant Restoration Corporation—a CDC developed in the 1960s with the bipartisan support of then senators Robert F. Kennedy and Jacob Javits—helped set the terms of reference for an institution that can now be found in thousands of communities.

In its initial ten years of operation, the Bedford Stuyvesant Restoration Corporation provided start-up capital and other assistance to 116 new businesses, helped create 3,300 jobs, arranged training programs or new jobs for 7,000 local residents, and renovated or built some 650 new housing units.[2] It also launched and still owns a major commercial development (Restoration Plaza), a property management company, and a construction firm. It receives two-thirds of the profits of a Pathmark supermarket that had over $28 million in annual sales by 2001. The Bedford Stuyvesant Restoration Corporation also operates a two-hundred-seat theater and a revolving loan fund for local start-up businesses. As of 2002, the CDC had roughly $26 million in assets. Its 2002 budget was $10.5 million, $7 million of which was funded by income from rental and other commercial ventures.[3]

Another leading example is the New Community Corporation in Newark, New Jersey, a CDC established after urban riots during the 1960s left many dead and over a thousand injured. New Community now owns an estimated $500 million in real estate and other ventures, including a shopping center, a supermarket, and three thousand units of housing. New Community Corporation enterprises employ 2,000 neighborhood residents and create roughly $200 million in economic activity each year. Profits help operate day care and after-school programs, a nursing home, and two medical day care centers for seniors. Proceeds from business activities help support job-training, educational, health, and other programs.[4] The New Community Corporation also runs a Youth Automotive Training

Center; young people who complete its courses are guaranteed jobs offering $20,000-plus starting salaries.[5]

A well-known rural example is the Kentucky Highlands Investment Corporation. This CDC provides both venture capital and small-business loans to assist rural firms. Over the last several decades Kentucky Highlands has made or helped generate more than $175 million in investments in 140 companies, creating some 7,900 jobs in rural southeast Kentucky. It has assets of roughly $30 million.[6]

Since the 1960s almost four thousand neighborhood-based CDCs have come into existence in U.S. communities. The majority are not nearly as large and sophisticated as the leaders, but all employ wealth-related principles to serve "small publics" in geographically defined areas. The assets that the far more numerous smaller CDCs commonly develop center, above all, on housing, but many also own retail firms and, in several cases, larger businesses.[7]

The more than thirty-five-year developmental trend that has produced the modern CDC is intimately related to the U.S. political economy's declining capacity to address problems of inequality and poverty directly through redistribution or through major job-creation strategies. Fiscal considerations have set the terms of reference from the beginning. At the time of the 1960s "War on Poverty," which gave the institution its first major backing, the Johnson administration explicitly rejected as financially and politically infeasible a large-scale public jobs program to deal with poverty in a more explicit and comprehensive manner.[8]

The trajectory of development has also been instructive. The first generation of CDCs began with a broad strategic conception that directly echoed Pluralist Commonwealth themes. The initial goal involved a community-building vision and included the provision of services, the ownership of productive enterprise, and advocacy on behalf of local residents. As the political scientist Rita Mae Kelly observes, institutional development, community control, and community ownership of property and other resources were "expected to foster, support, and sustain the development of managerial and entrepreneurial leadership within the community—and to keep it there."[9]

The advent of the Nixon administration, decisions by the Ford Foundation, and generally reduced funding in the Reagan years forced many CDCs to alter their initial approach. Two important ideas of the early period—direct ownership of assets beyond housing and community organizing and advocacy—were often abandoned or reduced to minor functions. Instead, most CDCs concentrated primarily on an important but narrow form of wealth ownership (the development of low-income housing); and secondarily on technical assistance and small-business loans to individual entrepreneurs.[10]

The basic concept, however, proved to be resilient. The number of CDCs expanded steadily; more than a thousand new CDCs emerged during the Reagan era alone. CDC housing development was strongly assisted by special tax incentives for investors who helped CDCs and others build low-income housing. (Numerous financial intermediaries now develop and market tax-based packages to facilitate the financing of a broad range of efforts.)[11] Although CDCs encountered financial difficulties, and some were victims of poor and occasionally corrupt leadership, the overall trial and error learning curve was impressive.[12]

Community Development Corporations also developed a number of new strategies that added to their strength during this period. "The lack of federal support," former Local Initiatives Support Corporation (LISC) president Paul Grogan and his coauthor Tony Proscio point out, "meant there was no federal bureaucracy prescribing what was supposed to happen." They go on:

"CDCs were free to develop and pursue their local agendas. And as they scrounged for dollars and technical help, they were building a web of relationships and a diversified funding base that would be with them for the long term, not for the short cycle of the latest federal program. . . . CDCs in city after city are now raising capital both for projects and for overhead from a wide range of charities, banks and other financial institutions, private corporations, city governments, and increasingly, state governments."[13]

CDC development also capitalized on the achievements of a parallel citizens movement that used the Community Reinvestment Act to fight redlining by banks—thereby helping allocate more than $60 billion to neighborhood investment by the early 1990s. The emergence of new Community Development Financial Institutions (CDFIs) like Chicago's South Shore Bank (now "Shore Bank") also provided new support for neighborhood development. During the Clinton years federal legislation gave CDFIs—and thus also CDCs— a further significant boost.[14]

A number of organized support efforts have also been critical. One of the most important, the Local Initiatives Support Corporation was established with broad foundation and corporate backing. Since 1979 LISC has raised over $4 billion—and leveraged almost $7 billion in additional investment—to help some 1,700 CDCs. In a development that acknowledged both the CDCs' important role and the coming-of-age of the movement in general, former Clinton treasury secretary Robert Rubin accepted chairmanship of the Local Initiatives board in 1999.*[15]

Some critics charge that in turning primarily to housing production during the second phase of development, many CDCs lost touch with their local communities. Urban Studies professor Robert Fisher writes that most "avoided political

---

* Another important organization, the Enterprise Foundation, founded by the late James Rouse, has made $3.9 billion in grants, loans, and investments to more than a thousand local organizations. In 1991 seventeen major foundations, banks, and corporations, together with HUD, established and funded the National Community Development Initiative—now known as Living Cities. Other significant support efforts include the Fannie Mae Foundation, the National Community Capital Association, the National Congress for Community Economic Development, and PolicyLink. Enterprise Foundation, "About Us," www.enterprisefoundation.org/about/index.asp (accessed 11/14/02); Living Cities, "History," www.livingcities .org/new_look/history.html (accessed 05/06/03).

controversy, were dominated by professionals with a technical orientation, had narrow membership bases, and rejected social action activity." On the other hand, another close observer—Andy Mott (at the time executive director of the Center for Community Change)—concluded in 2000 that an "increasing number of CDC coalitions are offering community organizing training to their members, and CDC associations . . . have taken on—and won—major policy battles on jobs, housing and reinvestment."[16]

In general, housing production remains central to Community Development Corporation efforts—along with the principle of public-benefiting ownership. Roughly three-quarters of new or rehabbed housing units are owned directly by the CDC that produces them. In addition, by 1998 CDCs had developed 71 million square feet of commercial and industrial space.[17]

In recent years a number of CDCs have also begun to explore (and return to) the broader ownership ideas envisioned in the early years of their development. Inspired in part by New Community Corporation's successful ownership of a supermarket, LISC established the Retail Initiative in 1994 to help CDCs develop shopping centers anchored by supermarkets or other large retailers in their neighborhoods. By 2002 the Retail Initiative had committed over $20 million to ten major projects in New Haven, Connecticut; North Philadelphia; Chicago; and other cities.[18]

The experience of Dudley Street Neighborhood Initiative in Boston—a nonprofit community-based institution similar to a traditional CDC—suggests additional possibilities for future change. The Initiative has won the right of eminent domain to acquire abandoned parcels of land, a unique development in modern urban policy. The Initiative also manages residential properties as part of a community land trust and has established several village commons, a series of "Tot Lots," two community centers, and commercial developments at key points in the neighborhood.[19]

In general, a 1998 survey found 40 percent of urban CDCs reported owning and/or operating a business (34 percent of rural CDCs did so). Over half also reported some form of business-lending activity with a total of nearly $2 billion in outstanding loans.[20]

Substantial economic projects continue to be exceptional. However, given the level of experience developed over the past several decades—and the example being set by the leaders—increasing numbers of CDCs appear likely to slowly broaden their ownership focus beyond housing and commercial real estate development in coming years.[21]

Louis Winnick of the Institute for Public Administration suggests that the "meteoric growth of CDCs and related grassroots initiatives owes much to their appeal across the political spectrum." As he observes: "The anti-statist Right saluted community development as a proxy for government, which might shield the succored poor from the dead hand of bureaucracy. . . . On the opposite end of the ideological spectrum, radical activists envisioned community-based organizations as weapons of political empowerment, instruments to liberate the poor from chronic neglect."[22]

Many states and local municipalities now back CDC activity—both directly and indirectly. In cities with a large number of cooperating CDCs, local governments have often become active development partners, making foreclosed properties available to them or earmarking Community Development Block Grant funds for housing subsidies. Particularly innovative state programs include New York's Neighborhood Preservation Companies Program, the North Carolina Community Development Initiative, and two efforts of the Commonwealth of Massachusetts: the Community Economic Development Assistance Corporation and the Community Enterprise Economic Development Program, the latter of which provides both financial and technical assistance to CDCs in economically depressed communities.[23]

Federal programs also provide significant support to CDCs, including Community Development Block Grants, the HOME Program, the Low Income Housing Tax Credit, and Empowerment Zone/Enterprise Communities tax credits. One of the last pieces of legislation of the Clinton administration, the Community Renewal Tax Relief Act of 2000, provides additional "new-market" tax and other assistance. The 2000 Act—which enjoyed the broad backing of Republican leaders in the House of Representatives—also suggests the potential for expanding the base of political support for housing and other wealth-ownership principles at the community and neighborhood level.[24]

There is little likelihood that the social and financial pressures that helped produce the CDC hybrid will let up—or that the steady step-by-step developmental trend will come to a halt. Indeed, given the fiscal problems facing the nation, the prospect is for more rather than less pressure to create additional forms of ownership—and of further forms of revenue-generating institutional change. Community organizing and advocacy efforts by CDCs also appear likely to increase.

Other nonprofit organizations with a service mission at the community, state, and national levels have picked up on the underlying principles exhibited by CDC development—and here, too, it is clear that the overarching fiscal crisis is producing forces that make ongoing evolutionary development all but certain.[25] Esperanza Unida, Inc., in Milwaukee suggests some of the possibilities.

Esperanza Unida began as an organization that initially focused on helping Hispanic workers deal with workplace issues and file unemployment and worker's compensation claims. In the early 1980s it started running businesses with a dual mission—raising funds for other operations and training. In what came to be called the "Training Business Model," Esperanza Unida now employs local citizens in enterprises involved in auto repair, construction, printing, child care, customer service skills, and welding. It also runs a coffeehouse/bookstore, ¿Que Pasa?, which hosts community events and offers books and periodicals in both Spanish and English. Roughly 50 to 70 percent of Esperanza Unida's annual revenues come from its business activities.[26]

Pioneer Human Services in Seattle, Washington—an organization initially established with donations and grants—is now almost entirely self-supporting. It provides drug-and-alcohol-free housing, employment, job training, counseling, and education to recovering alcoholics and drug addicts. Its annual operating budget is $54 million—over 99 percent is earned through fees for services or sales of products.

Pioneer Human Services and its subsidiaries own and manage a light-metal fabricator that employs people traditionally thought to be unemployable and that has contracts with Boeing, Xantrex, Leviton, and others; a Food Buying Service that distributes roughly 7 million pounds of food to nonprofit organizations in twenty states; a 132-room St. Regis Hotel that offers drug- and alcohol-free housing for tourists and low-income individuals; and a 150-seat Mezza Café, along with its satellite, Pronto, and two smaller Mezza Cafés.[27]

The Roberts Enterprise Development Fund in the San Francisco Bay Area works with nonprofit umbrella organizations. These, in turn, have operated roughly twenty businesses—from thrift stores and janitorial services to a bakery and a furniture manufacturer—that also both make money and help specific groups in the community. Revenues grew from $10 million in 1997 to $20 million in 2000, with profits increasing from $230,000 to $630,000. Enterprises target specific employee/trainee populations—including landscaping and packaging and shipping services for individuals with developmental disabilities; bike repair training for young people; and a cleaning service, a café, and a temp agency that provide jobs for individuals with psychiatric disabilities.[28]

Educational and health institutions in many areas, of course, have also long operated as nonprofits-in-business charging fees for services. A recent study found that in the twenty largest U.S. cities, sixty-nine of the two hundred largest private enterprises (35 percent) were universities and medical institutions, most of which were nonprofit. In four cities—Washington, Philadelphia, San Diego, and Baltimore—what the study called "eds" and "meds" accounted for more than 50 percent of all jobs generated.[29]

Some analysts who have studied hybrid nonprofits have raised serious questions about whether important service missions may be compromised by their economic activities; and several have suggested guidelines to maintain institutional integrity.[30] Conversely, others point out that by reducing the reliance of organizations on public (often politically influenced) funding and from foundation and individual donor support, new sources of revenue can often produce offsetting advantages in terms of institutional independence.

Such questions are certain to take on increasing urgency as time goes on. Given the fiscal pressures driving change and the growing support the strategies are beginning to attract, the trend is unlikely to be reversed. The real question is how the conflict between organizational goals can be managed intelligently—and whether those concerned with critical public missions organize themselves to ensure the integrity of the various efforts.*[31]

A recent *Chronicle of Philanthropy* study estimates that over $60 billion was earned from business activities by the fourteen thousand largest nonprofits in 1998. Income from fees, charges, and related business activities is estimated in other studies to have grown from 13 percent of nonprofit social service organization revenues in 1977 to 43 percent in 1996.[32]

A powerful indication of the developing and likely future trend—and of the growing sophistication of Pluralist

---

* A related, increasingly debated issue concerns taxation of unrelated business activities. For an overview of the questions involved, see Evelyn Brody and Joseph J. Cordes, "The Unrelated Business Income Tax: All Bark and No Bite?" Emerging Issues in Philanthropy Series Seminar No. 3, Urban-Brookings Tax Policy Center, March 1, 2001, www.urban.org/UploadedPDF/philanthropy_3.pdf (accessed 09/26/03).

Commonwealth–related strategies in general—is Harvard Business School's decision to launch a new "Initiative on Social Enterprise" offering research, teaching, and other programs to "catalyze . . . nonprofit, private, and public sector enterprises for the creation of social and economic value." Similar programs are under way at Yale, Stanford, and several other business schools.[33]

10

State and National Innovators

JUST BELOW THE RADAR OF conventional media reporting, a number of larger efforts based on Pluralist Commonwealth principles have also emerged in recent years, especially at the state level. Some are new and innovative; many are in advanced stages of development; several others illustrate long-standing but little-discussed practices that are likely to be extended if current trends continue—and if states continue to function in the future, as they have in the past, as laboratories for subsequent national activity.

Particularly interesting are a group of sophisticated developments that point in the direction of practical—even dramatic—applications of the most radical and far-reaching system-wide Pluralist Commonwealth strategies.

The Individual Development Accounts (IDAs) reviewed in Chapter 1, which match savings of the poor to build wealth-ownership, are no longer a matter of theory. Since 1990 some five hundred different projects and more than 20,000 IDA holders have been established. One of the most important is a four-year test conducted by the Corporation for Enterprise Development and the Center for Social Development, which has found that significant savings by even very low income participants can be achieved through IDA strategies.[1]

The federal government has also begun testing IDAs. Provisions for allocating funds to IDAs were included in the welfare reforms of 1996 (TANF, Temporary Assistance to

Needy Families). Passage in 1998 of the Assets for Independence Act established a five-year, $125 million demonstration effort aimed at creating roughly 50,000 IDAs. (As of 2003, $95 million had been appropriated.) Unexpected political alliances have also appeared in connection with this strategy. Significantly, the Bush administration included substantial funding for the Clinton-initiated IDA concept in each of its first four budgets.[*2]

Shortly after passage of the Assets for Independence Act, the *St. Louis Post-Dispatch* commented, "It's hard to decide if this is radical policy or an outgrowth of conservative economic ideals. Legislators who supported the idea in Congress didn't bother deciding. They came from both sides of the political aisle."[3]

Historically, several states have had considerable experience with the application of larger-scale Pluralist Commonwealth principles. The Bank of North Dakota—founded in 1919—currently has nearly $2 billion in assets. The bank's earnings (net income) now provide the fifth-largest source of revenue for the state government; an estimated $75 to $80 million will be returned to North Dakota for the two-year period, 2001 to 2003. The bank makes student loans (27 percent of the total), commercial loans (33 percent), agricultural loans (17 percent), and residential loans (23 percent). Return on equity was 21.3 percent for 2000, a year of record profitability; it was still 18.7 percent in 2001, a year of national economic difficulty.[4]

The Wisconsin State Life Insurance Fund, in operation since 1911, is also instructive. The fund has assets of over $75 million, manages roughly thirty thousand active life

---

* The Bush administration's proposed Faith Based Initiative legislation also includes $450 million in tax credits to support IDAs. If approved, banks that match the savings of the poor in IDAs would receive a 100 percent tax write-off for their contributions (up to $500 per person per year). Corporation for Enterprise Development, "Federal Policy Update," *Assets: A Quarterly Update for Innovators* (Winter 2002), www.idanetwork.org/assets/index.html (accessed 02/04/03), p. 3. Further references at www.idanetwork.org.

insurance policies, and has coverage in force totaling over $200 million. The fund distributed between $3.7 and $3.9 million annually in dividends to policyholders throughout the late 1990s. Premiums are 10 to 40 percent lower than comparable private insurance coverage. Such gains have been recorded even though the fund is subject to statutory restrictions—including a prohibition on advertising and maximum coverage of $10,000—which limit its capacity to compete with other companies.[5]

More recent state developments include venture capital initiatives that involve direct investment and stock ownership in local companies by state agencies. Though little discussed in the media, this form of public investment and ownership is extremely common. A recent National Governors Association survey found that more than half the states have allocated state funds to venture capital investments. Most involve direct investment by state agencies, often utilizing private firms to help manage the process.[6]

One of the most successful efforts, Maryland's Enterprise Investment Fund, provides promising high-tech start-ups with up to $500,000 in capital in exchange for equity shares and a guarantee from the firm that it will continue to operate in the state for at least five years. The fund has performed exceptionally well, investing $19 million in fifty-two Maryland companies and helping create an estimated 2,500 jobs as of this writing. From 1994 to 2002 the state made a 32 percent annual return on its investments—with total returns over $64 million. Successful ventures range from such companies as Visual Networks of Rockville, a network management and consulting firm, to Gene Logic of Gaithersburg, which specializes in "gene expression" technology—that is, examining tissues to determine whether particular genes are turned "on" or "off."[7]

Similar programs in Connecticut and Massachusetts also have achieved significant returns while at the same time helping create jobs in their respective states. Connecticut Innovations' return on investment rose from 17.3 percent in 1998 to 20.8 percent in 1999 to 39.7 percent in 2000. In

2001, a tough year when many high-tech investors lost money, it still managed a positive return (2.5 percent); and although along with many funds it experienced significant losses in 2002, its cumulative return for 1998 to 2002 was a respectable 8.4 percent. The Massachusetts Technology Development Corporation has invested in early-stage technology firms for a substantial period. Between 1980 and 2002 it recorded a 17.9 percent rate of return on total investments of $62 million in 115 companies.[8]

Assessments of such efforts are complicated by the fact that states commonly invest in ventures that one, have not already been selected as promising by private firms; and that two, offer the possibility of job creation and ancillary benefits of economic value to the state in question. Some state efforts have produced extremely positive results; others have achieved more modest gains, but in the process have contributed to larger state development goals.[9]

At the federal level, public ownership of stock in specific corporations is also a long-established strategy. In the recent airline bailout, for instance, the Bush administration demanded a ten-year option to purchase a third of America West's stock at $3 per share in exchange for federal guarantees that secured a $429 million loan. It granted a $900 million loan guarantee to US Airways—and received a 10 percent stake in the company in return.[10]

Similarly, in 1980 as part of a $1.5 billion loan guarantee for the Chrysler Corporation, the government received 14.4 million warrants (representing 10 to 15 percent of Chrysler stock). Again, the government through the FDIC took a controlling ownership position (over 80 percent) in connection with the 1984 $8 billion bailout of the Continental Illinois Bank (at the time the seventh-largest U.S. bank). Numerous other precedents can be traced back to World War II.*[11]

---

* Government loan guarantees (and related public insurance strategies) have long received bipartisan support in connection with many conventional economic development approaches and broad-based asset development efforts. These *(continues)*

We may add to this listing of Pluralist Commonwealth practices the long experience with public ownership of port authorities throughout the nation. By far the largest is the Port Authority of New York and New Jersey, which has approximately $16.9 billion in assets. The authority has planned, developed, and operated numerous enterprises that have been critical to the economic health of the region—including major airports and seaports, and the World Trade Center. In 2000 it paid $130 million in leases and payments in lieu of taxes to the cities of New York and Newark and to the states of New York and New Jersey. (Total payments were $96 and $140 million, even in the difficult years of 2001 and 2002.)[12]

The Port of Los Angeles owns several retail properties—including Ports O'Call Village, a large retail shopping and dining complex that generates between $650,000 and $1.5 million annually, and another retail/restaurant complex, the West Channel development, which is expected to bring in $1.2 million in leases plus healthy percentages of gross receipts. In fiscal year 2002 the port generated $289.8 million in total operating revenue, with a net income of $96.9 million.[13]

The Port of Seattle manages a cruise pier and several container ship loading facilities, the Seattle-Tacoma airport, and

---

(continued) provide additional precedents that might be adapted to the newer strategies. Thus, the Export-Import bank currently guarantees business loans of $7.4 billion per year. The Price-Anderson Act provides for insurance against risk in connection with the dangers associated with nuclear power plant development (without which little if any private investment would have taken place). Again, since the 1930s various government programs have expanded access to home-ownership by insuring mortgages, freeing up capital, and reducing initial asset thresholds. "Annual Report, Fiscal Year 2002," Export-Import Bank of the United States, 2002, www.exim.gov/about/reports/index.html (accessed 06/23/03); "Price Anderson Act: The Billion Dollar Bailout for Nuclear Power Mishaps," Public Citizen, October 10, 2001, www.citizen.org/documents/Anderson-wenonah.PDF (accessed 06/23/03); and John C. Weicher, *Housing: Federal Policies and Programs* (Washington, D.C.: American Enterprise Institute for Public Policy Research, 1980), pp. 38, 111. Ongoing discussion of new strategies that would help build community-benefitting ownership in exchange for government tax, loan, regulatory, and other support can be found at cog.kent.edu/.

a number of additional operations that lease commercial office space. In 2003 the port's operating revenues (from property rental, parking revenues, landing fees, etc.) were expected to exceed $375 million. When depreciation costs, accumulated tax income, and passenger facility charges are included, the port's total excess revenue in 2002 was projected to be $64 million.[14]

Such activity is not restricted to large cities: the Marine Administration of Portland, Maine, holds fifty leases—including a twelve-acre naval shipyard, an inter-island ferry system, and a pier—which together generate more than $2 million a year for the city.[15]

The history and successful record of different forms of public pension funds offer additional Pluralist Commonwealth precedents. There are currently more than 2,200 public employee retirement system boards operating at the municipal, state, and federal levels. The boards manage roughly $3 trillion in assets and have for many decades demonstrated the feasibility of public investment strategies.[16]

One of the most conservative of all public agencies at the national level—the Federal Reserve Board—has had an employee pension and retirement fund in operation since 1934. It manages roughly $8.2 billion in assets. Investments, as in most pension funds, are overseen by external fund managers. Again, the Federal Thrift Savings Plan, established in 1987, involves some 2.4 million federal employees in a similar plan; it has roughly $100 billion in assets.[17]

In Part I we noted that a number of state pension funds have begun to explore new forms of public oversight to make corporations more accountable. Additional possibilities are suggested by other aspects of the experience of California Public Employees' Retirement System (CalPERS) and by Retirement Systems of Alabama.

CalPERS (in operation now for more than sixty-five years) oversees more than $137 billion in pension funds for 1.4 million plan members (employees, retirees, and survivors). In addition to previously discussed innovations, CalPERS maintains a domestic portfolio "focus list" that singles out poorly performing companies and companies with poor governance practices. The results are illuminating. Companies that have been singled out in a particular year regularly outperform the S&P 500 by roughly 14 percent in the five years after CalPERS draws attention to their failings. CalPERS also places a great deal of emphasis on information disclosure and the independence of boards of directors. As noted, CalPERS is also beginning to enforce transparency, environmental performance and other standards in its international investments (see pp. 60–61).[18]

Alabama—a conservative state in which fiscal pressures are particularly intense and in which traditional tax proposals are commonly blocked—is also actively pursuing Pluralist Commonwealth–related strategies. Retirement Systems of Alabama, which manages pension investments for state employees and teachers, has been in operation for more than sixty years. Under the direction of CEO David Bronner, it has aggressively invested in numerous local Alabama industries, in some cases also using its assets to help create worker-owned firms. Investments range from aerospace to tourism development and include, among others, $100 million in the Alabama Pine Pulp Company; $60 million in a statewide golf course network, the Robert Trent Jones Golf Trail (maintaining a 33 percent ownership stake); and $250 million in Alabama-backed Ginnie Mae mortgages.[19]

Retirement Systems of Alabama has a total of $22 billion under management. It also has invested in office buildings in such cities as Montgomery and has helped form two media conglomerates involving hundreds of local newspapers and thirty-six television and radio stations. Stock in these is jointly owned by Retirement Systems and the employees of the companies.

Even more interesting politically—and suggestive of possible other larger-scale future strategies—in 2002 Retirement

Systems purchased a 36.6 percent controlling share of US Airways, in part to bring more jobs to the state.*[20]

A somewhat different but even more suggestive effort is that of the Alaska Permanent Fund. The Alaska state constitution directs that a significant portion of revenues derived from oil development be allocated to the fund for further investment on behalf of citizens of the state. Earnings are used to increase the size of the principal, offset the impact of inflation on long-run returns—and most important, provide annual dividends to the residents of the state. In 2000, a high-payout year, each individual state resident, as a matter of right, received dividends of just under $2,000 (almost $10,000 for a couple with three children).[21]

Permanent Fund operations have been efficient and economically successful. Competitively hired external managers invest roughly $25 billion in assets. In 2000 the fund earned an overall 9.18 percent rate of return, a figure well above expected benchmarks for its diversified low-risk portfolio. Operating costs were a low 1.83 percent (leaving a 98 percent profit margin). By way of comparison, the S&P 500 ended 2000 up 7.24 percent. During the stock market collapse of 2001 and 2002, the Permanent Fund outperformed its benchmark investments and also had operating costs below those of comparable large funds.[22]

Income inequality in Alaska is lower than most other states, and—unlike every other state and the nation as a whole—Alaska registered a decline in income inequality during the 1980s and 1990s. Research by University of Alaska economist Scott Goldsmith indicates that Permanent Fund operations played an important role in producing the recorded gains.[23]

CalPERS, Retirement Systems of Alabama, and similar efforts offer precedents for using investment strategies to achieve greater public oversight of corporate practices and to

---

* It is unclear whether this particular venture will succeed. As of this writing, US Airways, along with many other airlines, is experiencing considerable financial difficulty.

help achieve state and community economic goals. The Alaska Permanent Fund takes us one step further. It is an on-the-ground operating system that demonstrates the feasibility of the kinds of far-reaching proposals offered by Roemer, Meade, and Kelso—and of the Public Trust concept of the Pluralist Commonwealth. Although each approach differs in specifics, all are based on the principle that capital can and should be accumulated and managed in ways that provide individual citizens with an income stream from publicly backed investments.*

---

* See pp. 23–26. Roemer and Meade would accumulate capital through taxes and establish an agency to directly supervise investment management. Kelso proposed using government loan guarantees or insurance to develop investments—followed by temporary publicly accountable supervision before ultimately transferring ownership to individuals.

11

Coda

The Democratization of Wealth and the Era of Deepening Fiscal Crisis

F EW OBSERVERS HAVE AS yet grasped the extent—or further possibilities—of wealth-related strategies that benefit the public directly. It is obvious, however, that a great deal of hands-on experience now offers practical backing for ideas at the heart of the Pluralist Commonwealth vision—including (among others) worker ownership, cooperatives, municipal ownership, neighborhood ownership, nonprofit ownership, individual development accounts, and a wide range of major public investment strategies. There is also evidence that such efforts can be efficient, especially if adequate attention is paid to developing and refining management, training, and other strategies over time.

It would be a mistake either to exaggerate or to minimize the developments. On the other hand, the steady expansion of several of the most significant new forms has been impressive. In recent years the number of Employee Stock Option Plan firms has increased from a few hundred to more than eleven thousand; Community Development Corporations have grown from a few hundred to nearly four thousand. Municipal enterprise, though less well studied, is on the rise in cities across the nation. In other areas, long-standing experience—as with public utilities and pension funds—offers solid evidence both of the economic and political viability of larger wealth-owning approaches. Former New York State comptroller H. Carl McCall is also almost certainly correct to predict "a renewed era of activism by public institutional shareholders."[1]

Viewed in larger historical perspective, what stands out is the simple fact that the last several decades have established practical and policy foundations that offer a solid basis for future expansion. There is a body of hard-won expertise now available in each area—along with support organizations and technical and other experts who have accumulated a very great deal of direct problem-solving knowledge.

Significantly, in each area there has also been—and continues to be—a broad base of public backing for new approaches. Moreover, a converging trajectory of concern with community economic stability has added force to many of the newer strategies—especially as global economic pressures have intensified. As we have seen, a number of the new economic institutions are inherently anchored in local communities by virtue of their ownership structure.

Beyond this there has been growing recognition of the mutual interests of—and the organization of implicit alliances between—specific investors and firms, on the one hand, and engaged citizen groups developing new institutions, on the other. Tax benefits provided to corporations and retiring business owners have helped fuel ESOP development; other incentives provided to individual investors have helped CDCs develop low-income housing.

(The last several decades have also demonstrated that it is possible for new institutions to move beyond such origins. Thus, CDCs that develop momentum regularly transcend the limits of their initial financing strategies. Again, as ESOPs move toward majority ownership—at least in states that have been subjects of study, such as Ohio—they also begin to move increasingly toward greater democratic control.)

In general, and notwithstanding ideological opposition to government involvement in the economy, many of the new wealth-ownership efforts also transcend traditional left-right political distinctions—as is evident in connection with CDCs, ESOPs, bipartisan support of Individual Development Accounts, and the experience of mayors of both parties who embrace local public enterprise strategies. That a conservative state like Alabama can essentially socialize control of a major airline also suggests (win or lose) that politics in the future may well be far more open to innovative change than is commonly assumed.

The emerging direction is not without major challenges. Much greater democratization of CDCs, worker-owned firms (of all kinds), and other wealth-related institutions is clearly a priority for those seeking more far-reaching change. So, too, are new strategies to deal with the difficulties facing nonprofit organizations struggling with the conflict between service goals and economic support activities. Municipalities must not be allowed to raise fees for basic services in the name of new principles. Greater and more sophisticated citizen accountability and oversight of public pension investment efforts like those of CalPERS and Retirement Systems of Alabama need to be developed to ensure that worker, community, and other concerns are fully taken into account.[2] On the other hand, Americans already know—and in the future are likely increasingly to understand in their own communities—that a variety of ways of owning assets on behalf of small and large publics are now feasible.

What may well be of decisive importance in the coming period is that even as the various developments have gone forward, the nation as a whole has begun to move into a radically new and unrelenting fiscal environment—one that promises to force ever greater attention to strategies that offer ways to produce additional resources at all levels. Projections for the coming decade alone suggest a combined federal fiscal deficit that could easily reach more than $5 trillion—indeed, $7.5 trillion if Social Security Trust Fund reserves are left aside![3]

Nor is it likely that there will be an early reversal of the growing fiscal crisis. For one thing, the ongoing occupation of Iraq is likely to demand continuing large-scale financial support. Much more important is that the Bush tax cuts, though dramatic, are by no means unique. Indeed, fundamental and long-developing political-economic trends have been moving in this direction for some time.

Corporate taxes, as we have noted, were reduced from 35.4 percent of federal receipts in 1945 to 7.4 percent in 2003. Taxation of individuals in top brackets has also been reduced over the span of the last several decades—from 91 percent in the Eisenhower, Kennedy, and early Johnson eras to 35 percent today. And long before the Bush-era reductions (and proposed reductions), domestic discretionary spending by the federal government had moved down—from 4.7 percent of GDP a quarter-century ago to 3.6 percent now, a drop during this period alone of roughly 25 percent.[4]

An even greater fiscal squeeze is likely as time goes on. Critically, spending on Social Security benefits and Medicare will continue to rise as the baby-boom generation retires. So will spending on Medicaid. Recent studies project these three programs alone may ultimately consume a larger share of GDP than *all* of the money the federal government collects in taxes.[5]

A radically new context thus is being shaped that is forcing—and will continue to force—very difficult choices. Either there will be no solution to many problems, or something new will have to be tried. The growing fiscal pressures—intersecting now with growing global uncertainties—are, in fact, producing a political-economic environment in which alternatives of the kind we have reviewed may well become the only feasible way forward in many areas.

Although it is impossible to predict the degree and extent of potential expansion, a developmental perspective on past, present, and possible future stages of institutional and political change suggests that we are approaching a point in time when once controversial and seemingly novel strategies based on Pluralist Commonwealth principles are likely to become matter-of-fact and commonplace in everyday life.[6]

As we shall see, the question of interest is how this development, in turn, might contribute to further, much larger order change as the demanding terms of reference for twenty-first-century political-economic change continue to evolve.

PART III

LOCAL DEMOCRACY AND REGIONAL DECENTRALIZATION

QUITE APART FROM CHANGES in wealth ownership, the Pluralist Commonwealth vision rests firmly on the principle (following Alexis de Tocqueville, John Stuart Mill, and several modern writers) that over the long haul rebuilding local democracy with a small d, from the bottom up, is a necessary though obviously not sufficient requirement of renewing the basis of meaningful Democracy with a big D in the political-economic system as a whole.

At one level, this means nurturing the conditions in which networks of civil society associations can flourish. At another, it requires strategic changes that foster opportunities for more meaningful participation in local governmental decision making. Both, in turn, require more stable and robust local community economies.

The conventional wisdom is that the era of globalization makes such community priorities—especially local economic stability—all but impossible to achieve. The reality, however, is that sectoral changes and a broad range of economic, social, and psychological factors have begun to converge toward a resurgent community-building paradigm that complements the evolving wealth-oriented developmental trajectory. In addition, further opportunities for support appear likely to develop in connection with problems confronting specific groups concerned with environmental issues, on the one hand, and gender-related matters, on the other.

At quite another level of emerging change, a variety of domestic and global forces have begun to set the terms of reference for extensive forms of decentralization that have important implications for longer-term Pluralist Commonwealth regional ideas.

12

Is Local Democracy Possible in the Global Era?

MUST COMMUNITIES—AND therefore community democracy—rise and fall with every shift in the global economic winds? Can Americans ever really take charge of their common community life, given the realities of the modern political economy?[1]

Beyond this, might we have the wherewithal—the experience, knowledge, political sophistication—to one day achieve the idea of community?

Historical perspective provides insight into a critical economic trend which suggests that the economic stability required for a new community-based democratic vision is likely to become increasingly feasible in the coming period.

Fully 31 percent of the nation's nonfarm workforce were involved in manufacturing at the midpoint of the twentieth century, in 1950. By 1970 such employment had slipped to 25 percent. By 1990 it was 16 percent. As of 2003 those working in the manufacturing sector numbered only 11 percent of the labor force—and this figure is projected to decline to approximately 9 percent by 2045. Some experts expect that a mere 5 to 7 percent of the economy will be involved in manufacturing long before that time.[2]

The U.S. economy has for many years been dominated by services—a sector that is far more locally oriented and much more stable than manufacturing. Importantly, many service-sector industries are also much less dependent upon—and responsive to the vagaries and instabilities of—

global trade. Only approximately 5 to 7 percent of U.S. services are exported.[3]

Despite other problems associated with the larger trends, that more stable, locally oriented economic development is increasingly favored by sectoral changes even in an era of increasing globalization is documented in recent studies of the already high degree of localization of economic activity. "About 60 percent of U.S. economic activity is local and provides residents with the goods and services that make their lives comfortable," observes economist Thomas Michael Power. "This includes retail activities; personal, repair, medical, educational, and professional services; construction; public utilities; local transportation; financial institutions; real estate; and government services. Thus almost all local economies are dominated by residents taking in each other's wash."[4]

Power reports that locally oriented economic activity increased from 42 percent in 1940 to 52 percent in 1980. Over the roughly two-decade period between 1969 and 1992 "the aggregates of retail and wholesale sales, services, financial and real estate, and state and local government" have been making up "a larger and larger percentage of total earnings, rising from 52 to 60 percent."[5]

Paul Krugman offers a summary judgment: "Although we talk a lot these days about globalization, about a world grown small, when you look at the economies of modern cities what you see is a process of localization: A steadily rising share of the work force produces services that are sold only within that same metropolitan area."[6]

The long-term sectoral trends also have reduced the importance of location-related efficiency considerations that conflict with policies aimed at greater community stability. Opponents of policies designed to help local community economies have traditionally held that firms must be allowed to locate wherever managers think best. Many such arguments, however, are implicitly based on the assumption of a manufacturing-dominated economy—that is, one in which economic activity historically had to locate near raw material sources and transportation hubs, starting with water and evolving to rail and air.

Some service industries (e.g., international banking) require networks of related businesses, but most are not nearly as wedded to places that happen to provide access to natural resources or to cheap transportation. In addition, advances in communication technologies have made it economic for firms to locate in a number of different areas.

Community-oriented strategies throughout the nation now regularly build upon these realities to achieve greater stability. Some stress bottom-up development utilizing conventional tax, loan, procurement, and other strategies. Others emphasize measures that enhance the local community's physical and social environment so as to attract professionals and others looking for a supportive community in which to live and raise children. Successfully attracting new arrivals, in turn, stimulates new services, construction, and other economic activity. Attracting retirees and their pension income flows can also help bolster community stabilization efforts—a factor of increasing importance as the baby-boom generation reaches retirement age.[7]

In recent years numerous other policies have been developed to retain jobs, build greater local self-reliance, and increase local economic "multipliers" so that money spent in a community recirculates to produce additional jobs. In addition to tax, loan, training, and other traditional approaches:

- State governments now regularly target public procurement to boost local economies. Community-based small businesses, for instance, can receive a 5 percent preference on bids for state contracts in California, New Mexico, and Alaska. Louisiana allows a 7 percent preference for products "produced, manufactured, grown, harvested, or assembled" in the state.[8]

- Many cities increasingly use public contracts to help neighborhood-anchored Community Development Corporations—and to simultaneously improve the delivery of government services (roughly half the municipalities in a recent survey).[9]
- Publicly sponsored "buy local" programs are also widespread. The Rural Local Markets Demonstration in central North Carolina identifies products, services, parts, and raw materials that manufacturers would like to purchase locally—and then assists other local firms with the development of such products and/or helps establish new local firms to fill the supply gap.[10]
- Pension funds now also regularly seek ways to enhance local economic health. More than half the states have established Economically Targeted Investment programs to target investment to help communities. Several independent labor-backed programs—for example, the Landmark Growth Capital Fund and the Pittsburgh Regional Heartland Fund—also involve geographically targeted investments.[11]

As we have noted, an obvious line of convergence has also emerged between stabilization strategies and many new institutional efforts. Precisely because worker-owned firms, community development corporations, co-ops, municipal enterprises, and related efforts are increasingly regarded as important to achieving broader community economic goals, they have received additional backing from many states and localities (see Chapters 7, 8, and 9).

Research on the costs of "throwing away cities" has added to the economic arguments that favor new localist strategies. Allowing existing public and private investments in transportation, office buildings, schools, homes, and other local infrastructure to go to waste when companies leave town for small (possible) private advantage—and then having to rebuild them elsewhere—obviously creates very large expenses that, if saved, can significantly offset the costs of community-oriented policies.

One recent estimate is that taxpayers spent roughly $65 billion (2001 dollars) to pay for the infrastructure and other capital costs needed to serve individuals who moved out of declining cities to other locations over the 1980 to 1999 period. Work by University of Maryland researcher Tom Ricker suggests that adding private costs (e.g., redundant houses, stores, factories, etc.) brings the figure to over $350 billion—not including lost tax revenues and increased social spending borne by specific communities when jobs decline and citizens leave town.[12]

At the national level, both political parties have also shown themselves responsive to the practical and philosophical elements of a community-building paradigm—and to the concerns of local constituents. Among the many federal policies and precedents that now exist (and that suggest possible directions for future development) are:

- The strategic targeting, currently, of public contracts by federal agencies to small businesses in "HUBZones" (Historically Underutilized Business Zones)—that is, areas that have a high proportion of low-income households or those experiencing high unemployment.[13]
- Trade Adjustment Assistance to communities experiencing dislocation as a result of imports. Workers receiving TAA are eligible for an additional fifty-two weeks of income assistance (beyond the standard twenty-six weeks unemployment insurance) and for a variety of training and other programs.[14]
- The Community Adjustment and Investment Program, which uses funding from the North American Development Bank to make loans and grants to specific economically depressed communities.[15]
- Community Development Block Grants, which in fiscal year 2004 will provide $4.4 billion in support to various locally selected, largely community-based efforts.[16]

- The Empowerment Zone/Enterprise community programs, which, as of this writing, are expected to involve over $1 billion in public subsidies in 2004.[17]
- The previously cited New Markets Initiative, passed as part of the Community Renewal Tax Relief Act of 2000, which will make several billion dollars of federal tax credits available in the next six years. The credit (30 percent of funds invested) is available to specially certified entities that make investments in low-income communities.[18]

Unusual and often unexpected political alliances have developed around more controversial issues of importance to community stability—including the left-right coalition that blocked several "free trade" initiatives. After the passage of NAFTA in 1993, Congress refused Clinton administration requests to reestablish expired "fast-track" authority, which facilitates presidential trade negotiations. Again, fast-track legislation proposed by the Clinton administration in 1997 was withdrawn when it became clear that it faced substantial opposition in both parties, and as concern about the proposed Multilateral Agreement on Investment began to develop force.[19]

Although the Bush administration won approval of such authority (calling it "Trade Promotion Authority") in 2002, it did so only after yielding several major points of contention—especially those that impacted local communities. Among other things, Republicans from textile-producing states (in particular, North Carolina) secured language requiring that duty-free textile imports from the Caribbean, Africa, or Latin America be made with fabrics dyed and finished in the United States.[20]

The Bush administration also yielded much of the substance of the issue in connection with support for agricultural subsidies and protectionist measures for the steel industry—in large measure because of the economic threat to communities in Ohio and Pennsylvania. Given ongoing unemployment problems and the growing pressure from both left and right, the likelihood is for more rather than less support for trade measures of importance to specific communities in the future.*[21]

In connection with virtually every policy advance—local, state, and federal—there has been conflict, interest-group bargaining, and debate concerning effectiveness and efficiency. Viewed in a larger historical perspective, what is significant is the long-term trend. Detailed scholarly studies of numerous specific policies confirm the expanding use and refinement of a variety of new tools aimed in one way or another at community economic stability. "Sometime after the mid-1970s," observes urban policy expert Peter K. Eisinger, especially on the state and local level there emerged "an intense preoccupation with economic development that has been marked by a level of consensus and expectation unusual in American politics."[22]

The growing force and political appeal of locally oriented strategies is also evident in organizing efforts by engaged citizens. Although many studies show a decline in *national* citizen participation, the United States in fact is in the midst of an extraordinary resurgence of *local* community-building efforts. A recent comprehensive survey by professors Carmen Sirianni and Lewis Friedland confirms the findings of many scholars, and concludes that Americans at the local level "have created forms of civic practice that are far more sophisticated in grappling with complex public problems

---

* In addition, the Bush administration agreed to extend Trade Adjustment Assistance support to workers in firms supplying businesses disrupted by trade, to add six months to coverage, and to pay 65 percent of transitional health insurance for workers who lose jobs due to trade. A sign of related, growing concern: as of this writing, at least twenty-eight states were considering legislation to limit the "outsourcing" of jobs (see ALICE, www.highroadnow.org). In a highly unusual reversal the Bush administration rescinded the steel tariffs in December 2003 for complex reasons that included anger at high prices in Michigan and other politically important steel-using states, growing foreign (particularly Chinese) demand, and threats of retaliation by the European Union. Mike Allen, "President to Drop Tariffs on Steel, Bush Seeks to Avoid a Trade War and Its Political Fallout," *Washington Post*, December 1, 2003, p. A1.

and collaborating with highly diversified social actors than have ever existed in American history."[23]

The long-standing largely black BUILD alliance in Baltimore, for instance, challenges local insurance and home mortgage redlining, builds and rehabilitates homes, raises money for student scholarships, and—importantly—registers thousands of voters.[24] Since 1976 Citizens for Community Improvement in Iowa has spearheaded opposition to corporate concentration in state agriculture, helped create financing for small farms and low-income rural and urban housing, and fought for enforcement of environmental air and water regulations. A youth organizing project works on projects ranging from gun violence and crime education to drug addiction.[25]

In San Antonio, COPS—Communities Organized for Public Service—combines research and planning with public mobilizations of Hispanic American voters and other low-income groups. In the last several decades COPS campaigns have produced funds for libraries, playgrounds, schools, street paving, sewers, flood protection, and other infrastructure improvements. COPS has also forced support for health clinics, state funding of a community college, and federal backing for affordable housing programs from the Department of Housing and Urban Development. Taken together, COPS's organizing efforts have secured an estimated $1 billion for neighborhood development from these and other sources.[26]

New forms of local labor-community alliances have broken down traditional barriers between organizations in several cities. In Chicago the Association of Community Organizations for Reform Now (ACORN) and the Illinois Coalition for Immigrant and Refugee Rights jointly lead a Grassroots Collaborative of community and labor groups working on living wage and health care campaigns. In Oakland, California, the Labor Immigrant Organizers Network (LION) helped the hotel employees' union, HERE Local 2850, successfully challenge corporate efforts to prevent union organizing. In turn, the union supported LION's efforts to organize local residents around immigration issues.[27]

In many cities—from Boston and Baltimore to St. Louis and Los Angeles—"living wage" campaigns have succeeded in requiring public agencies and their contractors to pay a wage that allows employees to support themselves and their families, commonly $9 to $10 per hour, plus health benefits. Cincinnati established a floor of $8.70 per hour with health benefits ($10.20 an hour without benefits) for all city employees or any business with a city contract over $20,000. New York's law requires a wage of $9.10 an hour plus benefits (or $10.60 an hour without benefits) for about fifty thousand workers.[28]

Several related initiatives have achieved formal structures of greater democratic participation within larger municipalities. In Portland, Oregon, each of ninety largely autonomous neighborhood associations drafts its own plans detailing the form of development that is acceptable to its neighborhood. The city of St. Paul, Minnesota, has seventeen elected District Councils, each of which has considerable authority—including zoning powers and control over the allocation of certain city services and capital expenditures.[29]

In Seattle, a Neighborhood Matching Fund allocates public funds for neighborhood-initiated projects when local residents match such support with their own contributions. Neighborhood District Councils made up of representatives of neighborhood organizations make specific recommendations for project funding. In Birmingham, Alabama, each of the city's ninety-five neighborhood associations makes decisions about how public funds will be spent—with each also receiving an allocation of federal Community Development Block Grant funds.[30]

Political scientists Jeffery Berry, Kent Portney, and Ken Thompson—who have studied St. Paul, Birmingham, Portland, and Dayton, Ohio, in depth—conclude that such efforts alter the balance of power between businesses and neighborhoods. Although "general" participation does not increase because of formal changes of structure, there is an increase in "strong participation activities"—for example, "being involved in neighborhood or issue groups, contacting such groups," or "working with others to solve problems" (as opposed, for instance, to merely "working in social or service groups or contacting government officials"). A telling outcome is that it is commonly all but impossible for developers to win approval of projects that are strongly opposed by a neighborhood association—even when the association does not have formal power to reject proposals. In general, Berry, Portney, and Thompson observe: "Neighborhood-based government draws easily on people's sense of identity with the area they live in. People know they are going to have frequent interactions with their neighbors, so even if they attend meetings infrequently they have a powerful incentive to think about long-term relationships in addition to the policy questions at hand."[31]

None of this is to say that a new day of participatory democracy has arrived. In most cities power still largely resides in the hands of traditional economic interests. In some cases, too, civil society organizations have lost credibility and are deeply compromised politically. It is to say, however, that there is growing evidence of change and of new longer-term possibilities. In many communities the developing trend of activist organizing and local policy change has followed a logic similar to that which has forced a reassessment in connection with a number of other matters of strategic importance.

An inability to achieve solutions to growing problems through traditional means has repeatedly driven home a painful reality. In case after case, the choice presented has been between no solution, and the ultimately critical decision to begin the arduous long-term process of rebuilding, step by step—at home, within reach, from the bottom up.

Over the last several decades, community-building themes and paradigms related to the Pluralist Commonwealth vision have also attracted increasing interest and important support from writers, academics, and activists representing different philosophical perspectives. We have noted the emphasis given such ideas by progressives ranging from Hannah Arendt and Jane Jacobs to Benjamin Barber and Michael Sandel. Along with many modern conservatives, William Schambra of the Bradley Foundation holds that "conservatism wasted much of [the twentieth] century futilely extolling the virtues of rugged individualism and the untrammeled marketplace in the face of America's manifest yearning for some form of community."[32]

Similarly, communitarian theorist Amitai Etzioni echoes the oft-heard judgment that the "most common antidotes to mass society" are "intermediary bodies"—but Etzioni quickly goes on to stress, "It is often overlooked . . . that many of these bodies are not the vaunted voluntary associations, with their meager bonding power . . . but communities, with their much stronger interpersonal attachments."[33]

Environmentalists Herman Daly, Thomas Prugh, and Robert Costanza begin with a different question but come to a similar conclusion: "[M]ost of the individual behaviors and attitudes that support sustainability are best nurtured at the community level. The political structure and process necessary for a regionally, nationally, and globally sustainable society must be built on a foundation of local communities."[34]

Black scholars on both the right and the left now commonly also emphasize community-based themes. Thus, the conservative activist and writer Robert Woodson stresses, "The lives of young people cannot be salvaged through outside intervention that ignores the necessity of strengthening their communities." The progressive urban affairs and planning expert Sigmund C. Shipp emphasizes the importance of cooperative community-wide development: "The depth of the dilemmas that black communities face requires strategies that focus on the entire group and the total problem, that is, the collection of factors that constitute the quality of life of a community."[35]

Harry Boyte adds that such themes help reenergize a sense of commitment to "public work" in general.[36] And Betty Friedan, speaking for many feminists, writes, "I've spent 25 to 30 years focusing on women's issues. . . . I see no solutions in terms of power blocks. What is needed is a new vision of community, a higher vision of the good of a whole community that transcends polarization of groups. Groups have been effective in the past in achieving equality. Now we're in a position where the only way progress can continue is through a new definition of community."[37]

Many analysts believe the growing interest at various levels in rebuilding the foundations of community is ultimately traceable to the psychological dead end that individualism has reached for large numbers of Americans, and from a profound—and ongoing—personal reassessment process: "[M]any of those we talked to," sociologist Robert Bellah observes, "realize that though the processes of separation and individuation were necessary to free us from the tyrannical structures of the past, they must be balanced by a renewal of commitment and community if they are not to end in self-destruction."[38]

Research by University of Chicago sociologist Robert K. Sampson offers a summary overview. Sampson finds that "calls for a return to community values" now appear "everywhere"—especially (and, he urges, significantly) among the parents of the new generation: "Whatever the source, there has emerged a widespread idea that something has been lost in American society and that a return to community is in order. . . . Seeking an alternative to mainstream institutions such as old-line churches, urban sprawl, and market-induced conspicuous consumption, the baby boom is driving unforeseen demand for the good that is deemed community."[39]

The point is particularly important among those who will inevitably take over leadership of the nation—and of its communities—in coming decades. A recent survey found that two-thirds of young adults currently already do volunteer work in their own cities—and that a majority agree with the slogan "Think Globally, Act Locally." Two-thirds believe "the best way to make a difference is to get involved in your local community, because that's where you can best solve the problems that are really affecting people."[40]

13

Community, the Environment, and the "Nonsexist City"

AMERICANS CONCERNED WITH the environment, on the one hand, and gender-related issues, on the other, are also slowly coming to realize they now face systemically rooted challenges that are fundamentally different from those they once thought might easily be overcome. One clear requirement of a longer-run solution for both directly intersects with, and is likely to bolster, the strategic logic of the economically stable communities of the Pluralist Commonwealth vision.

Despite more than thirty years of modern achievement, the fact is many of the most important environmental trends—always allowing for exceptions that prove the rule—continue to move in a negative direction. We may distinguish between three quite different types of progress with regard to the environment.

First are what may be termed "Type A" gains—absolute breakthroughs in connection with discrete problems—like the near total elimination of DDT and lead. These are important but limited in number and in overall impact. Second, "Type B," are a range of policies, programs, and regulatory efforts that serve to "do something about" a major environmental problem; but often their positive effect, like the effect of many efforts to deal with inequality, is insufficient to reverse (as opposed to slow down) a major trend. Thus, without various national and international strategies to curb global warming, things would clearly be worse—*but the destructive negative trends continue nonetheless.* Again, the rate at which wetlands have been lost has slowed—yet net losses in the 1990s continued at over fifty thousand acres a year. Gains have been made in average passenger car fuel mileage, but these have been overwhelmed by a rise in the numbers of cars, a shift to less efficient light trucks and SUVs, and a doubling of miles driven since 1970.[1]

Third are "Type C" achievements that actually reverse the direction of destructive long-term environmental trends—including those involving certain components of air and water pollution, and the cleanup of Lake Erie. Reductions in U.S. emissions of volatile organic compounds, sulfur dioxide, and carbon monoxide since 1970, for instance, range between 15 and 40 percent.[2]

The reality is that, despite several significant "Type A" breakthroughs and a very few important "Type C" trend reversals, most environmental gains have been in the "Type B" category. They have done useful things, but the positive achievements have not been adequate to reverse long-term negative trends. A recent study of quarter-century patterns by the National Center for Economic and Security Alternatives demonstrates a general worsening of ecological outcomes in twenty-one key environmental factors. (Exceptions are certain aspects of air and water pollution.) Similarly, research covering the 1970 to 2000 period by Redefining Progress found improvement in air pollution, but negative trends in overall water pollution, noise pollution, loss of wetlands, loss of farmlands, depletion of nonrenewable resources, and ozone depletion. (The estimated magnitude of the worsening trends was roughly thirty-five times the improvement in positive trends.)*[3]

---

* A study of long-term trends by a consortium of several of the world's top environmental research groups also found that "conventional wastes, emissions, and discharges" in the United States rose from 5.3 billion metric tons in 1975 to 6.8 billion metric tons in 1996. The report noted that outputs of "some hazardous materials have been regulated and successfully reduced or stabilized," but "many potentially haz-

Such declines do not, of course, include the impact of many recent policy changes by the Bush administration that are likely to have a negative impact on the environment. Among others, these include abandoning the Kyoto treaty on climate change; allowing the expansion of older, dirtier power plants; loosening rules on mining wastes; weakening rules that protect wetlands; and seeking decreased public review of a range of activities, from offshore drilling to highway construction.[4]

The bottom line on many, many fronts is that the battle for ecological sustainability is being lost—despite positive "activity." The late Donnella Meadows put the situation succinctly in the title of one of her last essays: "Things Getting Worse at a Slower Rate."[5]

Environmentalists continue to organize in support of various regulations, and to express anger at major corporate and other polluters. However, the fundamental issue, like that which is increasingly obvious in other areas—is that many traditional strategies seem increasingly unable to achieve important defined goals. Yes, certain gains can be made, but unless some major shift occurs, the likelihood is that, no, many critical negative trends will not be reversed.

The development of a systematic capacity to achieve greater community economic stability, together with other features of Pluralist Commonwealth democratic reconstruction, offers a logically coherent strategic approach to moving beyond the impasse suggested by this reality (and accordingly, too, ultimately the possibility of additional political support for the policies and institutional changes it requires).

ardous flows in the United States increased by 25 to 100 percent." Emily Matthews, *The Weight of Nations: Material Outflows from Industrial Economies* (Washington, D.C.: World Resources Institute, 2000), pp. xi, 109. See Chapter 18 in this book for a discussion of additional trends and issues related to resource consumption and long-term sustainability. For a critical assessment of claims by Bjorn Lomborg and others that environmental gains have been much greater, see (among many sources): World Resources Institute, www.wri.org/press/mk_lomborg.html (accessed 12/16/02).

A basic reason environmental pollution is often difficult to deal with at the local level is that citizens and political leaders alike fear the loss of jobs that a challenge to corporate polluters might produce. The citizens of Pigeon River, Tennessee, for instance, chose to risk potentially carcinogenic emissions by North Carolina's Champion International paper mill because of fear they might otherwise lose a thousand jobs. A fifty-one-year-old worker who, despite the danger, supported keeping the plant open spoke for many: "What do you do when you're my age and faced with the prospect of being thrown out on the street?"[6]

For similar reasons, as the Nobel laureate economist Kenneth Arrow and others have observed, low-income nations typically have higher proportions of dangerous polluting industries. Conversely, several studies have found that economically successful states and localities have stronger and/or more effective environmental regulations.[7]

Strategies that bolster local economic stability offer a response to a common and critical dilemma: if community stability can be achieved through policies like those discussed in Chapter 12, then the fear of loss that a challenge to pollution may entail can be reduced—even, in principle, eliminated. Undercutting this source of strategic environmental weakness is thus a fundamental, not superficial, long-term requirement of significant change.

An additional foundational factor involves the inherent "embeddedness" of many new local economic institutions. Most of the growing numbers of worker-owned firms, non-profits-in-business, municipal enterprises, community-owned corporations, and the like that we have reviewed are enmeshed in, and deeply tied to, the community. Not only is it difficult for such entities to leave when challenged by local environmental regulation, but they are institutions with a stake in maintaining the general support of the community of which they are a part. Further, the people involved are themselves members of the community. All three reasons serve to increase the responsiveness of such enterprises to local environmental concerns.

Several firms in which workers have significant ownership are also on the cutting edge of specific environmental sustainability efforts: Cranston Print Works in Rhode Island has regularly won awards for reducing its use of toxic materials; Herman Miller, Inc., has been recognized by the National Wildlife Federation and the state of California for outstanding reductions in material waste; Kolbe and Kolbe has dramatically reduced its hazardous waste output as a result of suggestions by employee-owners.[8]

Environmentally oriented "civil society" associational development is also related to community economic stability. Local activism has produced a rich and broad grassroots tradition of environmental problem-solving—of efforts devoted to recycling, to encouraging community-supported agriculture, to challenging local pollution dangers, to organizing new forms of community transportation planning, to developing solar and other renewable energy projects, and the like. Instability obviously weakens all forms of civil society network-building. On the other hand, strategies that help achieve local stability produce a more supportive context for civil society associations in general—and for citizen organizations concerned with the environment in particular.

The longer-term involved citizen trend has also given rise to what is termed "civic environmentalism." Traditional regulatory methods have been applied to only a limited group of environmental problems—mainly those amenable to relatively easy compliance monitoring. The Clean Water Act, for instance, has focused largely on limiting concentrated dumping, but it has done far less to regulate the more difficult problem of "nonpoint source" pollution—that is, releases from widely dispersed locations. In contrast, flexible environmental agreements have been achieved in several areas by organized citizen groups that have negotiated directly with corporations in connection with such matters as habitat preservation, forestry, toxic release control, and green space preservation. Although there have been questionable compromises in some settings, the most interesting "civic environmental" experiments now provide sustained, rather than sporadic, citizen input into local corporate decision making.[9]

Beyond any particular project or strategy, what is ultimately at stake at the community level is the transformation over time of local culture in the direction of greater ecological consciousness—and this in turn is important for reasons that extend beyond the locality. Research by Giovanna Di Chiro and others has shown how the agendas of grassroots groups commonly evolve from defending a localized "place" orientation to supporting broader, more universal concepts of environmental justice. Similarly, Raymond DeYoung, Stefan Vogel, Stephen Kaplan, and others have demonstrated the diverse ways that direct local participation builds stronger environmentally oriented attitudes in general. The resulting changes in consciousness—and in "acceptable" standards and norms of environmental management—are critical, in turn, to establishing support for larger, longer-term national and regional policy change.[10]

We are back by another route to the Tocqueville-Mill axiom that direct local community experience is formative and essential—and to the question of whether local political and especially economic conditions provide a supportive context for such experience.

Sociologist Ronald Inglehart and others have traced the dramatic evolution of greater environmental consciousness at the national level throughout the Western world over the last four decades. Systematic support for the economic conditions that nurture the local sources of environmental norms may be understood as a way to add to and accelerate the longer-term developmental process—and thus also for consciously working to bolster the underlying society-wide cultural changes ultimately required for a renewal of support for environmentally important policies.[11]

Although the logic of such considerations—and the importance of local economic stability—is increasingly understood by many concerned with environmental matters, a key question is whether (when?) significant numbers might begin to confront the need to embrace a broader political-economic agenda aimed not only at immediate environmental threats, but explicitly at establishing the necessary foundations for longer-range change. Clearly, this is not a simple task; a great deal of energy is (and must be) absorbed in important day-to-day battles.

If the experience of other groups is any guide, however, the logic of failure here, too, may ultimately force a rethinking process, and perhaps one day may also help catalyze significant political alliances with others concerned with related political and economic matters—and with community economic stability in particular. Changes in the way sprawl issues have been conceived and addressed in recent years, in fact, already offer an example of how a greatly expanded environmental political agenda—and unexpected new alliances—can develop as the situational logic facing diverse groups forces them to confront new issues over time.

The American Farmland Trust calculates that almost a million acres of farm and open land are lost to sprawl each year. Chicago's expansion is illustrative: its metropolitan population grew only 4 percent between 1970 and 1990, but its urban land area increased 35 percent. In the same period Pittsburgh's population declined 9 percent, but its urban area continued to grow by 30 percent (180 square miles). Outward land expansion has, in fact, outpaced population growth in 94 percent of U.S. metropolitan areas in recent years.[12]

A particularly worrisome longer-range consequence of sprawl is the loss of biological diversity due to habitat destruction, especially wetlands. Water runoff problems are also exacerbated. In highly developed areas (with many buildings, parking lots, roads, etc.), the natural absorption of rainwater is greatly reduced, encouraging greater soil erosion, increased water pollution, and lower water tables. Again, sprawl increases reliance on the automobile—a primary source of air pollution and greenhouse emissions. A recent HUD study estimates that suburban families drive 30 percent more than city residents.[13]

Many of the outward-moving pressures that contribute to sprawl are derivative—in significant part the result of an absence of systematic job creation and economic development in central cities. Myron Orfield's study of the Washington, D.C., metropolitan area, for instance, found that "social decline and local fiscal stress 'push' people and businesses out of older declining communities," creating pressures on middle-class areas. Bruce Katz of the Brookings Institution puts it this way: the "flip side of the rise in concentrated urban poverty is the surge in suburban and exurban sprawl."[14]

Mass transit can help reduce commuting, but ultimately the provision of stable jobs near homes and schools—not only in the central city but in suburban communities as well—is the only way to undercut the forces producing the waste of ever greater expansion, commuting, and ever lower densities. For many years environmentalists mainly stressed policies to constrain the external sprawling thrust of metropolitan growth. During the last two decades, however, a number of groups have come to realize that it is important to deal with the deeper driving forces as well. Many have added community economic strategies to their once narrowly "environmental" agendas—and at the same time have formed new and previously unexpected alliances.

Maryland's Smart Growth & Neighborhood Conservation Initiative, for instance, is attempting both to limit sprawl and to develop communities ("conserving neighborhoods"). State infrastructure funding has been explicitly restricted to "designated growth areas," and efforts are under way to support brownfield redevelopment. Miami's Eastward Ho! Brownfields Partnership is a collaboration of government agencies, community organizations, and private groups working to redirect development in southeast Florida. A key strategy here involves "infill" development to revitalize Miami's urban core and other coastal communities. An explicit goal is to thereby reduce development pressures on the Everglades to the west.[15]

The sprawl issue offers a further lesson in political possibilities—and how change can occur even in times of long-term frustration and seeming stalemate. In the fall of 1998, suddenly and unexpectedly, more than 70 percent of 240 state and local antisprawl ballot measures were approved by voters around the nation. The 240 proposals were more than double the number reported just two years earlier in a similar survey. Taxpayers set aside a combined total of $7.5 billion to purchase land or development rights for preservation. In addition, they enacted numerous limits on suburban expansion.[16]

Both sides of the aisle got involved. Then Republican governor Christine Todd Whitman of New Jersey offered a plan to invest $1 billion to protect half the state's remaining 2 million acres of undeveloped land. Forty-three cities and six counties approved tax increases to finance the proposal. The liberal Democratic governor of Maryland, Parris Glendening, won passage of several antisprawl proposals—including the Smart Growth Areas Act, which "restricts state funding for road and sewer projects to those in older communities and areas already slated for growth."[17]

Two years later, in 2000, voters approved just under 80 percent of a record 257 similar measures on the ballot—something that would have seemed all but impossible even to the most optimistic in the politically difficult years only a short time before.[18]

"The most striking aspects of modern U.S. city spatial structure," University of Minnesota professor Ann Markusen points out, "are the significant spatial segregation of residence from the capitalist workplace, the increasing low-density settlement, and the predominant single-family form of residential housing. . . . [The] current forms . . . reinforce women's roles as household workers and as members of the secondary labor force."[19]

Many of the most commonly discussed issues of concern to American women can be traced to discriminatory attitudes and high levels of income inequality. (See Chapter 17 for further discussion.) In recent years, however, it has also become clear that critical matters of community economic stability, jobs, and land use planning must be addressed if fundamental goals of male-female equality are ever to be realized. The longer-term trajectory of learning and change here, too, points in the direction of the community-building Pluralist Commonwealth paradigm—and again, opens questions of how (whether) over time those concerned with gender issues might also begin to orient their efforts to foundational political-economic issues and principles, and to the alliances these suggest.

Markusen and others now forcefully argue that the spatial organization of the city must be addressed directly. What is needed (in Betty Friedan's formulation) is a "new kind of space for living that would be more human and less impersonal . . . and not so separated from the workplace, not so isolated as the suburbs." Friedan concludes: "We have to take new control . . . with not only new sharing of roles by women and men, but physical, spatial design of new kinds of housing and neighborhoods." The question for the future, Yale's Dolores Hayden declares, is, "What Would a Non-Sexist City Be Like?"[20]

One obvious requirement is a form of community planning and land use that brings men, women, and children into closer proximity throughout the workday. This is not simply a matter of reducing the commute to work and improving community ties; a change in proximity is also necessary if more meaningful shared male-female child-rearing is ever to be achieved. If one or both parents must leave home early in the morning to get to work "downtown"—and return late in the day—the possibility of rearranging roles and tasks is limited, to say the least (see pp. 208–213).

Even a preliminary approach to such planning, however, requires a systematic capacity to target stable jobs to both urban and suburban communities in a manner that brings home and work closer together. Although the logic of a gender-related form of community planning, which takes gender issues seriously, has become increasingly obvious—and, too, its relationship to the key policy elements of a general approach to achieving community economic stability clear—very few feminists have as yet embraced a *foundational* political-economic agenda that systematically addresses the underlying issues.

Partial movement in the direction of a new approach has, however, begun to emerge from a different quarter. City planners concerned with "New Urbanist" themes have begun to develop "village" groupings that attempt to bring work, home, school, and various community facilities closer together. Often such regrouping strategies are linked to new mass transit access points in so-called transit-oriented development designed to reduce automobile use. The issue goes well beyond city planning per se, and even beyond matters of gender equality. Ultimately, it involves questions of civic life and democratic participation, which are central to the Pluralist Commonwealth vision. New Urbanist leader Peter Calthorpe is devastating in his critique:

> Today the public world is shrunken and fractured. Parks, schools, libraries, post offices, town halls, and civic centers are dispersed, underutilized, and underfunded. Yet these civic elements determine the quality of our shared world and express the value we assign to community. The traditional Commons, which once centered our communities with convivial gathering and meeting places, is increasingly displaced by an exaggerated private domain: shopping malls, private clubs, and gated communities. Our basic public space, the street, is given over to the car and its accommodation, while our private world becomes more and more isolated behind garage doors and walled compounds. Our public space lacks identity and is largely anonymous, while our private space strains toward a narcissistic autonomy. Our communities are zoned black and white, private or public, my space or nobody's.

Calthorpe urges that we "need communities that are occupied full time and that provide a world of opportunity for kids, communities that support women (and men) in their efforts to weave together an ever more complex life of home and work."[21]

New Urbanists Andres Duany, Elizabeth Plater-Zyberk, and Jeff Speck point out that "we have rebuilt our nation every fifty to sixty years." We are likely to do so again, one way or the other, more than once over the course of the new century. As they observe: "The choice is ours: either a society of homogenous pieces, isolated from one another in often fortified enclaves, or a society of diverse and memorable neighborhoods, organized into mutually supportive towns, cities, and regions."[22]

New Urbanist efforts offer practical precedents for community planning—and, too, a further trajectory of intersecting thought and developing experience that reinforces the logic of a community-building approach to both environmental and gender issues. There are also signs that such efforts are developing increasing support—and in so doing are adding to the possibilities of a longer-term foundationally oriented politics in general.*[23]

The broad direction that begins with community stability and sprawl issues and moves on to New Urbanism—both in general and, now, in ways that facilitate new gender roles and civic renewal—recalls themes that have been evolving over the last hundred years that culminate, logically, in community-focused strategies aimed at the development of new towns and population centers in areas away from mass conurbations.

"The re-animation and re-building of regions, as deliberate works of collective art," Lewis Mumford wrote early in the twentieth century, "is the grand task of politics for the opening generation. . . . And as the new tasks of region-

---

* It is important to note that many New Urbanist strategies have been criticized as primarily middle- and upper-income efforts. Ultimately for such ideas to have society-wide impact, they clearly would have to be linked to strategies that address inequality. See chapters 1, 17, and 18.

building imply shifts in population, migration into more favored areas, and the building up or reconstruction of a multitude of new urban complexes, the politics of regional development become of critical importance."[24]

The creation of new population centers—and the construction of new homes, shops, and public facilities in new cities or around smaller older ones—is likely to become a matter of increasing concern as the U.S. population moves toward 400 million by midcentury and in the direction of even greater numbers by century's end. Either new community centers will be systematically encouraged, or the wasteful, ecologically destructive, traffic-congested and gendered development patterns of the last half-century will multiply, piling new cohort of population upon sprawling new cohort as time goes on.

Technological and other sectoral trends clearly permit far greater economically efficient dispersion of jobs. Numerous studies have also shown that smaller cities in the 100,000 to 200,000 range perform better than large cities with respect to a range of quality-of-life issues, including the environment, crime rates, and traffic management—and, too, that large majorities, if given a choice, would prefer living in smaller communities. Cities of smaller scale have also been shown to be more conducive to democratic participation than large cities. Ecologist David Orr suggests that the question is no longer "whether the urban tide will ebb, but when, how, how rapidly, and whether by foresight or happenstance."[25]

Many of the growing number of tax, loan, procurement, and institution-building policies aimed at bolstering community stability that we have reviewed could also obviously be used to help implement a coherent strategy to support new, more dispersed centers of population and economic activity. Precedents for using public job targeting to help stabilize and build up smaller towns are also well established in connection with the current placement of government offices and installations.[26]

Clearly, the near-term political odds against developing a systematic and fully realized approach to job and population dispersion are long. It would nonetheless be a mistake to dismiss the possible unfolding of such a strategy over the course of the century out of hand—and the logic of this possibility suggests one final perspective on the potential gains that might be achieved by bringing some of the key elements of the Pluralist Commonwealth theory and experience together in a comprehensive approach.

When new population centers are developed on new land or around existing small towns, the value of that land increases enormously. One of the founders of modern city planning, Sir Ebenezer Howard, long ago proposed that if such land were owned by some form of community corporation or land trust, the increase in value associated with new economic development would redound to the benefit of the community as a whole (and could ultimately be sufficient, he calculated, to repay investment costs and eliminate most local taxes).[27]

The key concept is essentially an expanded version of existing land trusts and value recapture efforts currently in common use in many parts of the nation.* Moreover, as we have seen, precedents for integrating such an approach with public investment strategies can be found in numerous cities—including Washington, D.C.; Atlanta; Miami; Cedar Rapids, Iowa; Santa Clara, California; and San Francisco—that have established community ownership of development around transit entrances in order to capture increased land values produced by public investment (see pp. 93–96).

A fully developed strategy aimed at helping create new population centers—one that brings together job-stabilizing policies and new land ownership institutions—offers dramatic opportunities not only for longer-term planning in general, but for capturing huge gains that might be plowed back into community development, housing, and other subsidies and even, perhaps, direct or indirect income supplements.

---

* It also recalls the municipal land ownership ideas urged by the conservative University of Chicago economist H. C. Simons (see above and pp. 56–57).

Intriguingly, Howard judged that the long-term possibilities suggested by the localist community-oriented ownership model he proposed might one day offer a way to bypass the difficulties of both historic political-economic "systems" through principles not unlike those at the very core of the Pluralist Commonwealth vision: "[O]n a small scale society may readily become more individualistic than now—if by Individualism is meant a society in which there is fuller and freer opportunity for its members to do and to produce what they will, and to form free associations, of the most varied kinds; while it may also become more socialistic—if by Socialism is meant a condition of life in which the well-being of the community is safeguarded, and in which the collective spirit is manifested by a wide extension of the area of municipal effort."[28]

14

The Regional Restructuring of the American Continent

THE PLURALIST COMMONWEALTH model attempts to deal seriously with long-standing arguments that the sheer continental size of the United States and its very large population are ultimately inimical to a robust system-wide vision of democratic practice. (See Chapter 5.) Community-oriented strategies appear to be within the range of realistic political possibility in coming years. What of the larger and seemingly utopian idea that much more far-reaching—indeed, radical—decentralization is both necessary and possible?

Five major considerations suggest that, contrary to conventional assumption, the logic of regional restructuring is likely to become of increasing importance as the twenty-first century develops. These include trends in Supreme Court and congressional decision making; an explosion of state-based initiatives; the impact of global political-economic forces on the current federal system; very large-order projected changes in the economy and population; and new trajectories of expanding ethnic political power concentrated in key regions experiencing economic distress.

Over the last several decades a series of Supreme Court and congressional decisions has begun to establish new principles of decentralization in the U.S. federal system that (for better or worse) are much more far-reaching than many understand. At the same time, numerous states have launched new initiatives that are slowly altering the locus of power in the system.

The trend in Supreme Court decision making has been well documented. In *United States v. Lopez* the Court ruled that Congress exceeded federal authority by attempting to keep firearms out of local school yards. In *Seminole Tribe of Florida v. Florida* and several subsequent cases involving state employees, savings banks, and violence against women, the Court held that Congress did not have authority to establish federal jurisdiction over states that did not consent to be sued. In *Printz v. United States* it ruled that requiring states to implement waiting periods for handgun purchases involved a similar overreach of federal power. The Court held in *Rush Prudential HMO v. Moran* that states had independent authority to protect patients' rights through legislation providing for "independent review"—a second opinion—in disputes with managed care companies (HMOs).[1]

An equally important trend in federal legislative actions has furthered the decentralization process. Among the most widely discussed is the 1996 Temporary Assistance to Needy Families reform, which gave states unprecedented power to "end welfare as we know it." This, however, is only one of a large number of less-publicized moves in the direction of greater state and local authority. We have noted the Community Development Block Grants, which allow great latitude in the use of federal money for various urban housing and community development programs. "Self-denying" legislation approved in 1995 limits the federal government's ability to impose unfunded mandates on the states. Again, the Children's Health Insurance Program allows states flexibility in designing benefits packages for uninsured children of low-income families.[2]

Similarly, the Intermodal Surface Transportation Efficiency Act gives states considerable discretion in developing transportation programs in accord with local priorities. The independent role of the states has also been augmented through widespread use of Medicaid "waivers" authorized under the Social Security laws. Innovative and widely publicized health insurance strategies in Oregon, Vermont,

Hawaii, and Maine, among others, have been developed on this basis.[3]

The states have also increased their powers through independent legislative and legal actions of their own—often because the federal government has been either deadlocked or opposed to change. After Congress failed to enact health care legislation in 1994, for instance, the states began passing patients' rights and prescription drug laws (more than half had enacted drug assistance legislation by 2003). "[O]ne can easily recount a long list of regulatory issues on which the feds have simply abdicated, leaving it to the states," observes Jonathan Walters of *Governing* magazine. States have moved into areas where federal inaction or minimalist action has been most obvious—including growth management, dirty-air emissions, gasoline additives, genetically engineered crops, questionable lending practices, and so on.[4]

Many states—most prominently, but hardly exclusively, California, Alabama, and Alaska—have also established innovative economic programs. (See Chapter 10.) Still others, like Washington and North Carolina, own or finance public railroad systems. New Mexico and California have radically reduced imprisonment for many drug offenders. Vermont has recognized gay partnerships. In 2002 California approved legislation requiring the "maximum feasible reduction" in tailpipe emissions of carbon dioxide and other greenhouse gases by cars and light trucks by 2009. Since 1993 Georgia has offered scholarships to all high school graduates with a B average that can be used at any public, private, or technical school in the state.[5]

The movement toward greater state authority is not an unbroken trend. A countermovement is evident in several Supreme Court decisions related to economic issues and in legislative efforts to enact "preemption clauses" mandating federal jurisdiction in connection with various regulatory matters. On the other hand, the state attorneys general have mounted important new legal challenges, most dramatically in connection with tobacco, but also with regard to inflated costs of prescription drugs, antitrust (Microsoft), and other issues ranging from securities fraud to global warming. In 2002 New York Attorney General Eliot Spitzer negotiated a settlement requiring Merrill Lynch and Company to pay $100 million in penalties to fifty states because of conflicts of interest between its sales, investment, and research services. Subsequent initiatives challenged other corporate practices and helped spur the Securities and Exchange Commission into more aggressive enforcement action.[6]

Nor are these simply progressive state initiatives. Typical of fraud cases was one brought by the Texas attorney general against Warrick Pharmaceuticals for allegedly attempting to gain market share by charging pharmacists $13.50 per prescription while arranging for Medicaid and Medicare to reimburse them at $40.30 per prescription. In February 2003 seven state attorneys general warned the federal government of possible litigation if it did not do more to force industry to lower emissions of greenhouse gases; in April 2003 five states helped push through the largest settlement ever under the Clean Air Act.[7]

Independent legal activism by the states has also arisen in large part because of federal inaction. Modern state attorney general initiatives first began to develop in response to the Reagan Justice Department's failure to do much to protect consumers and the environment. The $206 billion tobacco settlement in 1998 was a major victory that helped put the general movement into high gear.[*]

---

[*] As in the recent gay marriage decision of the Supreme Judicial Court of Massachusetts, state courts have also often been more protective of individual rights than the Supreme Court. Though public attention has rarely focused on such issues, modern studies of "judicial federalism" indicate that: (1) in general, Supreme Court decisions establish a federal rights protection floor below which state courts may not go; (2) in about one-third of recent cases, state courts have mandated greater protections for individual rights than is required; and (3) in general, this is true in so-called conservative states as well as in liberal states. See, for instance, James N. G. Cauthen, "Expanding Rights Under State Constitutions: A Quantitative Appraisal," *Albany Law Review,* vol. 63, no. 1183, 2000; and Barry Latzer, *State Constitutions and Criminal Justice* (New York: Greenwood Press, 1991). A *(continues)*

In general, University of Virginia political scientist Martha Derthick points out, the states have increasingly become the "default setting" of the American political-economic system—the level of government that acts when Washington does not because of gridlock or neglect. Alan Ehrenhalt of *Governing* magazine goes further: states are now increasingly the "level of government we go to because we don't expect the others to succeed."[8]

Many traditional liberals, fearing a weakening of federal standards, have opposed the general trend. Others feel the only option available may be a long-haul effort to rebuild power at the base, state by state. The important point for the future, Ehrenhalt emphasizes, is that "once states and their elected leaders begin thinking of themselves as the actors of first resort on crucial questions—rather than the actors of last resort—the logic of the whole system is in for a change."[9]

The implications of globalization reinforce this fundamental judgment. Especially significant are pressures that create new Washington-level restrictions on state decision making—and in turn produce new and angry resistance. A recent study by Columbia University professor Mark Gordon of the implications of World Trade Organization (WTO) regulations points out that WTO rules "strike at the heart of the types of policy decisions that States use to define some of

---

(continued) landmark 1977 article by Justice William J. Brennan Jr. pointed to state constitutions as "a font of individual liberties, their protections often extending beyond those required by the Supreme Court's interpretation of federal law." "State Constitutions and the Protection of Individual Rights," *Harvard Law Review,* vol. 90, no. 3, January 1977. The point could become of substantial importance as time goes on: Cass Sunstein observes that, contrary to widespread opinion, the U.S. Supreme Court has only occasionally made protection of civil rights and liberties a priority (in recent years, "a brief quirk of history," Sunstein suggests, "limited to a short time in the middle of the 20th century"). The more fundamental and far more conservative trend—further bolstered by modern Court appointees—has been exacerbated by post–September 11 security fears. See Cass Sunstein, "What We'll Remember in 2050: 9 Views on *Bush v. Gore,*" *The Chronicle of Higher Education,* vol. 47, no. 17 (January 5, 2001), p. B15.

their most basic beliefs." WTO regulations now increasingly challenge traditional state prerogatives in connection with "issues of environmental and consumer protection, set-asides to assist minority or small businesses, efforts to regulate the activities of large financial services institutions such as banks and insurance companies, and decisions about how to structure the raising of revenue through taxes and its expenditure through government procurement policies."[10]

Gordon and other analysts predict that as the impact of the new global trade regime hits home, an intense dynamic will be set loose that will force Washington to reach ever deeper into state power to enforce global agreements—and will, in turn, force states to develop ever more adamant counterstrategies: "[G]lobalization introduces a whole series of 'shocks' to the existing system."[11]

Numerous state leaders throughout the country have, in fact, already gone on record challenging WTO and NAFTA-imposed requirements. A resolution passed by the Oklahoma legislature—to cite only one of many examples—demands that the president and Congress "preserve the traditional powers of state and local governance" and "ensure that international investment rules do not give greater rights to foreign investors than United States investors enjoy under the United States Constitution."[12]

The long-term logic points to an ever more powerful "backlash" by the states—and demands for greater independence from the long arm of Washington in its role as enforcer of WTO rules. A test case currently being litigated involves Methanex, a Canadian corporation that manufactures a component of the chemical MTBE, a gasoline additive and suspected carcinogen that has run afoul of California environmental law. As of this writing, legislative hearings and other forceful initiatives have been launched in response to growing state anger.[13]

The likelihood of structural change in the federal system over the course of the century is intimately related to even more fundamental shifts—above all, to emerging economic and population trends.

As we have noted, the United States is much larger in geographic scale than most Americans commonly realize—in fact, larger geographically than all the other advanced industrial countries taken together when Canada and Australia (nations with large empty land masses) are excluded. In Kennan's phrase it is "a monster country" (see p. 67). Again, the current $10 trillion U.S. economy is over five times the size of the German economy, and more than seven times the economies of France and Britain. Leaving aside Germany and Japan, it is larger than the combined economies of all the remaining OECD countries taken together.[14]

The conservative estimating assumptions used in official Social Security projections suggest that the U.S. economy will more than double by midcentury to roughly $29 trillion (in 2003 dollars)—three times that of the current European Union. It will reach more than six times its current size (roughly $70 trillion in 2003 dollars) by the end of the century. If the more optimistic short-term economic assumptions used by the U.S. Council of Economic Advisors are projected forward, the figure could easily be $100 trillion or more by 2100. The latter estimate is roughly ten times the U.S. economy's current scale. Discounting either projection substantially, of course, still yields an extraordinary figure.[15]

The present U.S. population of over 280 million is also huge by world standards. It is the third largest after China and India and more than twice as large as any other OECD nation—greater, in fact, than the combined populations of twenty-one of the other twenty-nine OECD countries taken together. U.S. population is also projected to increase dramatically over the course of the twenty-first century. Midrange Census Bureau projections suggest it will reach 400 million by 2050—and 570 million by 2100. If the Census Bureau "high-series" projection is taken as a baseline, these numbers will increase to 550 million by 2050—and to 1.18 billion by 2100.[16]

Accurate demographic projections are notoriously difficult to make. The critical variables are future birth and death rates and immigration flows. Census Bureau demographers do not include political analyses in their projections, even though political factors can also be extremely important. When such factors are introduced, two quite obvious considerations suggest something in the direction of the higher-range projections may well be closer to reality than the mid- and lower-range estimates.

First, immigration from Mexico—now over 300,000 a year (roughly 160,000 a year documented and an estimated 150,000 undocumented)—is all but certain to be significantly affected by politics in the future. The Mexican American vote has now become sufficiently large to force both political parties to respond to its strong interest in immigration and in making immigrants already here citizens. It is all but impossible to win the presidency without winning either California or Texas, and in both states the Mexican American vote is critical.[17]

A political tipping point may well have been reached prior to the events of September 11, 2001, when both the Bush administration and leading Democrats signaled a desire to be responsive on immigration issues related to Mexico. Corporate interests in cheap labor have also encouraged Republican support for a relaxation of immigration policy; and new community alliances, especially in California and key Southwestern states, have brought labor to support Democratic positions favorable to immigration.[18]

Recent studies by the Census Bureau and the Center for Labor Market Studies at Northeastern University show that there was little change in (legal and illegal) immigration over the 2001 to 2002 period. And although new legislative activity was put on hold by war on terror concerns after September 11, Bush offered a proposal to allow undocumented immigrants already in the country permanent residence under certain circumstances in early 2004. "[T]he long-term dynamics encouraging a new approach to immigration remain in place," *Los Angeles Times* columnist Ron Brownstein observes—especially the fact that as the economy recovers, business demand for new workers will become increasingly important.[19]

A second political factor likely to impact immigration and thereby population growth is the Social Security financing problem. As has been noted repeatedly, although there were five active workers in the labor force for every retiree in 1960, currently active workers number only 3.4 per retiree. By 2030 the ratio of workers to retirees is projected to fall to around 2.1 (and to a mere 1.8 by 2080). Although such figures have commonly been used to bolster arguments for a reduction in Social Security benefits, an obvious alternative—as several economists have urged, and many other countries have realized—is to increase the number of workers per retiree through immigration (see Chapter 16).

If even a modest long-term immigration increase is included as a response to considerations related to the Hispanic vote—and as a political alternative to cutting Social Security benefits of great importance to large numbers—movement in the direction of the higher-range Census Bureau projections becomes more rather than less likely. A very cautious and respected analyst, Harvard sociologist Christopher Jencks, suggests in any event that 500 million, rather than 400 million, is a likely number by 2050. Political and quasi-political considerations—plus the fact that Mexican American Catholic immigrants have birth rates almost twice those of the general non-Hispanic U.S. population—suggest that long-range projections in the 1.18 billion range are not nearly as speculative as some may think.[20]

Even assuming more modest population projections, the numbers become very large as the century unfolds, no matter what. At some point, large enough in all probability to force even the most reluctant to consider large-order moves away from the current centralized concentration of major governmental decision making.

Twenty-one states have populations of less than 3 million (of these, seven have less than a million). Another nine have populations of less than 5 million. Most of these thirty states (and perhaps others) are too small to deal effectively with many economic, environmental, transportation, and other problems on their own.[21]

Long-term federal restructuring that might ultimately come to rest on a unit of scale larger than most states but smaller than the nation—the region—most likely would begin with states that: (1) are themselves very large; (2) have a sense of their own political and policy identity; (3) are experiencing trajectories of growing racial and ethnic change different from the rest of the nation; (4) are experiencing particularly painful economic and fiscal distress; and (5) are already constituted as organized "polities."

An obvious candidate to initiate long-range change is the regional-scale "mega-state" of California.

California, in fact, is already the equivalent of a very large semiautonomous political-economic system. Its economy is roughly the size of France's, the fifth-largest economy in the OECD.* The economy of the five-county Los Angeles area alone is roughly the size of Spain's, the OECD's ninth-largest economy—and is greater than the economies of Brazil, India, and South Korea.[22]

California's population of 35 million is greater than that of Canada (31 million), Australia (19 million), the Netherlands (16 million), Portugal (10 million), and all four of the Scandinavian countries combined (24 million). Los Angeles County is larger in population than forty-two of the fifty states. The state is also larger, geographically, than numerous important nations—including Germany, Japan, the United Kingdom, Poland, and Italy.[23]

In recent years state political leaders of both parties have also begun to take ever more challenging and independent

---

* The California economy is ranked either fifth or sixth largest, depending on the relative values of the U.S. dollar and the euro in any given year.

positions. In 1994 Republican governor Pete Wilson came head-to-head with Washington in a bitter fight over the results of Proposition 187, a ballot initiative that would have denied public services—including public education and subsidized health care—to undocumented immigrants. "California will not submit its destiny to faceless federal bureaucrats or even congressional barons," an angry Wilson all but shouted. "We declare to Washington that California is a proud and sovereign state, not a colony of the federal government."[24]

In 2001 Democratic governor Gray Davis confronted the Bush administration over its energy policy after rolling blackouts and extortionate prices had drained billions from consumers and the state treasury alike: "If you're looking for a culprit, I'll give you a culprit. The culprit is the Federal Energy Regulatory Commission." Representative Henry A. Waxman coolly observed that the issue sharpened battle lines; it was the state in general against Washington, not one party versus the other: "It didn't make any difference whether you were a conservative Republican or a liberal Democrat."[25]

The current California economy of $1.36 trillion is likely to increase to roughly $9.4 trillion—and possibly to $15.2 trillion—by 2100 (assuming no major order-of-magnitude changes in its share of national GDP). Under similar general baseline assumptions, its population will reach on the order of between 68.7 million and 83.3 million, on the basis of midrange census projections.[26]

Under all projections, California's population changes are also laying the demographic foundations for a different Hispanic-dominated political-economic identity and developmental path—one that is likely to further intensify the state's growing sense of independent direction and difference from the rest of the nation. In 1940 just 6 percent of the population was Latino (roughly 415,000 of the state population of 6.9 million). By 1970 it had reached 13.7 percent. The non-Hispanic white population in California is now a minority—less than 47 percent (in 2000), down from 57.2 percent just ten years earlier. Non-Hispanic whites are projected to constitute a mere 31 percent of the state in 2040.[27]

What will happen beyond 2040 is anybody's guess. "There will be no place in the state that is not touched by immigration and these racial and ethnic changes," observes Mark Baldassare of the Public Policy Institute of California. "We will be inventing a new kind of society."[28]

Though few have fully grasped the implications, such changes in fact point to the kinds of long-term regionally defined cultural and ethnic shifts that have intensified the logic of regional restructuring in nations throughout the world. A major difference is that the United States is, and will increasingly become, truly mammoth in comparison to most other advanced nations.

In addition to the MTBE case, California has also already been impacted by other globalization pressures, and numerous of its state programs are likely to run afoul of WTO and NAFTA regulations.* Its massive fiscal problems—and recent electoral events—suggest the likelihood of ongoing political volatility. Given its economic difficulties and the emerging pressures, in many ways it would be surprising, in fact, if a large and inherently wealthy regional-size state like California did not at some point *demand* greater powers to better manage its own affairs.

If (when?) it did, its example would likely be followed in one way or another by other large states. Texas, which now numbers 20.9 million, is projected to reach 27.2 million by 2025 and, on reasonable assumptions, 46 million by century's end. Within a decade non-Hispanic whites are projected to be

---

* Including (among many, many others) the California Export Finance Program (prohibited), the California Transportation Research and Innovation Program, the Energy Conservation and Development Program, the California Hardwoods Industry Initiative and California Technology Investment Program (all subject to "countervailing measures"), and "increased research activities tax credits." Mark C. Gordon, *Democracy's New Challenge: Globalization, Governance, and the Future of American Federalism* (New York: Demos, 2001), p. 41.

a minority—and a mere 33 percent of the population by 2040. Florida and New York are also of substantial interest. Florida is larger geographically than many midsize European countries; its current 15.9 million population is projected to reach 35 million by 2100. New York's population of 18.9 million could reach 33.5 million and its economy grow to over $8 trillion by 2100. All three states might follow the lead of California—or at some point launch independent initiatives of their own that would have repercussions throughout the system.[29]

Other plausible decentralization scenarios involve groups of smaller states. Numerous precedents and a long history of states working together could be drawn upon either in response to an assertion of power by larger states or simply in order to achieve positive goals that few small states can achieve on their own. Regional strategies have long been common, for instance, in connection with environmental issues. Some regions, such as New England, have developed multiple forms of interstate cooperation involving groupings of governors, attorneys general, environmental administrators, and others.[30]

Nearly two hundred Interstate Compacts—which are already authorized by the Constitution—also currently coordinate various state efforts in connection with matters ranging from economic development to high-speed intercity passenger rail service. Federal precedents also abound—including the Tennessee Valley Authority and previously noted presidential proposals for many similar authorities (see Chapter 5). The Appalachian Regional Commission currently involves some thirteen states in common efforts related to industrial development, energy resource coordination, tourism promotion, and other matters. Both the Johnson and Nixon administrations experimented with various additional forms of regionalization—the former by establishing regional commissions, the latter through regional administrative strategies.[31]

Such precedents for regional coordination do not reach to the many larger issues of political-economic authority and power that system-wide restructuring would clearly require. On the other hand, the historical record offers evidence that states working together when problems are larger than any one state can handle have been effective in many, many instances. The regular reappearance of regional efforts also points to a certain political appeal that regionalist ideas appear to have—especially when traditional alternatives are incapable of dealing with pressing political-economic problems.

Few in the United States are aware that in recent decades an intense exploration of regionalist constitutional changes has been under way throughout the world—in Britain and in nations as diverse as China, Italy, Indonesia, the former Soviet Union, and Canada. In 1989 a comprehensive international report concluded that decentralization had become a "subject of discussion in all countries regardless of whether they are old or young states or whether they have a long unitary or federal tradition."*[32]

It is possible that the United States will be immune to the global trend—and that as the nation moves toward 500 million and beyond, it will continue to be managed, administered, and fundamentally governed from Washington without significant change in what by century's end will be a constitutional structure that is more than three hundred years old. However—and even though few Americans have yet imagined the possibility—given the various changes under way, the odds are that population growth alone will ultimately create conditions that demand consideration of some form of major restructuring.

The specific shape a new Pluralist Commonwealth–oriented regionalism might take over the course of the century

* The first round of British regional devolution has focused on existing political units (Scotland and Wales); coming rounds are expected to produce new units within territorial England itself. A recent survey found almost two-thirds (63 percent) backing further regionalization; as of this writing, referenda on the establishment of regional assemblies are set to take place in three English regions (the North-East, North-West, and Yorkshire and the Humber) in 2004. Other countries are in various stages of debate, legislation, and implementation. See, for instance, Matthew Tempest, "Three Regions to Vote on Assemblies," "Q&A: Regional Government," and "Regional Government Around the World," all in *The Guardian,* June 16, 2003. United Kingdom survey at news.bbc.co.uk/1/hi/uk_politics/1976027.stm (accessed 04/24/03).

is obviously indeterminate. Initial changes would likely involve greater state/regional autonomy in connection with economic and environmental matters, reductions in federal preemptive powers with regard to corporate regulation, limitations on the impact of WTO and other trade treaties on state/regional legislative authority, and alterations in current Constitutional Commerce Clause restrictions related to state/regional economic rights. Beyond this, much larger issues concerning the apportionment of power might well be posed.

The nations of the European Union are currently groping toward a constitutional structure that begins with highly decentralized nation-state political units (roughly similar in scale to U.S. regions)—and attempts to move from this basis centripetally, toward greater power at the center. The United States may well find itself moving in the direction of a similar long-term structural end-point—beginning, however, from the other direction and moving outward, centrifugally, to greater independence of regional-scale units away from the center.*

Quite apart from population and other pressures that may force change—and the many uncertainties that would ultimately have to be confronted and resolved—over the long arc of the twenty-first century, Americans who are committed to a renewal of democracy are unlikely to be able to avoid the truth that in all probability this can only be meaningfully achieved in units of scale smaller than a continent but also of sufficient size to be capable of substantial semiautonomous functioning: the region.

---

* European experience also demonstrates that civil liberties and civil rights can be protected in systems involving substantial decentralization—indeed, sovereignty. In the opinion of many specialists the European Convention of Human Rights and subsequent protocols provide greater protections in many areas than U.S. practice. See, for instance, Nadine Strossen, "Recent U.S. and International Judicial Protection of Individual Rights: A Comparative Legal Process Analysis and Proposed Synthesis," *Hastings Law Journal*, vol. 41, no. 805 (April 1990); and Paul R. Dubinsky, "The Essential Function of Federal Courts: The European Union and the United States Compared," *American Journal of Comparative Law*, vol. 42, no. 295 (1994).

PART IV

TWENTY-FIRST-CENTURY
POPULISM

THE TRAJECTORIES OF EMERGING theory and the evolving new forms of ownership and community restructuring suggest that the opening decades of the twenty-first century are likely to establish significant foundations for what potentially could become much more far-reaching change in the direction of Pluralist Commonwealth ideas.

Is there any chance that the large-order power arrangements of the U.S. political economy might ever be challenged to permit a major rather than a minor political dynamic that builds upon such foundations over time?

An initial issue is whether longer-range system-oriented change is absolutely precluded. If so, even under the most favorable circumstances the steadily evolving developments are likely to remain at the margins of American politics— even if substantial advances are achieved.

The answer can never be certain, but as we have noted, larger-order political realignments have been common in U.S. history. During the last several decades alone, important political movements on both left and right have also developed unexpected power despite the conventional wisdom of the time that little of importance was likely to change.

Americans on the left commonly think of the unpredicted explosions of the civil rights, feminist, and environmental movements—but of equal interest was the rise against once seemingly impossible odds of the conservative movement over the second half of the twentieth century. Especially given the extraordinary technological changes now under way, it would be a mistake to assume that the possibility of very great future change is excluded.

Indeed, partly as a backlash phenomenon, partly in response to new domestic and global political-economic developments, and partly because of important demographic changes, a variety of growing pressures suggest the emergence and likely sharpening of a new and potentially explosive line of political cleavage—and a slowly evolving trajectory of political crisis—which converges with, and is likely to greatly reinforce, other evolving forms of Pluralist Commonwealth–related change.

The line of political cleavage, and the potential crisis, center on the privileged position of top elites and major corporate actors—and the question of who should own and control large-scale income and wealth as we move ever deeper into an era characterized by great technological abundance, on the one hand, and great social pain, on the other.

15

The Logic of Long-Term Political Refocusing

A T THE BEGINNING OF THE Bush era the Democrats were completely stymied. It was obvious no one wanted to risk proposing a tax increase—despite the fact that once in office, the new administration quickly pushed through $1.35 trillion in tax cuts largely favoring the rich, thereby squandering a massive surplus and limiting all future public programs.

Then it slowly began to dawn on several leading figures where a possible point of vulnerability might lie.

Gene Sperling, Bill Clinton's politically sophisticated former economic adviser, was one of the first to put his finger on the issue. Just before the events of September 11, 2001, Sperling proposed holding off "full repeal of the estate tax, and the second and third stage of the [Bush] tax cut for those in the top 2%"—so that funds could be made available to close at least half the Social Security deficit. The proposal would save more than $1 trillion and would ensure that 98 percent of Americans would still "get their full tax cut."[1]

A few months later the Senate's liberals joined in. The late Paul Wellstone proposed freezing future income tax reductions for the top 1 percent and retaining the corporate Alternative Minimum Tax—saving an estimated total of $134 billion over ten years. Ted Kennedy proposed delaying tax cuts for families with incomes over $130,000 and keeping the estate tax (while gradually raising the value of exempted estates from a then current $1 million to $4 million by

2010). Kennedy estimated this would save $350 billion over ten years.[2]

The political arithmetic of strategies that offered gains to 98 to 99 percent and losses only to the extremely wealthy 1 to 2 percent also began to capture the attention of those beyond traditional liberal ranks. In late May 2002 the centrist Democrat Joseph Lieberman urged postponing both the full repeal of the estate tax and reductions in the top tax bracket rates. Lieberman estimated that a trillion dollars could be saved over twenty years. The Bush tax cuts were simply unfair, he said, "giving the biggest benefit to those who needed it the least." By the fall of 2003 virtually all the Democratic presidential candidates had put forward one or another variation on the same general theme.[3]

What are we to make of such ideas?

The political logic of small versus large numbers has been present for much of history. It has also rarely led to sustainable large-order challenges to either the income or wealth of top elites. Moreover, even the more modest proposals that Democrats have offered face a highly uncertain future. Indeed, in its second major tax initiative the Bush administration secured passage of legislation to reduce dividend and other taxes of importance to the rich, and to accelerate the earlier tax reductions, and it continued to push for making repeal of the estate tax permament.[4]

On the other hand, the new round of tax proposals encountered growing resistance even among conservatives as the fiscal implications began to hit home. The critical longer-term question is: under what circumstances might new strategic alliances be developed that could ultimately achieve power and momentum following a thoroughgoing elite-challenging paradigm?

Put another way, might the situational logic of the emerging political-economic context open the way for a narrowly focused exception to the general rule that traditional progressive "after-the-fact" strategies are largely at a dead end—

and further, in so doing could this in turn define new political alignments of more far-reaching importance to longer-term Pluralist Commonwealth change?

Four key points stand out when such questions are considered in terms of their larger twenty-first-century possibilities. The first is negative. The experience of the last several decades suggests that any strategy that depends heavily on further taxation of the middle-class suburban 20 percent is simply unlikely to achieve significant gains (see Chapter 1).[5] This door is largely closed.

Second, an attempt to challenge the position of elites at the very top at least in principle inherently narrows the political focus to an extremely small number—either the top 1 to 2 percent, or perhaps the top 1 to 5 percent. It also implicitly places up to at least 95 percent of the electorate on the other side of the interest-group line.

Third, a political-economic strategy that targets elite income also inevitably brings into focus other related ideas— as in the case of estate taxes—for challenging concentrations of elite-owned wealth. Several experts have already begun to refine new approaches to such taxes, and the need for larger resources than can readily be attained by taxing income alone seems all but certain to force greater attention to wealth as well as income as time goes on.

Finally, there is an important connection between such efforts and new Pluralist Commonwealth wealth-ownership principles. Indeed, as we have seen in connection with certain "stakeholder" proposals, the strategy of challenging existing wealth concentrations, on the one hand, and building an alternative paradigm of wealth-ownership designed to benefit broad publics, on the other, has already been explicitly articulated in some proposals (see p. 23).

A certain perspective may also be gained by recalling that it was once thought impossible to tax income in general—until passage, after a long prehistory of debate and political agitation, of the Sixteenth Amendment to the U.S. Constitution in

1913. For many years the amendment in practice *meant* targeting elites: significant income taxation was largely restricted to roughly the top 2 to 4 percent until World War II.[6]

Even more important is a rarely discussed truth at the heart of the modern history of taxation. For many decades the current income tax has, in fact, been organized in a manner that rests directly upon the logic of elite targeting—even in the Bush era, and even in a society preoccupied with terrorism and war.

In 2000 the top 1 percent of households paid 36.5 percent of federal income taxes.[7] The top 5 percent paid 56.2 percent of income taxes. Although detailed calculations are not available as of this writing, the massive elite-benefiting Bush tax cuts are not expected to significantly alter these basic orders of magnitude. (It is estimated that the ultimate impact of the tax reductions may at most modify the figures by no more than two or possibly three percentage points.)[8]

Quite simply, the argument that challenging elites is politically impossible is belied by the realities of the contemporary income tax system—even under a very conservative Republican administration.

Moreover, far greater taxation of elites has been accepted policy for substantial periods of modern American history under both Democratic and Republican presidents. It also has often been associated with great economic success. Thus, throughout the post–World War II economic boom—including the Eisenhower years and up to the early Johnson era—income of those at the very top was taxed at 91 percent. The rate was reduced to 77 percent in 1964 and 70 percent in 1965, and it remained at that level or higher—including the Nixon years—until the Reagan era.[9]

There is also evidence of profound concern with the growing inequities of American society. In 1988 only 26 percent of those surveyed judged the United States to be a "have/have-not" society; in 2001 the figure had increased to 44 percent. A 1998 Gallup poll found that roughly seven in ten felt that "the rich just get richer while the poor get poorer." A full 63 percent agreed with the statement that "money and wealth in this country should be more evenly distributed." A report done for the conservative American Enterprise Institute at the same time noted that three-quarters of Americans consistently state that high-income families pay too little in taxes.[10]

Public attitudes shifted briefly after the events of September 11, 2001, but even during this period of high patriotism, 69 percent still complained that "the rich get richer and the poor get poorer." Again, although several polls indicated that roughly half of those surveyed approved the first major Bush tax cut, *when offered a choice,* large majorities (two-thirds to three-quarters) indicated they would have preferred to spend the surplus on Social Security, health care, or reducing the deficit.[11]

Sociologist S. M. Miller and activist Chuck Collins observe that public awareness of deep inequalities of wages, income, and wealth has moved through three distinct stages in recent decades:

> In the first stage, class and inequalities were forbidden topics. . . .
>
> In the second stage, data continued to show disturbing increases in income and wealth inequalities. Statistical debates followed: conservative economists contended that inequalities disappeared if the "right" years, the "right" data or the "right" statistical manipulations were used. Gradually, even they gave up the fight. . . .
>
> In the current stage, the scene has changed dramatically. . . . The heavy hand of an upper class or even an overclass is recognized as distorting the economy to its special advantage. A profound change has occurred in a very short time.[12]

The trend of growing awareness and underlying concern has been reinforced by a related trend of growing distrust of large corporations, the ownership of which is heavily skewed to elites. A 1966 Harris poll found that 55 percent of Americans surveyed had a great deal of confidence in major corporations. During the 1970s the figure collapsed to the low twenties (21.5 percent); in the 1980s and 1990s it fell further to the high teens (17 to 18.5 percent). By 2002 the number expressing a great deal of confidence in corporations had declined to 13 percent.[13]

Such surveys now regularly find that an extraordinary 80 to 85 percent of the public believe large corporations have excessive political influence. The Enron scandal and the many others that followed drew widespread attention to executive greed, only adding to long-standing and deeply rooted public distrust. A 2002 Harris poll reported, "Very large majorities of the public believe that big companies (87 percent) . . . have too much power . . . in Washington."[14]

Two fundamental contextual changes are likely to set the terms of reference in which new political alignments, new political targets, and new Pluralist Commonwealth–related issues will be considered in the coming period. The first involves the growing financial pain and increasingly stressful time pressures experienced by the average American family.

Critically, real hourly wages of the bottom 50 percent of wage earners went *down*, not up for more than two decades between 1973 and 1995. Wage changes for those even in the sixtieth and seventieth percentiles amounted respectively to a mere 1 cent per hour (down) and 41 cents per hour (up) over the twenty-two-year period. Though a slight upward blip occurred in these numbers at the end of the 1990s, with the slowing of the economy after 2000, the modest gains began to recede again (see p. 18).[15]

Total family income rose a bit more than hourly wages during the final decades of the century. The gains, however, were not large. Whereas median family (inflation-adjusted) income had more than doubled during the previous (1947 to 1973) quarter-century, more than a quarter-century later, in

2000, it had increased only modestly—from $42,590 to $52,977 (in 2002 dollars).[16]

Most of the increase came about because people worked many more hours, not because pay increased. Indeed, on average, individuals in 2000 worked more than an additional month each year to achieve the gains. Average hours worked increased from 1,679 in 1973 to 1,878 in 2000.[17]

In all of this, the contribution of wives was of central importance. Families with a wife in the paid labor force registered a substantial increase in median income—from $53,421 to $72,299 between 1973 and 2000 (2002 dollars). Families in which the wife was not in the paid labor force saw median income rise only very slowly during the same period, from $40,032 to $41,752 (in 2002 dollars).[18]

As noted in Chapter 1, we are fast approaching a limit to the number of wives who will be able to make additional contributions to family income. The annual rate of wives joining the labor force fell from 1.3 percent in the 1970s to 0.8 percent in the 1980s and 0.4 percent between 1989 and 2000. Unlike the final quarter century of the twentieth century, there will be no qualitative shift in the number of those working to help the family out during the twenty-first century (see p. 18).[19]

None of the underlying factors that have been at the root of growing inequality and stagnating family incomes—the decline in manufacturing, the reduction in union bargaining power, changes in technology, competition from low-skilled immigrant labor, and new global competitive pressures—are expected to change significantly in the coming period.[20]

At the same time, the rising cost of essential goods and services has created increasing pressures on family budgets and on family time alike. For families with children, two important changes have been particularly threatening.

Child care costs have been rising much faster than both income and inflation. Although the consumer price index increased only 29 percent during the 1990s, fees charged by child care centers and nursery schools shot up by 56 percent.[21]

The costs of college have been rising even more dramatically. The average tuition at public four-year universities increased from roughly 4 percent of a middle-class family income in 1980 to almost 7 percent in 2000. Private tuition costs increased even more—from 19.1 percent of median family income in 1975 to 37 percent of median family income in 1996. In the post-2000 period the overall fiscal crisis has especially impacted the public institutions to which most families send their children: State colleges and universities raised in-state tuition by an average of 14.1 percent for the 2003 to 2004 academic year (on top of a 9.6 percent hike for the 2002 to 2003 academic year). Overall, public tuition costs increased 47 percent for the decade 1993–1994 to 2003–2004.[22]

Housing expenses—the biggest single item in the family budget—have placed additional pressure on family budgets. The median sales price of homes increased from $23,000 in 1970 to $62,200 in 1980 to $147,800 in 2001. In constant dollars the increase was over 60 percent. A 2002 federal commission concluded that almost 28 million households— one in four—spend more on housing than the 30 percent of income commonly considered affordable. Again, the share of household income used to pay rent has been trending upward; it rose roughly 11 percent between 1984 and 2001. (Nearly 40 percent of renters spend more than 30 percent of their income on shelter, including about one in five who spend half or more of their income.)*[23]

The real "cost" of housing has, in fact, increased far more in recent decades than such figures suggest. Large numbers of families have chosen to pay more *in time* for the housing they need by moving farther and farther away from the city,

---

* Lower interest rates in 2001 to 2003 reduced mortgage payments for those who purchased homes or refinanced. Partly in response to the collapse of the stock market, however, housing prices also rose dramatically in many markets as investors rushed to real estate during this period.

where prices have not (yet) risen as dramatically. In 1983 the average miles driven to work per household totaled 3,538 each year. Miles driven rose to 4,853 by 1990 and to 6,492 by 1995—an overall increase of more than 80 percent.[24]

Health care costs and retirement costs will be taken up in Chapter 16. Suffice it to note at this point that as health costs have exploded, families in different income categories have inevitably felt the impact. A 2001 survey by the Pew Center for the People and the Press found that over a quarter of respondents (27 percent) said they didn't have enough money in the past year to afford health care—up from 15 percent in 1976. More than 43 million people were without health insurance in 2002. With the steady decline of unions, more and more corporations have begun to attack both health and pension benefits and are likely to continue to do so, increasingly, as time goes on.[25]

Needless to say, the general pressures facing families throughout the income distribution are most extreme among those at the low end of the scale. At the turn of the century almost one-third of all African American children were being raised in poverty. In African American female-headed households the figure for children under six was a chilling 54 percent.*[26]

---

* In all probability, the level of stress has risen even more because of a major historical shift in expectations. What a family now feels it is obliged to do with its limited resources has increased much more dramatically even than the costs it faces. A college education was once something reserved only for elites. In 1950 only 9 percent of Americans age twenty to twenty-four were enrolled in any kind of school. By 2000 fully 32.5 percent of twenty- to twenty-four-year-olds were attending college or other vocational schools (and fully 44 percent of twenty- to twenty-one-year-olds)—and millions of families knew that they had better plan for this major expense or their children would fall behind. And it was one thing to save for retirement in 1950 when a forty-year-old white male might expect to live only six years after stopping work at age sixty-five. Quite another financial challenge was posed by 2000, when post-sixty-five retirement life expectancy had doubled. National Center for Education Statistics, *Digest of Education Statistics, 2001*, chapter 1, table 6, nces.ed.gov/pubs2002/digest2001/tables/dt006.asp (accessed 04/09/03); *Historical Statistics of the United States: Colonial Times to 1970*, vol. 1, p. 56; and *Statistical Abstract of the United States: 2002*, table 93, p. 73.

Families under growing pressure—with no relief in sight from the fiscally constrained public sector—define one critical element of the emerging context. The long-term environment in which questions of large-order political-economic strategy will be posed will also be profoundly shaped by fundamental demographic trends.

California, as we have noted, already has a Hispanic and nonwhite majority, and Texas will join California by the end of the decade—possibly as early as 2004—as a state in which non-Hispanic whites will be in the minority. A similarly dramatic change in ethnicity and race will become the national norm as time goes on.[27]

By the midpoint of the century blacks, Hispanics, and other people of color are projected to become nearly a majority of the nation as a whole—and more than a majority ten years thereafter. Non-Hispanic whites, currently 70 percent of the population, are expected to decline to 53 percent of the population in 2050, then to just under 50 percent by 2060, and (on midrange census calculations) to a mere 40 percent by the end of the century.[28]

The changes have already been—and promise increasingly to be—historically revolutionary. Before World War II roughly nine out of ten Americans were non-Hispanic whites![29]

The extraordinary demographic changes that will occur over the coming period have been noted by many observers. Some analysts, impressed by the general voting patterns, see the numbers as leading to a resurgence of traditional liberal politics and programs. One of the most optimistic is *New Republic* senior editor John Judis: "[T]he two pillars of the McGovern coalition—minorities and highly educated social liberals—have been growing, as a proportion of the electorate, at an extraordinary rate. Combine them with labor . . . and you have an enduring political majority."[30]

Others disagree. Michael Lind argues that divisions between blacks and other minorities will make "rainbow coalition" politics highly problematic—and further, that over time intermarriage will lead to what he calls "a mostly white mixed-race majority." Many hold with Tom and Mary Edsall that racial divisions are now so easily exploited that traditional liberal alliances can no longer be sustained (see p. 16).[31]

These various perspectives miss a critical historic change. The long evolving, deeply entrenched political-economic patterns we have reviewed suggest that even if Democrats can be elected, it is highly unlikely a program can be enacted that alters fundamental distributional and public program trends—at least not through traditional strategies (see Chapter 1).

The question, in short, goes well beyond who gets elected to whether serious change can occur.

Such considerations return us to the contextual logic forcing consideration of new strategies over the long haul. The obstacles facing traditional approaches suggest that a coherent elite-targeting strategy is likely to continue to develop during the coming period, in the first instance in response to the fading away of all other alternatives.

Especially important are the long-term decline in union membership and the continuing inability to tax the suburban middle class. The two are related. Critically, although labor will inevitably still play a significant political role—and although occasional temporary progressive upswings may occur—union money and organizational efforts no longer have the capacity to undergird a sustained revival of traditional progressive strategy.

The larger and profoundly important result is that the emerging context of the twenty-first century is likely to steadily destroy the illusion that traditional strategies can achieve their most important goals, no matter how hard they are pressed—even as the growing fiscal crisis intensifies.

If so, the problems facing key groups under pressure must increasingly sharpen new choices. The most obvious initial place to secure significant resources is among the very top groups that control disproportionate shares of income. Related to this are challenges to the corporations that the elites overwhelmingly own and largely control.

The political choice facing the expanding numbers of black, Hispanic, and other minority groups, on the one hand, and white nonelite groups, on the other, is likely to be posed in ever more stark terms: either find a way to overcome traditional divisions, or allow those with opposing interests to divide and conquer the nonelite majority.

It is sometimes argued that Americans are opposed to taxing elites because they admire them and aspire to reach the same income levels. Steven R. Weisman has demonstrated in *The Great Tax Wars* that the central issue is neither admiration nor aspiration. What matters is necessity. When there is a strongly perceived need, "the historical record tells us that there will be a demand to impose those higher taxes especially on the wealthiest, who can bear them with the least amount of pain."*[32]

Sperling, Wellstone, Kennedy, and even Lieberman came to the realization that the way forward was to narrow the focus to an increasingly obvious—indeed, the only possible—political target allowing full exploitation of the logic of large versus small numbers: the extremely wealthy elites, and the corporations they control, at the very top.[33]

The same logic has begun to hit home where the greatest fiscal pain has been felt in recent years—at the state and local level. Under the pressure of declining resources and expanding needs, growing numbers of states have begun to increase taxes on elites. Many have acted to maintain estate taxes on the wealthy by "decoupling" from the federal system. Others have voted to raise corporate taxes or to

---

* Ronald Reagan even signed a signifiant rollback of corporate taxes into law when fiscal pressures intensified in 1982. George H. W. Bush in 1990 and Bill Clinton in 1993 both proposed and secured enactment of new taxes on the very top groups when faced with severe fiscal problems. See Paul Krugman, "The Great Taxer," The New York Times, June 8, 2004, p. A25; Leonard Burman and Deborah Kobes, "Income Tax Brackets Since 1985," Tax Notes, July 28, 2003, p. 557; and David E. Rosenbaum, "The Deficit Disappeared, But That Was Then," New York Times, September 21, 2003, p. D3.

"decouple" from favorable federal depreciation changes. In 2003 the Republication-controlled Virginia state Senate added higher tax brackets for incomes between $100,000 and $150,000 and for incomes above $150,000.[34]

The obvious question is how the overarching logic is likely to play out as the pain increases over time.

16

Social Security, Retirement, and Health Care

THE LOGIC OF GROWING pain and declining alternatives that has begun to confront key groups in American society is further illuminated by considering long-term financial problems developing in connection with Social Security, with retirement in general, and with health care. In each area, to varying degrees, there is little political prospect of finding a serious solution following traditional strategies. Accordingly, as fiscal difficulties continue to mount and social pain increases, other major constituencies are also increasingly being forced to consider their alternatives.

Indeed, in each area there are already indications of a refocusing and realigning of political targets—away from attempting to further tax the suburban middle class, and toward challenging top elites. In addition, several important initiatives have moved beyond income taxation to strategies based on wealth-related principles—a trend that is also likely to continue as fiscal pressures continue to intensify.

Although near-term Social Security funding problems have often been exaggerated, the long-term difficulties facing the system are quite real and will increase over the course of the century. Pressures are building in regard to the system's internal financial viability and in regard to an external environment of steadily growing crisis in connection with problems of retirement in general. The less commonly discussed general retirement crisis is likely to feed back into, and exacerbate, difficulties facing Social Security on its own terms.

A great deal of public discussion has focused on claims that a Social Security funding crisis already exists. On conservative assumptions, it will be necessary to begin to tap the Social Security Trust Fund to pay benefits by 2018, and the fund will be exhausted by 2042. Thereafter (again, on conservative assumptions) major cuts in benefits or substantial tax increases will be necessary.[1]

This, however, is the projected scenario if nothing is done in the interim. But that *if* is the rub. One analyst, Dean Baker, suggests the claim of a crisis is "a crisis in the same way that a car headed westward in the middle of Kansas faces a crisis. If it doesn't stop or turn, the car will eventually fall into the Pacific Ocean, but it's hard to get too worried about the possibility."[2]

Baker and many others point out that modest changes—especially raising the $87,000 limit on income subject to Social Security taxation, possibly postponing the age of retirement a bit, perhaps slightly increasing taxation rates, and/or slightly decreasing benefits—can easily manage the short-term problems. An International Monetary Fund report concurs: the "financing problems of Social Security are not large . . . and could be addressed through relatively small adjustments in the program's parameters."[3]

The longer-term problems Social Security will face over the course of the century, however, are more serious. Basically, the present "pay-as-you-go" system operates on the principle that today's generation will pay benefits for current retirees—just as current retirees once paid for those who retired while they were working and just as a subsequent group will pay for the benefits received by those now working when they retire. This kind of system works especially well when both the economy and population grow—and especially when population grows in a manner that increases the number of workers at each stage faster than the number of retirees (as it did for much of the postwar period).[4]

When, however, each new cohort of retirees expands faster than the current cohort of workers who pay the bills, problems begin to multiply.

In 2000 the census counted slightly fewer than 35 million elderly. By 2030 this number will more than double—to in excess of 70 million. By the end of the century midrange Census Bureau projections suggest there may be more than 131 million elderly. If such numbers are realized, the elderly will explode from a current 12.4 percent of the U.S. population to 20 percent by 2030 and 23 percent by the end of the century.[5]

The ratio of workers to retirees declined from 5.1-to-1 in 1960 to 3.3-to-1 in 2004, and under midrange assumptions it is projected to decline to 2.0-to-1 by 2040. By 2080 the ratio drops to 1.9 workers per retiree. The bottom line is that the system must face growing difficulties as these ratios continue to shift.[6]

An additional long-term financial challenge stems from the fact that the number of retirement years that must be financed has been increasing as average life spans have been increasing—and will continue to do so as time goes on. At the beginning of the twentieth century, the average American male could expect to live forty-six years. Currently male life expectancy is seventy-four years. The Census Bureau projects male life expectancy to grow to eighty-five years by the end of the twenty-first century.[7]

Given such realities, and depending upon the particular assumptions made, the current estimate of the underfunded Social Security liability "gap" rises to $3.7 trillion for the next seventy-five years—and considerably more for the century as a whole.[8]

In theory, answers to some of the longer-term problems can be found by raising the amount of income taxed, increasing the rate of taxation, postponing retirement, reducing benefits, and the like. In addition, increasing the number of workers (and thereby the ratio of workers to retirees) through greater immigration could obviously help.[9]

In the real world, however, there are limits to all of these responses—especially to significantly raising taxes or significantly cutting benefits. The political problems are especially challenging in connection with workers who might be more heavily taxed and among retirees who might lose important benefits.[10]

At a deeper level there is the fact that Social Security taxation is one of the most regressive parts of the overall tax system. It is a "flat tax," applied across the board to low- and middle-income earners alike—but one with limits set so as to *not* apply to the higher income of the rich. In fact most Americans (71 percent of households) now pay more in payroll taxes than they do in income taxes.[*11]

The trend is extraordinary: Social Security payroll taxes amounted to only 5 percent of federal revenues in 1950; they had increased to 17.4 percent by 1970; and are now 29 percent of such revenues.[†12]

Conservatives have attempted to focus blue collar anger at Social Security's growing costs by responding to the short- and long-term crises with much-discussed proposals for privatization—that is, permitting individuals to invest in stock by shifting part of their current payments into individually managed brokerage accounts. The stock market collapse of 2000 to 2003 temporarily undercut the politics of this idea, but there are fundamental problems with the approach—and little reason to believe it will ever offer anything other than a token "solution" to the growing difficulties.

First, if current payments are shifted into brokerage accounts, this will reduce funds needed to meet current Social Security obligations—and proponents have failed to offer a convincing proposal for how the "transitional" gap

---

* Moreover, of course, payroll taxes apply only to wages, not to capital income— rent, dividends, interest, and so on—which is heavily concentrated at the top of the income scale.

† This is for Social Security alone; all social insurance and retirement receipts rose from 11 percent to 23 percent to 40 percent over the same years.

(estimated at between $400 billion and $1.1 trillion) can be filled during the extended period before the investment of diverted payments might begin to pay off.[13]

Second, if individuals are allowed to invest freely in stocks, and if they invest badly, or if (as in 2000–2003) the stock market happens to fall at the time they retire—the entire premise of a system designed to establish a floor under retirement security collapses.*[14]

A number of liberal and other economists have responded to the longer-term crisis by offering reasonable proposals that emphasize raising the level of income that is taxed and, for instance, taxing all Social Security benefits received by upper-income groups. Others, like Ted Halstead of the New America Foundation, have proposed exempting the first $10,000 of wages from payroll taxation.[15]

Even if combined with other strategies, however, progressive lines of attack like those implicitly or explicitly require additional taxes on the upper range of the middle class to achieve the required financial flows—at a time when the political possibility of major gains in this direction is increasingly problematic.[16]

Given that neither side of the conservative-liberal debate appears to have much chance of dealing in a thoroughgoing way with the underlying problems, the prospect is likely to be one of continued frustration and political posturing. It is not surprising, given this context, that a number of analysts have

---

* Privatization is also expensive—especially in that: (1) the management of individual brokerage accounts, unlike pooled pension accounts, is extremely inefficient and costly; and (2) when individuals must provide for their individual security, they cannot take advantage of the actuarial benefits that accrue to large numbers, which—as in all insurance schemes—allow the pooling of risks so that those who end up living longer than average can be supported by the payments of those who live shorter than average. In addition, Social Security also provides disability insurance and survivor benefits for spouses and dependents. The value of the total package of services is often overlooked in comparison with alternatives, as is the fact that retirement benefits are provided as an inflation-adjusted annuity, while most private annuities are not protected against inflation.

recognized the need to look for other, more far-reaching alternatives—or that, once again, there is only one place where significant new resources are likely to be found.

We noted earlier Gene Sperling's proposal to postpone elite tax reductions in order to support Social Security. Sperling subsequently offered additional details in other writings: "I believe we should freeze at current levels only the top two tax rates (which affect families making over $190,000), avoid new measures to enhance deductions and exemptions for high-income taxpayers, and double the exemption from the estate tax from $2 million to $4 million (but not repeal the estate tax entirely). Then we should devote all of the savings to a Social Security Reserve Fund dedicated to lowering deficits and debt, unless it were part of a comprehensive reform to extend Social Security's 75-year solvency." Sperling stresses: "if it is made clear that these savings would be used for saving Social Security first—not last—it could be as politically viable as it is economically sensible."[17]

Similarly, Paul Krugman points out that the projected 2025 Social Security deficit ($419 billion) is far less than the elite-oriented provisions of the 2000 Bush tax cut—"which the administration insists is easily affordable—[and which] will reduce revenue in 2025 by $700 billion." Chuck Collins and William Gates Sr. urge: "Congress should explore the possibility of linking estate tax revenue to the Social Security Trust Fund, providing long-term solvency for the Fund without increasing payroll taxes or reducing retiree benefits."[18]

Hofstra law professor Leon Friedman has gone further. He suggests a 1 percent net worth tax levied on the top 1 percent of households. Friedman estimated such a tax (in 2000) "would allow us to eliminate the estate tax, thus solving the family-business problem, while still raising enough revenue to pay off the national debt, save Social Security, and have money left over for targeted tax cuts."[19]

In these and other recommendations the logical progression that begins with relatively routine tax and other changes moves directly to the targeting of elite income—and ultimately toward Pluralist Commonwealth–related questions of wealth, both in the most obvious case of estate taxation and in Friedman's further suggestion of a net worth tax. The logic that has begun to reorient discussions of Social Security is likely to further intensify as new factors add to the pressures shaping the longer-term context in which the central issues are posed.

The overall U.S. retirement security system has traditionally been described as a three-leg stool in which Social Security is only one of the basic elements. Although Social Security provides substantial support for some retirees, in many ways it is best understood as a bottom-line guarantee against true disaster for the elderly. The maximum monthly benefit in 2001 was $1,538; half of those on Social Security received less than $900 a month.[20]

The other two legs of the stool are private pensions and private savings. The problem is that both of these mainstays of the traditional system have also begun to decay as income has stagnated, as corporate practices have shifted, and as labor's power, on the one hand, and progressive politics, on the other, have faltered.

The second leg—a traditional pension—once provided many Americans with a certain level of guaranteed income they could count on in retirement—that is, an annuity. In 1975 just under 40 percent of private-sector workers had some form of traditional ("defined benefit") pension plan. The downward trend since that time has been dramatic. By 2003 only 20 percent of private-sector workers were covered by such pensions.*[21]

Traditional pensions have given way to the government-encouraged savings plan—commonly an IRA—and the

---

* Further complicating the picture is the severe underfunding of many plans. Retiring workers in airline and other companies facing bankruptcy are unlikely to receive full retirement benefits even if their pension plans are taken over by the Federal Pension Benefit Guaranty Corporation—a painful reality that many have already had to face in connection with the LTV, National Steel, Bethlehem Steel, and PanAm bankruptcies.

employee-sponsored defined contribution plan such as a 401(k). These do not guarantee any assured level of retirement income. The funds that can be drawn upon in retirement depend upon how much is contributed—and what happens to the investments selected over time. The percentage who have such individual retirement account plans has gone up dramatically—from 5.8 percent in 1975 to 40 percent in 2003.[22]

The amounts involved for the average person, however, are not large. The median net balance in the most common 401(k) form of plan was a mere $13,493 in 2000. The median IRA value in 2001 was $30,000. These figures include young and old alike. For those nearing retirement, such accounts taken together averaged roughly $50,000 in 2001—an amount that, invested at 5 percent, would yield $2,500 a year in income, far less at rates commonly available in 2003. With the decline of the stock market, moreover, many plans lost value—shrinking, as a bitter joke put it, to "201(k)" and "101(k)" plans.[23]

Strikingly, 41 percent of those working in the private economy simply do not have either a defined benefit pension or defined contribution plan!

The amount of retirement income generated by all forms of pensions taken together is modest. Median pension income for retirees who received such income in 2000 was $7,800. Since more than half received no pension, however, the average (mean) for all retirees was much less, roughly $4,000.[24]

Private savings, the third leg of the traditional three-leg retirement stool, have also not kept up—in part because a defined contribution plan is in practice an alternative form of savings that substitutes for, and currently does not significantly augment, traditional private savings. The growing financial pressures reviewed in Chapter 15 have had a devastating impact on the average family's capacity to save. The personal savings rate (which includes private savings and 401(k)s, IRAs, and the like) has declined dramatically in recent years (from 9.2 percent in 1985 to less than 3 percent in 2003). On average—which, of course, includes top groups—those over sixty-five draw upon assets (savings and home equity) for a modest $310 a month. (The median is a mere $160 per month.)[25]

The growing general retirement crisis thus adds to the long-term challenges confronting Social Security. This has helped create an environment in which, by necessity, much more far-reaching ideas have begun to be put forward. These in effect take up the key point of those who would privatize the Social Security system, but turn it on its head to produce an approach that is more coherent in its ultimate retirement support capacities.

Proponents of investing some part of Social Security's assets in equities are correct to suggest that over the long haul, a comprehensive retirement security plan that includes an investment component may be capable of paying higher benefits than a pay-as-you-go system—especially if new population cohorts do not grow faster than older ones. All traditional private pension plans and public employee pension plans are based on this understanding (including, as we have noted, the Federal Thrift Savings Plan, which currently serves federal employees and the employee pension plan provided by the Federal Reserve Board).

That with proper safeguards Social Security—or an even broader future system—might logically move in this direction is not in principle an unreasonable idea. Indeed, the U.S. Social Security system in its original form was based on precisely this concept. Instead of operating on a pay-as-you-go basis, it was planned initially as a system that would utilize contributions both to provide income support and for further long-term investment.*[26]

---

* The original plan was abandoned during the late 1930s in large part because Keynesian economists worried that the system's initial reserve buildup might undercut attempts to stimulate economic recovery from the Depression. See Henry J. Aaron and Lawrence H. Thompson, "Social Security and the Economists," in *Social Security After Fifty*, ed. Edward D. Berkowitz (New York: Greenwood Press, 1987), pp. 79–100.

In this same vein, one of the architects of the modern system, the former commissioner of the Social Security Administration, Robert Ball, has proposed investing roughly 40 percent of the Social Security Trust Fund in equities (the exact amount to be determined on the basis of an actuarial accounting of needs). The investments would be managed through several competing mutual funds. Ball offered his proposal in 1995 as a member of the Social Security Advisory Council and—importantly—was supported by a number of other progressive members of the council, including representatives of the Machinists and Electrical Unions, and by the president of the AFL-CIO.[27]

A first-step variation on the same theme was formally proposed by the Clinton administration in 1999. Clinton suggested allocating a portion of new Social Security contributions to an equity-invested fund that might be managed along the lines of the Federal Thrift Savings Plan. The fund would be limited to a maximum of 14.6 percent of the Social Security Trust Fund's overall assets. Clinton would have used the then available federal budget surpluses to close the transition "gap" that diverting a portion of the contributions to investment would create.[28]

Economists Henry Aaron and Robert Reischauer have suggested a related midrange strategy that would invest Social Security reserves in excess of one and a half years' expenditure requirements. A very expansive proposal to invest Social Security reserves based on state and other pension fund precedents—and the current Canadian national system—has been offered by management professor Alice H. Munnell and Brookings fellow R. Kent Weaver.[29]

The underlying logic of allocating publicly controlled funds to wealth-owning strategies of this kind has been fully extended by specialists on both the left and the right who have looked to still longer range solutions.

Economist Thomas Michl has put forward a proposal for what amounts to a return to the initial Social Security concept.

His plan would ultimately establish a "fully funded system [that] in an idealized model returns participants the same yield as a diversified portfolio of stocks." In 2001 Michl proposed revoking the Bush income tax cuts to begin funding such a system on a permanent basis. Significantly, after the kind of "reassessment" that has become increasingly common, Michl subsequently concluded that relying on a general increase in income taxation was probably futile, that the target had to be sharpened, and that a progressive wealth tax dedicated to funding Social Security now had to be considered.[30]

The conservative Nobel–prize winning economist Robert Fogel has also outlined a fully funded investment-based plan—one that would be subsidized in part for those with low incomes by "a tax of 2 or 3 percent applied progressively to the top half of the income distribution." In addition, Fogel put forward an important societal goal for a nation as richly endowed as the United States: unlike solutions offered by those on the left and the right that would save money by delaying the retirement age and thereby reducing the total years of retirement, his proposal would begin retirement earlier (routinely at age fifty-five)—and would increase the number of years free from work at the end of one's career as the nation's wealth increased over the course of the century.[31]

Finally, sociologist Robin Blackburn has offered a partly public, partly private long-term system that would use several sources of funding to achieve a major revolution in retirement financing. A first tier would expand and increase Social Security. A second would reform private pension efforts so as to increase their impact and make them more secure by, among other things, requiring companies to contribute stock to pooled funds in order to maintain greater investment diversification.[32]

Blackburn's third strategy draws upon the 1970s Swedish Meidner Plan (a watered-down version of which was implemented between 1983 and 1991). This would require firms to issue and set aside stock equivalent to 10 to 20 percent of profits each year in order to increase pension fund capital. The stock would be managed by new publicly accountable agencies and could not be sold for at least five years. Financing through a "share levy" of this kind (like current stock options given to top executives) dilutes the value of outstanding stock and in practice is thus similar to a wealth tax.*[33]

The first question of interest in connection with the trajectory of development traced by such proposals is over what time span the implications of the dead ends facing traditional strategies sink in. A second is how long it takes before growing problems in this area and elsewhere, along with increasing pain levels, force the inherent logic of such Pluralist Commonwealth–related principles they embody into ever sharper public and political focus.

The growing pressures that are steadily producing an explosion of new wealth and investment proposals are sharpening another very large-order, long-term challenge: extraordinary increases in the cost of health care. This is an area where growing distress, particularly among the elderly, has been generating new demands for change for some time.

The basic numbers are already staggering. Spending on health care more than doubled from 5.1 percent of GDP in 1960 to 14.9 percent in 2002. It is projected by the U.S. Center for Medicare and Medicaid Services to rise to 18.4 percent of GDP by 2013. Some well-informed experts predict that health care expenditures could reach as high as 25 percent of GDP by 2025—and potentially far more in the later years of the century as the baby-boom generation ages and the population cohorts continue to shift.[34]

Such estimates do not include, as yet, an attempt to provide assured care to the more than 43 million Americans who have no insurance coverage at all. And the financial problems facing Medicare and Medicaid far exceed those of Social Security: the long-term medicare funding gap alone is estimated to be at least five times that of Social Security.[35]

---

* In addition, Blackburn would use such funds for long-term investments aimed at achieving broad community, regional, infrastructure, and environmental goals.

The explosion in health care costs can be traced to many factors, including high personnel costs, technological improvements, the cost of drugs, and administrative inefficiencies. It is also fundamentally related to the dramatic changes in the percentage of elderly in the population and to their increased health needs.

Per capita health care expenditures after age sixty-five are commonly three times greater than before sixty-five—and the number of elderly, as we have seen, could well reach more than 131 million by the century's end. The share of the very old (eighty-five and older) among the elderly is also increasing, and those eighty-five and over commonly consume three times as much health care as those in the sixty-five to seventy-four range. Health economist Victor Fuchs observes that for such reasons the problem of financing health care for the elderly could "soon equal and then surpass the problem of financing retirement."[36]

Two points are especially worth emphasizing from the perspective of our overall concern. The first simply continues and underscores the line of analysis that has emerged in connection with several other issues: the growing difficulties must inevitably increase the pressure to find new solutions, both in this area and generally as problems in each sector ramify and feed back into other areas experiencing financial and political challenges. With traditional solutions blocked, the search for alternatives—and given the emerging logic, for Pluralist Commonwealth–related alternatives in particular—is all but certain to intensify.

A national campaign to cover the uninsured, led by former presidents Gerald Ford and Jimmy Carter, and backed by the Chamber of Commerce, the AFL-CIO, and many other groups, is already under way. In the last several years proposals for universal coverage have been introduced in numerous state legislatures. Several Democratic presidential candidates, including John Kerry, put forward a range of plans during the 2004 primaries—virtually all financed in whole or in part by rescinding Bush elite tax cuts. Further proposals are certain to be put forward as time goes on.[37]

The second point takes us beyond the logic, trends, and trajectories so far reviewed to the general observation that when pressures build that simply cannot be dealt with by traditional means—or even the kinds of alternatives now beginning to be discussed—very different possibilities and unexpected options and alliances often suddenly become thinkable.

It is rarely recalled that in the early 1990s, a number of leading corporations strongly urged President George H. W. Bush to do something dramatic about the health care costs that were consuming a growing proportion of corporate profits (56 percent of pretax company profits in 1991, up from just 8 percent in 1965).[38]

Similarly, early in the Clinton years, leading corporations urged enactment of a single-payer system like that of Canada. Chrysler, Ford, American Airlines, and General Motors (among others) joined in a coalition with labor and consumer advocates to support universal coverage plans—including both the single-payer model and the Clinton proposal.[39]

The three leading business lobbies—the Business Round-table, the U.S. Chamber of Commerce, and the National Association of Manufacturers—and business-oriented health coalitions such as the Washington Business Group on Health, the National Leadership Coalition for Health Care Reform, and the Jackson Hole Group—all also publicly endorsed universal coverage.[40]

Although a successful counterattack by the insurance industry and its allies thwarted Clinton's proposals for universal care, it is unlikely the issue will remain closed forever. Critically, however, the most obvious health-related cost-saving possibilities offered by managed care and HMO measures have now been largely exhausted. Conventional proposals for change based on private insurance models promise little in the way of cost-saving.[41]

In this situation, as the extraordinary financial pressures continue to build—and as political demands for a solution grow—ultimately, as many studies and the experience of other nations have demonstrated, an alternative in this area that involves radically different system-changing principles of public-benefiting ownership and control is also likely to offer the only way forward.*[42]

* Administrative costs of the current U.S. system are estimated to be almost 31 percent of health care expenditures—as compared with only 16.7 percent in Canada. See Steffie Woolhandler, Terry Campbell, and David U. Himmelstein, "Costs of Health Care Administration in the United States and Canada," *New England Journal of Medicine,* vol. 349, no. 8 (August 21, 2003), pp. 768–775. As we have noted, the U.S. system currently absorbs roughly 14 percent of GDP—and much higher percentages are expected in the future. The Canadian system absorbs far less—9.7 percent of GDP (2001); that of Sweden, 8.7 percent (2001); and that of Japan, 7.6 percent (2000). Organization for Economic Co-operation and Development, "Health Data 2003—Frequently Asked Data," table 10, www.oecd.org/document/ 16/0,2340,en_2825_495642_2085200_1_1_1_1,00.html (accessed 10/28/03); see also *OECD in Figures 2001* (Paris: OECD, 2001), pp. 8–9. Between 1997 and 2004, U.S. healthcare expenditures grew 2.3 times faster than GDP compared with 1.7 times faster in all other OECD countries. OECD, "Health Spending in Most OECD Countries Rises, with the U.S. far Outstripping all Others," www.oecd.org/ home/ (accessed 06/03/2004). In an August 2003 statement published in the *Journal of the American Medical Association,* some 7,782 doctors (including two former U.S. surgeons general) urged that the time had come for the United States to establish a universal single-payer health system. See Physicians for a National Health Program, "Doctors Call for National Health Insurance," August 14, 2003, www .pnhp.org/news/2003/august/doctors_call_for_nat.php (accessed 10/13/03).

17

A Twenty-Five-Hour Week?

THE LOGIC OF RESOURCE allocation between elites and nonelites and issues of retirement and health care open converging perspectives on the question of whether the privileged position of those at the top might ultimately be challenged—and on how, simultaneously, the pressure of events is forcing ever greater attention to nontraditional strategies related to Pluralist Commonwealth principles.

The longer-term logic of time use and of gender equality offers additional avenues of approach to the underlying issues—and to the dead ends, realignment possibilities, and new strategic and institutional options likely to face other important constituencies over the course of the twenty-first century.

Time and gender issues are also instructive in that they permit the analysis to begin to move beyond pain and difficulty to the question of how the resources of a very rich society might ultimately be used to achieve more fulfilling positive goals.

Scholars who have studied long-term patterns of work in the United States have documented a clear trend up to approximately the middle of the twentieth century: the typical workweek declined from roughly seventy hours in 1850, to sixty hours in 1900, to fifty hours in 1920, and—allowing for variation during the Depression and World War II—stabilized at a little over forty hours by the middle of the century. After that, further diminution of work-time largely ceased. Indeed, as we have seen, hours worked per week and per year have increased very substantially for large numbers of Americans in recent years.[*1]

The pattern is different in Europe: although most Western industrialized nations once lagged behind U.S. developments, in recent years most forged ahead while the United States fell back. In 2000, 76 percent of American workers put in forty or more hours a week—an increase from 73 percent in 1983. In England only about 50 percent worked forty or more hours a week, and in France the share of the employed working that many hours decreased from 36 percent to 22 percent between 1983 and 2000. The reduction in the workweek was even more pronounced in Germany: only 43 percent of the workforce worked forty or more hours in 2000, down sharply from 85 percent in 1983.[2]

In much of Europe four to six weeks of annual vacation is also now mandated by law for all workers (including newly hired workers). In the United States most workers don't receive four weeks of vacation until they've reached twenty years of service. Different methods of data collection make precise comparisons difficult. However, taking hours worked per week together with vacation time, workers in France and Germany reduced work enormously, compared to their American counterparts—by 260 hours per year between 1979 and 2000, the equivalent of cutting six and a half forty-hour-weeks out of the work year![3]

Not surprisingly, many U.S. workers would prefer to work less—if they could afford to do so. Research by the Families and Work Institute indicates that almost two-thirds (63 percent) would like to work fewer hours—up from 46 percent just a few years earlier. On average those questioned said

---

* See p. 175. Academic debate concerning various aspects of the trend (and the use of diary versus census data) is usefully reviewed in Barry Bluestone and Stephen Rose, "Overworked and Underemployed," *The American Prospect*, vol. 8, no. 31 (March 1, 1997–April 1, 1997); see also "The Unmeasured Labor Force: The Growth in Work Hours," Policy Brief #40 (Bard College, N.Y.: The Levy Institute, 1998).

they would reduce their workweek by more than ten hours if they could.[4]

It is theoretically possible, of course, that the richest nation in the world will never move forward in the direction that is increasingly common elsewhere. On the other hand, as technological progress continues—and as the capacity of one hour's work to produce three, four, or possibly even five times what it now produces continues to increase—at some point during the coming century, almost certainly Americans are likely to demand that the United States begin to follow the trend of other nations.

It is at this point that some of the most interesting questions come into play.

In 2003 the U.S. economy produced just over $38,000 for each individual, or just over $152,000 for every group or family of four. Per capita production in the United States increased more than sixfold during the twentieth century—even though the economy was jolted by two World Wars and the Great Depression. Although the gains might well have been greater had these costly events not intervened, we may use the twentieth-century trend as an initial rough baseline.

Projecting twentieth-century growth forward yields a very large number by the end of the twenty-first century—minimally $220,000 per capita and $880,000 for each group or family of four. (All in 2003 dollars—far more, of course, if inflation is considered.)

Per capita GDP will still be impressive by the century's end if the conservative assumptions used in the Social Security Trustees Report are followed: $125,000 per person, or $501,000 per group of four (again, all in 2003 dollars).[5] Even if such projections are substantially discounted (we shall explore ecological limitations shortly), they suggest some obvious possibilities.

In Chapter 2 we noted Segal's proposal that we should aim to reduce the average workweek for both men and women to something like twenty-five hours. The proposal appears utopian in terms of immediate prospects. On the other hand, it is hardly a major stretch beyond either European practices or the emerging technological possibilities. In France nearly 80 percent of all those in full-time employment worked thirty-six hours or less as of September 2002; in Germany metalworkers, who currently work a thirty-five-hour week, have been pushing to extend this to eastern Germany; and the union's longer-term goal is a workweek below thirty-five hours throughout the country. If the American workweek were even to be cut in half, the U.S. economy would still be able to produce an extraordinary amount for each family by the century's end.[6]

Indeed, greater work-time reductions are conceivable—and in principle could be achieved with no diminution of living standards (and plausibly an increase) for the vast majority of Americans. A recent estimate is that productivity gains of 2 percent per year—if fully translated into reduced work-time—would cut roughly seven hours off the workweek in the course of only one decade.[7]

Although many moderates and liberals have shied away from such questions, Robert Fogel has argued that as early as 2040 current trends and "technophysio evolution" could produce a 1,400-hour work-year, a 30-hour workweek, 30 holidays, and 12 sick days. Further movement in the direction of shorter working hours, he suggests, would continue as the century progresses.*[8]

The fundamental long-term political-economic problem is not whether major changes in the workweek are likely to be technologically feasible; it is how, specifically, the fruits of technological change can be translated into equitably distributed reductions in the workweek as time goes on. The specific question is how to allocate the financial gains made possible as the productivity of the economy improves.

---

* See p. 192. As we have seen, unlike many fellow conservatives who have been seeking ways to reduce Social Security costs by postponing retirement, Fogel has also urged that, given the technological possibilities, we should aim to *increase* the number of years individuals enjoy free from work during life's final years.

The logically available options are not difficult to define. The most straightforward but perhaps least likely method of achieving a reduction in working time is simply to enact legislation reducing the workweek—and then penalize companies that violate the law. The difficulty is that both workers and corporations oppose a mandatory approach. The legally set forty-hour week with pay increases for overtime is the basis of our current stalled system, and legislation making it more restrictive is not likely.[9]

Juliet Schor has proposed that companies be required to allow workers to choose whether they prefer to take the value of some portion of productivity gains in increased pay or in reduced hours. This would give workers the right to take more time off, something few now have as a matter of right. Here, however, powerful corporate opposition stands in the way of mandated requirements.[10]

Given the political realities, almost certainly a strategy that offers carrots as well as sticks will ultimately be necessary. One precedent is the thirty-five-hour-week legislation enacted in France in the late 1990s—an approach that required a reduction in hours worked but compensated employers through the tax system for continuing to provide workers the equivalent of full-time pay.* Variations on this theme can be found in other nations that (commonly to help spread employment) in one way or another also pass through compensatory payments to the company and the worker.

In Austria older workers (men at fifty-five, women at fifty) can reduce working hours and receive partial compensation

---

* The payments were initially to last for a five-year phase-in period. The conservative government elected in 2002 amended the law so that it could be more flexibly implemented—which, in some cases, means that more overtime is permitted. Although there is considerable left-right political dispute over other issues, as of this writing the basic financing principle appears all but certain to be retained (though for three years rather than the original five). See Victor Mallet, "French Face Longer Working Week," *Financial Times*, September 19, 2002; and Jeanne Fagnani and Marie-Thérèse Letablier, *Working Time and Family Life: The Impact of the 35 Hour Laws on the Work and Family Life Balance in France,* forthcoming paper.

for the loss of earnings involved: hours are cut in half, but workers receive 75 percent of their former salary and 100 percent of the employer contributions to the state health care and pension insurance systems. The employer is reimbursed through tax reductions by the government. In Italy full-time workers nearing retirement age who are replaced by new hires may move to part-time work and receive government support to bring wages up to previous levels.[11]

Segal has suggested an expansive work-reduction system that in certain respects both extends European precedents and links them to other well-tested U.S. policies. Segal proposes enacting a "Simple Living Credit" modeled on the current Earned Income Tax Credit (EITC). This would be structured so as to allow individuals to reduce hours worked with a less-than-proportional drop in income. The EITC has proven acceptable to many business groups because it in part implicitly subsidizes labor costs. The enactment of numerous state and local forms of EITC over the last decades also suggests the potential political feasibility of an expanded approach at some point in time. Segal estimates that a phased-in credit of $10,000 for families with combined income of $60,000 would permit a reduction in working hours of 25 percent—with a corresponding after-tax income decline of only 10.5 percent.[12]

A fully evolved long-term program would likely build upon either the indirect subsidy route of the French, Austrian, and Italian models, or on Segal's direct approach using EITC-related strategies, or on both so that the workweek could be progressively and systematically reduced over the course of the century.[13]

Drawing in part on the work of the Swedish economist Gösta Rehn, Carmen Sirianni has offered the additional suggestion that reductions in work-time should be tailored to individual preferences. Instead of everyone reducing the workweek by a certain number of hours at the same time, a person could choose to take an equivalent amount of time off in different ways—perhaps several months at a time for one, perhaps a year for another.*[14]

Low-income individuals who must work long hours to provide for their families obviously have far less choice than middle- and upper-income Americans. Even assuming support for a general reduction in work-time, a critical long-term question is whether time can be allocated equitably—which is to say, in a manner that also provides benefits to lower-income Americans. A coherent approach would ultimately likely entail both a major expansion of the current EITC and perhaps some form of basic income as proposed by Philippe Van Parijs, Bill Jordan, and others. Over the long haul, such an effort would inevitably also converge with a comprehensive general strategy to reduce inequality (see Chapters 1 and 18).

The obvious issue, again, is how a serious-scale program might ultimately be financed. We are once more back full circle to large-order questions of resource allocation and—given the dead ends facing traditional strategies—whether, over time, a transition to a new approach might one day be achieved. And again, if there is no way forward under current strategies, then either there can be no solution—or ultimately an alternative approach must be considered.

There has as yet been very little discussion of such matters in connection with time-allocation issues. A major shift would clearly require a buildup of understanding of strategies beyond traditional taxation, a much sharper focus on how resources are currently allocated, the systematic organization of an alliance of the majority, and finally a critical (if perhaps slow) return to a moral commitment to achieving equity in the U.S. system.

---

* Sirianni has also sketched the many ways productive use might be made of greater free time—including further education, the development of new skills, unpaid home and volunteer work, greater family and community time, and the like. See Carmen Sirianni, "The Self-Management of Time in Postindustrial Society," in *Working Time in Transition: The Political Economy of Working Hours in Industrial Nations,* eds. Karl Hinrichs, William Roche, and Carmen Sirianni (Philadelphia: Temple University Press, 1991), pp. 259–260.

There are reasons to believe the first of these require-ments—a buildup of understanding of the need for new approaches—is slowly beginning to develop: we have noted the Ackerman-Alstott suggestion of a 2 percent tax on wealth, the proposal of Thomas Michl for a net-worth tax, and the suggestion of Leon Friedman of a 1 percent tax on wealth owned by the top 1 percent. Kevin Phillips and Jeff Gates (among many others) have also urged that wealth taxation must now be put on the American agenda. Robert Kuttner adds that a wealth tax is "by definition, the most progressive way to raise revenue, since it hits only the very pinnacle of the income distribution." A large group of multimillionaires has launched a campaign opposing elimination of taxes on inher-ited wealth—paid only by the top 2 percent—as "bad for our democracy, our economy, and our society." Even Donald Trump has proposed a one-time 14.25 percent net worth tax on Americans with more than $10 million in assets.[15]

Economist Edward Wolff points out that most European nations have for years levied general taxes on wealth. Wolff suggests that the United States follow suit with a wealth tax based on the current modest Swiss effort—an approach that, if applied to America, would involve marginal rates of 0.05 to 0.30 percent after exempting the first $100,000 per house-hold. Existing European practice, in fact, offers precedents for a much more aggressive approach. Wealth taxation rates in ten other European countries are much higher—often between 1 and 3 percent—and would yield very considerable revenues if applied here.*[16]

---

* Wolff calculated that applying a Swiss-style tax in the United States would have pro-duced roughly $52 billion in revenues in 1998 (and would not have increased taxes for the vast majority—indeed, only 8.5 percent of families would have paid more than $300). An earlier 1989 estimate by Wolff showed that revenues produced by a Swedish-style wealth tax in the United States would have been far greater—equal, in fact, to 74 percent of all revenues from personal income taxes (or $545 billion in 1998). Although an updated current estimate is not available, the rough order of magnitude is suggested by the fact that nominal GDP increased roughly 19 percent between 1998 and 2002. See Edward N. Wolff, *Top Heavy: The Increasing Inequality of Wealth in America and What Can Be Done About It* (New York: The New Press, 2002), pp. 53–61.

Taxation of wealth, of course, has long been central to the American tax system *for the kind of wealth most Americans own—their home.** Broader wealth taxation—a "property tax on wealth"—of the kind increasingly being discussed would likely exempt home-ownership and middle-class levels of other assets and focus primarily on large-order elite wealth concentrations.[17]

A comprehensive long-term approach to managing major reductions in the workweek would also likely require new Pluralist Commonwealth–style investment strategies based in part on analyses like those of Roemer, Meade, and Kelso reviewed in Part I. Groundwork has begun to be laid for an understanding of these as well. The most obvious precedent that might be built upon is the Alaska Permanent Fund. In a good year this already produces an income stream (for a family with three children) that approaches Segal's goal of $10,000 in direct payments (see p. 117).

The numerous investment strategies now increasingly being offered in connection with Social Security also would assemble and invest capital in order to achieve income flows to individuals (in this case the elderly)—and as we have seen, the management mechanisms in common use by public pension funds also demonstrate the feasibility and efficiency of public strategies that invest assets on behalf of broad groups of citizens.

The longer-term logic of such precedents suggests the establishment ultimately of a public authority that would slowly build up a capital reserve for investment to support new time-use (and other) strategies. Such an authority— implicitly a Public Trust, one of the core institutions of the Pluralist Commonwealth—might ultimately draw upon a

---

* Taxation of real estate, moreover, is based upon the value of the asset in general— *not* the value of an individual's equity: an owner of a $200,000 home will be taxed on the full value of the asset, even if his or her actual ownership position (with a mortgage debt of, say, $190,000) is only one-twentieth this amount. The property tax rebellion in California and opposition to property tax increases in many states become readily understandable when such factors are considered—especially given the absence of taxation on other forms of wealth.

variety of additional sources, beyond income and wealth taxation, to finance major system-wide allocations over the long haul of the century (see Chapter 6).

Might clear targets of political attack ever be successfully defined in support of such demanding and far-reaching strategies? Several observers believe that the way to a much more challenging longer-term politics may quietly be developing because of what Paul Krugman terms "tectonic shifts" now taking place among American elites.[18]

The super-elite—the people Krugman, Kevin Phillips, and others have termed the new "plutocracy"—increasingly live in a very, very different world from most Americans and in a radically different culture. It is a world where homes cost $5 to $10 million and where $5,000 grills, $14,000 Hermès Kelly handbags, $17,500 Patek Philippe wristwatches, and $100,000 luxury automobiles are commonplace.[19]

The world of the new plutocracy is also a world of routine white-collar corruption. The former Enron CFO Andrew Fastow as of this writing faces a 109-count indictment for alleged manipulations that prosecutors believe garnered Fastow $30 million and an additional $12 million for his associate Michael Klopper (who has pleaded guilty to federal charges). Global Crossing's chairman, Gary Winnick, it appears, may have made off with more than half a billion dollars as his company was moving toward bankruptcy and its own federal investigation. WorldCom, another telecommunications giant facing bankruptcy and criminal investigations, paid out hundreds of millions in bonuses and loans to those at the top during its last years.[20]

Above all, the world of the super-elites is a world in which wealth ownership has become *extremely* concentrated—far more so than is commonly understood. Although many Americans own small amounts of stock, the ownership of wealth—particularly financial wealth—is medieval in character.

The richest 1 percent of households now owns half of all outstanding stock, financial securities, trust equity, and business equity in the United States. A mere 5 percent owns more than two-thirds of America's financial assets. In recent years those with incomes over $1 million—*a minuscule less than two-tenths of 1 percent of all taxpayers*—made more money from stock sales than all the rest of the nation combined![21]

"The rich have always been different from you and me," Krugman observes, "but they are far more different now than they were not long ago—indeed, they are as different now as they were when F. Scott Fitzgerald made his famous remark" that they were different from most Americans. Political scientist Alan Wolfe adds, "There are really only two classes in America now, the top 2 percent and everybody else."[22]

The Bush administration has showered the super-rich with special benefits—massive reductions in income taxation, in estate taxation, in capital gains taxation, and in dividend taxation. If—when—at some point a backlash occurs among the growing number of Americans experiencing economic pain and the stress of ever greater time pressures, there is a more than reasonable possibility that a target of ever greater clarity at the top may slowly be brought into sharp political focus as the century progresses.

It is even possible that at some point during the century, the majority will wake up to its power and create an alliance to demand change.

Quite apart from the equities involved, more free time is one of the most important requirements of any serious long-term system-wide approach to building solid foundations for individual liberty in the new century. Again, a systematic strategy for opening up free time is absolutely essential if there is to be a renewal of democratic participation (see above and Chapters 2 and 4).

Although such questions increasingly confront both men and women, the painful choices and pressures facing American women suggest that as a group, women are ultimately likely to have the greatest stake in a positive resolution of time-use issues—and a stake, too, in the difficult challenge of developing a long-term politics that offers hope of altering current work-versus-family patterns.

By now the situational logic facing U.S. families in general and women in particular is well-known. For all but the very well-to-do the choices are stark:

(1) The husband and wife both work, and someone else is hired to raise the children for many hours of the day.
(2) The husband and wife both work, and the wife (rarely the husband) does double-duty raising the children.
(3) Both the husband and wife work and both attempt to raise the children in a shared fashion.

The first choice not only involves leaving the child in the care of someone else for substantial periods; for most people, it increasingly means a series of several "someone elses," since good and sustained help at affordable cost is hard to find—and since most families do not make enough money to pay for such help either in the form of nannies or decent day care. Low-paid, poorly trained help tends to move on, leaving the children to make do as best they can with the next low-paid, poorly trained person . . . and the next . . . *

Aside from the personal and family costs involved, a substantial body of research suggests that consistent caregiving may be extremely important to both psychological and cognitive development in the very early infant years. This need

---

* With day care workers making an average of $7.14 an hour—less than $13,000 a year—turnover rates are well over 30 percent in most big cities. A study by the University of California at Berkeley and the Washington-based Center for the Child Care Workforce found that three-quarters of the staff employed at day care centers in 1996 were no longer on the job in 2000. In Missouri, for example, turnover amounted to 60 percent per year. *Then and Now: Changes in Child Care Staffing, 1994–2000* (Center for the Child Care Workforce and Institute of Industrial Relations, U.C. Berkeley, April 29, 2001), www.ccw.org/pubs/Then&Nowfull.pdf (accessed 03/23/03); for Missouri turnover rates, see Judy Greenwald, "Day Care Centers Pay Premium for Quality," *Business Insurance,* vol. 35, no. 38 (July 9, 2001), p. 3.

not be the parent; it does need to be someone regularly and lovingly there. The cornerstone of healthy emotional and intellectual development for very young children is also high-quality early child care.[23]

But high-quality care is even more expensive—from a low of $3,900 a year for minimal levels of quality care to more than $10,000 in many cities. In 2000, according to the Children's Defense Fund, "the average annual cost of child care for a four-year-old in an urban area center [was] more than the average annual cost of public college tuition in all but one state."[24]

Accordingly, the first option, though available in theory, is rarely available in practice for most Americans—that is, for all but those at the top, who can afford expensive care. The second of the bad choices often produces the anguish of the so-called Superwoman model—a thoroughly exhausted and depleted woman, a tense marriage, and an inadequate capacity to give full attention either to child-rearing or to a career. "There is no more time in the day than there was when wives stayed home," observes Arlie Hochschild, the author of *The Second Shift,* "but there is twice as much to get done."[25]

"Time use studies demonstrate that working mothers put in longer hours than almost anyone else in the economy," adds Ann Crittenden, the author of *The Price of Motherhood.* "On average . . . more than eighty hours a week . . . the equivalent of two full-time jobs."[26]

The problem is significant at all levels—not simply for those with low incomes. Professional women under the pressure of career competition (reinforced by widespread gender discrimination in the workplace) commonly feel they must put in more time on the job and after hours than nonprofessionals. Even when there is more money available, ironically, time may be tighter and the pressures and stress higher among many at the professional level.

The third option—that of the husband sharing a significant portion of child-rearing—offers the logical possibility of ultimately equalizing gender roles and, too, of a potentially nurturant model of sustained child-rearing. However, given real-world differences between male and female earning capacity, when the male reduces his work-time, this usually entails very substantial costs to family income.[27]

It is an option theoretically available to all, but one that in practice is limited, again, to a small number of families where money either is not important or where women earn far more than median salaries. As Crittenden observes, "[I]n a middle-income family, with one parent earning $30,000 per year as a sales representative and the other averaging $15,000 as a part-time computer consultant," the numbers just do not work. In the real world, it means the woman commonly severely compromises her goals and aspirations.[28]

Nontraditional families face many of the same fundamental dilemmas. For most families there are simply no satisfactory ways out of the three-sided box defined by current economic constraints; still fewer are there realistic possibilities for moving toward creative, equal, and more generous gender roles and definitions. There are only poor compromises.

For low-income families, the three-sided box often becomes a slowly tightening three-sided vise that makes any option an excruciating compromise. In all too many cases the painful reality is that two adults together work three or more jobs to make ends meet, and the children are left to their own devices or to be raised by television.[29]

In principle, logical long-term solutions to the basic problem are quite obvious. The first is simply to provide sufficient resources to pay for first-rate day care services. "First-rate" means ongoing caregiving by people who can—and want to—maintain sustained relationships with children. The costs of various national programs have been estimated at between $50 and $123 billion per year (the latter figure for free care for all). Brookings scholar Isabel Sawhill calculates that a French style (crèche) system of day care would cost about $8,000 a year per child (or $61 billion). Economist

Barbara Bergmann suggests beginning with a $15 billion program targeted to low-income children.[30]

But again, financing a serious strategy in this direction clearly would require confronting the dilemmas of the resource allocation problem in ways that point ultimately to strategies beyond those now at a dead end. Many advocates—Hochschild, Crittenden, Bergmann, and others—have urged that day care be made a priority; few have as yet confronted the need for a fundamentally new political-economic strategy, and new alliances, to achieve the resources necessary to finance it.

A second and more basic solution returns us to the long-term logic of time use. Over the course of the century a reduction in necessary work-time, say, to the twenty-five-hour week urged by Segal, offers the logical possibility of both the husband and wife sharing child-rearing duties if they so desire—or of either or both working more hours (without total exhaustion) to pay for good child care.

Political theorist Philip Green urges that a "democratic division of labor in reproduction requires that as a matter of course, that is of mutual expectation, men share parenting in some rough equality with women, regardless of how much time off from external employments this may require."[31] We cannot ultimately achieve real change, Joan Williams stresses, until—quite simply—we "redefine the nature of equality."[32]

But this, in turn, requires that the benefits of technological progress are translated into financial resources to make this possible. We are back by still another route to the basic questions of how new Pluralist Commonwealth approaches might be developed and how new alliances to achieve them might be fashioned over time. The challenging reality facing those concerned with gender roles and child-rearing, on the one hand, and those concerned with time use and allocation, on the other, is the same.

The strictly political implications are again obvious. If change is ever to occur, at some point women and others deeply concerned with time problems will have to confront the need for a new political-economic approach—and for a long, difficult struggle. They also will have to come to terms with the question of how to build common cause with others facing similar pressures so that together they can force serious proposals for change.*

The above formulations focus primarily on middle-income families. Unless problems at the bottom of the system also are addressed directly, however, the solution to a middle-class family's problem can all too easily become just another way to pass the buck to those below—especially to racial minorities and immigrant women. As social historians Linda Martin and Kerry Segrave observe, "Every time the house-wife or working woman buys freedom for herself with a domestic, that very same freedom is denied to the domestic, for the maid must go home and do her own housework."[33]

Sadly, Yale's Dolores Hayden points out, many women "may never ask how their private maid or child-care worker arranges care for her own children." Nor, we may add, do many men.[34]

In short, any serious consideration of the larger issue once more forces the profound question of overall income inequality to the surface—and suggests that, difficult as this may be, a serious solution will ultimately require radically new structural arrangements.

In all this we are beginning to confront some of the most fundamental issues posed by the coming technological opportunities, on the one hand, and current political arrangements, on the other. It is clear that quite new and positive possibilities will be well within technological reach. It is also clear that, given the power of existing arrangements,

---

* Additional reforms clearly are important—including (among others) equal pay for equal work by women and men, flexible leave laws, and (paid and unpaid) maternity leave for women and men.

a serious way forward may not be possible—even over very long stretches of time.

In larger historical perspective what is important at this point is not simply the question of how time might be allocated over the course of the century, or even the question of how gender roles might be altered. It is whether individuals at all levels begin to confront the emerging logic that suggests that either economic pain and social decay will continue, perhaps indefinitely—or that a new approach must at some point be clarified that allows diverse groups to come together around different strategies aimed at achieving long-term system-wide change.

18

Beyond Super-Elites
and Conspicuous Consumption

Real Ecological Sustainability
in the Twenty-First Century

THE OVERRIDING ISSUE OF ecological sustainability offers
a final perspective on the problem of resource allocation,
the need for new political-economic strategies, and the possibility of additional groups that might one day join in a
realignment of U.S. politics around Pluralist Commonwealth
themes. It also casts important light on how a number of initiatives might be combined to reinforce one another and to
undergird a longer-term model of sustainable development if
and when new political possibilities open up over the course
of the century.

Although there is dispute about the precise dimensions of the
problem, prudence alone suggests the importance of confronting basic ecological limits. The issue goes beyond the
narrow question of physical depletion of specific resources. A
deeper problem is the system's finite capacity to deal with the
secondary effects of our current mode of economic activity—
what ecologists call "sink" problems. The earth's atmosphere
simply cannot absorb infinite amounts of carbon dioxide produced by burning fossil fuels; its water systems cannot absorb
the runoff of nitrate-based fertilizers used in modern food
production without damage to the ecosystem.[1]

Again, the developed world in general—with the United
States leading the way—consumes an extraordinary proportion of the world's goods and services. In 1999 the World

Bank estimated that the world's wealthiest nations—with roughly 16 percent of the global population—were responsible for 80 percent of private consumption. The United States, with less than 5 percent of the global population, consumes roughly 25 percent of the world's beef. Americans use 26 percent of world oil, 26 percent of world coal, and 27 percent of world natural gas. The United States produces 24 percent of global carbon emissions. Research by two government metallurgists suggests that in the brief period from 1940 to 1976, Americans alone used up as large a share of the earth's mineral resources *as did everyone in all previous history.*[2]

The late Kenneth Boulding has put the central point acerbically: "[A]nyone who believes that exponential growth can go on forever is either a madman or an economist." (Boulding, himself a highly regarded economist, was impatient with many in his own profession who were unwilling to look beyond the limits of narrowly defined technical concerns.)[3]

"We are practicing a kind of commerce," adds Ed Ayres, the editor of *World Watch* magazine, "that is drawing down the Earth's finite resources—its topsoil, water tables, and genetic resources—far faster than natural processes can regenerate them."[4]

Numerous near-term proposals have been offered to promote greater ecological sustainability—from carbon taxes, recycling efforts, and renewable energy policies, to programs to reduce population growth. Most sophisticated observers understand, however, that even the most promising initiatives, like the "Type A" and "Type B" partial reforms considered in Chapter 13, are likely at best (possibly) to slow the growth of—rather than reverse—ever worsening trends. A coherent approach thus also requires a long-term strategy for dealing with the underlying drivers that create unsustainable growth.

At the outset of the twentieth century Thorstein Veblen coined the phrase "conspicuous consumption" to describe a form of materialism that has far more to do with demonstrating one's place in society than it does with meeting a physical or other need. Modern scholars have explored related concepts—including hunger for the kinds of "positional goods" that only elites can afford, pressures to emulate those ahead of one in career ladders, defensive strategies to keep from falling behind, and many similar efforts.[5]

Just how strong such pressures can be is suggested by studies of what Americans feel they need in order to achieve their hoped-for goals. In 1986, when median family income was only $29,458, survey researchers found that on average Americans felt they really needed far, far more—$50,000—if they hoped to fulfill their dreams. This benchmark, of course, only offers a snapshot at one moment in time. The ongoing moving picture reveals a deeper dynamic. Only eight years later, in 1994, what people felt they needed had more than doubled—to $102,000 (while actual median family income had risen to only $38,782 in current dollars).[6]

Not surprisingly, even as incomes have grown over time, Americans (and others) have not experienced greater happiness. Quite the contrary; given the expanding dimensions of their unsatisfied aspirations, millions feel they are on a treadmill running faster and faster simply to stay in place. Over the roughly four-decade period between 1957 and 1995, the U.S. economy and consumption expenditures both just about doubled. The proportion of Americans who described themselves as "very happy," however, did not change in any significant way.[7]

Ever more expansive materialism is driven in significant part by the pattern set by those who can afford high-level purchases. After "the rich and super-rich began a bout of conspicuous luxury consumption" in the early 1980s, Juliet Schor reports, members of "the upper middle class followed suit with their own imitative luxury spending." In turn, the 80 percent below who lost ground also "engaged in a round of compensatory keeping-up consumption."[8]

As we have noted previously, even when there is no worsening in the relative distribution of income, as economic growth continues over time there must be an expanding absolute gap between those at the top and those at the bottom. To recall, if I have $50,000 this year and you have $1,000—and next year I have $100,000 and you have $2,000—the *relative* distribution of income has not changed since the ratio between our incomes remains constant at 50 to 1. However, the real-world distance between us has gone from $49,000 to $98,000 (see p. 17).

Dynamic processes of the kind that systematically expand the gap between those at the top and those at the bottom generate a powerful "envy machine"—a social and cultural dynamic in which even those who climb the ladder, step-by-step, regularly experience the space between the rungs getting greater and greater and the distance to the top farther and farther away as they climb (if, in fact, they do climb).[9]

"Compensatory consumption" to keep up is also driven by factors that are not directly related to envy or status. Essential to getting into a top college is a high-quality primary and secondary education. However, as Robert Frank has observed, for those who can only send their children to public schools, this almost always requires purchasing a home in a neighborhood supportive of good schools—that is, a location where prices are inflated by high incomes at the top.*[10]

Again, the "arms race" among car buyers is not simply a matter of taste or status-striving. To the extent that drivers of small, relatively fuel-efficient cars face the possibility of

---

* A classic study by the late Fred Hirsch underscores a related logic of "positional" frustration in connection with education: (1) A Harvard degree is a "positional good"; only so many people can obtain one. Hence striving must always continue—and always also be futile for the vast majority, especially as population increases and the number of candidates relative to job openings grows. (2) If a Master's degree, rather than a Bachelor's degree, becomes a new "standard," then again, all must strive for it irrespective of whether an additional year or two of (any) college actually adds significantly to one's capacities. (If one person stands up to see better at a football game, others must do so, as well.) Fred Hirsch, *The Social Limits to Growth* (Cambridge, Mass.: Harvard University Press, 1976).

collision with a 7,500-pound Ford Expedition, they may understandably feel compelled to buy a larger car for the sake of safety alone.

The capacity of top elites to keep raising the bar in connection with consumption is almost unlimited. Income received by the ten most highly paid CEOs in the United States, as we have noted, rose from an average of $3.5 million in 1981 to an impressive $19.3 million in 1988. By 2000 it had skyrocketed to an average of $154 million. Meanwhile workers' wages did little more than slightly outpace inflation during the same decades (see pp. 10, 18, and 174).[11]

Several scholars have urged reforms that begin to suggest an initial line of attack on the expansive consumption and resource challenges created by such pressures and relationships. Schor, for instance, proposes ending the tax deductibility of advertising costs by corporations as a way to reduce some forms of unnecessary consumption. (A limited version of this approach has also been suggested by Senator John McCain.) Schor and others also urge new taxes on luxury items. One specific proposal would provide that "the high-end, status versions of certain commodities would pay a high tax, the mid-range models would pay mid-range taxes, and low-end versions would be exempt."[12]

It helps to be specific about the meaning of the term "luxury items." We have noted expensive grills, wristwatches, handbags, automobiles, and the like. The luxury (limited edition) fountain pen market, with prices ranging up to $230,000 for a single pen, is now large enough to have attracted thirty-five competitors. (One recent entrant, Renaissance Pen Company, offers a gold-and-diamond "Michel Perchin" line *averaging* $45,000 for each pen.) Nokia recently launched a line of handmade cell phones with sapphire crystal displays and precious jewels as buttons— with a price tag of $19,450. In 2002 Mercedes-Benz introduced a new Maybach sedan with base prices beginning at

$310,000 to $360,000; Ferrari had a three-and-a-half-year waiting list for its $170,000 360 Modena Spider.[13]

A somewhat broader approach is Frank's proposal for a progressive consumption tax to replace the federal income tax. This would exempt all savings from taxation—plus an additional $7,500 deductible amount per person ($30,000 for a family of four). It would then steadily increase the progressivity of taxes on the remaining income devoted to consumption—with a top marginal tax rate of 70 percent on income and consumption expenditures above $500,000.*[14]

Important as such measures are, addressing the huge and growing income disparities that drive wasteful consumption patterns would clearly ultimately require much more far-reaching strategies to deal with the underlying social and economic dynamics. One obvious element of a long-range approach converges with elite-challenging efforts that have emerged in connection with other Pluralist Commonwealth issues—namely, greater elite taxation, including wealth taxes and a return to income taxes that might range up to pre–Reagan era rates of 70 to 91 percent for the top 1 to 2 percent.

Long-haul strategies that challenge elite income and wealth, and thereby consumption, serve both an economic and a larger cultural purpose. They begin to give content to the ecologically—and for many, morally—important principle that at some point *enough is enough* (or should be). Just as the environmental standards developed in local community processes help lay the groundwork for longer-term change,

---

* General consumption tax proposals have typically been urged by conservatives—primarily as a way to increase savings and investment and to shift taxes away from business. Such legislation was introduced in 1995 by a bipartisan group in the Senate, and related proposals are discussed in the 2003 *Economic Report of the President*. A progressive consumption tax would also help achieve savings and investment, but its specific features flow in the first instance from ecologically defined and equity-oriented principles. Robert H. Frank, *Luxury Fever,* pp. 223–224, 227; and *Economic Report of the President* (Washington, D.C., Government Printing Office, February 2003), chapter 5.

such strategies contribute to the development of norms that might ultimately undergird a fully developed long-term "sustainability" policy regime (see p. 142).*

A proposal by the former chairman of the House Budget Committee, Martin Sabo, points to a further issue that a serious long-term approach would also need to address— namely, the ratio of income at the top to income at the bottom (i.e., not simply the extraordinary levels of elite income). Sabo has proposed legislation that would eliminate the deductibility to corporations of compensation at the top that is more than twenty-five times that at the bottom.[15]

Taxation that challenges excessive elite income and consumption—both economically and culturally—could also help generate resources that might in turn be channeled back to support an expanded EITC-type program to raise floor-level incomes, thereby reducing the social distances that contribute to compensatory consumption. Additional precedents for dealing with inequality from the bottom up include increasing minimum wage levels and enacting "living wage" requirements.[16]

Over the course of the century, a comprehensive strategy to undercut excessive materialism might slowly reduce ceiling levels of elite income (or minimally, slow the rate of increase of ceiling levels) at the same time that low-income floor levels are raised—so that ultimately the income distribution might begin to compress toward greater degrees of equality.

Additional sources of revenue could be tapped for these and related purposes. We have noted that corporate taxes declined from 35.4 percent of all federal budget receipts in 1945 to 7.4 percent in 2003. Even a partial return to levels of previous years would produce significant revenue flows. (Sev-

---

* As the ecological economist Herman Daly observes: first, "there *is* a limit to the total material production that the ecosystem can support"; second, "I conclude, therefore, that there must implicitly be some maximum personal income." Daly adds that "bonds of community break" if there is not some limit to inequality. *Beyond Growth* (Boston, Mass.: Beacon Press, 1996), pp. 202–203.

eral states have demonstrated that it is politically feasible to move much more aggressively in this area. New Jersey, for instance, more than doubled its corporate tax levy in 2002—after twenty years of decline.*[17]

David Bollier, the author of *Silent Theft,* has clarified the potential of another source of funding that might be drawn upon for such purposes—increasing the royalties from public mineral, timber, and other resource extraction; from the use of public airwaves and the electromagnetic spectrum; from government-funded research (particularly in connection with pharmaceuticals); and from the use of government's extensive information holdings and other segments of the public "commons." Bollier suggests establishing "stakeholder trusts that give all citizens a personal stake in public assets." In similar fashion, trusts might be used to fund such important public goods as education, public broadcasting, and land conservation.[18]

Bollier points out that the management of the public lands that comprise one-third of the nation has for decades been characterized by "sweetheart deals pushed through Congress and federal agencies." Corporations "have obtained discount access to huge quantities of publicly owned oil, coal, minerals, timber and grass-lands while wreaking serious environmental havoc."[19]

A related proposal is that of Peter Barnes, the author of *Who Owns the Sky?,* for a "Sky Trust" funded through the sale of permits for the right to release carbon into the atmosphere.

---

* Also suggestive is the political/policy reaction of several states to other recent Bush administration proposals. A central provision of Bush's 2002 legislation—a major increase in corporate depreciation write-offs—would have cost states $12 billion in revenue over three years if applied across the board. As of June 2002 thirty states and the District of Columbia had decoupled from federal depreciation changes—including Virginia, at the behest of the largely Republican legislature, and Mississippi, after a finding by the Republican Tax Commissioner that the new allowances were not "reasonable." Robert S. McIntyre, "States Blow Off Bush," *The American Prospect,* vol. 13, no. 10 (June 3, 2002). See also Chapter 15, note 34.

The Sky Trust would make annual payments to each U.S. citizen in a manner similar to that of the Alaska Permanent Fund. Barnes has also proposed a tax of perhaps 5 percent on all initial public offerings of stock to capture some of the value created by the public by virtue of its maintenance of the federal securities regulatory system.[20]

Large-order longer-term system-wide Pluralist Commonwealth Public Trust strategies could permit the development of additional income flows not dependent upon either taxation or increased royalties and the sale of permits. Here a key question is not only who owns the existing productive wealth of the nation, but who will own the new wealth that will inevitably be created in the future.

The United States will be built and rebuilt anew over the course of the twenty-first century. Much of the capital infrastructure—homes, roads, public and private buildings, all forms of equipment and transportation, virtually everything of significant durability—will be replaced and substantially increased. On conservatively estimated current replacement rates, new factories will take the place of old ones at least twice during the century (and the equipment within them will be replaced at least six times), new offices will take the place of old ones at almost the same rate (and office equipment will be replaced fourteen times), warehouses will be replaced twice— and then again early in the following century.[21]

As population moves from 270 million to 400 million and beyond, other entirely new productive investments will also be needed—adding the equivalent, minimally, of capital roughly half again as large as our current stock (far more, of course, if Census Bureau population projections moving toward the 1 billion range are realized).

As we have seen, Louis Kelso and others have put forward strategies that utilize public loan guarantees or other widely accepted forms of government-backed insurance to finance new capital formation aimed at broadening wealth ownership. Strategies based on the same principle could also provide a major long-term source of capital for Public Trust investment aimed at producing income flows to help narrow the growing income gap and for other public purposes.*

The invidious comparison and envy machine mechanisms associated with great inequality are not the only sources of ecologically unsustainable growth. Other underlying drivers involve the foundational conditions of everyday work and community life. Among the well-known pressures generating status-oriented consumption in this regard are economic insecurity, a dearth of meaningful personal relationships and a sense of community, and insufficient time and encouragement to pursue creative and fulfilling activities that do not require materialist consumption.

Psychologists Tom Kasser, Richard Ryan, and several other researchers have shown, for instance, that low levels of life satisfaction in social and family relationships are strongly correlated with high levels of materialism. "Faced with the loneliness and vulnerability that come with deprivation of a securely encompassing community," New York University professor Paul Wachtel writes, "we have sought to quell the vulnerability through our possessions."[22] What is often interpreted as materialism, adds Thomas Power, is in reality a

---

* See Chapter 1. U.S. asset-based property income currently amounts to 20 to 25 percent of national income (depending on definitions used). It is sometimes suggested that even if all income from capital were allocated entirely to public purposes, this could have only a relatively modest impact on distributional matters. Quite apart from the fact that 20 to 25 percent of current income is a substantial sum, income flows from such assets would have a much greater impact in the context of a long-term ecologically oriented consumption-reducing tax regime that placed severe limits on upper incomes. The reason is obvious: as absolute income (asset-based or other) increases in such a regime, higher and higher absolute amounts become available for distributional or other public purposes as the century progresses. Given high taxation at the top, the capacity of such absolute amounts to make very substantial changes in relative patterns is enormously enhanced. Moreover, as in case of the 1960s "fiscal drag," such flows would in any event have to be substantially redirected if economic activity is not to be retarded. (We may add that a balanced program would also include "asset-based" and other strategies to ensure that adequate savings occur.)

"demonstration of the pathologies of social deprivation." What is really being sought "is participation in authentic social and natural worlds."[23]

Sophisticated advertising professionals exploit this painful reality: Barry Feig, the author of *Marketing Straight to the Heart*, tells fellow marketers that one of the best ways to increase sales is to stress the "real reasons" (as opposed to the "logical reasons") people make purchases—"hot button" emotional needs, including "desire for control," "family values," the "nurturing response," and the "need for belonging."[24]

A number of the community-oriented strategies explored in Part II help open the door to dealing with foundational problems of this kind—especially specific policies aimed at achieving greater local economic stability and thereby individual job security, and the emphasis placed upon strategies designed to nurture community economic and social well-being. Locally anchored worker-owned firms, CDCs, municipal enterprises, and the like also further such goals (as well as the general principle that wealth ownership should benefit the larger community).

The development of a secure community, as we have seen, is of strategic—not simply tactical—importance for other reasons as well. In the absence of economic security localities have very little ability to resist corporate relocation threats that run counter to a variety of ecologically significant measures. This, in turn, weakens the general capacity of communities to develop ongoing support for ecologically significant standards.

Wealth-related approaches to financing changes in work pressures and free time could also obviously help increase community participation and contribute to nurturing the networks that sustain and create the reality of "community" as a lived experience. Free time is the precondition, too, of developing meaningful individual pursuits in the arts, crafts, and education—and thereby encouraging ways other than consumption to fulfill personal identity goals (see pp. 201–206).[25]

Viewed in broader historical perspective, it is clear that the growth and power dynamics of large economic enterprises (private and public alike) present fundamental environmental challenges in all political-economic systems.* Corporate growth-driven priorities that are inimical to a regime of reduced consumption, reduced material resource use, and ecological sustainability are particularly difficult to contain. In general, the Pluralist Commonwealth strategies attempt to slowly and steadily undercut the economic and social forces that permit unrestrained expansion by building up converging lines of foundational restructuring over time. Especially important are those that reduce key inequality and psychological consumption drivers, on the one hand, and measures designed to establish conditions needed to develop new community cultural norms, on the other. In addition, public accountability and transparency are basic principles of the Public Trust and other public wealth-investing institutions. We have previously also noted some of the ways public utilities have achieved high efficiencies and reduced energy consumption.[26]

In all of this, we are again obviously beginning to confront some of the most far-reaching and difficult issues likely to challenge not only the U.S. political economy but virtually every political economy over the coming century. It is by no means clear that viable solutions will ever be found to the problem of ecological sustainability—or that those concerned with the environment will come to terms with the need to form alliances with others beginning to confront some of the common resource-related issues and systemic questions involved.

What *is* clear is that any attempt to deal seriously with the central issues will ultimately require a self-conscious effort to move beyond the conceptual limits of traditional approaches to consider strategies that confront the underlying sources of the problem.

---

* Although the corporation's environmental performance is poor, that of its public management rivals has often been worse. The abysmal environmental record of Soviet enterprise is well documented—and the U.S. Army Corps of Engineers and the Atomic Energy Commission evidence large-order ecological failures in public management in the United States as well.

19

Coda

Twenty-First-Century Populism

WE MAY STAND BACK from these various considerations to reflect upon a larger analytic point. The difficulties facing progressive strategies do not stem simply from the election of George Bush or from the massive and growing fiscal difficulties that his time in office has produced. We are entering an era in which systemic problems are slowly coming ever more forcefully into play. In the first instance the deeper challenges involve the decay of political-economic forces that once helped maintain a modicum of balance in the American system.

For much of the twentieth century organized labor provided powerful backing for progressive politics in general, and for strategies aimed at securing gains for Americans not among the upper ranks of society in particular. Even allowing for the continued importance of unions, this is no longer true. With corporate power increasing as labor declines, and with upper-middle-class suburban-based economic power firmly entrenched, the politics of the twenty-first century will be very different from that which many Americans once took for granted.

One result is that the fundamental stance of social democracy in general, and American liberalism in particular, will continue to come under increasing pressure. A second result is that traditional ameliorative strategies must lose force as time goes on. A third result is that larger, more fundamental institutional issues are likely to become increasingly obvious—and ultimately unavoidable.

History reminds us that the faltering of one form of change is rarely the end of all forms of change. It is commonly observed that when reform is blocked, a radicalization of politics often occurs. Targets of political attack become more sharply focused, anger increases, moderate tactics are abandoned, often violence explodes. We know the scenario—sometimes successful (as, for instance, in the American Revolution); sometimes not (as, for instance, in the radical Southern challenge to the Union that led to the Civil War).

What the situational logic of the emerging context suggests is a new twenty-first-century possibility—one related to, but also different from, the radicalization option. The beginning point is not the total blockage of traditional progressive strategy but a substantial and continual fading away of its promise. Moreover, the nation is extremely rich, meaning that desperation levels are unlikely to reach revolutionary levels (except among tiny groups) or give rise to major—as opposed to occasional—violence.

Something appears likely to "give," but the traditional posture, tone, and style of reform no longer offer sufficient meaning or hope to mobilize the energies needed for major change. A likely result is the emergence of an intermediate position that involves a more angry, militant, and aggressive (but not revolutionary or necessarily violent) style of politics, on the one hand, and a more aggressively and narrowly focused targeting of politics, on the other.

The term "twenty-first-century populism" points to far more than the mere rhetorical framing of issues implied in some usages. Indeed, it designates a specific and historically distinct strategic arrangement of groups and a distinct and considered understanding of the sharpening of issues required both to mobilize effective long-term political activity and to blunt inevitable elite-driven efforts to divide and conquer those striving for reform.

The politics of the intermediate form of change is inherently hospitable to the simultaneous and converging development of new Pluralist Commonwealth wealth-holding strategies and principles. Indeed, it requires the kinds of new economic approaches that, as we have seen, are now developing in all parts of the country. The new politics is thus also likely to accelerate and nurture the further development of practical system-shifting institutional efforts.

The overall arc of development also offers the promise of new ways to undergird individual choice—and the time and security to exercise such choice creatively and in the context of communities sustained by new political-economic strategies. It is not, accordingly, simply about social and economic matters or systemic change writ large. It is about individual fulfillment in the context of community.

Historian Lawrence Goodwyn's studies of nineteenth-century populism suggest the emerging changes may offer one additional possibility. Individuals who come together to demand a new way forward, in so doing, may well also rebuild the foundations of "unintimidated self-respect . . . the one essential ingredient of an authentic mass democracy."[1]

PART V

TOWARD A MORALLY COHERENT POLITICS

AT THE TIME OF THE DECLARATION of Independence, the United States comprised a modest line of settlements along a thin shelf of land bordering the Atlantic Ocean, plus a smattering of inland farms and small community groupings. The first census in 1790 registered a total population of less than 4 million. Only five cities numbered more than ten thousand; the two largest, New York and Philadelphia, fewer than fifty thousand.[1]

The majority of Americans earned their living in agriculture; technologically, the horse and iron plow were standard. Commerce was mainly restricted to traders and small manufacturers. Neither men without significant property, nor women, nor slaves could vote. For them—a large majority of the population—there was no democracy. Government constituted a tiny percentage of the small postcolonial economy; federal spending had reached only a little over $7.5 million by 1795.[2]

By the year 2000 dramatic shifts in geographic scale and population had transformed the postcolonial settlements

229

into a continental nation of over 280 million—more than seventy times the population at the time of the Declaration. Nearly 65 percent of Americans now lived in metropolitan areas of more than a million; with over a third (35 percent) living in areas of more than 2.5 million.[3]

Revolutionary changes had relegated the once dominant independent farmer and individual entrepreneur to the secondary margins of economic life. The large for-profit limited liability corporation had been elevated to a central role in ongoing American life, radically different from anything ever envisioned by classical free-market theory (the most important text of which, by Adam Smith, had just begun to circulate shortly after the Revolution).[4]

Transformative changes in technology had taken the nation from the horse and buggy to the steam locomotive to the automobile and on to manned flight and the jet airplane—to say nothing of penicillin, antibiotics, and DNA, on the one hand, and the development of computers and the Internet, on the other. The average person could now earn approximately seventeen times what his or her counterpart in the late eighteenth century could with roughly the same expenditure of time and energy.[5]

Evolutionary changes in public institutional structure had transformed government from a tiny force to almost 40 percent of direct activity in the modern economy—plus a vast array of regulations, loans, loan guarantees, tax provisions and related incentives, and other indirect activities. At the same time, extraordinary changes in culture forced the elimination of slavery and much (though hardly all) racial discrimination—and ended many (though hardly all) obstacles to women's equal participation in virtually every institution of modern society.

It would be surprising if the coming era did not experience large-order transformative shifts at least as great as these. Indeed, given that technological change is now extraordinarily rapid (there are more scientists alive today than in all of previous human history)—and given that the constitutional structure of the nation was scripted in the time of the horse and the plow—it would be even more surprising if far greater changes than had ever previously occurred were not to dominate the coming stages of American development.[6]

Conclusion

The Challenge of the Era of Technological Abundance

THE UNITED STATES IS THE wealthiest nation in the history of the world. By the end of the twenty-first century it will have the technological capacity to increase the income of all its citizens many times over or to radically reduce work-time and thereby allow a new flowering of democracy, liberty, and personal and community creativity. The new century could be—should be—one of innovation, hope, even excitement.[1]

Few Americans approach the century this way. The future is clouded by problems rather than opportunities; it appears as an era of great political difficulty and danger. At the most obvious level is the threat posed by terrorism and war—and the many challenges to liberty that overly zealous approaches to both have produced. At another level are the growing social, economic, racial, and other difficulties catalogued in the preceding pages. Critically, confidence that the great traditional values at the very heart of the American experience can be sustained has been declining rapidly.

A society committed to enhancing equality, liberty, and democracy that is unable to achieve such values in practice—indeed, that is moving in precisely the opposite direction—is committed to a morally incoherent politics. If such a politics continues through time, ever greater cynicism must develop; and with it, an ever deepening sense that American society has lost its moral compass, that government policies are merely the result of power plays and brokering between

232

interested parties that do not and cannot claim any deeper democratic or moral legitimacy.

A political-economic system can continue to violate the values it affirms for a very long time without major consequences. It is unlikely, however, to be able to do so forever. The question is: can a meaningful, morally coherent, and ultimately positive politics be constructed in the emerging era of technological abundance?

Can a new direction be set that acknowledges the systemic nature of our problems and openly posits a concrete alternative and a process that might move in a new direction? Can the system be changed?

It is important to stand back from the current moment to consider underlying issues of principle that will frame the politics of the coming era—to and through times of war and terrorism . . . and beyond. Leaving aside the question of near- or long-term political-economic feasibility, four fundamental contentions are suggested by the evolving political-economic developments we have reviewed:

First, that there is no way to achieve movement toward greater equality without developing new institutions that hold wealth on behalf of small and large publics.

Second, that there is no way to rebuild Democracy with a big D in the system as a whole without nurturing the conditions of democracy with a small d in everyday life—including the economic institutions that allow and sustain greater stability of local community life.

Third, that there is no way to achieve democracy in a continental-scale system with a population moving toward 400 million people—and possibly a billion or beyond—without radical decentralization, ultimately in all probability to some form of regional units.

Fourth, that there is no way to achieve meaningful individual liberty in the modern era without individual economic security and greater amounts of free time—and that neither of these, in turn, is possible without a change in the owner-ship of wealth and the income flows it permits.

These four contentions stand on their own. Indeed, at this point in American history, the ball is in the court of those who hold that equality, liberty, and meaningful democracy can be achieved *without* meeting the challenges suggested by the four basic points. Further related questions are whether there is any other way to achieve gender equality, ecological sustain-ability, and the sustained reality of meaningful community.

The Pluralist Commonwealth model holds, beyond this, that democratic control of large economic enterprise—a cen-tral problem confronting all political-economic systems—can never be achieved without transforming and making public the ownership of large-scale wealth and without developing a new culture—and further, that this can only be done by building on the four key elements.

Without local democracy, there can be no culture of demo-cratic practice; without security and time, there can be only a weak citizenry; without decentralization, it is difficult to mobi-lize democratic practice and accountability; and without major and far-reaching new forms of wealth holding, there can never be adequate support for the conditions and policies needed to build a more egalitarian and free democratic culture.

Finally, the model is based on the judgment that greater equality, greater individual economic security, greater amounts of free time, and—upon this basis—the reconstitu-tion of a culture of common responsibility are ultimately required if we are ever to reorient our community and national priorities in general.[2]

The central argument of this book is that the first decades of the twenty-first century are likely to open the way to a serious debate about these and other systemic questions—and further, that real-world conditions during the coming period are likely to offer opportunities for establishing substantial foundations for a possible longer-term systemic transformation thereafter.

The prospects for near-term change are obviously not great—especially when such change is conceived in traditional terms. Indeed, although there may be an occasional progressive electoral win, there is every reason to believe that the underlying trends will continue their decaying downward course. In many ways times are likely to get worse before they get better.

On the other hand, fundamental to the analysis presented in the preceding pages is the observation that for precisely such reasons, there is likely to be an intensified process of much deeper probing, much more serious political analysis, and much more fundamental institutional exploration and development. We have also noted that there are important signs of change in the traditional "laboratories" of democratic process. States from Alaska to California, and from Alabama to Ohio, have moved forward to create—and systematically build political support for—many new political-economic experiments and strategies. Federal fiscal and other decisions are now producing pain and reassessment at every level.

Traditionally, a distinction has been made between reform, on the one hand, and revolution, on the other. The former implies nonviolent improvement in the outcomes of a given system—with no fundamental change in its basic institutional structure. It cleans up around the edges of the existing system, as it were—sometimes slowly, sometimes in major political outbursts. The latter commonly implies abrupt and often violent change—above all, of the fundamental institutional structures of the system.

The kind of change that appears in the various trajectories of emerging U.S. development involves an unusual combination of strategic approaches. Like reform, in the main it involves step-by-step nonviolent change. But like revolution, its process is oriented to the development of different institutional structures to replace traditional corporate forms over time. It might appropriately be called "evolutionary reconstruction."

A politics based on evolutionary reconstructive principles does not abandon reform when it can achieve important gains. On the other hand, such a politics explicitly seeks to understand—and to foster—the longer-term foundational requirements of the values it affirms. It is not satisfied with, or misled by, occasional electoral gains that do little to alter the direction of long-term trends. It is a politics of historical perspective and commitment to the long haul.

Few predicted either the upheavals of the 1960s or the conservative revolution that followed. Major eruptions and political realignments are the rule, not the exception in U.S. history. Large numbers of working Americans; blacks and Hispanics who will become a majority as the century develops; senior citizens (and those who shortly will become seniors); women who seek practical ways to achieve thoroughgoing gender equality; liberals and conservatives alike who value family and community; environmentalists who cannot secure protections either for endangered goals or sustainable growth along current lines of development—all are finding it increasingly difficult to realize their objectives through traditional means.

A fundamental question is what may happen as various groups, each beginning with more narrowly defined interests, come to the realization that what they value most cannot be achieved without a new approach. If, as appears increasingly likely, such awareness begins to intersect with the knowledge and experience gained through the development of new strategies and ideas, new possibilities are likely to become available to politics in the coming era.

There are numerous indications of underlying political instability in the U.S. system. Millions have expressed their discontent by breaking with the major political parties to vote for Ross Perot, Pat Buchanan, and Ralph Nader; to elect Jesse Ventura in Minnesota; and to support Howard Dean's insurgent campaign for the Democratic Party nomination in 2004. Such "unexpected" developments also suggest that beneath the surface level of politics-as-usual, it is by no means clear that the public is or will remain quiescent forever—especially if social and economic pain continues, if political elites continue to overreach, and if new directions begin to be clearly defined.[3]

The term "conjunktur" designates a coming together at one moment in time of diverse trends to create new, unforeseen, and often dramatic opportunities for change. A major electoral shift or political realignment is easily conceivable—and with it the truly interesting question of the first decades of the century: whether foundations for something much more far-reaching might be established for the period beyond.

The legitimacy of the present economic arrangements and entitlements is also likely to be called into question by large-order developments that intersect with—and strengthen—ongoing efforts to achieve change.

In the late 1990s economist William Baumol pointed out that per capita GDP in the United States had increased ninefold since 1870—and that almost 90 percent of this growth was due to innovations developed over the previous 130-year period. Even pre-1870 innovations such as the steam engine and the railroad, he observed, "still add to today's GDP."[4]

Nobel laureate Robert Solow has similarly pointed out that current economic growth must overwhelmingly be attributed to "residual" factors that, broadly speaking, involve the huge contributions of inherited technological knowledge. Again, research by economist Edward Denison has shown that advances in knowledge are "the biggest and most basic reason for the persistent long-term growth of output per unit of input."[5]

The moral—and hence, ultimately, political—implications of this growing understanding are beginning to be recognized. Above all, as historian Joel Mokyr observes, the vital knowledge we receive from the past comes to us through no effort of our own as a "free lunch." The implicit question is inherently explosive: if so, who should rightly benefit, and in what proportions, from this extraordinary inheritance—this free gift that produces so much of our common abundance?[6]

Seth Shulman, the author of *Owning the Future,* has made the obvious connection. The elites who hold most of the rights to modern technologies "are legally sanctioned, but the legitimacy of their claims often remains dubious because of the debt they owe to innovations that have been made possible only by years or decades of collective advances."[7]

The current technological contributions that produce such huge rewards for the fortunate few, in short, are a mere pebble placed atop a Gibraltar of received science and technology that makes the modern additions possible—and that was often paid for by the public, and that can be traced back through many generations, indeed, centuries. Current elites, William Gates Sr. urges, disproportionately reap the harvest of what is inherently a collective investment. Gates proposes their estates be taxed accordingly.[8]

The late Herbert Simon, another Nobel laureate, defined the central issue this way: "[A]ny causal analysis explaining why American GDP is about $25,000 per capita [1998] would show that at least two-thirds is due to the happy accident that the income recipient was born in the U.S." Simon termed the vast gift of the past a sort of "patrimony" received simply by the chance of birth—and like Gates, urged that this should be subject to large-order taxation.[9]

We have noted growing anger at the extreme wealth of some amid the great poverty of others—and, too, at the corrupt practices of many leading corporate executives. We have seen that elite ownership has very little to do with the demands of efficiency and productivity, and that a variety of institutional forms can manage wealth effectively—indeed, often more effectively than traditional forms.

The new understandings that the computer, satellite communication, and the World Wide Web increasingly underscore are the moral wild cards of the era of technological abundance. Nobel laureate Joseph Stiglitz urges in general that "just as the importance of land in production changed dramatically as the economy moved from agriculture to industry, so too does the movement to a knowledge economy necessitate a rethinking of economic fundamentals." As recognition that the sources of modern abundance are deeply rooted in the legacy we all commonly receive from the past continues to develop, it is likely to bring with it a powerful critique of all justifications of current wealth ownership patterns and a powerful rationale for new, broader allocations and institutional strategies.*[10]

Little has been said in the preceding pages about global issues and international relations. The reason is not only that this book is devoted primarily to U.S. developments. It is that it is extremely difficult to imagine a fundamental shift in America's stance toward the rest of the world absent a transformation of our own ways at home. The argument of Alexis de Tocqueville and John Stuart Mill—that ultimately democracy in a nation depends upon the development of democracy in its communities—is echoed in the judgment that America is unlikely to play a different role in the world until it is a different America—until it finds ways once again to realize values of equality, liberty, democracy, and, one day, perhaps even of community in our own land. Efforts to alter the excesses of America's international stance and to persuade the United States to respond more humanely to global problems are both essential and laudable. If we Americans truly hope to help others around the world, however, we have much hard work to do, first and foremost, here at home.

---

* The evolving recognition that the technologies and other gifts of the past at the heart of the modern economy are different—and that they are not primarily the result of current effort or merit—also recalls the understanding of leading figures of the early Chicago school of economics. Here, for instance, is Frank Knight: "Existing capacities to render service, including ownership of wealth, are in turn the result of the working of the economic process in the past." Knight continues, "There is no visible reason why anyone is more or less entitled to the earnings of inherited personal capacities than to those of inherited property in any other form; and similarly as to capacity resulting from impersonal social processes." Frank Knight, *Freedom and Reform* (New York: Harper & Brothers, 1947), pp. 9, 151.

Large-order institutional restructuring, we tend to forget, is exceedingly common in the long sweep of world history. The difficulty lies in pulling ourselves out of the present moment to consider our own possibilities in broader historical perspective.

The current years of terrorism and war are not the first time our nation has been challenged by grave danger, nor is this the only time it has experienced great violence at home. Indeed, we have survived even civil war and losses many times those of recent years. The fundamental questions posed throughout this book may or may not be answered. They will not, however, go away.

We have begun a new century. The coming decades will establish the terms of reference for further, future change. It is not possible to know whether a new direction based on the developing ideas, models, practical experiments, and new alliance explorations can lay the foundations for the next political-economic system. Or whether, over time, a new basis can thereby be established for a politics capable of unleashing the moral energies that can flow from a renewed commitment to achieving equality, liberty, and democracy.

It *is* possible, however, for one person—each person—to help refine our understanding and our strategies and to help establish the practical and political elements needed in the first stage of any realistic forward-moving developmental process. Each step is valuable on its own terms, no matter what.

Long before the civil rights movement, there were many years of hard, quiet, dangerous work by those who came before. Long before the feminist explosion there were those who labored to establish new principles in earlier decades. It is within the possibilities of our own time in history that—working together and openly charting an explicit new course—this generation can establish the necessary foundations for an extraordinary future and for the release of new energies.

It may even be that far-reaching change will come much earlier and much faster than many now imagine.

Notes

PREFACE

1. For the story of Youngstown see Staughton Lynd, *The Fight Against Shutdowns: Youngstown's Steel Mill Closings* (San Pedro: Singlejack Books, 1982); Gar Alperovitz and Jeff Faux, *Rebuilding America: A Blueprint for the New Economy* (New York: Pantheon, 1984).
2. David J. Garrow, *Bearing the Cross: Martin Luther King, Jr., and the Southern Christian Leadership Conference* (New York: William Morrow, 1986), pp. 469–545.
3. See John Egerton, *Speak Now Against the Day: The Generation Before the Civil Rights Movement in the South* (Chapel Hill: University of North Carolina Press, 1995); John Dittmer, *Local People: The Struggle for Civil Rights in Mississippi* (Urbana: University of Illinois Press, 1994).
4. See, for instance, Gar Alperovitz, *Atomic Diplomacy: Hiroshima and Potsdam* (New York: Simon & Schuster, 1965); *The Decision to Use the Atomic Bomb and the Architecture of an American Myth* (New York: Alfred A. Knopf, 1995); *Cold War Essays* (New York: Doubleday, 1970); Gar Alperovitz and Kai Bird, "The Fading of the Cold War—and the Demystification of Twentieth Century Issues," in *The End of the Cold War: Its Meaning and Implications,* ed. Michael J. Hogan (Cambridge: Cambridge University Press, 1992).

INTRODUCTION

1. In 2000 the top 1 percent received 17.8 percent of income while the bottom 40 percent earned 12.6 percent of income. After-tax income was slightly less unequal, with 15.5 percent going to the top 1 percent and 14.6 percent going to the bottom 40 percent. Congressional Budget Office, "Effective Federal Tax Rates, 1997 to 2000," August 2003, www.cbo.gov/ftpdoc.cfm?index=4514&type=1 (accessed 10/10/03), table B1-C. Richard Posner quoted in Alexander Cockburn, "The Prosecutorial State," *The Nation,* vol. 268, no. 7 (February 22, 1999), p. 9.
2. Peter Levine, "Expert Analysis vs. Public Opinion: The Case of Campaign Finance Reform," *Philosophy and Public Policy,* vol. 17, no. 3 (Summer 1997), p. 1. Alan F. Kay, Hazel Henderson, Frederick T. Steeper, Stanley B. Greenberg, and Christopher Blunt, "Who Will Reconnect with the People: Republicans, Democrats, or . . . None of the Above?" Americans Talk Issues Foundation Survey #28, Conducted June 1995 (Washington, D.C.: Americans Talk Issues Foundation, 1995), p. 7. Ronald Brownstein, "Poll Says Americans Deeply Discouraged with State of Nation," *Houston Chronicle,* November 5, 1995, p. 2.

3. Kevin Phillips, *Wealth and Democracy* (New York: Broadway Books, 2002), p. xv.

4. Robert D. Kaplan, "Was Democracy Just a Moment?" *Atlantic Monthly,* vol. 280, no. 6 (December 1997), pp. 56, 73.

5. The specific contributions of numerous scholars over many years are cited throughout this book. Among conservatives, the early work of Louis Kelso and Robert Nisbet deserves special mention. Important early progressive contributions include those, especially, of E. F. Schumacher, Martin Carnoy and Derek Shearer, Jane Mansbridge, Samuel Bowles and Herbert Gintis, Benjamin Barber, Bertell Ollman, Murray Bookchin, Noam Chomsky, Robin Hahnel and Michael Albert, and Robert Dahl. In recent years the ongoing work of the Real Utopias project led by Erik Olin Wright has been particularly valuable. The trajectory of my own concern begins with an initial effort in the late 1960s, "Notes Towards a Pluralist Commonwealth," which is most easily available in Staughton Lynd and Gar Alperovitz, *Strategy and Program* (Boston: Beacon Press, 1973). See also Thad Williamson, *What Comes Next? Proposals for a Different Society* (Washington, D.C.: National Center for Economic and Security Alternatives, 1998). See also John Cavanagh and Jerry Mander, et al., *Alternatives to Economic Globalization: A Report of the International Forum on Globalization* (San Francisco: Berrett-Koehler, 2002); Roberto Mangabeira Unger, *Democracy Realized* (New York: Verso, 1998); Hazel Henderson, *Creating Alternative Futures* (San Francisco: Kumarian, 1996); Jeff Gates, *The Ownership Solution: Toward a Shared Capitalism for the Twenty-First Century* (Reading, Mass.: Addison-Wesley, 1998); and Immanuel Wallerstein, *After Liberalism* (New York: The New Press, 1995). I have not attempted to cite in this work the vast literature and numerous important contributions made by many others who have offered significant "market socialist" strategies, or the many insights provided by earlier guild socialist and anarcho-communitarian theorists. However, for a useful overview of the market socialist debate see Bertell Ollman (ed.), *Market Socialism: The Debate Among Socialists* (New York: Routledge, 1998).

6. "Changes in Household Wealth in the 1980s and 1990s in the U.S," in *International Perspectives on Household Wealth,* ed. Edward N. Wolff (Elgar Publishing Ltd., forthcoming), p. 12 and table 6. See also Arthur Kennickell, "A Rolling Tide: Changes in the Distribution of Wealth in the U.S., 1989–2001," Federal Reserve Board, March 2003. Lawrence Mishel, Jared Bernstein, and Heather Boushey, *State of Working America: 2002–2003* (Ithaca, N.Y.: ILR Press, 2003), table 4.1 (47.3 percent of financial wealth was held by the top 1 percent in 1998). See also Lisa A. Keister, *Wealth in America* (Cambridge: Cambridge University Press, 2000); Melvin L. Oliver and Thomas M. Shapiro, *Black Wealth/White Wealth* (New York: Routledge, 1995); and Dalton Conley, *Being Black, Living in the Red* (Berkeley: University of California Press, 1999). While there is an obvious relationship between wealth and income, households in the wealthiest 1 percent are not necessarily the same as those in the richest 1 percent by income, and vice versa.

7. In addition to the first founding period, commonly cited political realignments include the changes that created the second party system, resulting in the election of Jackson in 1828; which produced the new Republican Party in 1860 and opened the way to the Civil War; which established "the system of 1896," and reoriented politics in favor of triumphant industrial capitalism; and which created the 1932 New Deal coalition during the Great Depression. A sixth realignment, centered on the takeover of Southern politics by the Republican Party

after 1964, is cited by some analysts. A classic work is Walter Dean Burnham, *Critical Elections and the Mainsprings of American Politics* (New York: W. W. Norton & Co., 1970).

PART I: THE PLURALIST COMMONWEALTH

1. Ervin K. Zingler, "Wealth and Power in America—An Analysis of Social Class and Income Distribution (Book Review)," *American Economic Review*, vol. 53, no. 3 (June 1963), p. 462; James N. Morgan et al., *Income and Welfare in the United States* (New York: McGraw-Hill, 1962), p. 3; and John Kenneth Galbraith, *The Affluent Society* (Boston: Houghton Mifflin, 1958).

2. Michael Harrington, *The Other America: Poverty in the United States* (New York: Macmillan, 1962); John Kenneth Galbraith, "The Heartless Society," *New York Times Magazine*, September 2, 1984, pp. 20, 44; and Dwight MacDonald, "Our Invisible Poor," *The New Yorker*, vol. 38, no. 82 (January 19, 1963), pp. 82–132.

3. Paul Krugman, "Plutocracy and Politics," *New York Times*, June 14, 2002, p. A37; Krugman's data drawn from Kevin Phillips, *Wealth and Democracy* (New York: Broadway Books, 2002), pp. 151–153.

4. Paul A. Samuelson, *Economics: An Introductory Analysis* (New York: McGraw-Hill, 1948), p. 63.

5. Paul A. Samuelson and William Nordhaus, *Economics* (Boston: Irwin/McGraw-Hill, 1998), p. 359.

6. Lester C. Thurow, *The Future of Capitalism: How Today's Economic Forces Shape Tomorrow's World* (New York: William Morrow, 1996), p. 42.

7. Robert D. Putnam, *Making Democracy Work: Civic Traditions in Modern Italy* (Princeton: Princeton University Press, 1993), p. 3.

8. Steven Kull, *Expecting More Say: The American Public on Its Role in Government Decisionmaking* (Washington, D.C.: Center on Policy Attitudes, May 10, 1999), pp. 4, 10.

9. Data from Committee for the Study of the American Electorate, published by the Center for Voting and Democracy, www.fairvote.org/turnout/index.html (accessed 10/25/02); Center for Voting and Democracy, *Monopoly Politics 2002: How "No Choice" Elections Rule in a Competitive House*, September 30, 2002, www.fairvote.org/2002/mp2002.htm (accessed 08/22/03); and Steven Hill and Rob Richie, "Drawing the Line on Redistricting," *Washington Post*, July 1, 2003, p. A13.

10. Ronnie Dugger, "Crimes Against Democracy," *The Progressive Populist*, vol. 5, no. 13 (December 15, 1999), p. 14.

11. Charles E. Lindblom, *The Market System: What It Is, How It Works, and What to Make of It* (New Haven: Yale University Press, 2001), p. 237.

12. Carl Boggs, *The End of Politics: Corporate Power and the Decline of the Public Sphere* (New York: Guilford Press, 2000), pp. 70–71.

13. Michael J. Sandel, *Democracy's Discontent: America in Search of a Public Philosophy* (Cambridge, Mass.: Belknap Press, 1996), pp. 201–202.

14. David Cole, "National Security State," *The Nation*, vol. 273, no. 20 (December 17, 2001), p. 5.

15. William Safire, "Seizing Dictatorial Power," *New York Times*, November 15, 2001, p. A31.

16. William Safire, "The Great Unwatched," *New York Times*, February 18, 2002, p. A15.

17. Carl Rowan, "Who Will Stop the Erosion of Civil Liberties?" *The Buffalo News,* July 5, 1997, p. C3; and Paige M. Harrison and Jennifer C. Karberg, "Prison and Jail Inmates at Midyear 2002," *Bureau of Justice Statistics Bulletin,* U.S. Bureau of Justice Statistics, April 2003, p. 11.

18. The Bush administration's first budget proposal projected federal government spending at 18.1 percent of GDP. Clinton's last budget projected government spending at just under 18 percent. Office of Management and Budget, *Budget of the United States 2002: Historical Tables* (Washington, D.C.: Government Printing Office, 2001), w3.access.gpo.gov/usbudget/ (accessed 11/11/02), tables 1.1, 10.1; Office of Management and Budget, *Budget of the United States 2003: Historical Tables* (Washington, D.C.: Government Printing Office, 2002), w3.access.gpo.gov/usbudget/ (accessed 11/11/02), tables 1.1, 10.1; and Robert Higgs, *Crisis and Leviathan: Critical Episodes in the Growth of American Government* (New York: Oxford University Press, 1987), p. 262.

19. Bureau of Labor Statistics, "Incorporated Self-Employed in the United States, Annual Averages 1989-2001," and "Self-Employment in the United States, Annual Averages 1948-2002," unpublished tables provided by the BLS economist Marissa Di Natale. See also John E. Bregger, "Measuring Self-employment in the United States," *Monthly Labor Review,* vol. 119, nos. 1 and 2 (January/February 1996), pp. 3-9.

1. EQUALITY: BEYOND TAX-AND-SPEND

1. George E. Johnson, "Changes in Earnings Inequality: The Role of Demand Shifts," *The Journal of Economic Perspectives,* vol. 11, no. 2 (Spring 1997), pp. 41-54; James K. Galbraith, *Created Unequal: The Crisis in American Pay* (New York: The Free Press, 1998); Frank Levy, *The New Dollars and Dreams* (New York: The Russell Sage Foundation, 1998), pp. 3-4; George Borjas, *Heaven's Door: Immigration Policy and the American Economy* (Princeton: Princeton University Press, 1999), p. 11; and Barry Bluestone, "The Inequality Express," *The American Prospect,* vol. 6, no. 20 (Winter 1995), pp. 81-93.

2. The mid-1950s estimate is widely cited and is included in the text for this reason. However, it is not fully comparable to more recent estimates. Since 1973, the official source of union membership statistics has been the Current Population Survey. In 1973, 24 percent of the workforce were members of unions. Barry T. Hirsch and David A. Macpherson, "Union Membership and Coverage Database from the Current Population Survey: Note," *Industrial and Labor Relations Review,* vol. 56, no. 2 (January 2003), pp. 349-354. The wartime peak was slightly higher: 35.5 percent in 1945. U.S. Census Bureau, *Historical Statistics of the United States, Colonial Times to 1970, Part 1* (Washington, D.C.: Government Printing Office, 1975), p. 178; Bureau of Labor Statistics, "Union Members Summary," Current Population Survey, January 2004, www.bls.gov/news.release/union2.toc.htm. Projections of continuing union decline are offered by Henry S. Farber and Bruce Western, "Accounting for the Decline of Unions in the Private Sector, 1973-1998," *Journal of Labor Research,* vol. 22, no. 3 (Summer 2001), pp. 459-485; Paul C. Weiler, "The Representation Gap in the North American Workplace," Larry Sefton Memorial Lecture, February 22, 1989, mimeo, p. 7; and Bruce E. Kaufman, "The Future of U.S. Private Sector Unionism: Did George Barnett Get It Right After All?" *Journal of Labor Research,* vol. 22, no. 3 (Summer 2001), pp. 433-457.

3. David Card, "The Effect of Unions on Wage Inequality in the U.S. Labor Market," *Industrial and Labor Relations Review*, vol. 54, no. 2 (January 2001), pp. 296–315; and Michael Wallerstein, "Union Organization in Advanced Industrial Democracies," *American Political Science Review*, vol. 83, no. 2 (June 1989), pp. 481–501 and 481. For discussions of the relationship between labor movements and welfare state protections see Seymour Martin Lipset and Gary Marks, *It Didn't Happen Here* (New York: Norton, 2000), pp. 284–285; and Alexander M. Hicks, *Social Democracy and Welfare Capitalism* (Ithaca, N.Y.: Cornell University Press, 1999).

4. Bjorn Gustafsson and Mats Johansson, "In Search of Smoking Guns: What Makes Income Inequality Vary Over Time in Different Countries?" *American Sociological Review*, vol. 64, no. 4 (August 1999), pp. 585–605.

5. Nelson Lichtenstein, *State of the Union: A Century of American Labor* (Princeton: Princeton University Press, 2002); Michael Goldfield, *The Decline of Organized Labor in the United States* (Chicago: University of Chicago Press, 1987); and Fernando Gapasin and Michael Yates, "Organizing the Unorganized: Will Promises Become Practices?" *Monthly Review*, vol. 49, no. 3 (July–August 1997), pp. 46–62.

6. Thomas I. Palley, "The Economics of Globalization: Problems and Policy Responses," Paper prepared for the plenary meeting of the Pontifical Academy of Social Sciences, March 3–6, 1999, The Vatican (revised July 1999), p. 9.

7. Office of Management and Budget, *Budget of the United States 2005: Historical Tables*, (Washington, D.C.: Government Printing Office, 2004) w3.access.gpo .gov/usbudget/fy2004/pdf/hist.pdf (accessed 08/22/03), table 2.2, pp. 31–32. For 2003 numbers see Congress of the United States, Joint Economic Committee, "U.S. Corporate Taxes are Very Low from Both an Historical and International Perspective," November 6, 2003, jec.senate.gov/democrats/Documents/Releases/ dc6nov2003.pdf (accessed 05/25/04). The welfare state, Dani Rodrik concludes, "can work as long as international economic integration is not too advanced. But once globalization moves beyond a certain point, the government can no longer finance the requisite income transfers because the tax base becomes too footloose." Dani Rodrik, *Has Globalization Gone Too Far?* (Washington, D.C.: Institute for International Economics, 1997), p. 55. See also Lucas Bretschger and Frank Hettich, "Globalisation, Capital Mobility and Tax Competition: Theory and Evidence for OECD Countries," Paper for the Dynamics, Economic Growth, and International Trade, V Conference, June 22–24, 2000. For other views see Geoffrey Garrett, *Partisan Politics in the Global Economy* (New York: Cambridge University Press, 1998); and Duane Swank and Sven Steinmo, "The New Political Economy of Taxation in Advanced Capitalist Democracies," *American Journal of Political Science*, vol. 46, no. 3 (July 2002), pp. 642–655. General Accounting Office, "Tax Administration: Comparison of the Reported Tax Liabilities of Foreign and U.S. Controlled Corporations, 1996–2000," GAO-04-358, February 2004, table 4. The study further distinguished between large and small corporations ("large" indicates assets of at least $250 million or gross receipts of at least $50 million in constant 2000 U.S. dollars). In 2000 more than 45 percent of large U.S. companies paid no federal taxes, ibid, table 6.

8. Juliet F. Gainsborough, *Fenced Off: The Suburbanization of American Politics* (Washington, D.C.: Georgetown University Press, 2001), pp. 76–77; J. Eric Oliver, *Democracy in Suburbia* (Princeton: Princeton University Press, 2001), p. 86; and Thomas Byrne Edsall with Mary D. Edsall, *Chain Reaction* (New York:

W. W. Norton, 1991), pp. 5–6. See also Jill Quadagno, *The Color of Welfare: How Racism Undermined the War on Poverty* (New York: Oxford University Press, 1994).

9. August B. Cochran III, *Democracy Heading South* (Lawrence: University of Kansas Press, 2001), p. 23.

10. On market-generated inequality see Lester C. Thurow, *Zero-Sum Society* (New York: Basic Books, 1980), pp. 199–200; see also Claudia Goldin and Robert A. Margo, "The Great Compression: The Wage Structure in the United States at Mid-Century," *Quarterly Journal of Economics*, vol. 107, no. 1 (February 1992), pp. 1–34; and Robert D. Plotnick, Eugene Smolensky, Eirik Evenhouse, and Siobhan Reilly, "The Twentieth-Century Record of Inequality and Poverty in the United States," in *The Cambridge Economic History of the United States*. Vol. 3, *The Twentieth Century*, ed. Stanley Engerman and Robert Gallman (New York: Cambridge University Press, 2000), pp. 249–300, cited material on p. 286. See also U.S. Census Bureau, "Index of Income Concentration (Gini Index), by Definition of Income: 1979 to 2001," table RDI-5, www.census.gov/ hhes/income/histinc/rdi5.html (accessed 12/03/02). In general, and in connection with shifts that took place prior to 1950, note especially the tax structure put in place as a result not of "normal politics" but of World War II; note also the ongoing post–World War II impact of such critical programs as AFDC and Social Security, enacted in the special political environment of the Depression. A possible exception to the general rule was the enactment of Medicare and Medicaid in 1965 in the highly unusual Great Society Congress elected in the wake of the Goldwater defeat of 1964. The debacle resulted in the temporary defeat of thirty-eight Republican members of the House—the equivalent in many instances of a shift of seventy-six votes in the House.

11. Congressional Budget Office, "Effective Federal Tax Rates, 1997 to 2000," August 2003, www.cbo.gov/ftpdoc.cfm?index=4514&type=1 (accessed 10/06/03), table B1-C. Average income of the bottom 20 percent increased from $13,700 in 1973 to $14,600 in 2001 while average income for the top 5 percent increased from $205,500 to $434,300 (all figures are adjusted by the Congressional Budget Office to 2000 dollars using the CPI-U-RS).

12. Lawrence Mishel, Jared Bernstein, and Heather Boushey, *The State of Working America: 2002–2003* (Ithaca, N.Y.: ILR Press, 2003), tables 1.7, 2.6, pp. 47, 128.

13. While favorable economic conditions in the second half of the 1990s modestly raised both median real wages and median family income, the return of slow growth and recession undermined these slight gains. Median income fell and poverty increased in both 2001 and 2002—and recent data suggest continuing difficulties in 2003. Between 2000 and 2002 the number of those in poverty increased by 3 million; the average income of the poor in 2002 was lower relative to the poverty line than in any year since 1979. Center on Budget and Policy Priorities, "Poverty Increases and Median Income Declines for Second Consecutive Year" (September 29, 2003), www.cbpp.org/9-26-03pov.htm (accessed 05/20/04). Mishel, Bernstein, and Boushey, *The State of Working America*, table 2.1, pp. 98, 117.

14. See Bureau of Labor Statistics, "Labor Force Statistics from the Current Population Survey," Bulletin 2307 (August 1988). The rate of married women joining the labor force slowed from 1.3 percent per year in the 1970s to 0.4 percent in the 1990s. Over the postwar period, the share of families with a spouse to add to the labor force also declined as marriage rates declined. Currently, 62

percent of wives are working—which may be close to a "ceiling" participation rate, according to Mishel and Bernstein. Mishel, Bernstein, and Boushey, *The State of Working America,* table 1.7 and pp. 46–47; and Lawrence Mishel, Jared Bernstein, and John Schmitt, *The State of Working America: 2000–2001,* table 1.6. On wives' labor participation rates, see Chapters 1 and 15 in this book.

15. John Kenneth Galbraith, *The Culture of Contentment* (Boston: Houghton Mifflin, 1992), p. 179. See also Lester C. Thurow, *The Future of Capitalism* (New York: William Morrow, 1996), p. 245.

16. Richard B. Freeman, "Solving the New Inequality," in *The New Inequality: Creating Solutions for Poor America,* ed. Joshua Cohen and Joel Rogers (Boston: Beacon Press, 1999), p. 11.

17. Freeman, "Solving the New Inequality," p. 14.

18. Robert B. Reich, "To Lift All Boats," *Washington Post,* May 16, 1999, pp. B1, B4.

19. Jeff Gates, *The Ownership Solution* (Reading, Penn.: Addison-Wesley, 1998), p 17.

20. Worker-ownership ideas, of course, were widely discussed in the nineteenth century. For a discussion of the earlier era see Terence V. Powderly, *The Path I Trod,* ed. Harry J. Carman, Henry David, and Paul N. Guthrie (New York: Columbia University Press, 1940), pp. 206, 273–285; and Kim Voss, *The Making of American Exceptionalism: The Knights of Labor and Class Formation in the Nineteenth Century* (Ithaca, N.Y.: Cornell University Press, 1993), pp. 84–85.

21. Samuel Bowles and Herbert Gintis, "Efficient Redistribution: New Rules for Markets, States, and Communities," in *Recasting Egalitarianism: New Rules for Communities, States, and Markets,* ed. Erik Olin Wright (New York: Verso Books, 1998), pp. 10, 58, 37.

22. Bowles and Gintis, "Efficient Redistribution," pp. 37–38. Economic arguments in support of worker ownership have been offered by a range of scholars. See, for instance, David Schweickart, *Against Capitalism* (Boulder, Colo.: Westview Press, 1996); Gregory K. Dow *Governing the Firm: Workers' Control in Theory and Practice* (New York: Cambridge University Press, 2003); and Joseph Blasi, Douglas Kruse, and Aaron Bernstein, *In the Company of Owners: The Truth About Stock Options (And Why Every Employee Should Have Them)* (New York: Basic Books, 2003), among others. For an overview of pros and cons and a theory that emphasizes the costs of decision making, see Henry Hansmann, *The Ownership of Enterprise* (Cambridge, Mass.: The Belknap Press, 1996). For a recent empirical study that emphasizes the gains of participatory decision making, see John Logue and Jacquelyn Yates, *The Real World of Employee Ownership* (Ithaca, N.Y.: ILR Press, 2001). For critical views see Michael C. Jensen, *A Theory of the Firm: Governance, Residual Claims and Organizational Forms* (Cambridge, Mass.: Harvard University Press, 2000), chapter 6 in particular; and Armen A. Alchian and Harold Demsetz, "Production, Information Costs, and Economic Organization," *American Economic Review,* vol. 62, no. 5 (December 1972), pp. 777–795. See Chapter 7 in this book for a discussion of studies of the efficiency of the most common form of worker ownership.

23. Jeff Gates, *The Ownership Solution* (Reading, Penn.: Addison-Wesley, 1998), p. 167, support from others cited in Gates, pp. 167–169; and Robert Kuttner, "Broaden the Wealth: An Idea Even Conservatives Love," *Business Week,* no. 3545 (September 22, 1997), p. 22.

24. Joint Committee on Taxation, *Estimates of Federal Tax Expenditures for Fiscal Years 2004–2008* (JCS-8-03) (Washington, D.C.: Government Printing Office, 2003), table 1, pp. 22, 28. Estimated tax expenditures in 2004 for home-ownership

include deductions for mortgage interest ($61.4 billion), property taxes ($18.7 billion), and the exclusion of capital gains on the sale of homes ($17.9 billion). Tax expenditures related to pension contributions include those for employer plans ($94.6 billion), individual plans ($13 billion), and Keoghs ($6.2 billion).

25. Michael Sherraden, *Assets and the Poor* (Armonk, N.Y.: M.E. Sharpe, Inc., 1991), p. xv (emphasis in the original).

26. Social Security Solvency Act of 1999, S.21, 106th Congress, Sec. 11, Part C— KidSave Accounts. Robert B. Reich, "To Lift All Boats," *Washington Post,* May 16, 1999, p. B1.

27. Senators Moynihan, Lieberman and Breaux cosponsored S.2184, Kerrey's "KidSave" bill in the 105th Congress. Robert Kuttner, "Rampant Bull," *The American Prospect,* vol. 9, no. 39 (July–August 1998), pp. 30–36. Similar proposals have been offered by Republican Senator Rick Santorum of Pennsylvania. J. Larry Brown and Larry W. Beeferman, "From New Deal to New Opportunity," *The American Prospect,* vol. 12, no. 3 (February 12, 2001), pp. 24–27; and Ray Boshara, "The $6,000 Solution," *Atlantic Monthly,* vol. 291, no. 1 (January–February 2003), pp. 91–95.

28. Freeman, "Solving the New Inequality," pp. 16–17.

29. Bruce Ackerman and Anne Alstott, *The Stakeholder Society* (New Haven: Yale University Press, 1999). Ultimately, Ackerman and Alstott hope the stakeholder grant will become largely self-financing. At the end of the stakeholder's life, the $80,000 would be returned to the government.

30. John E. Roemer, *A Future for Socialism* (Cambridge, Mass.: Harvard University Press, 1994); John E. Roemer, *Equal Shares: Making Market Socialism Work,* ed. Erik Olin Wright (New York: Verso Books, 1996). Roemer would also prohibit private investment in stock other than through the use of coupons, thus making this the only source of investment.

31. Leland Stauber, *A New Program for Democratic Socialism* (Carbondale, Ill.: Four Willows Press, 1987), p. 339.

32. J. E. Meade, *Liberty, Equality, and Efficiency* (New York: New York University Press, 1993), p. 199. Anthony B. Atkinson, "James Meade's Vision: Full Employment and Social Justice," *National Institute Economic Review,* no. 157 (July 1996), pp. 90–96.

33. Louis Kelso and Mortimer Adler, *The Capitalist Manifesto* (New York: Random House, 1958), pp. 241–251. For further detail on the design of the plan see Louis Kelso and Mortimer Adler, *The New Capitalists* (New York: Random House, 1961).

34. Stuart Speiser, *Superstock* (New York: Everest House Publishers, 1982), pp. 50–51 (emphasis in the original).

35. William Greider, *One World Ready or Not: The Manic Logic of Global Capitalism* (New York: Simon & Schuster, 1997), p. 418. See also his book *The Soul of Capitalism: Opening Paths to a Moral Economy* (New York: Simon & Schuster, 2003).

2. LIBERTY: MONEY, TIME, AND REAL FREEDOM OF CHOICE

1. Milton Friedman, *Capitalism and Freedom* (Chicago: University of Chicago Press, 1962), pp. 2–3, 8, 15; Friedrich A. Hayek, *The Road to Serfdom* (Chicago: University of Chicago Press, 1944); and Henry C. Simons, *Economic Policy for a Free Society* (Chicago: University of Chicago Press, 1948), p. 23.

2. Friedman, *Capitalism and Freedom,* p. 201.
3. The 1902 figure, based on statistics then available and not directly comparable to the modern 2002 figure, is nonetheless a serviceable approximation. Total government expenditures as a share of GDP were 30.6 percent in 2003: Office of Management and Budget, *Budget of the United States Government: Historical Tables, Fiscal Year 2005* (Washington, D.C.: Government Printing Office, 2004), www.gpoaccess.gov/usbudget/, table 15.3. For 1902 figures see U.S. Census Bureau, *Historical Statistics of the United States, Colonial Times to 1970, Bicentennial Edition* (Washington, D.C.: Government Printing Office, 1975), pp. 1, 120 (government expenditures), 224 (GDP). A more comprehensive measure of state and local government expenditure (including government enterprises and insurance trusts) brings total government expenditure to around 36–37 percent of GDP. U.S. Census Bureau State and Local Government Finances, www.census.gov/govs/www/estimate.html (accessed 10/21/03); for an explanation of the difference between the two measures, see Bureau of Economic Analysis National Income and Product Accounts Table 3.19, www.bea.gov/bea/dn/nipaweb/ (accessed 10/21/03). Milton Friedman estimates that "roughly 40% of our income . . . is spent by government—federal, state and local" and an "additional 10% or so of income [is spent by] residents or businesses in response to government mandates and regulation." Milton Friedman, "What Every American Wants," *Wall Street Journal,* January 15, 2003, p. A10. Bureau of Economic Analysis National Income and Product Accounts Table 1.1, www.bea.gov/bea/dn/nipaweb/ (accessed 10/21/03). The percentages, of course, vary from year to year—in part depending on whether the economy is in boom or recession (thereby altering the denominator of the fraction of government's share). For the 8 percent estimate of regulatory costs see W. Mark Crain and Thomas D. Hopkins, "The Impact of Regulatory Costs on Small Firms," U.S. Small Business Administration, Washington, D.C., July 2001, www.sba.gov/ADVO/research/rs207tot.pdf (accessed 10/21/03). For a recent overview—and interpretation of—the literature on regulation, see Edward L. Glaeser and Andrei Shleifer, "The Rise of the Regulatory State," *Journal of Economic Literature,* vol. 41, no. 2 (June 2003), pp. 401–425.
4. Eisenhower left office with federal spending at 18.4 percent of GDP, the Nixon/Ford administrations ended with spending at 20.8 percent of GDP, Reagan at 21.2 percent, and the first Bush administration at 21.5 percent. See *Economic Report of the President 2003* (Washington, D.C.: Government Printing Office, 2003), table B-79, p. 370. The current Bush administration's first two budgets both anticipated an increase in the ratio of government spending to GDP. Office of Management and Budget, *Budget of the United States 2002: Historical Tables* (Washington, D.C.: Government Printing Office, 2001), w3.access .gpo.gov/usbudget/ (accessed 11/11/02), tables 1.1, 10.1; and Office of Management and Budget, *Budget of the United States 2003: Historical Tables,* (Washington, D.C.: Government Printing Office, 2002), w3.access.gpo.gov/usbudget/ (accessed 11/11/02), tables 1.1, 10.1.
5. Regarding conservative dismay, see also Stuart M. Butler, "The Medicare Drug Bill: An Impending Disaster for All Americans," The Heritage Foundation, Web-Memo #293, June 13, 2003, www.heritage.org/Research/HealthCare/wm293 .cfm (accessed 09/05/03). Another indicator of the unyielding reality is the number of people employed directly and indirectly (through contracts and grants) by government—a figure which increased from 11 million in October

1999 to 12.1 million in October 2002. See Paul C. Light, "Fact Sheet on the New True Size of Government," Center for Public Service, Brookings Institution, Washington, D.C., September 5, 2003, www.brookings.org/dybdocroot/gs/cps/light20030905.pdf (accessed 09/10/03); and Office of Management and Budget, *Budget of the United States Government, Fiscal Year 2005* (Washington, D.C.: Government Printing Office, 2004), www.gpoaccess.gov/usbudget/, table S.13.

6. For a statement of continuing conservative strategies aimed at starving government through fiscal crowding-out, see Grover Norquist, "Step-by-Step Tax Reform," *Washington Post,* June 9, 2003, p. A21. For a review of various failed attempts to curtail the general size of government, see Joseph White and Aaron Wildavsky, *The Deficit and the Public Interest: The Search for Responsible Budgeting in the 1980s* (Berkeley: University of California Press, 1989), pp. 78–81. The frustration of conservatives is captured in Fred Barnes and Grover Norquist, "The Politics of Less: A Debate on Big-Government Conservatism," *Policy Review,* no. 55 (Winter 1991), pp. 66–71. Similar frustrations are expressed in Murray Weidenbaum, "Progress in Federal Regulatory Policy, 1980–2000," *Contemporary Issues Series 100* (St. Louis: Center for the Study of American Business, 2000); and Stephen Moore, "Not-So-Radical Republicans," *Reason,* vol. 30, no. 3 (July 1998), pp. 24–32.

7. Mancur Olson, *The Logic of Collective Action: Public Goods and the Theory of Groups* (Cambridge, Mass.: Harvard University Press, 1965); James M. Buchanan and Gordon Tullock, *The Calculus of Consent* (Ann Arbor: University of Michigan Press, 1962); James Buchanan, *The Limits of Liberty: Between Anarchy and Leviathan* (Chicago: University of Chicago Press, 1975), pp. 147–165; Anthony Downs, *An Economic Theory of Democracy* (New York: Harper & Row, 1957); and George Stigler, "The Theory of Economic Regulation," in *The Politics of American Economic Policy Making,* 2nd ed., ed. Paul Peretz (Armonk, N.Y.: M. E. Sharpe, 1987), pp. 60–75.

8. Robert Higgs, *Crisis and Leviathan: Critical Episodes in the Growth of American Government* (New York: Oxford University Press, 1987).

9. David A. Stockman, *The Triumph of Politics: How the Reagan Revolution Failed* (New York: Harper & Row, 1986), p. 13; and Milton and Rose Friedman, *Two Lucky People: Memoirs* (Chicago: University of Chicago Press, 1998), p. 588.

10. "The Share-of-Market Picture for 1999: 1999 Core Appliance Market Share," *Appliance,* vol. 57, no. 9 (September 2000), p. 85; "Discounters Continue to Make Gains," *Chain Drug Review,* vol. 24, no. 2 (January 21, 2002), p. 17; "Big Business: Why the Sudden Rise in the Urge to Merge and Form Oligopolies?" *Wall Street Journal,* February 25, 2002, p. A1; and "Coke's Share of Market Rises," *Atlanta Journal-Constitution,* February 25, 2003, p. D1. The modern literature on market concentration is primarily concerned with the impact concentration may have on prices; it largely eschews questions related to liberty and other political matters. One of the few recent articles to address broader issues, albeit through the lens of aggregate as opposed to market concentration, is Lawrence White, "Trends in Aggregate Concentration in the United States," *Journal of Economic Perspectives,* vol. 16, no. 4 (Fall 2002), pp.137–160; see also Edward Nissan, "Measuring Trends in Sales Concentration in American Business," *Quarterly Journal of Business and Economics,* vol. 36, no. 1 (Winter 1997), pp. 17–34. An important related study of corporate trends is Naomi R. Lamoreaux, Daniel M. G. Raff, and Peter Temin, "Beyond Markets and Hierar-

chies: Toward a New Synthesis of American Business History," *American Historical Review*, vol. 108, no. 2 (April 2003), pp. 404–433.

11. David C. Korten, *When Corporations Rule the World* (San Francisco: Berrett-Koehler, 2001), p. 210; and Noreena Hertz, *The Silent Takeover: Global Capitalism and the Death of Democracy* (London: William Heinemann, 2001), pp. 7, 33–34.

12. William E. Simon, *A Time for Truth* (New York: McGraw-Hill, 1978), p. 196.

13. Simons, *Economic Policy for a Free Society*, p. 34.

14. Hayek, *The Road to Serfdom*, pp. 194–195. It is often forgotten that Hayek saw the general movement in this direction as "planned mainly by the capitalist organizers of monopolies, and they are thus one of the main sources of this danger."

15. Marc Eisner, *Antitrust and the Triumph of Economics* (Chapel Hill: University of North Carolina Press, 1991), p. 235; and Walter Adams, "Dissolution, Divorcement, Divestiture: The Pyrrhic Victories of Antitrust," in *Antitrust, the Market, and the State: The Contributions of Walter Adams*, ed. James Brock and Kenneth Elzinga (Armonk, N.Y.: M.E. Sharpe, 1991), p. 191.

16. Eisner, *Antitrust and the Triumph of Economics;* Robert Bork, *The Antitrust Paradox: A Policy at War with Itself* (Chicago: University of Chicago Press, 1978), pp. 7–9; and William Safire, "The Urge to Converge," *New York Times*, March 7, 2002, p. A31.

17. Thomas Jefferson, "Notes on the State of Virginia," and Letter to John Adams, "The Natural Aristocracy," October 28, 1813, in *The Portable Jefferson*, ed. Merrill D. Peterson (New York: Penguin Books, 1977), pp. 217, 538.

18. Woodrow Wilson, *The New Freedom* (Englewood Cliffs, N.J.: Prentice-Hall, 1961), pp. 166–167, quoted in Michael J. Sandel, *Democracy's Discontent: America in Search of a Public Philosophy* (Cambridge, Mass.: Belknap Press, 1996), p. 216; and Louis Brandeis, *Business: A Profession* (New York: Augustus M. Kelley, 1971), p. 53.

19. Friedrich A. Hayek, *The Constitution of Liberty* (Chicago: The University of Chicago Press, 1960), pp. 118–132.

20. Robert Nisbet, *Twilight of Authority* (New York: Oxford University Press, 1975), p. 195; and Robert Nisbet, *The Quest for Community: A Study in the Ethics of Order and Freedom* (San Francisco: Institute for Contemporary Studies Press, 1990), p. 237.

21. Nisbet, *The Quest for Community*, p. 238. Recent scholarship has challenged the theory that atomization led to the rise of Nazism: see, for example, Sheri Berman, "Civil Society and the Collapse of the Weimar Republic," *World Politics*, vol. 49, no. 3 (April 1997), pp. 401–429.

22. Peter Berger, *Facing Up to Modernity* (New York: Basic Books, 1977), pp. 137, 141 (emphasis in the original).

23. Peter F. Drucker, "The Job as Property Right," *Wall Street Journal*, March 4, 1980, p. 24.

24. The Humphrey-Hawkins Full Employment and Balanced Growth Act, as initially offered in 1975, would have established a Federal Job Guarantee office and the right of "all adult Americans able and willing to work" to opportunities for "useful paid employment at fair rates of compensation." It directed "all practical means" to the achievement of full employment (set at 3 percent unemployment). The bill that passed into law omitted or watered down these provisions, and simply set "as a national goal the fulfillment of the right to full

opportunities for useful paid employment at fair rates of compensation of all individuals able, willing, and seeking to work." See Equal Opportunity and Full Employment Act, S. 50, 94th Congress; and Full Employment and Balanced Growth Act, H.R. 50, 95th Congress. On the subject of tenure and academic freedom see Anthony O'Hear, "Academic Freedom and the University," in *Academic Freedom and Responsibility,* ed. Malcolm Tight (Philadelphia: Open University Press, 1988).

25. Edward Luttwak, *Turbo-Capitalism* (New York: HarperCollins, 1999), p. 68.

26. Alan Ryan, "Please Fence Me In," *New York Review of Books,* vol. 46, no. 14 (September 23, 1999), pp. 68–72; and Alan Ryan, *Property* (Minneapolis: University of Minnesota Press, 1987), p. 87.

27. Stephen Holmes and Cass R. Sunstein, *The Cost of Rights: Why Liberty Depends on Taxes* (New York: W. W. Norton, 1999), pp. 14–15.

28. Walter Lippmann quoted in Benjamin Kline Hunnicutt, *Work Without End: Abandoning Shorter Hours for the Right to Work* (Philadelphia: Temple University Press, 1988), p. 262; John Maynard Keynes, "Economic Possibilities for Our Grandchildren," (1930) in John Maynard Keynes, *Essays in Persuasion* (New York: W. W. Norton, 1963), pp. 365, 367; and Herbert Marcuse, *Eros and Civilization* (Boston: Beacon Press, 1966), p. 152.

29. Joseph Zeisel, "The Workweek in American Industry, 1850–1956," *Monthly Labor Review,* vol. 81, no. 1 (January 1958), pp. 23–29; Juliet B. Schor, *The Overworked American: The Unexpected Decline of Leisure* (New York: Basic Books, 1991); Hunnicutt, *Work Without End*; and Jerome M. Segal, *Graceful Simplicity: Toward a Philosophy and Politics of Simple Living* (New York: Henry Holt, 1999).

30. The Bush Administration proposed regulatory changes to overtime laws in 2003 that could have made more than 8 million white-collar employees ineligible for overtime pay. However, as of this writing, both the Senate and the House of Representatives have voted to block the changes. See Ross Eisenbrey and Jared Bernstein, "Eliminating the Right to Overtime Pay: Department of Labor Proposal Means Lower Pay, Longer Hours for Millions of Workers," EPI Briefing Paper (Washington, D.C.: Economic Policy Institute, June 2003), www.epinet.org/briefingpapers/flsa_jun03.pdf (accessed 09/05/03); and Juliet Eilperin, "In a Switch, House Rejects Bush Overtime Proposal," *Washington Post,* October 3, 2003, p. A2.

31. Segal, *Graceful Simplicity,* pp. 93–94.

32. Philippe Van Parijs, *Real Freedom for All: What (If Anything) Can Justify Capitalism?* (Oxford: Clarendon Press, 1995), p. 33 (emphasis in the original). Thomas Paine may have been the first to argue for a basic income grant in 1796: Thomas Paine, "Agrarian Justice," in *The Life and Major Writings of Thomas Paine,* ed. Philip S. Foner (Secaucus, N.J.: Citadel Press, 1974). Others arguing for a basic income, for various reasons, include: Bill Jordan, *The State: Authority and Autonomy* (Oxford: Basil Blackwell, 1995), pp. 266–269; Alan Carling, *Social Division* (London: Verso, 1991); James E. Meade, *Liberty, Equality, and Efficiency* (New York: New York University Press, 1993); Bruce Ackerman and Anne Alstott, *The Stakeholder Society* (New Haven: Yale University Press, 1999); *Arguing for Basic Income,* ed. Philippe Van Parijs (London: Verso, 1992); and Robley E. George, *Socioeconomic Democracy: An Advanced Socioeconomic System* (Westport, Conn.: Praeger, 2002).

33. James M. Buchanan, "Can Democracy Promote the General Welfare," *Social Philosophy and Policy,* vol. 14, no. 2 (1997), p. 171. Regarding the Negative

Income Tax see Friedman, *Capitalism and Freedom*, p. 192. (The Earned Income Tax Credit differs from the Negative Income Tax in that it is available only to those who earn some income.)

34. Eric Foner, *The Story of American Freedom* (New York: W. W. Norton, 1998), p. 20. Alexis de Tocqueville, *Democracy in America* (New York: Knopf, 1946), vol. 1, p. 3.

35. John Dewey quoted in Foner, *The Story of American Freedom*, p. 153. E. J. Dionne, *They Only Look Dead: Why Progressives Will Dominate the Next Political Era* (New York: Simon & Schuster, 1996), p. 291.

36. Alan Ryan, *Property* (Minneapolis: University of Minnesota Press, 1987), p. 84; and Amartya Sen, *Development as Freedom* (New York: Knopf, 1999), p. 75.

3. DEMOCRACY: FROM THE GROUND UP

1. Robert D. Putnam, *Making Democracy Work: Civic Traditions in Modern Italy* (Princeton: Princeton University Press, 1993), p. 3; and Ronald Brownstein, "Poll Says Americans Deeply Discouraged With State of Nation," *Houston Chronicle*, November 5, 1995, p. 2. See also Jeffrey C. Isaac, *The Poverty of Progressivism: The Future of American Democracy in a Time of Liberal Decline* (Lanham, Md.: Rowman & Littlefield, 2003).

2. Robert D. Putnam, *Bowling Alone: The Collapse and Revival of American Community* (New York: Simon & Schuster, 2000); and "Better Together," revised ed., Report of the Saguaro Seminar (Cambridge, Mass.: Harvard University, 2002), www.bettertogether.org/report.php3 (accessed 04/04/03).

3. William A. Galston, "Won't You Be My Neighbor?" *The American Prospect*, vol. 7, no. 26 (May–June 1996), p. 16–18. For assessments of Putnam's thesis, see Eric Uslaner, *The Moral Foundations of Trust* (New York: Cambridge University Press, 2002); *Civil Society, Democracy, and Civic Renewal*, ed. Robert K. Fullinwider (Lanham, Md.: Rowman & Littlefield, 1999); and *Civic Engagement in American Democracy*, ed. Theda Skocpol and Morris P. Fiorina (Washington, D.C.: Brookings Institution Press, 1999).

4. Alexis de Tocqueville, *Democracy in America*, ed. J. P. Mayer, trans. George Lawrence (Garden City, N.Y.: Doubleday, 1969), p. 517; and Robert Nisbet, *The Quest for Community* (San Francisco: ICS Press, 1990).

5. Alexis de Tocqueville, *Democracy in America* (New York: Vintage Books, 1960), vol. 1, p. 63, as quoted in Benjamin Barber, *Strong Democracy* (Berkeley: University of California Press, 1984), p. 234; John Stuart Mill, *On Liberty*, ed. Elizabeth Rapaport (Indianapolis: Hackett Publishing, 1978), p. 108; and John Stuart Mill, "Tocqueville on Democracy in America (Vol. I)," in *Essays on Politics and Culture*, ed. Gertrude Himmelfarb (Garden City, N.Y.: Doubleday, 1962), pp. 200–201.

6. Stephen L. Elkin, "Citizen and City," in *Dilemmas of Scale in America's Federal Democracy* (Woodrow Wilson Center series), ed. Martha K. Derthick (New York: Cambridge University Press, 1999), p. 59.

7. Jane J. Mansbridge, *Beyond Adversary Democracy* (New York: Basic Books, 1980), p. 289; Michael J. Sandel, *Democracy's Discontent: America in Search of a Public Philosophy* (Cambridge, Mass.: Belknap Press, 1996), p. 202. For recent developments in participatory theory and practice—including the participatory budget in Porto Alegre, Brazil—see Archon Fung and Eric Olin Wright (eds.), *Deepening Democracy: Institutional Innovations in Empowered Participatory Gover-*

nance (New York: Verso, 2003); and Hilary Wainwright, *Reclaim the State: Experiments in Popular Democracy* (New York: Verso, 2003).

8. Barber, *Strong Democracy,* pp. 234–235.

9. Friedrich A. Hayek, *The Road to Serfdom* (Chicago: University of Chicago Press, 1944), p. 235.

10. Hannah Arendt, *On Revolution* (New York: Viking Press, 1963), p. 257; and Jane Jacobs, *The Death and Life of Great American Cities* (New York: The Modern Library, 1961), p. 423.

11. J. Phillip Thompson III, "Universalism and Deconcentration: Why Race Still Matters in Poverty and Economic Development," *Politics and Society,* vol. 26, no. 2 (June 1998), p. 208.

12. Amie Jamieson, Hyon B. Shin, and Jennifer Day, "Voting and Registration in the Election of November 2000," U.S. Census Bureau, Current Population Reports, P20-542 (February 2002), available online at www.census.gov/prod/2002pubs/p20-542.pdf (accessed 10/24/02); and Sidney Verba, Kay Lehman Schlozman, and Henry E. Brady, *Voice and Equality: Civic Voluntarism in American Politics* (Cambridge: Harvard University Press, 1995), pp. 452–455. See also Putnam, *Bowling Alone,* pp. 204–205 and related citations. Thad Williamson, David Imbroscio, and Gar Alperovitz, *Making a Place for Community: Local Democracy in a Global Era* (New York: Routledge, 2002), p. 350, note 6.

13. Paul E. Peterson, *City Limits* (Chicago: University of Chicago Press, 1981), p. 30. See also Gerald E. Frug, "The City as a Legal Concept," *Harvard Law Review,* vol. 93, no. 6 (April 1980), pp. 1053–1154; *The Politics of Urban Development,* ed. Clarence N. Stone and Heywood T. Sanders (Lawrence: University Press of Kansas, 1987); *Beyond the City Limits: Urban Policy and Economic Restructuring in Comparative Perspective,* ed. John R. Logan and Todd Swanstrom (Philadelphia: Temple University Press, 1990); and David L. Imbroscio, "The Necessity of Urban Regime Change," *Journal of Urban Affairs,* vol. 20, no. 3, pp. 261–268.

14. David L. Imbroscio, "Restructuring the Urban Political Economy: Local States, Urban Regimes, and the Centrality of Mobile Capital," Paper presented at the Annual Meeting of the Midwest Political Science Association, Chicago, Illinois, April 5–7, 1990, p. 26. See also James DeFilippis, "Alternatives to the 'New Urban Politics': Finding Locality and Autonomy in Local Economic Development," *Political Geography,* vol. 18, no. 8 (1999), pp. 973–990.

15. On public "anchors," see David L. Imbroscio, *Reconstructing City Politics* (Thousand Oaks, Calif.: Sage, 1997), pp. 32–33; Ann Markusen, Peter Hall, Scott Campbell, and Sabina Deitrick, *The Rise of the Gunbelt: The Military Remapping of Industrial America* (New York: Oxford University Press, 1991), pp. 244–245; Arthur C. Nelson, "Theories of Regional Development," in *Theories of Local Economic Development,* ed. Richard D. Bingham and Robert Mier (Newbury Park, Calif.: Sage, 1993), p. 47; John R. Logan and Harvey L. Molotch, *Urban Fortunes* (Berkeley: University of California Press, 1987), pp. 292–293; and Wim Wiewel, Michael Teitz, and Robert Giloth, "The Economic Development of Neighborhoods and Localities," in *Theories of Local Economic Development,* ed. Richard D. Bingham and Robert Mier (Newbury Park, Calif.: Sage, 1993), p. 96.

16. Michael H. Shuman, "Going Local: Devolution for Progressives," *The Nation,* vol. 267, no. 11 (October 12, 1998), pp. 11–15. See also Michael H. Shuman, *Going Local: Creating Self-Reliant Communities in a Global Age* (New York: Routledge, 2000).

4. DEMOCRACY: INEQUALITY
AND GIANT CORPORATIONS

1. Robert A. Dahl, *Democracy and Its Critics* (New Haven: Yale University Press, 1989), p. 326.
2. John Green, Paul Herrnson, Lynda Powell, and Clyde Wilcox, "Individual Congressional Campaign Contributors: Wealthy, Conservative and Reform-Minded" (Center for Responsive Politics, June 9, 1998), www.opensecrets.org/pubs/donors/donors.htm (accessed 10/24/02); and Sidney Verba, Kay Lehman Schlozman, and Henry E. Brady, "The Big Tilt: Participatory Inequality in America," *The American Prospect*, no. 32 (May–June 1997), p. 76.
3. Michael Lind, *The Next American Nation* (New York: The Free Press, 1995), p. 156.
4. Larry Makinson, *The Big Picture: The Money Behind the 2000 Elections* (Washington, D.C.: The Center for Responsive Politics, 2001), p. 7.
5. William Greider, *Who Will Tell the People: The Betrayal of American Democracy* (New York: Simon & Schuster, 1992), p. 35.
6. "Squash the Jell-O," *Washington Post* editorial, February 13, 2002, p. A26; and CNN/*USA Today*/Gallup, February 13, 2002, via Polling the Nations database.
7. Benjamin R. Barber, *A Place for Us: How To Make Society Civil and Democracy Strong* (New York: Hill and Wang, 1998), pp. 127, 141.
8. There is an extensive literature on both the left and the right on these issues—including, by way of introduction, the works by George Stigler, Marver Bernstein, James Q. Wilson, and Charles Lindblom cited below. See also Thomas Ferguson, *Golden Rule: The Investment Theory of Party Competition and the Logic of Money-Driven Political Systems* (Chicago: University of Chicago Press, 1995); Kevin B. Grier, Michael C. Munger, and Brian E. Roberts, "The Industrial Organization of Corporate Political Participation," *Southern Economic Journal*, vol. 57, no. 3 (1991), pp. 727–738; Kim McQuaid, *Uneasy Partners: Big Business in American Politics, 1945–1990* (Baltimore: Johns Hopkins University Press, 1994); G. William Domhoff, *Who Rules America? Power and Politics*, 4th ed. (Boston: McGraw-Hill, 2002); Charles Perrow, *Organizing America: Wealth, Power, and the Origins of Corporate Capitalism* (Princeton: Princeton University Press, 2002); and Lawrence R. Jacobs and Robert Y. Shapiro, *Politicians Don't Pander* (Chicago: University of Chicago Press, 2000).
9. For union labor force decline, see pp. 14–15 in this book. For data on corporate income taxes, see pp. 15–16 in this book. For business donations versus labor donations, see OpenSecrets.org, "Election Overview, 2000 Cycle, Business-Labor-Ideology Split in PAC, Soft and Individual Donations to Candidates and Parties," www.opensecrets.org/overview/blio.asp?Cycle=2000 (accessed 10/25/02).
10. Robert D. Kaplan, "Was Democracy Just a Moment?" *Atlantic Monthly*, vol. 280, no. 6 (December 1997), pp. 55–80, esp. pp. 71, 73.
11. Charles E. Lindblom, *Politics and Markets* (New York: Basic Books, 1977), p. 356.
12. Jacob M. Schlesinger, "What's Wrong? The Deregulators: Did Washington Help Set Stage for Current Business Turmoil?" *Wall Street Journal*, October 17, 2002, p. A1.
13. OMB Watch, "Safeguards Weakened or Revoked," March 28, 2002, www.ombwatch.org/article/articleview/195/110 (accessed 04/04/03); David S. Broder, "Bush's Stealthy Pursuit of a Partisan Agenda," *Washington Post*,

January 2, 2002, p. A13; "Environmental Policy: A Scorecard," *New York Times*, February 23, 2003, p. A23; "An Unsettling Settlement," *The Economist*, November 10, 2001; and Stephen Labaton, "F.C.C. Votes to Relax Rules Limiting Media Ownership," *New York Times*, June 3, 2003. As of this writing the FCC's move has been challenged in Congress, and may be reversed.

14. Marver H. Bernstein, *Regulating Business by Independent Commission* (Princeton: Princeton University Press, 1955), pp. 155–156.

15. George Stigler, "The Theory of Economic Regulation," *Bell Journal of Economics and Management Science*, vol. 2, no. 1 (1971), pp. 3–21, esp. p. 3. James Q. Wilson, *The Politics of Regulation*, ed. James Q. Wilson (New York: Basic Books, 1980), p. x; and Ralph Nader, "Introduction," *The Monopoly Makers: Ralph Nader's Study Group Report on Regulation and Competition*, ed. by Mark J. Green (New York: Gossman Publishers, 1973), p. ix.

16. William E. Simon, *A Time for Truth* (New York: Berkeley Books, 1979), p. 210; and William Greider, "The Education of David Stockman," *Atlantic Monthly*, vol. 248, no. 6 (December 1981), p. 52.

17. Henry C. Simons, *Economic Policy for a Free Society* (Chicago: University of Chicago Press, 1948), pp. 44, 51, 87–88, 195.

18. See Robert Kuttner, *Everything for Sale: The Virtues and Limits of Markets* (Chicago: University of Chicago Press, 1999).

19. The corporation was granted many of the rights of a natural "person" by Supreme Court interpretation of the Fourteenth Amendment in 1886. Histories written from different perspectives include Alfred D. Chandler Jr.'s *Scale and Scope: The Dynamics of Industrial Capitalism*, reprint ed. (Cambridge, Mass.: Belknap Press, 1994) and *The Visible Hand: The Managerial Revolution in American Business* (Cambridge, Mass.: Belknap Press, 1977); *The Nature of the Firm: Origins, Evolution, and Development*, ed. Oliver E. Williamson and Sidney G. Winter (New York: Oxford University Press, 1991); William G. Roy, *Socializing Capital: The Rise of the Large Industrial Corporation in America* (Princeton: Princeton University Press, 1997); and Naomi R. Lamoreaux, Daniel M.G. Raff, and Peter Temin, "Beyond Markets and Hierarchies: Toward a New Synthesis of American Business History," *American Historical Review*, vol. 108, no. 2 (April 2003), pp. 404–433. Marjorie Kelly, the publisher of *Business Ethics*, has proposed a "national dialogue on redefining the corporation" to replace the current patchwork of legal precedent and to clarify and redefine the legal status of the corporation. Hofstra Law professor Carl Mayer, among others, has suggested a constitutional amendment stating the corporation is not a natural person. Marjorie Kelly, *The Divine Right of Capital: Dethroning the Corporate Aristocracy* (San Francisco: Berrett-Koehler, 2001), pp. 165–166.

20. For proposals to federalize and reform corporate charters, see Kent Greenfield, "It's Time to Federalize Corporate Charters," *TomPaine.com* (July 26, 2002) and *Alternatives to Economic Globalization: A Better World Is Possible*, A Report of the International Forum on Globalization (San Francisco: Berrett-Koehler, 2002), pp. 126–130; and Charles Derber, *Corporation Nation* (New York: St. Martin's Press, 1998), pp. 256–257.

21. Michael Lerner, "Social Responsibility Amendment and Initiative," *Tikkun*, vol. 12, no. 4 (July–August 1997).

22. An early proposal was made by R. Edward Freeman, a University of Virginia business ethics professor, in *Strategic Management: A Stakeholder Approach* (Boston: Pitman, 1984). British journalist and chief executive of the London-

based Work Foundation, Will Hutton did much to popularize the idea: see Ben Webb, "The Big Idea?" *New Statesman and Society,* vol. 9, no. 396 (March 29, 1996), pp. 18–20; and Ralph Estes, "New Millennium Capitalism: Business for the Benefit of All Stakeholders," www.stakeholderalliance.org/newmillen.html (accessed 06/15/02). See also Derber, *Corporation Nation,* pp. 218–219, 250–254; and Kelly, *Divine Right of Capital,* pp. 138–139, 147–150.

23. See, for example, Kim Moody, *Workers in a Lean World: Unions in the International Economy* (New York: Verso, 1997), pp. 93–108. This has long been a criticism from the Left: see Tony Benn, *Arguments for Socialism* (London: Penguin, 1979), p. 64.

24. Seymour Melman, *After Capitalism* (New York: Knopf, 2001), p. 395; David Ellerman, "The Democratic Firm: A 'Non-Economic' Approach to the Problem of Distribution Based on Property Theory and Democratic Theory," Paper presented at a 1998 conference at the Brookings Institution on the Corporation and Human Capital, www.ellerman.org/Econ&Pol-Econ/Brookings%20(1). DOC (accessed 10/10/02); and Robert A. Dahl, *A Preface to Economic Democracy* (Berkeley: University of California Press, 1985), p. 110. Ellerman's early work informed Dahl's book.

25. "Largest Study Yet Shows ESOPs Improve Performance and Employee Benefits" (NCEO, n.d.), www.nceo.org/library/esop_perf.html (appeared 11/08/02); NCEO, "Employee Ownership and Corporate Performance" (NCEO, 2001), www.nceo.org/library/corpperf.html (appeared 11/08/02); and Justin Fox, "Giving Workers a Voice Increases Productivity," *NBER Digest* (May 1998).

26. Peter F. Drucker, *The Unseen Revolution: How Pension Fund Socialism Came to America* (New York: Harper & Row, 1976); Jeremy Rifkin and Randy Barber, *The North Will Rise Again: Pensions, Politics and Power in the 1980s* (Boston: Beacon Press, 1978); Robin Blackburn, *Banking on Death* (London: Verso, 2002); and Archon Fung, Tessa Hebb, and Joel Rogers, ed., *Working Capital: The Power of Labor's Pensions* (Ithaca, N.Y.: Cornell University Press, 2001). William Greider's book, *The Soul of Capitalism: Opening Paths to a Moral Economy* (New York: Simon & Schuster, 2003), which appeared as this work was in the final stages of preparation, is a useful introduction to many of these themes.

27. Robert Collier, "State Employees' Pension Fund Flexes Its Muscle Around the World," *San Francisco Chronicle* (July 21, 2002), p. A12; Carolyn Said, "Risk a Bigger Factor for Funds: Scandals Force New Strategies," *San Francisco Chronicle,* July 28, 2002, p. G1; Anitha Reddy, "Calif. Funds Urged to Bar Tax-Haven Investments," *Washington Post,* July 26, 2002, p. E1; and Julie Earle, "When Public and Private Worlds Collide: A Series of Market Crises Has Pushed US Pension Funds into Taking Stronger Action," *Financial Times* (London), July 8, 2002, p. 20.

28. See John E. Roemer, *A Future for Socialism* (Cambridge, Mass.: Harvard University Press, 1994). For a critical view see Doug Henwood, *Wall Street: How It Works and for Whom* (New York: Verso, 1998), pp. 289–293.

29. Joan Pryde, "Shareholder Activists to Flex New Muscle," *Kiplinger Business Forecasts,* vol. 2002, no. 1011 (October 8, 2002), via LexisNexis.

5. DEMOCRACY: IS A CONTINENT TOO LARGE?

1. Quoted in David McCullough, *John Adams* (New York: Simon & Schuster, 2001), p. 397. For a discussion of Montesquieu's arguments on scale and democracy—in particular, his *The Spirit of the Laws*—see Robert A. Dahl and

Edward R. Tufte, *Size and Democracy* (Stanford, Calif.: Stanford University Press, 1973), pp. 6–9.

2. For an insightful discussion related to the Civil War, see William Appleman Williams, *The Contours of American History* (New York: World Publishing Company, 1961), pp. 255–300 and specific citations therein to the ideas of Calhoun.

3. Frederick Jackson Turner, *The Significance of Sections in American History* (New York: Henry Holt, 1932), pp. 45, 194.

4. William Yandell Elliott, *The Need for Constitutional Reform: A Program for National Security* (New York: McGraw-Hill, 1935), p. 193.

5. Henry C. Simons, *Economic Policy for a Free Society* (Chicago: University of Chicago Press, 1948), pp. 12, 21.

6. William Bennett Munro, *The Invisible Government* (New York: Macmillan, 1928), pp. 137, 153–154.

7. Philip Selznick, *TVA and the Grass Roots* (New York: Harper & Row, 1966); and Martha Derthick, *Between State and Nation: Regional Organizations of the United States* (Washington, D.C.: Brookings, 1974).

8. Paul Taylor, "Free and Fair TV Spots," *Washington Post,* July 8, 2001, p. B7; and Dave Umhoefer, "Bush Camp Was Outspent on TV Spots in 2 Markets," *Milwaukee Journal Sentinel,* December 12, 2000, p. B2.

9. *OECD in Figures: Statistics on the Member Countries* (Paris: OECD, 2002), pp. 6–7.

10. Dahl and Tufte, *Size and Democracy*, p. 2. A related academic statement of the problem is that of Larry Diamond, Hoover Institution senior fellow and coeditor of the *Journal of Democracy:* "Since most states are not likely to get smaller in size . . . other ways must be found to reduce the scale of democracy as it is experienced by citizens in their daily lives. This means devolution of power: federalism and regional autonomy in countries whose scale and complexity call for it and whose culture and politics permit it." Larry Diamond, *Developing Democracy: Toward Consolidation* (Baltimore: Johns Hopkins University Press, 1999), pp. 119–120.

11. Daniel Bell, "The World and the United States in 2013," *Dædalus,* vol. 116, no. 3 (Summer 1987), p. 14.

12. George F. Kennan, *Around the Cragged Hill: A Personal and Political Philosophy* (New York: W.W. Norton, 1993), pp. 143, 149.

13. William Appleman Williams, *The Great Evasion* (Chicago: Quadrangle Books, 1964), p. 175; Donald Livingston, "Dismantling Leviathan," from *Chronicles* (January 2002), reprinted in *Harper's,* vol. 304, no. 1824 (May 2002), pp. 13–17, esp. p. 17.

14. Thomas H. Naylor and William H. Willimon, *Downsizing the U.S.A.* (Grand Rapids, Mich.: William B. Erdmans, 1997); Joel Garreau, *The Nine Nations of North America* (Boston: Houghton Mifflin, 1981); and Robert Goodman, *The Last Entrepreneurs: America's Regional Wars for Jobs and Dollars* (New York: Simon & Schuster, 1979).

15. Mary Graham, "Why States Can Do More," *The American Prospect,* vol. 9, no. 36 (January–February 1998), pp. 63–60, 70; Kirkpatrick Sale, *Dwellers in the Land: The Bioregional Vision* (San Francisco: Sierra Club Books, 1985); and World Wildlife Fund, "Ecoregions Project Snapshot," www.worldwildlife.org/ecoregions/related_projects.htm (accessed 04/09/03). Frank Popper has proposed a Great Plains Agency to deal with common problems of the ten-state area between the Rockies and Corn and Cotton belts. Frank J. Popper, "Thinking Globally, Acting Regionally," *Technology Review,* vol. 95, no. 3 (April 1992), p. 46.

16. Herman E. Daly and John B. Cobb, Jr., *For the Common Good* (Boston: Beacon Press, 1989), pp. 174, 293.
17. See Peter J. Katzenstein, *Small States in World Markets: Industrial Policy in Europe* (Ithaca, N.Y.: Cornell University Press, 1985).
18. Michael Wallerstein, "Union Organization in Advanced Industrial Democracies," *American Political Science Review,* vol. 83, no. 2 (June 1989), pp. 481–501.

6. THE PLURALIST COMMONWEALTH

1. For early formulations of these ideas see Gar Alperovitz, "Notes Toward a Pluralist Commonwealth," in Staughton Lynd and Gar Alperovitz, *Strategy and Program* (Boston: Beacon Press, 1973), pp. 49–109; Gar Alperovitz, "Toward a Tough-Minded Populism," *Dissent,* vol. 33, no. 2 (Spring 1986), pp. 156–160; Gar Alperovitz, "The Coming Break in Liberal Consciousness," *Christianity and Crisis,* vol. 46, no. 3 (March 3, 1986), pp. 59–65; and Gar Alperovitz, "Building a Living Democracy," *Sojourners,* vol. 19, no. 6 (July 1990), pp. 11–23.
2. For the operations of large enterprises under state socialism, see, for example, Bartlomiej Kamínski, *The Collapse of State Socialism: The Case of Poland* (Princeton, N.J.: Princeton University Press, 1991); János Kornai, *Contradictions and Dilemmas: Studies on the Socialist Economy and Society,* trans. Ilona Lukács (Cambridge, Mass.: M.I.T. Press, 1986); János Kornai, *The Socialist System: The Political Economy of Communism* (Princeton: Princeton University Press, 1992); Michael Ellman, *Socialist Planning* (Cambridge: Cambridge University Press, 1979); Paul R. Gregory and Robert C. Stuart, *Soviet Economic Structure and Performance* (New York: Harper & Row, 1974); and Alec Nove, *The Soviet Economic System* (London: G. Allen & Unwin, 1977).
3. There is a vast literature on changes in corporate accountability, and in particular, the growing independence and power of corporate executives. A recent assessment of "the rise of the imperial chief executive" is that of New York University finance professors Roy Smith and Ingo Walter: "Institutional Investors Hold the Key to Better Governance," *Financial Times* (London), July 21, 2003, p. 17. See also SEC Chairman William H. Donaldson, "Corporate Governance: What Has Happened and Where We Need to Go," *Business Economics,* vol. 38, no. 3 (July 2003), p. 16. For a representative sample of the broad literature, see Adolf A. Berle and Gardiner C. Means, *The Modern Corporation and Private Property,* revised ed. (New York: Harcourt, Brace & World, 1932, 1968); Peter F. Drucker, *The New Society: The Anatomy of the Industrial Order* (New York: Harper & Brothers, 1949); Charles E. Lindblom, *Politics and Markets: The World's Political-Economic Systems* (New York: Basic Books, 1977); Edward S. Herman, *Corporate Control, Corporate Power* (Cambridge: Cambridge University Press, 1981); and Scott R. Bowman, *The Modern Corporation and American Political Thought: Law, Power and Ideology* (University Park, Penn.: Penn State Press, 1996).
4. Alan G. Hevesi, *Impact of the Corporate Scandals on New York State* (Albany, N.Y.: Office of the State Comptroller, August 2003), www.osc.state.ny.us/press/releases/aug03/corpgovernrpt.pdf (accessed 08/21/03), pp.18–21. The cost to New York State is based, in part, on a recent Brookings study estimating that such problems cost the overall economy roughly $35 billion; see Carol Graham, Robert E. Litan, and Sandip Suhktankar, *Cooking the Books: The Cost to the Economy,* Policy Brief #106 (Washington, D.C.: Brookings Institution, August 2002), www.brook.edu/comm/policybriefs/pb106.htm (accessed 10/22/03).

5. Total California energy costs were estimated at nearly $27 billion a year in 2001 and 2000, as opposed to only $10 billion in 2002. "2002 Annual Report on Market Issues and Performance," California Independent System Operator, www. caiso.com/docs/2000/07/27/2000072710233117407.html (accessed 10/22/03), pp. E1–E2. For calculations on the portion that can be attributed to market power, see Severin Borenstein, James B. Bushnell, and Frank A. Wolak, "Measuring Market Inefficiencies in California's Restructured Wholesale Electricity Market," *American Economic Review*, vol. 92, no. 5 (December 2002), pp. 1376–1405. "Over $10 billion" from personal communication to Alex Campbell from Frank Wolak (06/11/03). For higher estimates see Kathleen Sharp, "Price-Gouging Inquiries Target Enron, Overcharges in California May Exceed $40 Billion," *Boston Globe*, March 3, 2002, p. A12; and William J. Kilberg "From the Editor: Enron: The Studebaker of the 21st Century?" *Employee Relations Law Journal*, vol. 28, no. 1 (Summer 2002), pp. 1–6. For estimates of the cost of resolving the savings and loan crisis and related funding crises, see General Accounting Office, "Financial Audit: Resolution Trust Corporation's 1995 and 1994 Financial Statements," GAO/AIMD-96-123 (Washington, D.C.: GAO, July 1996), pp. 13, 19.

6. On the efficiency of ESOPs, in particular, see Chapter 7, note 14 in this book. For other literature on the efficiency of worker ownership, and for critical arguments in general, see also Chapter 1, note 22 in this book. On the efficiency of public utilities, see Chapter 8, note 19 in this book. See also *The Rise and Fall of State-Owned Enterprise in the Western World*, ed. Pier Angelo Toninelli (Cambridge: Cambridge University Press, 2000); and Malcolm Sawyer and Kathy O'Donnell, *A Future for Public Ownership* (London: UNISON, 1999). On public pension fund investment see Wilshire Associates, "Private Versus Public Pension Fund Investment Performance," February 4, 1999, www.calpers.ca.gov/whatshap/hottopic/w-study.htm (accessed 06/10/03); Cost Effectiveness Management, "Do Public Funds Underperform Corporate Pension Funds?" February 5, 1999, www.calpers.ca.gov/whatshap/hottopic/cem-study.htm (accessed 06/10/03); General Accounting Office, "Public Pension Plans: Evaluation of Economically Targeted Investment Programs," GAO/PEMD-95-13 (Washington, D.C.: GAO, March 1995); and Gordon L. Clark, *Pension Fund Capitalism* (Oxford: Oxford University Press, 2000). See also Geoffrey M. Hodgson, *Economics and Utopia: Why the Learning Economy Is Not the End of History* (New York: Routledge, 1999); Joseph S. Berliner, *The Economics of the Good Society: The Variety of Economic Arrangements* (Malden, Mass.: Blackwell, 1999); and the *Annals of Public and Cooperative Economics*. Recent contributions to the larger theoretical debate on efficiency versus equality include: Louis Putterman, John E. Roemer, and Joaquim Silvestre, "Does Egalitarianism Have a Future?" *Journal of Economic Literature*, vol. 36, no. 2 (June 1998), pp. 861–902; *Meritocracy and Economic Inequality*, ed. Kenneth Arrow, Samuel Bowles, and Steven Durlaf (Princeton: Princeton University Press, 2000); and Samuel Bowles and Herbert Gintis, *Recasting Egalitarianism* (New York: Verso, 1998). For an estimate of waste and inefficiency throughout the U.S. economy see Samuel Bowles, David M. Gordon, and Thomas E. Weisskopf, *Beyond the Waste Land* (Garden City, N.Y.: Anchor Press/Doubleday, 1984). See also pp. 96–97, 115–118 in this book.

7. Figures for public sector compensation do not include retirement benefits. For McDonough's salary, see "Are CEOs Worth Their Salaries? As Firms Founder, Critics Question the Pay Formula," *Washington Post*, October 2, 2002, p. E1. Private sector CEO compensation numbers are from the AFL-CIO Paywatch data-

base, which catalogs executive compensation from SEC filings: www.aflcio.org/ corporateamerica/paywatch/ceou/database.cfm (accessed 06/10/03) and Louis Lavelle, "Executive Pay," *Business Week*, no. 3829 (April 21, 2003), p. 86. Bill Wallace, "CalPERS Names Interim CEO," *San Francisco Chronicle*, August 22, 2002, p. B1; Arthur M. Louis, "CalPERS Investment Chief to Resign," *The San Francisco Chronicle*, November 14, 2001, p. B2; TVA Office of the Inspector General, *30th Semiannual Report, October 1, 2000–March 31, 2001* (Knoxville, Tenn.: TVA, 2001), p. 8, www.oig.tva.gov/semiannu.htm (06/11/03); and Nancy Zuckerbrod, "Wamp-Requested Report Examines How TVA Pays Execs," *The Oak Ridger,* Thursday, March 1, 2001, www.oakridger.com/stories/030101/stt_ 0301010025.html (accessed 06/11/03). On the weak relationship between pay and performance for corporate CEOs, see Gretchen Morgenson, "The Rules on Bosses' Pay Seem Written with Pencil," *New York Times,* May 25, 2003, p. C1.

8. Michael S. McPherson and Morton Owen Schapiro, "Reinforcing Stratification in American Higher Education: Some Disturbing Trends," Paper written for the Macalester Forum on Higher Education Conference, Diversity and Stratification in American Higher Education, Macalester College, June 1999, p. 15, www .macalester.edu/president/MACFORUM99+stats.pdf (accessed 12/02/02).

7. A DIRECT STAKE IN ECONOMIC LIFE: WORKER-OWNED FIRMS

1. In 2003 there were 8.4 million workers in private-sector unions and 8.8 million workers working in ESOP employee-owned firms. See Bureau of Labor Statistics, "Union Members in 2003," table 3, "Union Affiliation of Employed Wage and Salary Workers by Occupation and Industry," www.bls.gov/news.release/ union2.t03.htm (accessed 05/31/04); and National Center for Employee Ownership (NCEO), "A Statistical Profile of Employee Ownership" (NCEO, December 2003), www.nceo.org/library/eo_stat.html (accessed 05/31/04), p.1.

2. Appleton, www.appletonideas.com (accessed 06/25/03); Joel Dresang, "It's A Gamble on Paper," *Milwaukee Journal Sentinel* (Wisconsin), November 11, 2001, p. 1D; and John Case, "E.O.Y. 1992: Collective Effort," *Inc.,* vol. 14, no. 1 (January 1992), p. 32.

3. *Red Herring,* "Science Applications International Corp.: Massive, Employee-owned, and Proud of It," May 7, 2001, www.redherring.com/mag/issue97/ 520019052.html (accessed 04/10/03); SAIC, "*Business Week* Names SAIC the Largest Private IT Firm," www.saic.com/cover-archive/saicarchive/busweek. html (accessed 01/06/03); "Largest Private Companies," Forbes.com, www. forbes.com/finance/lists (accessed 04/10/03); SAIC, "Employee Ownership," www.saic.com/empown/ (accessed 04/10/03); www.saic.com/about/profile.html (accessed 09/23/03); personal communication to Alex Campbell from David Binns, the Beyster Institute (11/01/02); and Karen M. Young, Corey Rosen, and Edward J. Carberry, *Theory O: Creating an Ownership Style of Management* (Oakland, Calif.: The National Center for Employee Ownership, 1999), pp. 93–94.

4. National Center for Employee Ownership (NCEO), "A Statistical Profile of Employee Ownership" (NCEO, December 2003), www.nceo.org/library/eo_stat .html (accessed 05/31/04), p. 1; NCEO, "A Comprehensive Overview of Employee Ownership" (NCEO, 2002), www.nceo.org/library/overview.html (accessed 11/07/02), p. 2. See note 8 on the next page for information on benefits. Although these are the most widely cited estimates, several efforts are

currently underway to improve and refine information on ESOP numbers, members, scale, etc. General information on specific companies is available in "The Largest 100 Majority Employee Owned Companies," *Employee Ownership Report*, vol. 12, no. 4 (July–August 2002), pp. 6–7 and "The Employee Ownership 100," *Business Ethics*, vol. 15 (September–October 2001), pp. 14–15. See also Joseph Blasi, Douglas Kruse, and Aaron Bernstein's *In the Company of Owners* (New York: Basic Books, 2003); the Capital Ownership Group's on-line library, cog.kent.edu/Title/Title.htm; and Jeff Gates, *The Ownership Solution: Toward a Shared Capitalism for the Twenty-first Century* (Reading, Mass.: Addison-Wesley, 1998).

5. Karen M. Young, Corey Rosen, and Edward J. Carberry, *Theory O: Creating an Ownership Style of Management* (Oakland, Calif.: The National Center for Employee Ownership, 1999), p.135; "Fast Facts," www.gore.com/about/fastfacts.html (accessed 10/02/03); and "W. L. Gore & Associates Again One of the 100 Best," www.gore.com/news/100best.html (accessed 04/10/03). Gore ranked number twenty-seven in the most recent survey.

6. See www.westonsolutions.com; and "Roy F. Weston, Inc. Changes Name to Weston Solutions, Inc.," *Business Wire*, June 5, 2002.

7. Fetter Printing, "Honors and Awards," www.fetterprinting.com/news/awards/main.htm (accessed 03/07/03); "Fetter Printing Co.," Experian Business Reports, 2003, via Lexis Nexis; "How Have Ohio Employee Owned Companies Fared?" *Owners At Work* (Winter 1999–2000), p. 13; Center for Economic and Social Justice, "The Nuts and Bolts of a Modern Ownership Culture: Fastener Industries," www.cesj.org/vbm/casestudies-vbm/fastener.html (accessed 01/06/03); Marjorie Kelly, "Fastener Industries, Employee Ownership Award," *Business Ethics*, vol. 16, nos. 5, 6 (Fall 2002), p. 12. Parametrix, "Parametrix Firm Overview," www.parametrix.com/pdf/FirmOverview.pdf; "Awards," www.parametrix.com/profile/awards.htm (accessed 01/06/03); ComSonics, "Our Company," www.comsonics.com/html/company.htm (accessed 03/07/03); and "Comsonics Inc," Experian Business Reports, 2003, via Lexis Nexis.

8. Peter Kardas, Adria L. Scharf, and Jim Keogh, "Wealth and Income Consequences of ESOPs and Employee Ownership: A Comparative Study from Washington State," *Journal of Employee Ownership Law and Finance*, vol. 10, no. 4 (Fall 1998). Median holdings were just under $25,000 (personal communication to Gar Alperovitz from Adria Scharf). The 1990 study was NCEO, *Employee Stock Ownership Plans: How the Average Worker Fares* (Oakland, Calif.: National Center for Employee Ownership, 1990). Comparative data are from 1992 because data are only available every three years: see Edward N. Wolff, "Recent Trends in Wealth Ownership," in *Assets for the Poor*, ed. Thomas M. Schapiro and Edward N. Wolff (New York: Russell Sage Foundation, 2001), p. 38. Christopher Mackin, Loren Rodgers, and Adria Scharf, Ownership Associates, Inc., "An Open Letter to the Massachusetts Congressional Delegation," February 15, 2002, www.ownershipassociates.com/congress.shtm (accessed 03/07/03). A 2001 study of a large national sample by Joseph R. Blasi and Douglas Kruse found that ESOP firms were much more likely to have retirement plans than comparable non-ESOP firms—and that they were four times as likely to have defined benefit plans, and more than five times as likely to have 401(k)s, profit sharing, or other defined contribution plans. NCEO, "Largest Study Yet Shows ESOPs Improve Performance and Employee Benefits," www.nceo.org/library/esop_perf.html (accessed 11/08/02).

9. For tax support, see Joint Committee on Taxation, *Estimates of Federal Tax Expenditures for Fiscal Years 2002–2006*, JCS-1-02 (Washington, D.C.: Government Printing Office, 2002), p. 25; see also John Logue and Jacquelyn Yates, *The Real World of Employee Ownership* (Ithaca, N.Y.: ILR Press, 2001), p. 171. In 1980 the Small Business Administration (SBA) was also authorized to provide loan guarantees to ESOP firms. SBA assistance to ESOPs continues today under the Qualified Employee Trusts Loan Program: SBA, "Qualified Employee Trusts Loan Program," www.sba.gov/financing/loanprog/trusts.html (accessed 06/10/03). The Job Training Partnership Act, which provided funds for a variety of purposes, was used by a number of states to conduct worker-ownership feasibility studies in the event of plant closures or substantial layoffs at existing firms. John Logue, Richard Glass, and John Grummel, "Employees and Ownership: Trends, Characteristics, and Policy Implications of State Employee Ownership Legislation" (Ohio Employee Ownership Center, Kent State University, n.d.). Funding of this kind continues under the rapid response program of the Workforce Investment Act, which includes prefeasibility studies for employee ownership as an "accepted usage" for funds. Interview by Alex Campbell, Bill Bujalos, director, MidAtlantic Trade Adjustment Assistance Center, May 6, 2002. A small-scale pilot program, the National Steel/Aluminum Retention Initiative, provides technical assistance to explore possible worker buyouts to companies in these industries. Ohio Employee Ownership Center, "National Steel/Aluminum Retention Initiative," (06/03/02) dept.kent.edu/oeoc/nsari/index.htm (accessed 11/08/02). Another small-scale demonstration effort supported by HUD is the Vermont Workers' Ownership Center, which provides similar support services to encourage employee ownership. David Mace, "Sanders Lands Federal Money for Employee Ownership Projects," *Rutland Herald Online* (November 27, 2001), www.rutlandherald.com/To_Print/38210.html (accessed 11/08/02).

10. More than half the states have provided direct support for worker ownership in recent decades—seven through explicitly mandated financial and technical assistance efforts. Typical state programs have included a mix of policies. Some have collected information and established resource centers or published pamphlets and guides (Michigan, New York, Ohio, and Maryland). Several states have provided seminars to interested citizens and companies. Michigan and New York provided training to a range of state officials to facilitate access of interested firms to state assistance. A number have provided financial assistance, through loan guarantees or similar programs. Williamson, Imbroscio, and Alperovitz, *Making a Place for Community*, p. 196. For information on one of the most innovative efforts (in Ohio), see Logue and Yates, *The Real World of Employee Ownership*, pp. 168–169. For information on one of the most expansive, see Michigan Department of Career Development, "Workforce Investment Act (WIA) Services for Workers Affected by Plant Closures or Mass Layoffs," www.michigan.gov/mdcd/0,1607,7-122-1683_2988_2991-12926—,00.html (accessed 11/07/02). For information on the Massachusetts program, see Commonwealth Corporation, "Employee Ownership and Involvement," www.commcorp.org/BES/Trust/EIO.htm (accessed 11/07/02). For information on the Massachusetts program, see the Massachusetts Office for Employee Involvement and Ownership at www.masseio.org.

11. For information on voting rights pass-throughs, see NCEO, "A Statistical Profile of Employee Ownership" (NCEO, December 2003), www.nceo.org/library/eo_stat.html (accessed 05/31/04), p. 5. For an analysis of the potential impact

on overall income distribution, see Thad Williamson, "Is Employee Ownership a Road to Anywhere? (That Is, Anywhere Economic Democrats Want to Go?)," paper presented at Democracy Collaborative Affiliates Conference: The State of Democratic Practice, University of Maryland, College Park, Md., January 25–26, 2002.

12. NCEO, "A Statistical Profile of Employee Ownership" (NCEO, December 2003), www.nceo.org/library/eo_stat.html (accessed 05/31/04), p. 5; NCEO, "A Comprehensive Overview of Employee Ownership" (NCEO, December 2003), www.nceo.org/library/overview.html (accessed 05/31/04), p. 2; "ESOP Survey," (The ESOP Association, n. d.); compare with NCEO, "A Statistical Profile of Employee Ownership" (NCEO, November 2001), p. 3.

13. "The Real Strengths of Employee Ownership, *Business Week,* no. 3222 (July 15, 1991), p. 156; and Logue and Yates, *The Real World of Employee Ownership,* p. 32.

14. Douglas Kruse, "Research Evidence on Prevalence and Effects of Employee Ownership," Testimony before the Subcommittee on Employer-Employee Relations, Committee on Education and the Workforce, U.S. House of Representatives, February 13, 2002, www.nceo.org/library/kruse_testimony.html (accessed 11/08/02). For evidence on sales growth, see "Largest Study Yet Shows ESOPs Improve Performance and Employee Benefits" (NCEO, n.d.), www.nceo.org/library/esop_perf.html (accessed 11/08/02). For a review that emphasizes the importance of efforts to increase participation, see NCEO, "Employee Ownership and Corporate Performance" (NCEO, 2001), www.nceo.org/library/corpperf.html (accessed 11/08/02). See also Logue and Yates, *The Real World of Employee Ownership,* chapters 3 and 4; Justin Fox, "Giving Workers a Voice Increases Productivity," *NBER Digest* (May 1998); Joseph Blasi, Michael Conte, and Douglas Kruse, "Employee Stock Ownership and Corporate Performance Among Public Companies," *Industrial and Labor Relations Review,* vol. 50, no. 1 (1996), pp. 60–79; and David R. Francis, "Motivating Employees with Stock and Involvement," *NBER Digest* (Cambridge, Mass: National Bureau of Economic Research, May 2004).

15. NCEO, "A Statistical Profile of Employee Ownership" (NCEO, December 2003), www.nceo.org/library/eo_stat.html (accessed 05/31/04), p. 2.

16. Joseph Blasi, "Memorandum to Clinton Administration on Employee Ownership," December 1992; copy provided to author by Blasi.

17. "Will America Be 30% Employee Owned in 2010," *Owners at Work* (Summer 1999), p. 4, dept.kent.edu/oeoc/PublicationsResearch/OwnersAtWork.htm (accessed 04/11/03).

18. John Logue and Marjorie Kelly, "It's Time to Renew Our National Enthusiasm for Employee Ownership," *Business Ethics,* vol. 14, no. 5 (September–October 2000), pp. 16–17.

19. In the wake of the Enron scandal of 2002, many were concerned that workers owning stock in their own corporations might risk significant losses. ESOP advocates offered several responses: (1) most ESOP firms do not concentrate all pension funds in company stock; more than one retirement vehicle is common in approximately three-quarters of such firms (and significantly more common than in comparable non-ESOP firms); (2) financial problems have been less common in ESOPs than among conventional firms; (3) putting worker-representatives on boards with access to company books would permit more careful oversight; (4) allowing workers to withdraw from ESOPs over specified periods of time can further reduce risk; and (5) additional forms of

pension insurance might be provided through federal guarantees. An NCEO study in the late 1990s found that "employees in ESOP companies had about as much in diversified (noncompany stock) assets as employees had in all assets in non-ESOP companies." NCEO, "Wealth and Income Consequences of ESOPs and Employee Ownership," www.nceo.org/pubs/wealth.html (accessed 05/18/03); Corey Rosen, "Enron and Employee Ownership," *San Diego Union-Tribune*, February 28, 2002; Corey Rosen, "Questions and Answers About Enron, 401(k)s, and ESOPs," January 2002, www.nceo.org/library/enron.html (accessed 04/09/03); NCEO, "Largest Study Yet Shows ESOPs Improve Performance and Employee Benefits," www.nceo.org/library/esop_perf.html (accessed 11/08/02); Nien-hê Hsieh, "Employee Ownership and Workplace Democracy: A Protective Account," paper presented at Democracy Collaborative Affiliates Conference: The State of Democratic Practice, University of Maryland, College Park, Md., January 25–26, 2002; and "Employee Governance," *Business Ethics*, vol. 16, nos. 5, 6 (Fall 2002), pp. 14–16.

20. The National Cooperative Bank, "A Day in the Life of Cooperative America," "Introduction"(NCB, n.d.), www.ncb.com/homepage/dayinlife.nsf/intro.htm (accessed 11/22/02). Credit Union National Association, "United States Credit Union Statistics," doig.cuna.org/download/us_totals.pdf (accessed 11/22/02); National Cooperative Business Association, "About Cooperatives, Co-op Statistics," www.ncba.org/abcoop_stats.cfm (accessed 05/31/04). See also *From Community Economic Development and Ethnic Entrepreneurship to Economic Democracy: The Cooperative Alternative*, ed. Jonathan Michael Feldman and Jessica Gordon Nembhard (Umea, Sweden: Partnership for Multiethnic Inclusion, 2002); and Greg MacLeod, *From Mondragon to America: Experiments in Community Economic Development* (Sydney, Nova Scotia: University of Cape Breton Press, 1997).

21. "REI Facts," "About REI," "Patronage Refund 101," www.rei.com (accessed 05/07/03); and Fortune.com, "REI," www.fortune.com/fortune/bestcompanies/snapshot/0,15154,73,00.html (accessed 04/10/03).

8. ENTERPRISING CITIES: RIGHT, LEFT, AND CENTER

1. David Osborne and Ted Gaebler, *Reinventing Government* (New York: Addison-Wesley, 1992), p. 196. See also Adria Scharf with Thad Williamson, Alex Campbell and Jeff Pope, *Municipal Enterprise: A Strategy for Job Creation and Stabilization*, ed. Sondra Myers (College Park, Md.: The Democracy Collaborative at the University of Maryland and the National Center for Economic and Security Alternatives, 2003); and The Public Strategies Group Web site www.psgrp.com/. For recent overall statistical trends, see Beverly Bunch, "Changes in the Usage of Enterprise Funds by Large City Governments," *Public Budgeting and Finance* (Summer 2000), pp. 15–29; Christopher W. Hoene and Michael A. Pagano, "Enterprising Cities: An Exploratory Analysis of Municipal Enterprise Revenues, User Fees and Charges, and Service Delivery," paper presented at the Association for Budgeting and Financial Management Conference, 2001; and Gary Paul, "Measuring the Effects of Municipal Enterprise on the Budgets of Local Government," *Western Journal of Black Studies* (Winter 1999), pp. 217–228.

2. B. J. Frieden and L. B. Sagalyn, *Downtown, Inc.* (Boston: M.I.T. Press, 1989), p. 169. See also *Leasing Public Land: Policy Debates and International Experiences,*

eds. Steven C. Bourassa and Yu-Hung Hong (Cambridge, Mass.: Lincoln Institute of Land Policy, 2003).

3. David Imbroscio, "Nontraditional Public Enterprise as Local Economic Development Policy," *Policy Studies Journal,* vol. 23, no. 2 (Summer 1995), pp. 218–230, note 2.

4. R. F. Babcock, "The City as Entrepreneur," in *City Deal Making,* ed. T. Lasser (Washington, D.C.: Urban Land Institute, 1990), p. 14.

5. City of Alhambra, "Commercial Projects," www.cityofalhambra.org/government/development_services/economic/commercial_projects.html (accessed 12/19/02); Thad Williamson, David Imbroscio, and Gar Alperovitz, *Making a Place for Community,* pp. 157, 158; "Plans for Convention Center Hotel Moving Forward," *City Development,* vol. 3, no. 2 (Fall 2002), www.louky.org/mayor/development/page5.htm (accessed 12/18/02); and City of San Diego, FY 2003 budget, "Real Estate Assets," www.sannet.gov/budget/annual/volume3/pdf/v3real.pdf (accessed 12/19/02).

6. Glasgow Electric Plant Board, "Cable TV," www.glasgow-ky.com/cabletv/channel.htm (accessed 04/08/03).

7. Cedar Falls Municipal Communications Utility, www.cfunet.net/commun/index.htm; Click! network, www.click-network.com/ (accessed 06/02/04). As of this writing 278 public power utilities provided such services; of these, 109 provided cable TV. In addition, almost 570 offered broadband services for either community or municipal government use. Diane Moody, Director of Statistical Analysis, American Public Power Association, "Public Power Utilities Offering Community Broadband Services" (from *2004–2005 Statistical Directory*) provided to Katharine Nelson, June 3, 2004. "Community Broadband: Separating Fact From Fiction," (Washington, D.C.: American Public Power Association, January, 2004), pp. 24, 25. For a partial list of municipally owned networks, see "Public-Owned Communications Networks," www.townofcary.org/agenda/specialcoms/Fiber/pocn.htm (accessed 6/02/04).

8. Ann O'M. Bowman, "Tools and Targets" (Washington, D.C.: National League of Cities, 1987), p. 4; Susan E. Clarke and Gary L. Gaile, *The Work of Cities* (Minneapolis: University of Minnesota Press, 1998), p. 84; and Newyorkbiz.com, "Giuliani Administration to Reinvest in Successful High-Tech Venture Capital Fund," July 18, 2000, www.newyorkbiz.com/About_Us/getPressReleasePreview2000_detail38.htm (accessed 11/20/02).

9. Charles Mahtesian, "Memo to the Cities: If You Can't Bribe the Owner, Maybe You Can Buy the Team," *Governing,* vol. 9, no. 6 (March 1996), pp. 42–45; and David Imbroscio, "Reformulating Urban Regime Theory: The Division of Labor Between State and Market Reconsidered," *Journal of Urban Affairs,* vol. 20, no. 3 (1998), pp. 239–240.

10. Sue Halpern, "Home Field Advantage," *Mother Jones* (November–December 2002), pp. 30–33.

11. Denver Health, "Denver Health Financial Data," www.denverhealth.org/ovr-finance.cfm?hand=4, "Denver Health: A Public Health Care System Model for the Next Century," www.denverhealth.org/ovr-chs.cfm?hand=2 (accessed 04/08/03); and J. Duncan Moore Jr., "Denver Role Model: City Turns Public Hospital into Integrated System," *Modern Healthcare,* (April 14, 1997). Due to state funding cuts and an increase in uninsured patients, Denver Health ran a deficit in 2003 and as of this writing may be forced to reduce some programs: "Denver Health May Cap Care for Uninsured 'Safety-Net'," *Denver Post,* April 21, 2004.

12. DTE biomass, "Success Stories," www.dtebe.com/stories/stories.html (accessed 11/08/02). NCESA interviews. The U.S. EPA reports that as of November 2002, over 340 projects were in operation (a number of these are privately owned and operated); see "LFG Energy Projects," www.epa.gov/lmop/projects/projects.htm (accessed 12/18/02). For information on Riverview see DTE biomass, "Success Stories," www.dtebe.com/stories/stories.html (accessed 11/08/02). EPA, "Case Studies," www.epa.gov/lmop/products/products.htm#4 (accessed 04/09/03).

13. Williamson, Imbroscio, and Alperovitz, *Making a Place for Community*, p. 252.

14. Heather McCulloch, *Sharing the Wealth: Resident Ownership Mechanisms* (Oakland, Calif.: PolicyLink, 2001), p. 96, based on interview with Julie Orvis. See also *Property and Values: Alternatives to Public and Private Ownership*, ed. Charles Geisler and Gail Daneker (Washington, D.C.: Island Press, 2000) and the Institute for Community Economics, www.iceclt.org/.

15. Sheila Muto, "Nonprofit Becomes Landlord to Help Other Organizations," *Wall Street Journal*, June 20, 2001, p. B10; and Williamson, Imbroscio, and Alperovitz, *Making a Place for Community*, p. 253.

16. Miami-Dade Transit, "Dadeland South Metrorail Station," www.co.miami-dade.fl.us/transit/metrorail/jointdev/dadeland_south.htm (accessed 06/12/03); Miami-Dade Transit, "Dadeland North Metrorail Station," www.co.miami-dade.fl.us/transit/metrorail/jointdev/dadeland_north.htm (accessed 06/12/03).

17. Valley Transportation Authority (VTA), "Transit-Oriented Development Program," www.vta.org/projects/tod.html (accessed 11/19/02); VTA, "Almaden Lake Village Housing Fact Sheet" (San Jose, Calif.: VTA, n.d.). The VTA's Ohlone-Chynoweth project includes two hundred units in two- and three-story town houses, a community recreation center, a child care center, and small retail components that together are expected to generate $250,000 a year in revenue. VTA, "Ohlone-Chynoweth Fact Sheet" (San Jose, Calif.: VTA, n.d.). Income figures confirmed, interview by Alex Campbell with Terry Sullivan, executive secretary to the CFO of VTA (December 5, 2002); and WMATA, "Metro Transit Oriented Development Program marks a twenty-six-year history of success, board approves FY 2003 program," www.wmata.com/about/MET_NEWS/200206/pr_transitproject.cfm (accessed 10/07/03).

18. American Public Power Association, *2002 Annual Directory and Statistical Report* (Washington, D.C.: APPA), available at www.appanet.org/about/statistics/statistics.cfm (accessed 11/19/02); and Energy Information Administration, *Financial Statistics of Major U.S. Publicly owned Electric Utilities 2000* (Washington, D.C.: U.S. Department of Energy, November 2001).

19. Had the municipalization of a large, high-rate private utility on Long Island not increased average costs, average savings for public utility customers would have been substantially higher compared with recent years. American Public Power Association, *2003 Annual Directory and Statistical Report* "Public Power Costs Less" (Washington, D.C.: APPA, 2002), p. 36, available at www.appanet.org/about/statistics/statistics.cfm (accessed 11/19/02). For a discussion of the basis of the public power price advantage, see American Public Power Association, "Straight Answers to More False Charges Against Public Power" (2002), pp. 18, 20, 22, 23; and www.appanet.org/about/why/answers/answers.cfm (accessed 11/19/02). See also Bay Area Economic Forum, *The Economics of Electric System Municipalization* (Bay Area Economic Forum: October 2001);

Energy Information Administration, *Financial Statistics of Major U.S. Publicly Owned Electric Utilities 2000* (Washington, D.C.: U.S. Department of Energy, November 2001), esp. tables 1, 3, 12, 23; and Elaine and Richard Davis, "Municipalization and Subsidized Utility Competition: The Taxpayers' Perspective," *Cal-Tax Digest*, April 1997. On public utility reliability and service during the California energy crisis, see John G. Edwards, "California Survey Suggests Publicly Owned Power Companies Offer Lower Fees," *Knight Ridder Tribune Business News*, September 12, 2002, via ProQuest. See also Williamson, Imbroscio, and Alperovitz, *Making a Place for Community*, pp. 148–151. On sustainability, see, for instance, American Public Power Association (APPA), *Shades of Green: Public Power's Environmental Profile* (Washington, DC: APPA, June 2001), esp. pp. 15–17, 20, 22.

20. Elliott D. Sclar, *You Don't Always Get What You Pay For* (Ithaca, N.Y.: Cornell University Press, 2000), chapters 2, 3, p. 49.

21. Alan A. Altshuler and William B. Parent, "Breaking Old Rules: Four Themes for the 21st Century" (Cambridge, Mass.: Harvard University, Institute for Government Innovation, n.d.), www.ksg.harvard.edu/innovations/4themes21st.htm (accessed 11/22/02); and Innovations in American Government, "Competition and Costing, 1995 Winner, City of Indianapolis," www.ksg.harvard.edu/innovations/winners/ccin95.htm (accessed 11/22/02).

22. Sclar, *You Don't Always Get What You Pay For*, pp. 144–146.

9. BUILDING COMMUNITY: NEIGHBORHOODS AND NONPROFITS WITH A MISSION

1. Jack Newfield, *Robert Kennedy: A Memoir* (New York: Bantam, 1969), pp. 89–115.
2. Gar Alperovitz and Jeff Faux, *Rebuilding America* (New York: Pantheon, 1985), p. 252; and Pratt Institute Center for Community and Environmental Development (PICCED), "Community Development Corporation (CDC) Oral History Project, Bedford Stuyvesant Restoration Corporation (BSRC)," www.picced.org/advocacy/bsrc.htm (accessed 11/07/02).
3. BSRC, "Background" (n.d. Bedford Stuyvesant Restoration Corporation Subsidiaries and Controlled Affiliates), "Combined Statement of Activities (Unaudited) for the Year Ended June 30, 2002," "Combined Statement of Activities for the Year Ended June 30, 2001," and "Financial Statements as of June 30, 2001 Together with Independent Auditor's Reports." For further information see www.restorationplaza.org/. Communication to the author by Bob Brandwein, June 1, 2004.
4. All figures based on NCC estimates; $500 million asset is based on replacement cost accounting. New Community Corporation, www.newcommunity.org/main.htm (accessed 11/13/02); Kristin Rusch, *The Emerging New Society* (College Park, Md.: The Democracy Collaborative, 2001), p. 5; and interview by Joe Guinan, Mary Abernathy of New Community Corporation, August 26, 2003. Interview by Steve Dubb, Dale Anglin, Director of Resource Development, New Community Corporation, June 2, 2004.
5. Rusch, *The Emerging New Society*.
6. Kentucky Highlands Investment Corporation (KHIC), "Background," www.khic.org/page2.htm (accessed 02/22/02); and "Equity Investments," www.khic.org/equity.htm (accessed 11/08/02).

7. NCCED, *Coming of Age—Trends and Achievements of Community-Based Development Organizations* (Washington, D.C.: NCCED, 1998), p. 3; and Carmen Sirianni and Lewis Friedland, *Civic Innovation in America* (Berkeley: University of California Press, 2001), p. 59.

8. Daniel P. Moynihan, *On Understanding Poverty* (New York: Basic Books, 1969), pp. 12–13.

9. Rita Mae Kelly, *Community Control of Economic Development* (New York: Praeger, 1977), p. 22.

10. Robert J. Fisher, "Community Organizing in the Conservative '80s and Beyond," *Social Policy*, vol. 25, no. 1 (Fall 1994), pp. 11–20.

11. Neal R. Peirce and Carol F. Steinbach, *Corrective Capitalism: The Rise of America's Community Development Corporations* (New York: The Ford Foundation, 1987), p. 30; Paul S. Grogan and Tony Proscio, *Comeback Cities* (New York: Westview, 2000), p. 94; and Michael Rubinger, Testimony Regarding Housing Affordability and Availability before the Subcommittee on Housing and Community Opportunity, Committee on Financial Services, U.S. House of Representatives, May 3, 2001, www.liscnet.org/whatsnew/testimony.shtml (accessed 11/08/02).

12. There have been some highly publicized instances of malfeasance in CDC management. Whether the incidence of white collar crime is higher than in private corporations, however, is impossible to assess. The total dollar amounts involved, of course, are far less than the huge losses recorded in recent corporate scandals.

13. Grogan and Proscio, *Comeback Cities*, p. 86.

14. Sirianni and Friedland, *Civic Innovation in America*, pp. 58–60, 80–81; "CDFIs: Opening the Door to a More Inclusive Banking System" (Corporation for Enterprise Development: 2003), pp. 9–10, www.cdfi.org/whatare.asp (accessed 04/24/04).

15. Grogan and Proscio, *Comeback Cities*, pp. 88, 254; LISC, "Annual Report, 2001" (New York: LISC, n.d.), p. 3; LISC, "LISC Facts at a Glance," www.liscnet.org/whatwedo/facts (accessed 11/14/02); and Enterprise Foundation, "About Us," www.enterprisefoundation.org/about/index.asp (accessed 11/14/02).

16. Robert J. Fisher, "Community Organizing in the Conservative '80s and Beyond," *Social Policy*, vol. 25, no. 1 (Fall 1994), p. 14; Andrew Mott, "Twenty Five Years of Building Power and Capacity," *Shelterforce*, no. 110 (March–April 2000), www.nhi.org/online/issues/110/mott.html (accessed 12/18/02). For other views on the merits and level of "professionalization" of CDC management, see Pablo Eisenberg, "Time to Remove the Rose-Colored Glasses," *Shelterforce*, no. 110 (March–April 2000), www.nhi.org/online/issues/110/eisenberg.html (accessed 12/18/02); and Pierre Clavel, Jessica Pitt, and Jordan Yin, "The Community Option in Urban Policy," *Urban Affairs Review*, vol. 32, no. 4 (March 1997), p. 445.

17. NCCED, *Coming of Age—Trends and Achievements of Community-Based Development Organizations* (Washington, D.C.: NCCED, 1999), pp. 11, 13, 14.

18. TRI, "TRI Commitments," provided to the author by Dwain Brown, personal communication, February 12, 2003.

19. Holly Sklar, "Dudley Street Neighborhood Initiative: Building on Success, 1984–2002" (La Jolla, Calif.: Waitt Family Foundation, July 10, 2002), www.waittfoundation.org/CommunityBuild/DSNI.asp (accessed 11/14/02); and Gloria Negri, "A Sense of Renewal Stirs in Roxbury," *Boston Globe*, November 26, 2000, City Weekly section, p. 6.

20. General CDC statistics from NCCED, *Coming of Age—Trends and Achievements of Community-Based Development Organizations* (Washington, D.C.: NCCED, 1998), pp. 11, 13, 14.

21. Some observers (e.g., the authors of *Comeback Cities*) are optimistic about the future of CDCs, others have focused on potential warning signs—including management problems and the insecurity of federal funding. See Christopher Walker and Mark Weinheimer, *Community Development in the 1990s* (Washington, D.C.: The Urban Institute, September 1998), chapter 7. For a discussion of potential new federal funding sources, see Marcus Weiss, "CDCs Access New Economic Development Resources," *Shelterforce Online* (July–August 1999), www.nhi.org/online/issues/106/fundraising.html (accessed 12/18/02). See also Avis C. Vidal, "Rebuilding Communities: A National Study of Urban Community Development Corporations" (New York: Community Development Research Center, New School for Social Research, 1992); and Rachel G. Bratt, et al., *Confronting the Management Challenge: Affordable Housing in the Nonprofit Sector* (New York: Community Development Research Center, New School for Social Research, 1994).

22. Louis Winnick, "Community Action for the 1990s," *Public Interest,* vol. 138 (Winter 2000), pp. 124–127.

23. New York State, "Neighborhood Preservation Companies Program (NPP)," www.dhcr.state.ny.us/ocd/progs/npp/ocdprgnp.htm (accessed 11/14/02); North Carolina Community Development Initiative, www.ncinitiative.org/home.cfm (accessed 11/14/02); and Community Economic Development Assistance Corporation, www.cedac.org/ (accessed 11/14/02). For information on CEED, see Massachusetts Department of Housing and Community Development, "Annual Report 2001," www.state.ma.us/dhcd/publications/annual_report/default.htm (accessed 11/14/02).

24. See Williamson, Imbroscio, and Alperovitz, *Making a Place for Community,* chapter 9.

25. For a recent review of developments of this kind and others with "blended values," see James E. Emerson, "Total Foundation Asset Management: Exploring Elements of Engagement Within Philanthropic Practice," Stanford Graduate School of Business Research Paper #1803, February 2003, gobi.stanford.edu/ResearchPapers/Library/RP1803.pdf (accessed 09/26/03); and Cynthia W. Massarsky and Samantha L. Beinhacker, "Enterprising Nonprofits: Revenue Generation in the Nonprofit Sector," Yale School of Management—The Goldman Sachs Foundation Partnership on Nonprofit Ventures, www.ventures.yale.edu/docs/Enterprising_Nonprofits.pdf (accessed 09/26/03).

26. Esperanza Unida, "Our History," www.esperanzaunida.org and "Training and Job Placement Businesses," www.esperanzaunida.org/training/training.htm (accessed 11/15/02).

27. Pioneer Human Services, "Overview of Pioneer Human Services," www.pioneerhumanserv.com/PHSCondensedOverview2001.htm (accessed 11/15/02); Rusch, *The Emerging New Society,* p. 9; and PHS, "Annual Report 2002," p. 2.

28. Thomas J. Billitteri, "Roberts Fund Puts Its Venture-Philanthropy Approach to the Test," *Chronicle of Philanthropy,* June 1, 2000, www.philanthropy.com/free/articles/v12/i16/16000801.htm (accessed 04/11/03); and REDF, "REDF Portfolio Organizations and Enterprises as of November 2002," www.redf.org/download/other/portfoliolist_1102.doc (accessed 06/06/03). REDF has

recently reassessed its operations in order to target resources to the more productive ventures.

29. Ira Harkavy and Harmon Zuckerman, "Eds and Meds: Cities' Hidden Assets," Brookings Institution Survey Series (Washington, D.C.: Brookings Institution Center on Urban and Metropolitan Policy, August 1999), www.brookings.edu/ dybdocroot/es/urban/eds&meds.pdf (accessed 11/15/02). Roughly 60 percent of community hospitals are nonprofit; 15 percent for-profit; the rest government owned. American Hospital Association, "Fast Facts on U.S. Hospitals," www.hospitalconnect.com/aha/resource_center/fastfacts/fast_facts_US_ hospitals.html (accessed 02/07/03).

30. See Derek Curtis Bok, *Universities in the Marketplace: The Commercialization of Higher Education* (Princeton: Princeton University Press, 2003).

31. For a discussion of concerns, see Jon Van Til, *Growing Civil Society: From Non-profit Sector to Third Space* (Bloomington: Indiana University Press, 2000), part 3; and Bok, *Universities in the Marketplace.* Karen Froelich's studies, on the other hand, suggest that "there is little evidence of goal displacement, as commercial revenues seem less restricted than other revenue sources. On balance, it appears that commercial revenues enable greater flexibility and autonomy for nonprofit organizations than traditional forms of support." Karen A. Froelich, "Diversification of Revenue Strategies: Evolving Resource Dependence in Non-profit Organizations," *Non-profit and Voluntary Sector Quarterly,* vol. 28, no. 3 (September 1999), pp. 246–268. For further discussion, see Jerr Boschee, *The Social Enterprise Sourcebook* (Minneapolis: Northland Institute, 2001), available online at: www.northlandinst.org/sourcebook.cfm; the Partnership on Non-profit Ventures Web site, www.ventures.yale.edu; *Private Action and the Public Good,* ed. Walter W. Powell and Elisabeth S. Clemens (New Haven: Yale University Press, 1998); and *Annals of Public and Cooperative Economics,* in particular vols. 62 and 68. Support organizations have also begun to emerge as the sector has developed. The National Center for Social Entrepreneurs provides consulting and training programs to local and national nonprofits—including significant regional projects in Orlando, Seattle, Milwaukee, and Columbus, Ohio. Community Wealth Ventures, Inc., a for-profit consulting firm that also provides such services, is itself a model. It is a wholly owned subsidiary of Share Our Strength, a major antihunger group that raises over half its operating budget through revenues from business ventures and corporate partnerships. The National Center for Social Entrepreneurs, www.socialentrepreneurs.org/; Community Wealth Ventures, Inc., www.communitywealth.com/; and Share Our Strength, www .strength.org/learn/index.htm (accessed 11/18/02). Share Our Strength revenues figure from personal communication from Malia Miller (November 26, 2002) and "Share Our Strength and Subsidiary Consolidated Financial Statements, August 31, 2001."

32. Harvy Lipman and Elizabeth Schwinn, "Nonprofit Groups Reap Billions in Tax-Free Income Annually," *The Chronicle of Philanthropy* (October 18, 2001); Lester M. Salamon, *America's Nonprofit Sector: A Primer,* 2nd ed. (New York: The Foundation Center, 1999), p. 117; and Stephanie Strom, "Nonprofit Groups Reach for Profits on the Side," *New York Times,* March 17, 2002.

33. Harvard Initiative on Social Enterprise, "Overview of Strategy, Goals, and Focus," www.hbs.edu/socialenterprise/ (accessed 11/18/02); Stanford Center for Social Innovation, www.gsb.stanford.edu/csi/ (accessed 04/10/03); and Yale

School of Management—Goldman Sachs Foundation Partnership on Non-profit Ventures, www.ventures.yale.edu/ (accessed 04/10/03).

10. STATE AND NATIONAL INNOVATORS

1. Steven Shepelwich and Melissa Koide, "Engaging Financial Institutions in the IDA Marketplace," *Assets: A Quarterly Update for Innovators* (Winter 2002), p. 1; www.idanetwork.org/assets/index.html (accessed 02/04/03). Larry W. Beeferman, "The Promise of Asset-Development Policies," *Communities and Banking* (Federal Reserve Bank of Boston) (January 2002), www.centeronhunger.org/pubs/adipubs.html (accessed 06/23/03); and Mark Schreiner, et al., *Savings and Asset Accumulation in Individual Development Accounts* (St. Louis: Center for Social Development, February 2001), www.gwbweb.wustl.edu/csd/Publications/2001/ADDreport2001/index.htm (accessed 02/04/03). See also Mark Schreiner, Margaret Clancy, and Michael Sherraden, *Final Report: Saving Performance in the American Dream Demonstration* (St. Louis: Center for Social Development, October 2002), www.gwbweb.wustl.edu/csd/Publications/2002/ADDreport2002.pdf (accessed 02/04/03).

2. For details on the Assets for Independence demonstrations, see Ray Boshara, "Assets for Independence Act (AFIA) Overview," Center for Social Development (October 28, 1998), www.gwbweb.wustl.edu/csd/Areas_Work/Asset_building/IDAs/AFIA/index.htm (accessed 01/09/03) and "Assets for Independence Demonstration," Corporation for Enterprise Development (April 23, 2003), www.idanetwork.org/index.php?section=initiatives&page=afi.html (accessed 06/10/03). Office of Management and Budget, *Budget of the United States 2002: Appendix* (Washington, D.C.: Government Printing Office, 2001), w3.access.gpo.gov/usbudget/ (accessed 06/09/03), p. 470; and Office of Management and Budget, *Budget of the United States 2003: Appendix* (Washington, D.C.: Government Printing Office, 2002), w3.access.gpo.gov/usbudget/ (accessed 06/09/03), p. 462. The Assets for Independence Act is in the reauthorization process as of this writing: see *Assets: A Quarterly Update for Innovators*, 2004, no. 1; and Corporation for Enterprise Development, "Assets for Independence Act Reauthorization" (Washington, D.C.: March 2004).

3. Editorial, "IDAs Are a Good Idea," *St. Louis Post-Dispatch*, November 5, 1998, p. B6.

4. Bank of North Dakota, "Annual Report, 2002" (Bismarck: Bank of North Dakota, 2003), www.banknd.com/pdf/BND2002AnnualReport.pdf (accessed 06/19/03); Bank of North Dakota, "Annual Report, 2000" (Bismarck: Bank of North Dakota, 2001), www.banknd.com/pdf/BND_ANNUAL_REPORT_2000.pdf (accessed 06/09/03); and Bank of North Dakota, "Annual Report, 2000" (Bismarck: Bank of North Dakota, 2001), p. 3.

5. Wisconsin Legislative Audit Bureau, "An Audit of the State Life Insurance Fund," Report 02-18 (November 2002), www.legis.state.wi.us/lab/PastReportsByDate.htm (accessed 02/04/03); and Williamson, Imbroscio, and Alperovitz, *Making a Place for Community*, p. 154.

6. Robert G. Heard and John Sibert, *Growing New Businesses with Seed and Venture Capital: State Experiences and Options* (Washington, D.C.: National Governors Association, 2000), pp. 48–49. Also see David Barkley, et al., *Directory of State-Assisted Venture Capital Programs, 2000* (Columbia, Mo.: Rural Policy Research

Institute, 2000), www.rupri.org/pubs/archive/wpapers/WP2000–1/index.html (accessed 06/03/03).

7. Maryland Department of Business and Economic Development, "Venture Capital Funds Annual Report July 2002" (Baltimore, Md.: Department of Business and Economic Development, 2002), pp. 5–7. As of 2002 the fifty-two firms in which the fund invested, four went public, five were purchased by public firms, and one was liquidated. The other forty-two companies remain in the funds' portfolio. See also Dana Hedgpeth, "Fund for Start-Up Firms Yields Big Payoff for Md.," *Washington Post,* March 6, 2000, p. A1. The state of Pennsylvania has used proceeds from the tobacco settlement to create three regional seed funds dedicated to developing the biotechnology industry across the state. See www.bioadvance.com/ (accessed 06/06/03); and Michael Hardy, "Md. Biotechs Envy Philly Fund: Pennsylvania Uses Tobacco Cash to Boost Fledgling Industry," *Baltimore Business Journal,* December 6, 2002.

8. Connecticut Innovations, "Annual Report, 2002" (Rocky Hill: Connecticut Innovations, 2002), p. 1. Massachusetts Technology Development Corporation financials can be accessed at www.mtdc.com/annualfinance.html (accessed 04/11/03) and details regarding their investment portfolio can be found at www.mtdc.com/portfolio.html (accessed 04/11/03).

9. Peter K. Eisinger, "State Venture Capitalism, State Politics, and the World of High-Risk Investment," *Economic Development Quarterly,* vol. 7, no. 2 (May 1993), pp. 131–139.

10. David Kesmodel, "United Holds Loan Talks with Feds," *Rocky Mountain News* (Denver), April 13, 2002, p. C1; Edward Wong, "US Airways Makes Cuts and Leaves Bankruptcy," *New York Times,* April 1, 2003, p. C3. The federal government guaranteed $380 million of America West's $429 million loan package and $900 million of US Airways' $1 billion loan. As of this writing the Air Transportation Stabilization Board has approved loans to five additional smaller carriers; see www.ustreas.gov/offices/domestic-finance/atsb/index.html (accessed 01/09/03).

11. Robert B. Reich and John D. Donahue, *New Deals: The Chrysler Revival and the American System* (New York: Times Books, 1985), pp. 178, 186, 254–257. The Chrysler bailout legislation also required Chrysler to create an ESOP; see Logue and Yates, *The Real World of Employee Ownership,* p. 85. William Greider, *Secrets of the Temple: How the Federal Reserve Runs the Country* (New York: Simon & Schuster, 1987), pp. 624–631; Irvine Sprague, *Bailout: An Insider's Account of Bank Failures and Rescues* (New York: Basic Books, 1986); and Stacey R. Kole and J. Harold Mulherin, "The Government as a Shareholder: A Case from the United States," *Journal of Law and Economics,* vol. 40, no. 1 (April 1997), pp. 1–22. The federal government took between 35 and 100 percent of the ownership in seventeen firms during World War II and held its ownership stake for up to twenty-three years.

12. The Port Authority of New York and New Jersey, "Financial Statements and Appended Notes, Year 2002" (The Port Authority of New York and New Jersey, 2003), www.panynj.gov/annualreport/financial2002.pdf (accessed 09/29/03), p. 6; and The Port Authority of New York and New Jersey, "Financial Statements and Appended Notes, Year 2001" (The Port Authority of New York and New Jersey, 2002) www.panynj.gov/ (accessed 01/06/03).

13. Williamson, Imbroscio, and Alperovitz, *Making a Place for Community,* p. 158; and Port of Los Angeles, "Facts" www.portoflosangeles.org/about/facts.htm (accessed 04/11/03). The port also generated $1.4 billion in tax revenues in 2002.

14. Port of Seattle, www.portseattle.org/portandyou/works/2002Budover.pdf (accessed 09/29/03).

15. Williamson, Imbroscio, and Alperovitz, *Making a Place for Community,* p. 158; and City of Portland, Maine, "Comprehensive Annual Financial Report, 2002," p. 86.

16. U.S. Census Bureau, "2001 State and Local Government Public Employee Retirement Systems," *State and Local Government Public Employee Retirement System Survey,* www.census.gov/govs/www/retire01.html (accessed 01/09/03), tables 4, 5; and U.S. Census Bureau, *2002 Statistical Abstract of the United States* (Washington, D.C.: U.S. Bureau of the Census, 2003), table 521. In 2001 state and local public employee pension plans had over $2.1 trillion in assets—over $1 trillion of which was invested in corporate stocks and bonds. Fact Sheet "Retirement Plan Assets: Year-end 2001," Employee Benefits Research Institute, September 2002; and Jennifer D. Harris, "Survey of State and Local Government Employee Retirement Systems," Public Pension Coordinating Council, March 2002, ppcc.grsnet.com/PPCC2001Report.pdf (accessed 02/04/03). On the efficiency of public pension investment practices, see Wilshire Associates, "Private Versus Public Pension Fund Investment Performance," February 4, 1999, www.calpers.ca.gov/whatshap/hottopic/w-study.htm (accessed 06/10/03); Cost Effectiveness Management, "Do Public Funds Underperform Corporate Pension Funds?," February 5, 1999, www.calpers.ca.gov/whatshap/hottopic/cem-study.htm (accessed 06/10/03); General Accounting Office, "Public Pension Plans: Evaluation of Economically Targeted Investment Programs," GAO/PEMD-95-13 (Washington, D.C.: GAO, March 1995); and Gordon L. Clark, *Pension Fund Capitalism* (Oxford: Oxford University Press, 2000).

17. Financial Markets Center, "Uncivil Service: Pension Rebellion Stirs the Fed," *FOMC Alert,* vol. 4, no. 5 (August 2000), pp. 1–9; Thrift Savings Plan, "Financial Statements of the Thrift Savings Plan—2002 and 2001," www.tsp.gov/forms/financial-stmt.pdf (accessed 09/29/03); and U.S. Census Bureau, *2002 Statistical Abstract of the United States* (Washington, D.C.: U.S. Census Bureau, 2003), table 521, p. 348.

18. "Comprehensive Annual Financial Report, California Public Employees Retirement System, Year Ended June 30, 2002"; "Facts at a Glance: Investments," California Public Employees Retirement System, July 2003 www.calpers.ca.gov/about/factglan/factglan.htm (accessed 06/12/03); "Facts at a Glance: Retirement," California Public Employees Retirement System, May 2003, www.calpers.ca.gov/about/factglan/factglan.htm (accessed 06/12/03); and Stephen L. Nesbitt, "The 'CalPERS Effect' on Targeted Company Share Prices," *Directorship,* vol. 27, no. 5 (May 2001), pp. 1–3. CalPERS corporate governance principles include that a substantial majority of the board be filled by independent directors, and that the board's audit and compensation committees be comprised entirely of independent directors. CalPERS has been a strong voice urging additional reforms in the wake of the Enron and other scandals. An initiative launched in February 2002 stresses the separation of accounting and consulting functions, empowering audit committees and boards to facilitate the assessment of audited statements, and other related reforms. See www.calpers-governance.org (accessed 06/17/03).

19. For the fiscal crunch in Alabama—and the defeat of Governor Bob Riley's tax proposals—see Adam Cohen, "What Alabama's Low-Tax Mania Can Teach the Rest of the Country," *New York Times*, October 20, 2003, p. A16; and "Retirement System of Alabama, 2001 Annual Report," Retirement System of Alabama, www .rsa.state.al.us/Publications/publications_and_forms.htm (accessed 04/22/03); Williamson, Imbroscio, and Alperovitz, *Making a Place for Community*, p. 182.

20. "Retirement System of Alabama, 2002 Annual Report," Retirement System of Alabama, www.rsa.state.al.us/Publications/publications_and_forms.htm (accessed 04/22/03); Williamson, Imbroscio, and Alperovitz, *Making a Place for Community*, p. 182; US Airways press release, March 31, 2003, www.usairways.com/about/ press/nw_03_0331.htm (accessed 06/02/03); and Michael Tomberlin, "Bronner to Steer US Airways' New Course," *Birmingham News*, April 1, 2003. For more recent difficulties, see (among many reports) Keith L. Alexander, "US Airways Maps a New East Coast Strategy," *Washington Post*, April 22, 2004, p. E1.

21. "Permanent Fund Dividend Program," Alaska Permanent Fund Corporation, www.apfc.org/alaska/dividendprgrm.cfm?s=4 (accessed 06/06/03). The annual dividend rose steadily over the years to a high of $1,963 in 2000. With the stock market collapse, such payments went down to $1,850 in 2001 ($9,250 for a family with three children) and $1,541 in 2002 ($7,705 for a family with three children). Dividends are paid to individuals who have lived in the state for one year.

22. The fund finished 2002 down 2.2 percent overall, but outperformed benchmarks and the median public pension fund. Operating costs were 0.15 percent of the average market value of the fund in 2001 (and slightly higher in 2002 as the average value of the fund fell and operating costs rose slightly). By way of comparison, median large investment funds had operating costs of 0.2 percent of their average market value. "2002 Annual Report," Alaska Permanent Fund Corporation, www.apfc.org/library/AnRptArch.cfm (accessed 02/04/03), pp. 5, 33; "2001 Annual Report," Alaska Permanent Fund Corporation, www.apfc.org/library/ AnRptArch.cfm (accessed 02/04/03), p. 24; and "2000 Annual Report," Alaska Permanent Fund Corporation, www.apfc.org/library/AnRptArch.cfm (accessed 02/04/03), pp. 3, 5, 10.

23. Income inequality is measured here as the ratio between the average income of the richest 20 percent of families and the poorest 20 percent of families. Jared Bernstein, et al., "Pulling Apart: A State-by-State Analysis of Income Trends" (Washington, D.C.: Center on Budget and Policy Priorities and Economic Policy Institute, 2000), pp. 8, 9; and Scott Goldsmith, "The Alaska Permanent Fund Dividend: An Experiment in Wealth Distribution," Presented at the Ninth Congress of Basic Income European Network [BIEN], Geneva, Switzerland, September 12–14, 2002.

11. CODA: THE DEMOCRATIZATION OF WEALTH AND THE ERA OF DEEPENING FISCAL CRISIS

1. David Cay Johnston, "Officials of 14 States Pledge Protection of Pension Assets," *New York Times*, August 13, 2002, p. C7. See also chapter 3 in this book.

2. The issue here is the developmental trajectory of citizen concern and control. Unless made accountable to broader public purposes, pension fund strategies can undercut worker and other priorities. See Doug Henwood, *Wall Street: How It Works and for Whom* (New York: Verso, 1998), pp. 289–293, and Greider, *The Soul of Capitalism*, for differing views.

3. For a $5.1 trillion deficit projection over ten years, see Richard Kogan, "Deficit Picture Even Grimmer Than New CBO Projections Suggest," Center on Budget and Policy Priorities, August 26, 2003, www.cbpp.org/8-26-03bud.htm (accessed 10/03/03). A very similar number ($5.2 trillion) can be reached using the Congressional Budget Office numbers directly. The most recent CBO estimates show $1.397 trillion over the next decade (2004–2013). Obvious additions include: (1) extending the expiring tax cuts ($1.564 trillion); (2) reforming the alternative minimum tax ($400 billion); (3) Medicare prescription drug benefit ($400 billion); and (4) an ongoing increase of discretionary appropriations at the growth rate of nominal GDP ($1.392 trillion)—for a total estimate of $5.153 trillion dollars. CBO Current Budget Projections, August 26, 2003, www.cbo.gov/showdoc.cfm?index=1944&sequence=0#table5 (accessed 10/03/03). The $5.153 trillion in cumulative deficits over the next ten years includes a $2.436 trillion surplus in the Social Security trust fund. If the Social Security surplus is excluded, the projected deficits rise to $7.589 trillion. Note that the cost of prescription drug benefits are now estimated at between $500 and $600 billion: see Amy Goldstein, "Medicare Official Cites Cost Warning; White House Given Data, He Says," *Washington Post*, March 25, 2004, p. A3.

4. Much of this took place during the Reagan era. Office of Management and Budget, *Budget of the United States 2004: Historical Tables* (Washington, D.C.: Government Printing Office, 2003) w3.access.gpo.gov/usbudget/fy2004/pdf/hist.pdf (accessed 08/22/03), table 2.2, pp. 31–32; Congress of the United States, Joint Economic Committee, "U.S. Corporate Taxes are Very Low from Both an Historical and International Perspective," November 6, 2003, jec.senate.gov/democrats/Documents/Releases/dc6nov2003.pdf (accessed 05/25/04); Internal Revenue Service, "Personal Exemptions and Individual Income Tax Rates, 1913–2002," SOI Bulletin, Data Release, June 2002, www.irs.gov/taxstats/article/0,,id=96679,00.html (accessed 12/10/03); and Office of Management and Budget, *Budget of the United States Government: Historical Tables Fiscal Year 2005* (Washington, D.C.: Government Printing Office, 2004), www.gpoaccesss.gov/usbudget/, table 8.4. For a useful early discussion of the longer-term fiscal crisis that approaches the issue from a different perspective, see James O'Connor, *The Fiscal Crisis of the State* (New York: St. Martin's Press, 1973).

5. Alan J. Auerbach, William G. Gale, and Peter R. Orszag, "Reassessing the Fiscal Gap: The Role of Tax-Deferred Saving," *Tax Notes*, July 28, 2003, p. 570.

6. For listings of organizations that study and/or support the various institutional models discussed in Part II (and others), see Appendix, "Resources for Rebuilding," in Williamson, Imbroscio, and Alperovitz, *Making a Place for Community*, pp. 323–347; *An Economy of Hope: Annotated National Directory of Worker Co-ops, Democratic ESOPs, Sustainable Enterprises, Support Organizations and Resources* (Stillwater, Penn.: Grassroots Economic Organizing, n.d.); Appendix, "Around the World Economy in 80 Ways," in Shuman, *Going Local*, pp. 205–283; and the Fourth Sector Network, www.fourthsector.net/.

12. IS LOCAL DEMOCRACY POSSIBLE IN THE GLOBAL ERA?

1. For a detailed survey of many of the policies discussed in this chapter, see Williamson, Imbroscio, and Alperovitz, *Making a Place for Community*. For an earlier exploration of related themes see Alperovitz and Faux, *Rebuilding America*.

2. For historical data see Bureau of Labor Statistics, "National Employment, Hours, and Earnings," Public Data Query, www.bls.gov/data/home.htm (accessed 06/11/03). For projection to 2045 see Bureau of Economic Analysis, "Regional Projections to 2045: Volume 1, States," July 1995, www.beadata.bea. doc.gov:80/bea/ar/rprj2045.htm (accessed 06/01/98). For 5 to 7 percent projection see Peter F. Drucker, Interview, "The Future Manufacturing," *Industry Week,* vol. 247, no. 17 (September 21, 1998), p. 97. See also Richard B. Freeman, "The World of Work in the New Millennium," in *What the Future Holds,* ed. Richard N. Cooper and Richard Layard (Cambridge, Mass.: M.I.T. Press, 2002), p. 167.

3. For service share exports see U.S. Census Bureau, *Statistical Abstract of the United States: 2002* (Washington, D.C.: U.S. Government Printing Office, 2003), tables 633, 1277 and pp. 419, 793. For a discussion of service sector stability see Andrew J. Filardo, "Cyclical Implications of the Declining Manufacturing Employment Share," *Federal Reserve Bank of Kansas City Economic Review,* vol. 82, no. 2 (1997), pp. 63–88. See also Todd M. Godbout, "Employment Change and Sectoral Distribution in 10 Countries, 1970–1990," *Monthly Labor Review,* vol. 116, no. 10 (October 93), pp. 3–21, esp. p. 10. The growth of the (lower wage) service sector is one of the key factors producing greater inequality—and demanding new strategies of the kind explored throughout this book.

4. Thomas Michael Power, *Lost Landscapes and Failed Economies* (Washington, D.C.: Island Press, 1996), p. 37.

5. This is a minimum estimate for smaller cities (e.g., 200,000), which for obvious reasons have less internal trade than larger cities. For cities of over 1 million, the proportion of "locally oriented economic activity" increased at an annual rate of 0.7 percent from 1969 to 1989—and at a rate of over 0.8 percent from 1979 to 1989. "Locally oriented manufacturing's share increased at a rate of almost 2 percent per year during the same period." Power, *Lost Landscapes and Failed Economies,* p. 49.

6. Paul R. Krugman, *Pop Internationalism* (Cambridge, Mass.: M.I.T. Press, 1996), p. 211.

7. Jason White, "States Mine for Gray Gold," Stateline.org, September 12, 2002, www.stateline.org/story.do?storyId=259278 (accessed 11/25/02); Genaro C. Armas, "Luring Retirees Becomes Lucrative Business for States," Associated Press, December 26, 2000, via Lexis Nexis; "Hopkins County Hoping to Lure Retirees to the Area," Associated Press, January 22, 2001, via Lexis Nexis; Penelope Lemov, "Welcome to Eldertown," *Governing* (October 1996), www.governing.com/archive/1996/oct/elderly.txt (accessed 11/25/02); and Grant Smith, "Senior Migration Means Revenue, Study Says," *Arizona Capitol Times,* August 23, 2002, www.twaaconsulting.com/ PDFs/~REV%20AZ%20CAPITOL%20TIMES.pdf (accessed 06/11/03).

8. National Institute of Governmental Purchasing, *NIGP 1998 Preference Report* (Herndon, Va.: NIGP, 1998).

9. Christopher Walker and Mark Weinheimer, "Community Development in the 1990s" (Washington, D.C.: The Urban Institute, September 1998), pp. 90–93. The survey gave eleven of the twenty-three cities examined a 4 or 5 on a 5-point scale on the question, "Do public agency funding and policy decisions give CDCs a central role in the delivery of government programs in low-income neighborhoods?" An additional four cities had shown significant improvement in this area in the period examined (but had not reached a 4 or 5 on the scale).

10. "Local to Local Buying Programs Aid Rural Economies," *Economic Development Digest,* vol. 4, no. 11 (1995), p. 6.

11. According to the GAO (www.gao.gov/archive/1995/pe95013.pdf), at least twenty-nine states had some type of Economically Targeted Investment (ETI) program in 1992. See also Isamu Watson, *Investment Intermediaries: Model State Programs* (Washington, D.C.: Center for Policy Alternatives, June 1995), p. 2. Quite separately, a 2001 study of forty state and local pension investment systems found that 27 percent had ETI plans or included "collateral benefits" when considering investment decisions. Nicholas Greifer, "Pension Investment Policies: The State of the Art," *Governance Finance Review* (February 2002), www.sso.org/nasra/pension2.pdf (accessed 05/09/02), p. 4. The Landmark Growth Fund, which supports employee-owned firms or firms with strong employee participation in management, and the Pittsburgh Regional Heartland Fund both draw on pension fund investments. For more information see the Heartland Network, www.heartlandnetwork.org.

12. The study was based on cities of 25,000 or larger and does not include costs for smaller towns. For a discussion see Williamson, Imbroscio, and Alperovitz, *Making a Place for Community,* p. 12.

13. Small Business Administration, "HUBZone 'Historically Underutilized Business Zone'," www.sba.gov/hubzone/ (accessed 11/01/02).

14. U.S. Department of Labor, Employment and Training Administration, "Fact Sheet: Trade Adjustment Assistance," www.doleta.gov/programs/factsht/taa .htm (accessed 04/16/03). Benefits have been recently increased, see note 20 on the following page.

15. North American Development Bank, "US Community Adjustment Investment Program," www.nadbank-caip.org/ (accessed 11/01/02).

16. Department of Housing and Urban Development, "Fiscal Year 2004 Budget Summary," www.hud.gov/about/budget/fy04/budgetsummary.pdf (accessed 09/29/02).

17. The administration requested no new direct expenditures for these programs in 2003; see source in note 16 above. Tax expenditures are expected to exceed $1.2 billion in fiscal 2004. *Analytical Perspectives, Budget of the United States 2004* (Washington, D.C.: Government Printing Office, 2003), p. 108, w3.access.gpo.gov/usbudget/fy2004/pdf/spec.pdf (accessed 09/19/03).

18. The legislation originally made $15 billion in tax credits available; see Rapoza Associates, "New Markets Tax Credit Fact Sheet," www.rapoza.org/focus/ factsheet2.pdf (accessed 11/01/02). The Bush administration's most recent budget estimates tax expenditures (2004 to 2008) at $760 million for corporations and $2.3 billion for individuals. *Analytical Perspectives, Budget of the United States 2004* (Washington, D.C.: Government Printing Office, 2002), p. 107, w3.access.gpo.gov/usbudget/fy2004/pdf/spec.pdf (accessed 10/06/03). For two different perspectives on the developmental trajectory of federal programs and their possibilities, see Alice O'Connor, "Swimming Against the Tide: A Brief History of Federal Policy in Poor Communities," and the reply by Joseph McNeely, in *Urban Problems and Community Development,* ed. Ronald F. Ferguson and William T. Dickens (Washington, D.C.: Brookings Institution Press, 1999), pp. 77–138.

19. Lenore Sek, "Trade Promotion Authority (Fast-Track Authority for Trade Agreements): Background and Developments in the 107th Congress," Congressional Research Service Issue Brief, January 14, 2003, fpc.state.gov/docu-

ments/organization/16806.pdf (accessed 04/16/03); and Peter Beinart, "The Next NAFTA," *New Republic*, December 15, 1997, p. 4.

20. Joseph Kahn, "Wheeling, Dealing and Making Side Deals—Vow to Scrap Latin Textile Deals Wins Vote on Bush Trade Powers," *New York Times*, December 8, 2001, p. C1.

21. See footnote on page 131. Juliet Eilperin and Helen Dewar, "Accord Reached on Trade Authority; President Would Gain Power to Cut Deals," *Washington Post*, July 26, 2002, p. A1; Elizabeth Becker and Edmund L. Andrews, "Performing Free Trade Juggling Act, Offstage," *New York Times*, February 8, 2003, p. C1; and Leon Hadar, "Bush's Incomplete Victory on Trade," *Business Times Singapore*, August 7, 2002, via Lexis Nexis.

22. In particular, Eisinger found that a large number of innovative policy tools designed to support economic development have emerged which complement—and in some areas even supplant—more traditional locational incentives to attract business. He also found "increasing numbers and a growing use of economic development tools . . . designed to distribute firms to particular locales within a state," including "site-development programs, financial assistance to firms in distressed areas, tax-increment financing, and state enterprise zones." Peter K. Eisinger, *The Rise of the Entrepreneurial State* (Madison: University of Wisconsin Press, 1988), pp. 3, 173. Subsequent work by Susan Clarke and Gary Gaile confirmed that the trends continued into the 1990s. Utilization of what they term "third-wave" economic development strategies by localities in 1996 was significantly higher than in 1980. For example, over 70 percent of cities surveyed worked with or through local development corporations (compared to 38 percent before 1980), 64 percent used enterprise zones, and 56 percent had some form of equity participation program; one-third used equity pools and venture capital funds—and 75 percent using these tools had only begun doing so since 1989. Susan E. Clarke and Gary L. Gaile, *The Work of Cities* (Minneapolis: University of Minnesota Press, 1998), pp. 81, 84.

23. John Gardner, "National Renewal," Speech delivered to the National Conference on Governance (NCG) in November 1994, www.ncl.org/anr/speeches/gardner.html (accessed 12/02/02); G. Thomas Kingsley, Joseph B. McNeely, and James O. Gibson, *Community Building Coming of Age* (Washington, D.C.: The Development Training Institute and The Urban Institute, 1997); and Sirianni and Friedland, *Civic Innovation in America*, p. 1. Among many other studies, see also Harry C. Boyte and Nancy N. Kari, *Building America: The Democratic Promise of Public Work* (Philadelphia: Temple University Press, 1996).

24. BUILD, "Build Highlights," www.buildiaf.org/new_page_2.htm (accessed 10/17/01); and David Harvey, *Spaces of Hope* (Berkeley: University of California Press, 2000), pp. 124–127. BUILD was instrumental in the enactment of the first modern living wage law, in Baltimore in 1994.

25. All information from www.iowacci.org/ (accessed 08/21/03).

26. Mark R. Warren, *Dry Bones Rattling* (Princeton: Princeton University Press, 2001), pp. 41, 55, 56, 83, 165.

27. See the Grassroots Collaborative's web site at www.igrassroots.org/mission.html (accessed 11/07/02). David Bacon, "Labor Fights for Immigrants," *The Nation*, vol. 272, no. 20 (May 21, 2001), pp. 15–18. See also Paul Saba, Amy Simon, Frank Mitchell, and Jeremy Brecher, "Forging Closer Ties: Case Studies of Labor's Role in Progressive State Coalitions" (Amherst, Mass.: Proteus Fund, 2002), www.proteusfund.org/grantmaking/ssf/ssf.pdf (accessed 05/09/03).

28. By 2004 the Cincinnati rates were $8.79 and $10.30. See "Living Wage Successes," ACORN, www.livingwagecampaign.org/victories.php (accessed 06/03/04); City of Cincinnati, "Living Wage Requirements," www.cincinnati-oh .gov/cdap/pages/-3816-/ (accessed 05/31/04); and City of New York Office of the Comptroller, "Prevailing Wage Schedules," www.comptroller.nyc.gov/ bureaus/bll/2004_pdf_files/109-Living-Wage-Schedule-03to04.pdf (accessed 05/31/04).

29. Jeffrey M. Berry, Kent E. Portney, and Ken Thompson, *The Rebirth of Urban Democracy* (Washington D.C.: Brookings Institution, 1993), pp. 13, 113.

30. The National Commission on Civic Renewal, "A Nation of Spectators" (College Park, Md.: The National Commission on Civic Renewal, 1998), p. 14. For Seattle see "City of Seattle Neighborhood Involvement Structure," www. cityofseattle.net/neighborhoodcouncil/involvementstructure.htm (accessed 11/4/02); and Berry, Portney, and Thompson, *The Rebirth of Urban Democracy*, pp. 12, 65.

31. Berry, Portney, and Thompson, *The Rebirth of Urban Democracy*, pp. 12, 91, 286–291.

32. William A. Schambra, "Local Groups Are the Key to America's Civic Renewal," *Brookings Review*, vol. 15, no. 4 (Fall 1997), pp. 20–22. Important works on the larger problem of "community" from diverse perspectives include Raymond Williams, *The Long Revolution* (London: Chatto & Windus, 1961); Martin Buber, *Paths in Utopia*, trans. R.F.C. Hull, paperback ed. (Boston: Beacon Press, 1958); Paul and Percival Goodman, *Communitas: Means of Livelihood and Ways of Life*, 2nd ed. (New York: Vintage Books, 1960); and Wendell Berry, *The Unsettling of America*, 3rd ed. (San Francisco: Sierra Club Books, 1977). Robert B. Westbrook's *John Dewey and American Democracy* (Ithaca, N.Y.: Cornell University Press, 1991) is a useful introduction to Dewey's thought.

33. Amitai Etzioni, *The New Golden Rule* (New York: Basic Books, 1996), p. 27.

34. Thomas Prugh, Robert Costanza, and Herman E. Daly, *The Local Politics of Global Sustainability* (Washington, D.C.: Island Press, 2000), pp. xv–xvi. See also Murray Bookchin, *From Urbanization to Cities: Toward a New Politics of Citizenship*, revised ed. (London: Cassell, 1995).

35. Robert L. Woodson, "Reclaiming the Lives of Young People," *USA Today*, vol. 126, no. 2628 (September 1, 1997), pp. 56–59, via ProQuest; Sigmund C. Shipp, "The Road Not Taken: Alternative Strategies for Black Economic Development in the United States," *Journal of Economic Issues*, vol. 30, no. 1 (March 1996), pp. 79–95. See also James B. Stewart, "Building a Cooperative Economy: Lessons from the Black Experience," *Review of Social Economics*, vol. 42, no. 3 (December 1984), pp. 360–368; *Race, Politics and Economic Development*, ed. James Jennings (New York: Verso, 1992); and Jessica Gordon Nembhard, "Entering the New City as Men and Women, Not Mules," in *The Black Urban Community*, ed. Lewis Randolph and Gail Tate (forthcoming).

36. See Boyte, Booth, and Max, *Citizen Action and the New American Populism;* Evans and Boyte, *Free Spaces;* Boyte and Kari, *Building America;* and Harry C. Boyte, *Everyday Politics* (September 2004).

37. Betty Friedan, quoted in Kathleen Erickson, "Betty Friedan," *The Region*, vol. 8, no. 3 (September 1994), p. 10.

38. Robert N. Bellah, Richard Madsen, William M. Sullivan, Ann Swidler, and Steven M. Tipton, *Habits of the Heart* (Berkeley: University of California Press, 1985), p. 277. See also Bellah et al., *The Good Society*, (New York: Knopf, 1991).

39. Robert J. Sampson, "What 'Community' Supplies," in *Urban Problems and Community Development,* ed. Robert F. Ferguson and William T. Dickens (Washington, D.C.: Brookings Institution, 1999), pp. 241, 242.

40. Tracey C. Rembert, "Generation E," *E: The Environmental Magazine,* vol. 8, no. 5 (September–October 1997), p. 4, www.emagazine.com (accessed 01/08/03). See also poll research by the Mellman Group and Peter D. Hart Research Associates for the Panetta Institute, www.panettainstitute.org/ (accessed 11/03/02).

13. COMMUNITY, THE ENVIRONMENT, AND THE "NONSEXIST CITY"

1. DDT use was banned in the United States and most other industrialized countries in the 1970s, but continues to be manufactured for export in many developed nations. Paul R. Ehrlich and Anne H. Ehrlich, *Betrayal of Science and Reason* (Washington, D.C.: Island Press, 1996), pp. 164–165. Lead was largely phased out as a gasoline additive between 1973 and 1986, banned from residential paints (1978), banned from drinking fountains (1988), and limited in drinking water pipes (1986). While lead still remains a problem due to releases from old pipes and old paint, total national atmospheric emissions are down 98 percent from their high point in the early 1970s. United States Environmental Protection Agency, "National Air Pollutant Emission Trends, 1990–1998," EPA 454/R-00-002 (Research Triangle Park, N.C.: Office of Air Quality Planning and Standards, March 2000), pp. 3–15. The U.S. State Department estimated that in 2000, national policies lowered greenhouse gas releases by the equivalent of 241.9 teragrams of carbon dioxide. United States Department of State, *U.S. Climate Action Report 2002* (Washington, D.C.: Government Printing Office, May 2002), p. 69. However, total greenhouse gas emissions were still more than 14 percent higher than the 1990 level. United States Environmental Protection Agency (EPA), "Inventory of U.S. Greenhouse Gas Emissions and Sinks: 1990–2000" (Washington, D.C.: EPA, Office of Atmospheric Programs, April 15, 2002), p. ES-2. For wetlands trend see Thomas E. Dahl, *Status and Trends of Wetlands in the Conterminous United States 1986 to 1997* (Washington, D.C.: U.S. Department of the Interior, Fish and Wildlife Service, 2000) and "Summary Findings," www.nwi .fws.gov/bha/SandT/SandTSummaryFindings.html (accessed 11/04/02). For information on automobile fuel economy see United States Environmental Protection Agency, "Light-Duty Automotive Technology and Fuel Economy Trends 1975 Through 2001," EPA420-R-01-008 (Washington, D.C.: EPA, Office of Transportation and Air Quality, September 2001). For trend in miles traveled see EPA, "Latest Findings on National Air Quality: 1999 Status and Trends," EPA-454/F-00-002 (Research Triangle Park, N.C.: EPA, Office of Air Quality Planning and Standards, August 2000), p. 5. See also my chapter (with Thad Williamson and Alex Campbell), "Ecological Sustainability: Some Elements of Longer-term System Change" in *Nature, Production, Power: Towards an Ecological Political Economy,* ed. Fred P. Gale and R. Michael M'Gonigle (Northampton, Mass.: Edward Elgar, 2000).

2. For positive trends in water quality, see Ehrlich and Ehrlich, *Betrayal of Science and Reason,* pp. 51–53; Gregg Easterbrook, *A Moment on Earth* (New York: Viking, 1995), pp. 628–629; and Council on Environmental Quality, *Environmental Quality,* 25th Anniversary Report (Washington, D.C.: U.S. Government Printing Office, 1997), pp. 225–231. As of 2000 carbon monoxide emissions

were down 15.6 percent from the 1971 high, volatile organic compound emissions were down 35.2 percent from the 1970 high, and sulfur dioxide emissions were down 42.8 percent from their 1973 high. For historical data see United States Environmental Protection Agency, "National Air Pollutant Emission Trends, 1990–1998," EPA 454/R-00-002 (Research Triangle Park, N.C.: Office of Air Quality Planning and Standards, March 2000), table 3-13. For 2000 levels see EPA, "Tables for 2000 Air Quality Trends Report," www.epa .gov/ttn/chief/trends/trends00/trends2000.pdf (accessed 11/04/02).

3. National Center for Economic and Security Alternatives (NCESA), "Index of Environmental Trends" (Washington, D.C.: NCESA, April 1995). The 2000 Redefining Progress figures are from Clifford Cobb, Mark Glickman, and Craig Cheslog, "The Genuine Progress Indicator, 2000 Update," Redefining Progress Issue Brief (Oakland, Calif.: Redefining Progress, December 2001), p. 3; for historical data see Mark Anielski and Jonathan Rowe, "The Genuine Progress Indicator—1998 Update" (San Francisco: Redefining Progress, March 1999), pp. 53–54. Magnitude estimate is based on Redefining Progress data (the total estimated value of negative change in environmental costs over the period divided by the value of the positive change in trends).

4. "Environmental Policy: A Scorecard," *New York Times,* February 23, 2003, p. A23; and Natural Resources Defense Council, "Rewriting the Rules, Year-End Report 2002," "Executive Summary," www.nrdc.org/legislation/rollbacks/ execsum.asp (accessed 01/22/03).

5. Donnella Meadows, "Things Getting Worse at a Slower Rate," *Progressive Populist,* vol. 6, no. 14 (August1–15, 2000), p. 10.

6. Michael Satchell, "Fight for Pigeon River," *U.S. News and World Report,* vol. 107, no. 22 (December 4, 1989), pp. 28, 32. For a further description and evidence of these dynamics, see Thomas Michael Power, "The Pursuit of Quality," *Orion,* vol. 12, no. 3 (Summer 1993), pp. 30–35; Kent E. Portney, *Taking Sustainable Cities Seriously* (Cambridge, Mass.: M.I.T. Press, 2003), p. 101; James K. Boyce, "Inequality and Environmental Protection," in *Inequality, Collective Action and Environmental Sustainability,* ed. Jean-Marie Baland, Pranab Bardhan, and Samuel Bowles (Santa Fe, N.M.: Santa Fe Institute, 2002); James K. Boyce, Andrew R. Klemer, Paul H. Templet, and Cleve E. Willis, "Power Distribution, the Environment, and Public Health: A State-level Analysis," *Ecological Economics,* vol. 29 (1999), pp. 127–140; Frank Ackerman and Sumreen Mirza, "Waste in the Inner City: Asset or Assault?" Global Development and Environment Institute Working Paper No. 00–08 (Medford, Mass.: Tufts University, June 2000), p. 1; and Robert W. Williams, "Environmental Injustice in America and Its Politics of Scale," *Political Geography,* vol. 18, no. 1 (1999), pp. 49–73.

7. Kenneth Arrow, Bert Bolin, Robert Costanza, and Partha Dasgupta, "Economic Growth, Carrying Capacity and the Environment," *Science,* vol. 268, no. 5210 (1995), pp. 520–521; William R. Lowry, *The Dimensions of Federalism* (Durham, N.C.: Duke University Press, 1992), pp. 123–125; and Chris Kromm and Keith Ernst, "Gold and Green 2000" (Durham, N.C.: Institute for Southern Studies, 2000), available online at: www.southernstudies.org/goldgreen2000.html.

8. For information on Cranston and on Kolbe and Kolbe see Jacquelyn Yates and Marjorie Kelly, "The 100 Largest Majority-Employee-Owned Companies (and What Makes Them Great)," *BusinessEthics,* vol. 14, no. 5 (September–October 2000), p. 15. For Herman Miller, Inc., see Jeff Gates, *The Ownership Solution* (Reading, Mass.: Addison-Wesley, 1998), pp. 134–137.

9. Barbara Scott Murdock and Ken Sexton, "Community-Based Environmental Partnerships," in *Better Environmental Decisions,* eds. Ken Sexton, Alfred A. Marcus, K. William Easter, and Timothy D. Burkhardt (Washington, D.C.: Island Press, 1999), pp. 377–400. Some experimentation with civic environmentalism is undoubtedly mainly a public relations effort by companies seeking to gain credibility by involving local activists (but not permitting them to have any significant role in decision making). For a range of views see "A New Environmentalism Takes Root," New Democracy Forum, *Boston Review,* vol. 24, no. 5 (October–November 1999). See also Portney, *Taking Sustainable Cities Seriously,* and *Toward Sustainable Cities,* ed. Daniel A. Mazmanian and Michael E. Kraft (Cambridge, Mass.: M.I.T. Press, 1999).

10. Giovanna Di Chiro, "Local Actions, Global Visions: Remaking Environmental Expertise," *Frontiers* (Boulder), vol. 18, no. 12 (1997), pp. 203–231; Raymond De Young, "Some Psychological Aspects of Reduced Consumption Behavior: The Role of Intrinsic Satisfaction and Competence Motivation," *Environment and Behavior,* vol. 28, no. 3 (May 1996), pp. 358–409; Stefan Vogel, "Farmers' Environmental Attitudes and Behavior: A Case Study for Austria," *Environment and Behavior,* vol. 28, no. 5 (September 1996), pp. 591–613; and Stephen Kaplan, "Human Nature and Environmentally Responsible Behavior," *Journal of Social Issues,* vol. 56, no. 3 (Fall 2000), pp. 491–508. See also James B. Allen and Jennifer L. Ferrand, "Environmental Locus of Control, Sympathy, and Proenvironmental Behavior," *Environment and Behavior,* vol. 31, no. 3 (May 1999), pp. 338–353; Sherry Cable and Beth Degutis, "Movement Outcomes and Dimensions of Social Change: The Multiple Effects of Local Mobilizations," *Current Sociology,* vol. 45, no. 3 (July 1997), pp. 121–135; and Nicholas Freudenberg, *Not in Our Backyards!: Community Action for Health and the Environment,* foreword by Lois Marie Gibbs (New York: Monthly Review Press, 1985).

11. Sociologist Ronald Inglehart, among others, has demonstrated that long trends in overall economic abundance have tended to increase the relative prevalence of "post-material" values. There has also been an ongoing positive intergenerational shift in values among younger-age cohorts as time goes on. Ronald Inglehart, *Modernization and Postmodernization: Cultural, Economic, and Political Change in 43 Societies* (Princeton: Princeton University Press, 1997). See also John R. McNeill, *Something New Under the Sun: An Environmental History of the Twentieth-Century World* (New York: W. W. Norton, 2000).

12. American Farmland Trust, "Farming on the Edge," Executive Summary (Washington, D.C.: American Farmland Trust, October 2002), www.farmland. org/farmingontheedge/downloads.htm (accessed 11/05/02); Bruce Katz, "Give Community Institutions a Fighting Chance," *Brookings Review,* vol. 15, no. 4 (Fall 1997), pp. 32–35; and William Fulton, Rolf Pendall, Mai Nguyen, and Alicia Harrison, "Who Sprawls Most? How Growth Patterns Differ Across the U.S.," July 12, 2001, www.brookings.edu/es/urban/issues/smartgrowth/ growthtrends.htm (accessed 01/23/02).

13. Between 1985 and 1995 new development accounted for roughly one-fifth of the decline in wetlands. F. Kaid Benfield, Matthew D. Raimi, and Donald D.T. Chen, *Once There Were Greenfields: How Urban Sprawl Is Undermining America's Environment, Economy, and Social Fabric* (New York: Natural Resources Defense Council, 1999), pp. 64–72. For problems related to runoff see Benfield, Reimi, and Chen, *Once There Were Greenfields,* pp. 78–84. For data on

suburban driving patterns see United States Department of Housing and Urban Development, *The State of Our Cities* (Washington, D.C.: Government Printing Office, 1999), p. iv.

14. Myron Orfield, "Washington Metropolitics: A Regional Agenda for Community and Stability," Brookings Institution Discussion Paper (Washington, D.C.: The Brookings Institution Center on Urban and Metropolitan Policy, July 1999), p. 55; and Bruce Katz, "Give Community Institutions a Fighting Chance," *Brookings Review,* vol. 15, no. 4 (Fall 1997), p. 33.

15. Maryland Department of the Environment, "Managing for Smart Growth Results," www.mde.state.md.us/Programs/MultimediaPrograms/Smart_Growth/Implementation/index.asp (accessed 11/05/02); and EPA, "Brownfields Showcase Community Fact Sheet, Eastward Ho!, FL," www.epa.gov/brownfields/html-doc/sc_estwr.htm (accessed 08/16/02). On the role of CDCs in regional "smart growth" coalitions, see Roland V. Anglin and Charles Hill, "The Changing Nature of Community-Based Development," New Jersey Public Policy Research Institute Research Paper 02–02 (New Brunswick, N.J.: Rutgers Center for Urban Policy Research, 2002), policy.rutgers.edu:16080/njppri/pdf/wp0202.pdf (accessed 04/17/03).

16. Phyllis Myers, "Livability at the Ballot Box: State and Local Referenda on Parks, Conservation, and Smarter Growth, Election Day 1998," Brookings Discussion Paper (Washington, D.C.: The Brookings Institution Center on Urban and Metropolitan Policy, January 1999).

17. On the New Jersey plan, see Jennifer Preston, "New Jersey Legislature Puts Plan to Conserve Open Land on Ballot," *New York Times,* July 31, 1998, p. A1; and Timothy Egan, "Dreams of Fields: The New Politics of Urban Sprawl," *New York Times,* November 15, 1998, p. 1. On the Maryland plan, see Peter S. Goodman, "Glendening vs. Suburban Sprawl," *Washington Post,* October 6, 1998, p. B1.

18. Phyllis Myers and Robert Puentes, "Growth at the Ballot Box: Electing the Shape of Communities in November 2000," Brookings Discussion Paper (Washington, D.C.: The Brookings Institution Center on Urban and Metropolitan Policy, February 2001), p. 21. Though results were more mixed in the 2002 midterm elections, over the four-year period 1998 to 2002 voters allocated $20 billion to the purchase of open space, with $2.6 billion coming from measures passed in 2002. In a number of communities new coalitions of environmentalists and antitax conservatives defeated highway expansion proposals. See Urban Mobility Corporation, *Innovation Briefs* (Special Post-Election Issue), vol. 13, no. 7 (November 2002), www.innobriefs.com/abstracts/2002/novelection02.html (accessed 10/24/03); "Greening the Garden State," *New York Times,* November 16, 2002, p. A16; and Haya El Nasser, "Voters Picky on Transportation Issues," *USA Today,* November 7, 2002, p. A13.

19. Ann Markusen, "City Spatial Structure, Women's Household Work, and National Urban Policy," in *Women and the American City,* eds. Catherine R. Stimpson, Elsa Dixler, Martha J. Nelson, and Kathryn B. Yatrakis (Chicago: University of Chicago Press, 1981), pp. 20–41, cited material on p. 24.

20. Betty Friedan, *The Second Stage* (New York: Summit Books, 1981), pp. 285, 287; and Dolores Hayden, "What Would a Non-Sexist City Be Like? Speculations on Housing, Urban Design, and Human Work," in *Women and the American City,* eds. Stimpson, Dixler, Nelson, and Yatrakis, pp. 167–184.

21. Peter Calthorpe, *The Next American Metropolis: Ecology, Community, and the American Dream* (New York: Princeton Architectural Press, 1993), pp. 19, 23.

22. Andres Duany, Elizabeth Plater-Zyberk, and Jeff Speck, *Suburban Nation: The Rise of Sprawl and the Decline of the American Dream* (New York: North Point Press, 2000), p. xiv.

23. See also Mike Davis's discussion of the progressive possibilities of the New Urbanism in his "Las Vegas Versus Nature," in Mike Davis, *Dead Cities* (New York: New Press, 2002), pp. 85–103.

24. Lewis Mumford, *The Culture of Cities* (New York: Harcourt Brace and Company, 1938), p. 348.

25. Richard P. Applebaum, *Size, Growth, and U.S. Cities* (New York: Praeger, 1978), pp. 100–101; and Roper Organization Poll, February 1993, via Polling the Nations. Recent work by Princeton political scientist J. Eric Oliver indicates that smaller cities appear to be more conducive to participation in local politics than very large cities. J. Eric Oliver, *Democracy in Suburbia* (Princeton: Princeton University Press, 2001), chapter 2. See also Robert A. Dahl and Edward R. Tufte, *Size and Democracy* (Stanford, Calif.: Stanford University Press, 1973); and David W. Orr, "Our Urban Future?" *The Ecologist,* vol. 29, no. 1 (January–February 1999), pp. 12–15.

26. Williamson, Imbroscio, and Alperovitz, *Making a Place for Community,* p. 118.

27. Ebenezer Howard, *Garden Cities of To-Morrow* (Cambridge, Mass.: The M.I.T. Press, 1965), chapters 2–5.

28. Howard, *Garden Cities of To-Morrow,* p. 131. Murray Bookchin has also forcefully argued that community ownership of this kind is essential to achieving ecological goals. See Murray Bookchin, *Remaking Society: Pathways to a Green Future* (Boston: South End Press, 1990). See also the argument of Henry C. Simons for municipal land ownership on pages 56–57 of this book.

14. THE REGIONAL RESTRUCTURING OF THE AMERICAN CONTINENT

1. *United States v. Lopez* (93-1260), 514 U.S. 549 (1995), supct.law.cornell.edu/supct/html/93-1260.ZO.html (accessed 10/24/02); *Seminole Tribe of Florida v. Florida* (94-12), 517 U.S. 44 (1996), supct.law.cornell.edu/supct/html/94-12.ZO.html (accessed 10/24/02); *Printz v. United States* (95-1478), 521 U.S. 98 (1997), supct.law.cornell.edu/supct/html/95-1478.ZO.html (accessed 10/24/02); *Rush Prudential HMO, Inc. v. Moran* (00-1021), 230 F.3d 959, affirmed, supct.law.cornell.edu/supct/html/00-1021.ZO.html (accessed 10/24/02); and Linda Greenhouse, "Court, 5-4, Upholds Authority of States to Protect Patients," *New York Times,* June 21, 2002, p. A1.

2. John H. Cushman Jr., "Congress Limits Federal Orders Costly to States," *New York Times,* February 2, 1995, p. A1; Robert Tannenwald, "Implications of the Balanced Budget Act of 1997 for the 'Devolution Revolution,'" *Publius: The Journal of Federalism,* vol. 28, no. 1 (Winter 1998), pp. 23–48; and Malcolm L. Goggin, "The Use of Administrative Discretion in Implementing the State Children's Health Insurance Program," *Publius,* vol. 29, no. 2 (Spring 1999), pp. 35–51.

3. John D. Donahue, *Disunited States* (New York: Basic Books, 1997), p. 8; Robert Jay Dilger, "TEA-21: Transportation Policy, Pork Barrel Politics, and American Federalism," *Publius,* vol. 28, no. 1 (Winter 1998), pp. 49–69; Saundra K. Schneider, "Medicaid Section 1115 Waivers: Shifting Health Care Reform to the States," *Publius,* vol. 27, no. 2 (Spring 1997), pp. 89–109; and Linda

Greenhouse, "Justices Allow Drug-Cost Plan to Go Forward," *New York Times,* May 20, 2003, p. A1.

4. National Conference of State Legislatures, "2001 Prescription Drug Discount, Bulk Purchasing, and Price-Related Legislation" (February 2003), www.ncsl. org/programs/health/drugdisc01.htm (accessed 04/17/03); Milt Freudenheim and Melody Petersen, "The Drug-Price Express Runs Into a Wall," *New York Times,* December 23, 2001, p. C1; Jonathan Walters, "Save Us from the States!" *Governing,* vol. 14, no. 9 (June 2001), pp. 20–27; and Tom Arrandale, "The Pollution Puzzle," *Governing,* vol. 15, no. 11 (August 2002), pp. 22–26. See also Alan Ehrenhalt, "Demanding the Right Size Government," *New York Times,* October 4, 1999, p. A27.

5. Ellen Perlman, "Rail's Resurgence," *Governing,* vol. 12, no. 12 (September 1999), pp. 28–30; North Carolina Railroad Company, "About NCRR," www. ncrr.com/about/about.htm (accessed 12/06/02); Evelyn Nieves, "California Gets Set to Shift on Sentencing Drug Users," *New York Times,* November 10, 2000, p. A18; Leonard Sykes Jr., "Attacking the Cause of Crime: Group Pushing Drug Treatment Instead of Prison for Offenders," *Milwaukee Journal-Sentinel,* December 28, 2001, p. B1; John Bacon and Haya El Nasser, "Vermont Governor Signs Gay-union Bill," *USA Today,* April 27, 2000, p. A3; Danny Hakim, "At the Front on Pollution," *New York Times,* July 3, 2002, p. A1; and Georgia Student Finance Commission, "Georgia's HOPE Scholarship Program," www.gsfc.org/Hope/dsp_hopefaq.cfm (accessed 04/16/03). Georgia's HOPE Scholarship program, while in principle a worthy idea, is funded in an extremely regressive manner.

6. Jonathan Walters, "Save Us from the States!" *Governing,* vol. 14, no. 9 (June 2001), pp. 220–227; Russell Gold and Andrew Caffrey, "United Crime Busters—Chasing Bad Guys Together, State Attorneys General Win Big Cases, Attain New Clout," *Wall Street Journal,* August 1, 2002, p. B1; and David Usborne, "Now Spitzer Turns His Guns on the Rich But Fallen Idols of Corporate America," *The Independent* (London), August 2, 2002, p. 20. The Spitzer initiatives helped spur the SEC into further action—resulting in a broader settlement that included other firms and ultimately amounted to over $1 billion. See Stephen Labaton, "10 Wall St. Firms Reach Settlement in Analyst Inquiry," *New York Times,* April 29, 2003, p. A1; and Ben White, "Wall Street Agrees to Mend Its Ways," *Washington Post,* December 21, 2002, p. A1.

7. Alice Dembner and Shelley Murphy, "Fraud Probe Targets US Drug Firms Sales Tactics, Pricing Under Juries' Scrutiny," *Boston Globe,* August 8, 2002, p. A1; Jeff Nesmith, "Seven States to Sue EPA to Reduce Carbon Dioxide," *Atlanta Journal-Constitution,* February 21, 2003, p. B1; and Jennifer Lee, "Vowing to Enforce, and Change, the Clean Air Act," *New York Times,* April 22, 2003. As of this writing the attorneys general of New York, Connecticut, and New Jersey are also suing the EPA to prevent a relaxation of the agreed standards under the Clean Air Act settlement. See also Eric Pianin, "EPA Will Reconsider Enforcement Policies," *Washington Post,* July 28, 2003, p. A2.

8. Alan Ehrenhalt, "The Monkey or the Gorilla," *Governing,* vol. 15, no. 10 (July 2002), pp. 6–8.

9. Ibid.

10. Mark C. Gordon, *Democracy's New Challenge: Globalization, Governance, and the Future of American Federalism* (New York: Demos, 2001), p. 34.

11. Ibid., p. 6.

12. A partial list of resolutions and letters of protest—including the Oklahoma State Legislature's resolution—can be found at Public Citizen, "State and Local Opposition to NAFTA Chapter 11," www.citizen.org/trade/nafta/CH_11/articles.cfm?ID=7619 (accessed 10/31/02).

13. Chris Mooney, "Localizing Globalization," *The American Prospect,* vol. 12, no. 12 (July 2, 2001—July 16, 2001), pp. 23–26; and Public Citizen, *NAFTA Chapter 11 Investor-to-State Cases: Bankrupting Democracy—Lessons for Fast Track and the Free Trade Area of the Americas* (Washington, D.C.: Public Citizen, September 2001), pp. 23–25.

14. Such comparisons, of course, are subject to movements in exchange rates and have not been adjusted for purchasing power parity (PPP). However such adjustment does not substantially change the size of the U.S. GDP in relation to other countries—the next-largest economy (Japan) in 2001 had a gross domestic product (GDP) of $3.4 trillion (when adjusted for PPP) compared to the $10 trillion U.S. GDP. The U.S. economy is bigger than twenty-five of the other twenty-nine OECD economies combined. See *OECD in Figures: Statistics on the Member Countries* (Paris: OECD, 2002), pp. 12–13.

15. The Social Security Trust Fund assumes average real GDP growth rate of 2.9 percent over the next decade, lower than the average for the last four decades (3.4 percent). After 2012 it projects the growth rate to slow and to approach 1.8 percent by 2080. Projecting this historically low growth rate through the end of the century leads to a real GDP estimate of $71 trillion by 2100 (in chained 2002 dollars). The 1998 Economic Report of the President used a long-term growth rate projection of 2.4 percent, closer to historical growth rates. *The 2004 Annual Report of the Board of Trustees of the Federal Old-Age and Survivors Insurance and Disability Insurance Trust Funds* (Washington, D.C.: Government Printing Office, 2004), p. 99; *2003 Economic Report of the President* (Washington, D.C.: Government Printing Office, 2003), p. 63; and *1998 Economic Report of the President* (Washington, D.C.: Government Printing Office, 1998), p. 78.

16. See U.S. Census Bureau, International Data Base, www.census.gov/ipc/www/idbnew.html (accessed 09/19/03). China and India each have over a billion people. The U.S. population is larger than the combined populations of Australia, Austria, Belgium, Canada, the Czech Republic, Denmark, Finland, Greece, Hungary, Iceland, Ireland, Luxembourg, the Netherlands, New Zealand, Norway, Poland, Portugal, the Slovak Republic, Spain, Sweden, and Switzerland. See *OECD in Figures: Statistics on the Member Countries* (Paris: OECD, 2002), pp. 6–7. U.S. Census Bureau, Population Division, Population Projections Branch, "Annual Projections of the Total Resident Population as of July 1: Middle, Lowest, Highest, and Zero International Migration Series, 1999 to 2100," www.census.gov/population/www/projections/natsum-T1.html (accessed 12/20/02).

17. According to the Bureau of Citizenship and Immigration Services (the new INS), there were 206,426 legal immigrants admitted in federal fiscal year 2001, up from 131,575 in 1998. The average from FY1998 to FY2001 is 164,873. See www.immigration.gov/graphics/shared/aboutus/statistics/IMM2001.pdf (accessed 09/19/03). Also according to BCIS, immigration from Mexico has been adding about 150,000 undocumented immigrants per year. See www.immigration.gov/graphics/shared/aboutus/statistics/Est2000.pdf, p. 5 (accessed 09/19/03). For Republican attempts to woo the largely Mexican Hispanic vote, see James G. Gimpel and Karen Kaufmann, "Impossible Dream or Distant

Reality? Republican Efforts to Attract Latino Voters" (Washington, D.C.: Center for Immigration Studies, August 2001), www.cis.org/articles/2001/back901 .html (accessed 10/31/02).

18. Mike Allen, "Fox, Bush Urge Route to Legalization for Immigrants," *Washington Post*, September 7, 2001, p. A16; Mark Krikorian, "Con Game: The GOP Is Being Taken for a Ride," National Review Online (August 20, 2001), www.nationalreview.com/comment/comment-krikorian082001.shtml (accessed 10/31/02); Harold Meyerson, "California's Progressive Mosaic," *The American Prospect*, vol. 12, no. 11 (June 18, 2001), pp. 17–23; Eric Brazil, "Reaching Out: Unions Widen Their World; Ex-Foes of Undocumented Workers Now See Them as Membership Targets," *San Francisco Chronicle*, September 2, 2001, p. W1; and Steven Greenhouse, "Labor Urges Amnesty for Illegal Immigrants," *New York Times*, February 17, 2000, p. A26.

19. D'Vera Cohn, "Feeble Economy, Tighter Borders Don't Stem Immigrant Tide," *Washington Post*, March 10, 2003, p. A7; Andrew Sum, Paul Harrington with Sheila Palma, "The Impacts of the Recession of 2001 and the Jobless Recovery of 2002 on the Native Born and Immigrant Workforce of the United States" (Boston: Center for Labor Market Studies, Northeastern University, February 2003), www.nupr.neu.edu/3-03/immigration_march.pdf (accessed 04/18/03); and Ronald Brownstein, "Green Light, Red Light," *The American Prospect*, vol. 12, no. 20 (November 19, 2001), p. 29. See Lynette Clemetson, "Hispanic Population Is Rising Swiftly, Census Bureau Says," *New York Times*, June 19, 2003, p. A22. The 2004 Bush proposals were challenged by a broad range of critics on both left and right. See Elisabeth Bumiller, "Bush Would Give Illegal Workers Broad New Rights," *New York Times*, January 7, 2004, p. A1.

20. Christopher Jencks, "Who Should Get In? Part II," *New York Review of Books*, vol. 48, no. 20 (December 20, 2001), pp. 94–102; see also Christopher Jencks, "Who Should Get In?" *New York Review of Books*, vol. 48, no. 19 (November 29, 2001), pp. 57–63. Mexican American women (i.e., women of Mexican descent living in the United States) had a fertility rate of 115 births per 1,000 women in 2000. The fertility rate for Hispanics in general was 106 per 1,000. The fertility rate for non-Hispanics was 62 per 1,000. Joyce A. Martin, Brady E. Hamilton, Stephanie J. Ventura, Fay Menacker, Melissa M. Park, and Paul D. Sutton, "Births: Final Data for 2001," *National Vital Statistics Reports*, vol. 51, no. 2 (December 18, 2002), table 9, pp. 39–40, www.cdc.gov/nchs/data/ nvsr/nvsr51/nvsr51_02.pdf (accessed 05/14/03).

21. State populations as of the 2000 Census, quickfacts.census.gov/qfd/ (accessed 10/02/03).

22. Los Angeles County Economic Development Corporation, Press Release, *2002–2003 Southern California Five-County Area Economic Forecast and Industry Outlook*, September 16, 2002, www.laedc.org/data/press/PR65.shtml (accessed 10/29/02).

23. U.S. Census Bureau, *State and County QuickFacts:* California quickfacts .census.gov/qfd/states/06000.html (accessed 10/31/02); *OECD in Figures: Statistics on the Member Countries* (Paris: OECD, 2002), pp. 6–7; and U.S. Census Bureau, *RadioZone Quotes and Sound Bites: County Population Estimates and Rankings: 2002*, www.census.gov/pubinfo/www/radio/sb_2002countypopest.html (accessed 04/23/03).

24. William Claiborne, "Wilson Challenges Hill to Match His Hard Line," *Washington Post*, January 10, 1995, p. A7.

25. Mitchell Landsberg and Miguel Bustillo, "Davis Says All Power Costs to Be Recovered," *Los Angeles Times*, April 14, 2001, pp. A1, A21; and Dan Morain and Richard Simon, "Energy Deal May Take a Month, Davis Tells Analysts," *Los Angeles Times*, March 1, 2001, pp. A3, A18.

26. On the conservative assumption that California's gross state product (GSP) of $1.36 trillion (2001 dollars) remains at its current 13.5 percent share of GDP even as its (currently projected) population share increases, the figure rises to $9.4 trillion (2003 dollars) or $15.1 trillion following extensions, respectively, of either the Social Security or the Council of Economic Advisers projections. See estimates (by Jeff Chapman) in note 15. See Bureau of Economic Analysis, "Regional Accounts Data: Gross State Product Data," www.bea.gov/bea/regional/gsp (accessed 12/16/02). California had a population of just under 34 million in 2000, accounting for 12 percent of the national population. By 2025 this figure is projected by the Census Bureau's middle series to increase to 14.6 percent. If California ends the century as it began it—with 12 percent of the national population—such estimates suggest there will 68.4 million Californians. If it ends the century with 14.6 percent of the population, the number will be 83.3 million. See U.S. Census Bureau, "Projections of the Total Population of States: 1995 to 2025," www.census.gov/population/projections/state/stpjpop.txt (accessed 01/02/03); and U.S. Census Bureau, "Census 2000 Data for the State of California," www.census.gov/census2000/states/ca.html (accessed 12/16/02).

27. Campbell Gibson and Kay Jung, "Historical Census Statistics on Population Totals by Race, 1790 to 1990, and by Hispanic Origin, 1970 to 1990, for the United States, Regions, Divisions, and States," Population Division, U.S. Census Bureau, Working Paper Series, No. 56 (September 2002), table 19, www.census.gov/population/www/documentation/twps0056.html (accessed 05/14/03); U.S. Census Bureau, American Factfinder, table DP-1, "Profile of General Demographic Characteristics: 2000," Census 2000 Summary File 1 (SF 1), Geographic Area: California; and State of California Department of Finance, "County Population Projections with Age, Sex and Race/Ethnic Detail, July 1, 1990–2040 in 10-year Increments" (Sacramento, Calif.: Department of Finance, Demographic Research Unit, December 1998), www.dof.ca .gov/HTML/DEMOGRAP/projca.pdf (accessed 05/29/03).

28. Tanya Schevitz, Lori Olszewski, and John Wildermuth, "New Demographics Changing Everything," *San Francisco Chronicle*, August 31, 2000, p. A1. See also Mark Baldassare, *California in the New Millennium* (Berkeley: University of California Press and Public Policy Institute of California, 2000).

29. Utilizing the same approach as in the case of California (see note 26 in this chapter), in 2025 Texas is projected to comprise 8 percent of the population (up from a current 7 percent). The two percentages yield a projected population in 2100 of 46 million and 42 million, respectively. See U.S. Census Bureau, "Projections of the Total Population of States: 1995 to 2025," www.census.gov/population/projections/state/stpjpop.txt (accessed 01/02/03); U.S. Census Bureau, "Census 2000 Data for the State of Texas," www.census.gov/census2000/states/tx.html (accessed 12/16/02); and "2001 Population Projections—State of Texas: Projections of the Population of Texas and Counties in Texas by Age, Sex and Race/Ethnicity for 2000–2040," Population Estimates and Projections Program, Texas State Data Center, Texas A&M University System and Office of the State Demographer, December 2001, txsdc.tamu.edu/

tpepp/2001_txpopprj_txtotnum.php (accessed 01/02/03). Following the 0.5 immigration (middle) series, Texas is projected to have a total population of 35 million in 2040. Of the total, 11.4 million are projected to be non-Hispanic white, 18.4 million Hispanic, and 3.3 million black. New York is currently 6.7 percent of the national population and is projected to be 5.9 percent of the population by 2025. If New York ends this century as it began it—with 6.7 percent of the national population, there will 38.2 million New Yorkers under the same assumptions. If it ends the century with 5.9 percent of the population, it will have 33.5 million residents. See U.S. Census Bureau, "Projections of the Total Population of States: 1995 to 2025," www.census.gov/population/projections/state/stpjpop.txt (accessed 01/02/03); and U.S. Census Bureau, "Census 2000 Data for the State of New York," www.census.gov/census2000/states/ny.html (accessed 12/16/02). For ethnicity projections, see U.S. Census Bureau, "Projected State Populations by Sex, Race, and Hispanic Origin: 1995–2025," www.census.gov/population/projections/state/stpjrace.txt (accessed 01/02/03). The New York GSP in 2000 was $754.6 billion (7.6 percent of GDP). The New York GSP in 2001 was $826.5 billion (8.2 percent of GDP). If New York maintains its current share of GDP in 2100, its GSP would be $5.9 trillion using the conservative Social Security Trust Fund Trustees' Report projections, and over $8 trillion using more realistic projections (see note 15 in this chapter). See Bureau of Economic Analysis, Regional Accounts Data, www.bea.gov/bea/regional/gsp (accessed 12/16/02). Non-Hispanic whites, currently 62 percent of the state population, appear likely to diminish to 53.4 percent by 2025 and in all probability reach minority status by midcentury.

30. See, for example, Dan Fagin, "Ill Winds Blow: As Progress on Clean Air Stalls, Regional Fights and Attacks on Rules Intensify," *Newsday*, October 17, 1999, p. A7; Scott Allen, "Cut Is OK'd in Emissions of Mercury; New England Governors Join Canadian Premiers in Accord," *Boston Globe*, June 9, 1998, p. A1; Robert Gavin, "States Rediscover Energy Policies," *Wall Street Journal*, March 21, 2001, p. B13; and Kirk Johnson, "A Changing Climate in Ideas About Pollution," *New York Times*, May 20, 2001, p. 39.

31. Council of State Governments, "Compacts Believed to Be in Effect in 2001," ssl.csg.org/compactlaws/comlistlinks.html (accessed 10/29/02). For federal regional precedents, see Martha Derthick, *Between State and Nation* (Washington, D.C.: Brookings Institution, 1974); and Ann Markusen, *Regions: The Economics and Politics of Territory* (Totowa, N.J.: Rowman & Littlefield, 1987). For information on the continuing work of the Appalachian Regional Commission, see www.arc.gov/ (accessed 11/04/02).

32. Michael Keating and John Loughlin (eds.), *The Political Economy of Regionalism* (London: Frank Cass & Co., 1997); Paul Balchin and Luděk Sýkorla with Gregory Bull, *Regional Policy and Planning in Europe* (London: Routledge, 1999); Yehua Wei, "Economic Reforms and Regional Development in Coastal China," *Journal of Contemporary Asia*, vol. 28, no. 4 (1998), pp. 498–517; Matthew Tempest, "Regional Government Around the World," *The Guardian*, June 16, 2003, politics.guardian.co.uk/localgovernment/story/0,9061,978755,00.html (accessed 06/17/03); and Klaus Konig, "Appraisal of National Policies of Decentralization and Regionalization," Report for Research Committee I: Law and Science of Public Administration, International Institute of Administrative Sciences, XXIst International Congress, Marrakech, 1989, p. 3. James Manor observes that "[n]early all countries worldwide are now experimenting with decentralization."

James Manor, *The Political Economy of Democratic Decentralization* (Washington, D.C.: World Bank, 1999), pp. vii, 1.

15. THE LOGIC OF LONG-TERM POLITICAL REFOCUSING

1. Gene Sperling, "Fiscal Chutzpah," *Washington Post,* July 31, 2001, p. A23.
2. Helen Dewar, "Wellstone, Facing Reelection, Isn't Retreating on Taxes," *Washington Post,* February 17, 2002, p. A5; Senator Paul Wellstone, Press Release, "Wellstone Presses to Put Education First in Federal Budget" (February 12, 2002); and Remarks of Senator Edward M. Kennedy at the National Press Club, "America's New Challenges: National Security, Economic Recovery and Progress for All Americans" (January 16, 2002), www.senate.gov/~kennedy/statements/02/01/2002117616.html (accessed 12/05/02).
3. Remarks by Senator Joseph Lieberman to the Economic Club of Detroit, "The Need to Lead: The Case for a New Economic Growth Strategy" (May 20, 2002), www.senate.gov/~lieberman/speeches/02/05/detroitecon.html (accessed 12/05/02). Lieberman went further a year and a half later, proposing an overhaul of the federal tax code that would lower rates for the middle classes while shifting more of the tax burden to top income groups and corporations. See Edward Wyatt, "Citing Fairness, Lieberman Proposes Tax-Rate Changes," *New York Times,* October 14, 2003, p. A21.
4. The 2003 tax cut lowered the top rate on long-term capital gains from 20 percent to 15 percent, made dividends taxable at the capital gains rate (previously taxed at the same rate as other income), accelerated the rate reductions passed earlier, and cut small business taxes by allowing accelerated business depreciation rates. Albert B. Crenshaw, "A Tax Cut of Varied Proportions," *Washington Post,* May 25, 2003, p. A1; and Citizens for Tax Justice, "Final Plan Tilts Even More Toward Richest," May 22, 2003, www.ctj.org/pdf/sen0503.pdf (accessed 10/16/03). See page 185 in this book for a related discussion of payroll tax issues.
5. "The class gap in American politics is extraordinary. Turnout among those at the bottom of the income and education ladders is only half that of those at the top." Thomas E. Patterson, *The Vanishing Voter* (New York: Knopf, 2002), pp. 45–46. For a study of the dynamics of suburbanization and the impact on redistributive politics, see Juliet F. Gainsborough, *Fenced Off: The Suburbanization of American Politics* (Washington, D.C.: Georgetown University Press, 2001), pp. 75–77, 120–121.
6. Sidney Ratner, *American Taxation* (New York: W. W. Norton, 1942), p. 511–512; and Lawrence Seltzer, "The Place of the Personal Exemptions in the Present-Day Income Tax," *Tax Revision Compendium,* vol. 1 (Washington, D.C.: Government Printing Office, U.S. House Committee on Ways and Means, 1959), pp. 493–514. See also Joseph J. Thorndike and Dennis J. Ventry Jr. (eds.), *Tax Justice: The Ongoing Debate* (Washington, D.C.: Urban Institute Press, 2002).
7. Congressional Budget Office, "Effective Federal Tax Rates, 1997 to 2000," August 2003, www.cbo.gov/ftpdoc.cfm?index=4514&type=1 (accessed 11/04/03), table B1-B.
8. Limiting case projections can be derived from work by Citizens for Tax Justice: CTJ estimated in 2002 (before the third Bush tax cut was passed) that the share of income taxes paid by the top 1 percent would fall to 34.4 percent in

2010. "White House Reveals Nation's Biggest Problems: The Very Rich Don't Have Enough Money and Workers Don't Pay Enough in Taxes," December 16, 2002, www.ctj.org/pdf/flat1202.pdf (accessed 11/04/03). CTJ also estimated in 2003 that the impact of the three Bush tax cuts taken together would reduce the share of *total* federal taxes paid by the top 1 percent from 23.7 percent to 21.3 percent. Citizens for Tax Justice, "Effects of First Three Bush Tax Cuts Charted," June 4, 2003, www.ctj.org/pdf/allbushcut.pdf (accessed 11/04/03).

9. Internal Revenue Service, "Personal Exemptions and Individual Income Tax Rates, 1913–2002;" SOI Bulletin, Data Release, Spring 2002 (June 2002), www.irs.gov/taxstats/article/0,,id=96679,00.html (accessed 12/10/03).

10. Pew Research Center for the People and the Press, "Economic Inequality Seen As Rising, Boom Bypasses Poor" (June 21, 2001), www.people-press.org/reports/display.php3?ReportID=8 (accessed 5/31/02); The Gallup Organization, "Have and Have-Nots: Perceptions of Fairness and Opportunity–1998," section 5, p. 1, section 7, p. 3, www.gallup.com/poll/socialaudits (accessed 12/06/02); and Everett Carll Ladd and Karlyn H. Bowman, *Attitudes Toward Economic Inequality* (Washington, D.C.: A.E.I. Press, 1998), p. 97.

11. Humphrey Taylor, "Dramatic Decline in Alienation," *The Harris Poll*, No. 1 (January 2, 2002), www.harrisinteractive.com/harris_poll/index.asp?PollYear=2002 (accessed 12/06/02). Related to this: a 1999 poll that asked what bothered people most about taxes found 46 percent objecting that "some rich people get away with not paying their fair share." "A Taxing Dilemma: Public attitudes on the issue of government spending," *American Demographic,* vol. 23, no. 3 (March 2001), p. 22, via Academic Search Premier. In the previously noted report done for the American Enterprise Institute, the late Everett Carll Ladd and Ann Bowman suggested that if such sentiments evolve into judgments that the economic system is unfairly distributing the nation's wealth and income, "Social unrest and demands for protectionism and for tax policies designed to soak the rich could follow." Ladd and Bowman, *Attitudes Toward Economic Inequality,* p. 84. Overarching economic problems are also clearly relevant. Another recent poll found that a majority (51 percent) of Americans felt the "American dream has become impossible for most people to achieve." *Time*/CNN poll, "American Dream," January 16, 1998, via Polling the Nations. Regarding priorities, in 2002, 69 percent said it would have been "better to have spent the money on programs like Social Security and Medicare" rather than cut taxes, in a CBS News/*New York Times* poll, November 20–24, 2002. An AP poll in March 2002 found 72 percent would vote for candidates who would balance the budget rather than cut taxes. "Federal Budget and Taxes," PollingReport.com, www.pollingreport.com/budget.htm (accessed 01/21/03). On this point, see also Ruy Teixeira, "A Snapshot of American Public Opinion at the End of 2002," *Indicators,* vol. 2, no. 2 (Spring 2003), pp. 116–121; and "Toplines: National Survey of Americans' Views on Taxes," National Public Radio/Kaiser Family Foundation/Kennedy School of Government Poll, April 2003, www.npr.org/news/specials/polls/taxes2003/20030415_taxes_survey.pdf (accessed 10/22/03).

12. S. M. Miller and Charles Collins, "Growing Economic Fairness," *Social Policy,* vol. 26, no. 4 (Summer 1996), pp. 41–55, esp. p. 41.

13. Humphrey Taylor, "While Confidence in Leaders and Institutions Has Dropped from the Extraordinary Post-9/11 High, It Is Still Higher Than It Was for Most of the Late 70s, 80s, and 90s," *Harris Poll,* no. 4 (January 22, 2003), available online at www.harrisinteractive.com/harris_poll/index.asp?PID=351

(accessed 09/11/03). See also Ruy Teixeira, "Is the Big-Business Era Over?" *The American Prospect,* vol. 13, no. 15 (August 26, 2002), pp. 12–13.

14. Humphrey Taylor, "Large Majorities Believe Big Companies, PACs, Media and Lobbyists Have Too Much Power and Influence in Washington," *Harris Poll,* no. 17 (April 10, 2002), www.harrisinteractive.com/harris_poll/index.asp?PID=294 (accessed 09/11/03). See also "Americans Have a Beef with Big Business," *Business Week* Online, August 31, 2000, www.businessweek.com/bwdaily/dnflash/aug2000/nf20000831_923.htm (accessed 05/08/01).

15. Mishel, Bernstein, and Boushey, *The State of Working America: 2002–2003,* table 2.6, p. 126. For a discussion of recent trends, see Jared Bernstein and Lawrence Mishel, "Labor Market Left Behind: Evidence Shows That Post-Recession Economy Has Not Turned into a Recovery for Workers," EPI Briefing Paper #142, September 2003, www.epinet.org/content.cfm/briefingpapers_bp142 (accessed 10/06/03).

16. U.S. Census Bureau, March CPS "Table F-5: Race and Hispanic Origin of Householder-Families by Median and Mean Income: 1947 to 2002," www.census.gov/hhes/income/histinc/f05.html (accessed 10/06/03). Median family income fell to $52,225 in 2001 and then again to $51,680 in 2002 (2002 dollars).

17. For married couples with children the situation was even more challenging. Increases in hours of work for such couples dwarfed the general average: over the past thirty years they added twenty more weeks—around five months—to their joint annual work load. Mishel, Bernstein, and Boushey, *The State of Working America: 2002–2003,* pp. 16, 117. Other studies differ on the precise number of annual hours but confirm the trend: the International Labour Organization, which tracks working time as one of its key labor market indicators, estimates that hours worked per year in the United States rose from 1,883 in 1980 to 1,979 in 2000; see *Key Indicators of the Labour Market* (Geneva: International Labour Organization, 2001), table 6-B, "Annual Hours Worked Per Person," www.ilo.org/public/english/employment/strat/kilm/table.htm (accessed 05/02/03). Economists from the Bureau of Labor Statistics estimated that between 1976 and 1993, average annual hours for men rose by 100 hours and for women by 233 hours: see Philip Rones, Jennifer Gardner, and Randy Ilg, "Trends in Hours of Work in the United States," in *Working Time in Comparative Perspective, Vol. I: Patterns, Trends, and the Policy Implications for Earnings Inequality and Unemployment,* eds. Ging Wong and Garnett Picot (Kalamazoo, Mich.: W. E. Upjohn Institute for Employment Research, 2001).

18. U.S. Census Bureau, March CPS "Table F-7. Type of Family (All Races) by Median and Mean Income: 1947 to 2001," www.census.gov/hhes/income/histinc/f07.html (accessed 04/23/03).

19. Mishel, Bernstein, and Schmitt, *The State of Working America: 2000–2001,* p. 48. "It could be that, at 62 percent . . . the country is approaching the 'ceiling' of the share of wives that are able or willing to spend time in the labor market;" Mishel, Bernstein, and Boushey, *The State of Working America, 2002–2003,* p. 46. Related to this: during the 1960s the growth rate of the female labor force was 3.1 percent, compared to 1.0 percent for men. However, the Bureau of Labor Statistics estimates that between 1998 and 2015 the growth rate of the female labor force will only slightly outpace that of men (1.2 percent vs. 0.8 percent annually), and between 2015 and 2025 will actually be lower than that for men (0.1 percent vs. 0.3 percent). Howard N. Fullerton Jr.,

"Labor Force Participation: 75 Years of Change, 1950–1998 and 1998–2025," *Monthly Labor Review,* vol. 112, no. 12 (December 1999): pp. 3–12, esp. p. 11.

20. Barry Bluestone, "Understanding Growth in the New Economy," *Antipode,* vol. 33, no. 1 (January 2001), pp. 72–83; Freeman, *The New Inequality,* pp. 3–4.

21. Suzanne W. Helburn and Barbara R. Bergmann, *America's Child Care Problem: The Way Out* (New York: St. Martin's Press, 2002), p. 21. See also Kimberly Blanton, "Study: Families Don't Earn Enough to Cover Needs," *Boston Globe,* September 23, 1998, p. F3.

22. Public university figure from "Losing Ground," National Center for Public Policy and Higher Education (NCPPHE) (San Jose, Calif.: NCPPHE, May 2002), p. 5, www.highereducation.org (accessed 12/06/02). Private institution figure from Jerome Segal, *Graceful Simplicity* (New York: Henry Holt, 1999), p. 62. The College Board, *Trends in College Pricing 2003* (Washington, D.C.: The College Entrance Examination Board, 2003), www.collegeboard.com/prod_downloads/press/cost03/cb_trends_pricing_2003.pdf (accessed 05/05/04). The figure for the ten-year increase is in constant 2002 dollars.

23. *Statistical Abstract, 2002,* table 926, p. 593; and Millennial Housing Commission (MHC), *Meeting Our Nation's Housing Challenges* (Washington, D.C.: MHC, May 30, 2002), pp. 2, 15, 17. In 2001 the average renter spent 34.5 percent of expenditures on housing costs, up from 31.5 percent in 1985. Bureau of Labor Statistics, Consumer Expenditure Survey, table 7, 1984 and 2001 data, www.bls.gov/cex/csxstnd.htm (accessed 10/30/03). *Out of Reach 2003,* a report by the National Low Income Housing Coalition, found in 2003 that in every state in the nation the fair market rent for a two-bedroom home was beyond the means of many low-income families. See *Out of Reach 2003* (Washington, D.C.: National Low Income Housing Coalition, September 2003), available online at www.nlihc.org/oor2003/ (accessed 09/10/03); and Lynette Clemetson, "Poor Workers Finding Modest Housing Unaffordable, Study Says," *New York Times,* September 9, 2003, p. A15.

24. *Statistical Abstract, 2001,* table 1091, p. 683. This is not due to an increase in workers per household. The percentage of households with two or more earners changed only marginally over the period: 43.5 percent in 1983 and 45 percent in 1995. U.S. Census, "Historical Income Tables," table H-12, www.census.gov/hhes/income/histinc/h12.html (accessed 04/24/03). Even as miles driven increased, there was also a modest increase in residential ownership: from 62.9 percent owner-occupied units in 1970, to 64.4 percent in 1980, and to 67.8 percent percent in 2001. *Statistical Abstract, 2002,* table 939, p. 600; and *Statistical Abstract, 1990,* table 1274, p. 720.

25. Pew Research Center for the People and the Press, "Economic Inequality Seen As Rising, Boom Bypasses Poor" (June 21, 2001), www.people-press.org/reports/display.php3?ReportID=8 (accessed 05/31/02); and Robert J. Mills and Shailesh Bhandari, "Health Insurance Coverage in the United States: 2002," U.S. Census Bureau, September 2003, www.census.gov/prod/2003pubs/p60-223.pdf (accessed 12/09/02). For a discussion of the decline in poverty in the 1990s and the likely increase in the future, see William Julius Wilson, "There Goes the Neighborhood," *New York Times,* June 16, 2003, p. A19.

26. Center on Budget and Policy Priorities, "Poverty Rates Fell in 2000 as Unemployment Reached 31-Year Low" (September 26, 2001), www.cbpp.org/9-25-01pov.htm (accessed 12/09/02).

27. U.S. Department of the Census, Census 2000 Data for the State of California, Profile of General Demographic Characteristics, table DP-1, www.census

.gov/census2000/states/ca.html (accessed 12/13/02); and Jim Yardley, "Non-Hispanic Whites May Soon Be a Minority in Texas," *New York Times*, March 25, 2001, p. A22.

28. U.S. Census Bureau, (NP-T4) Projections of the Total Resident Population by 5-Year Age Groups, Race, and Hispanic Origin with Special Age Categories: Middle Series, 1999 to 2100 (August 2, 2002), www.census.gov/population/www/projections/natsum-T3.html (accessed 12/09/02).

29. Campbell Gibson and Kay Jung, "Historical Census Statistics on Population Totals by Race, 1790 to 1990, and by Hispanic Origin, 1970 to 1990, for the United States, Regions, Divisions, and States," U.S. Census Bureau Working Paper Series, No. 56, September 2002, www.census.gov/population/documentation/twps0056/tab01.pdf (accessed 10/06/03). Changes in terms of politics, of course, have been even more dramatic. Before World War II a very large share (approximately three out of four) of the black population was concentrated in Southern states where voting was often all but impossible. U.S. Bureau of the Census, *Historical Statistics of the United States, Colonial Times to 1970, Bicentennial Edition, Part 1* (Washington, D.C.: U.S. Government Printing Office, 1975), pp. 14, 23.

30. John B. Judis, "For Richer and Poorer," *New Republic*, vol. 223, no. 23 (December 4, 2000), pp. 18–19. Princeton sociologist Paul Starr also believes there is a potential for "flipping the sunbelt" by bringing together progressive Hispanic and elderly voters. Paul Starr, "An Emerging Democratic Majority," in *The New Majority*, eds. Stanley B. Greenberg and Theda Skocpol (New Haven: Yale University Press, 1997), pp. 221–237. See also William Julius Wilson, *The Bridge Over the Racial Divide: Rising Inequality and Coalition Politics* (Berkeley: University of California Press, 2001); Manuel Pastor Jr., Peter Dreier, J. Eugene Grigsby III, and Marta López Garza, *Regions That Work: How Cities and Suburbs Can Grow Together* (Minneapolis: University of Minnesota Press, 2000); Angela Glover Blackwell, Stewart Kwoh, and Manuel Pastor, *Searching for the Uncommon Common Ground* (New York: W.W. Norton, 2002); and Karen M. Kaufmann, "Black and Latino Voters in Denver: Responses to Each Other's Political Leadership," *Political Science Quarterly*, vol. 118, no. 1 (Spring 2003), pp.107–125.

31. Michael Lind, "The Beige and the Black," *New York Times*, August 16, 1998, Section 6, pp. 38–39; and Thomas Byrne Edsall with Mary D. Edsall, *Chain Reaction* (New York: W.W. Norton, 1991), p. 5.

32. Steven R. Weisman, *The Great Tax Wars: Lincoln to Wilson—The Fierce Battles Over Money and Power that Transformed the Nation* (New York: Simon & Schuster, 2002), p. 367.

33. Note in this regard that Lieberman also supported legislation to establish a commission to cut corporate welfare in 2002: S. 2181 (Corporate Subsidy Reform Commission Act of 2002), "A bill to review, reform, and terminate unnecessary and inequitable federal subsidies." Senator Joe Lieberman, Press Release, "Agenda for Economic Prosperity," October 18, 2002, www.senate.gov/~lieberman/press/02/10/2002A18719.html (accessed 04/23/03).

34. Seventeen states and the District of Columbia have decoupled from federal estate tax changes. Elizabeth C. McNichol, "Many States are Decoupling from the Federal Estate Tax Cut" (December 6, 2002), www.centeronbudget.org/5–23–02sfp.htm (accessed 01/20/03). Regarding corporate "bonus depreciation" decoupling: Thirty states and the District of Columbia, which had

previously followed federal depreciation guidelines, have decoupled. (In twenty-three states and in D.C., decoupling was the result of, or has been confirmed by, the legislature. Six states decoupled following laws already in place. Mississippi, the thirtieth state, decoupled following a ruling by the state tax commissioner.) Nicholas Johnson, "Many States Are Decoupling from Federal 'Bonus Depreciation' Tax Cut" (September 26, 2002), www.centeronbudget .org/5-8-02sfp.htm (accessed 12/06/02). In the face of severe budget problems, several Republican governors have also reluctantly reneged on pledges of "no new taxes"; among them Bob Taft (Ohio), Mike Huckabee (Ark.), Dirk Kempthorne (Idaho), and Sonny Perdue (Ga.). Jim McGreevey (D-N.J.) successfully pushed through an $824 million corporate tax increase that went into effect in 2003. Dale Russakoff and Edward Walsh, "GOP Governors Grit Teeth and Raise Taxes," *Washington Post*, January 19, 2003, p. A1; Josh Flory, "Missouri Budget Has Tax Hikes for Smokers, Casinos, Wealthy," *Columbia Daily Tribune*, January 15, 2003, via Lexis Nexis; William Hershey, "Taft Unveils $2.3B Tax-Hike Proposal; Some Republicans Stunned by Governor's Plan," *Dayton Daily News*, January 31, 2003, via Lexis Nexis; National Conference of State Legislatures, "State Budget and Tax Actions Preliminary Report 2002" (August 28, 2002), www.ncsl.org/ (accessed 10/13/03), p. 9; Randall Chase, "Delaware Governor Proposes Mix of Cuts, Tax Increases to Balance Budget," Associated Press, January 31, 2003, via Lexis Nexis; Jo Becker and Michael D. Shear, "Va. House Prepares Plan That Avoids Big Tax Rise; Senate Passes Competing Bill Providing $3.9 Billion Increase," *Washington Post*, February 21, 2004, p. B1; see also Senate bill "SB 635 Tax Reform"on the web site of the Virginia General Assembly Legislative Information System, leg1.state.va.us/cgi-bin/legp504.exe?041+sum+SB635S (accessed 03/29/04). It is worth noting, too, that George H. W. Bush in 1990 and Bill Clinton in 1993 both proposed and secured the enactment of new taxes on the very top groups when fiscal pressures intensified. See also Leonard Burman and Deborah Kobes, "Income Tax Brackets Since 1985," *Tax Notes*, July 28, 2003, p. 557; and David E. Rosenbaum, "The Deficit Disappeared, But That Was Then," *New York Times*, September 21, 2003, p. D3. The Republican-controlled Virginia State Senate voted to add new, higher tax brackets for incomes between $100,000 and $150,000 and for incomes above $150,000. The Democratic governor of Missouri proposed a 5 percent surcharge on state income taxes paid by the top 2 percent.

16. SOCIAL SECURITY, RETIREMENT, AND HEALTH CARE

1. Social Security Trustees, *The 2004 Annual Report of the Board of Trustees of the Federal Old-Age and Survivors Insurance and Disability Insurance Trust Funds* (Washington, D.C.: Government Printing Office, 2004), p. 8.
2. Dean Baker, "The Assumptions Are Too Pessimistic," *Challenge*, vol. 39, no. 6 (November–December 1996), pp. 31–32.
3. Baker, ibid.; Dimitri B. Papadimitriou and L. Randall Wray, "Does Social Security Need Saving?" Levy Institute Public Policy Brief, No. 55A, August 1999; Teresa Ghilarducci, "Myths and Misinformation About America's Retirement System," in *Unconventional Wisdom: Alternative Perspectives on the New Economy*, ed. Jeff Madrick (New York: The Century Foundation, 2000),

pp. 69–92; International Monetary Fund, "Staff Report for the 2001 Article IV Consultation" (International Monetary Fund: Washington, D.C., June 28, 2001), p. 30; and Paul Krugman, "Fabricating a Crisis," *New York Times*, August 21, 2001, p. 17. Social Security Administration estimates suggest that removing the tax cap could close between 74 percent and 98 percent of the financing gap, benefit cuts of up to 5 percent could close 30 percent of the gap, raising the retirement age could reduce the gap by 20 to 26 percent. Social Security Administration Memorandum, Keith Fontenot, "Information on the Distributional Effects of Various Social Security Solvency Options, by Gender and Income" (May 18, 1999). Others who have suggested altering the tax cap include Thomas Palley, "Social Security: Prefunding Is Not the Answer!" *Challenge*, vol. 45, no. 2 (March–April 2002), pp. 97–118; and Gary Burtless of the Brookings Institution, who argues that removing the cap not only would bring Social Security significantly closer to long-term solvency, but "would dampen the enthusiasm for giving raises to upper-income workers. Employers would think twice about having to pay more payroll tax. Wage inequality might even lessen." Louis Uchitelle, "A Retirement Plan That Wall Street Likes," *New York Times*, November 12, 2000, p. C6. Financing problems have been exacerbated because wage growth has been concentrated at the top in recent years—and the tax cap has not kept up with such growth. As a result, a decreasing proportion of total wages have been taxed. In 1983, 90.2 percent of earnings in covered employment were taxable (i.e., only 10 percent of earnings occurred above the tax cap). The covered share was 85.4 percent in 2002. It is projected to fall to 83.8 percent by 2012. See Social Security Trustees, *The 2003 Annual Report of the Board of Trustees of the Federal Old-Age and Survivors Insurance and Disability Insurance Trust Funds* (Washington, D.C.: Government Printing Office, 2003), p. 110.

4. Gary Burtless, "Reforming Social Security to Boost Contributors' Returns and Assure Retirement Income Security," Testimony for the Senate Committee on the Budget, January 19, 1999; Paul Samuelson, "An Exact Consumption Loan Model with or without the Social Contrivance of Money," *Journal of Political Economy*, vol. 66, no. 6 (1958), pp. 467–482; and Paul Samuelson, "Social Security," *Newsweek*, February 13, 1967, p. 88. Samuelson's model depicts a pay-as-you-go system as sustainable so long as the labor force and wage rate grow faster than inflation. As Sylvester Scheiber and John Shoven write, "[E]verything changed in 1973, and many of the socioeconomic underpinnings so important for Social Security have never been the same since." See Sylvester J. Scheiber and John B. Shoven, *The Real Deal: The History and Future of Social Security* (New Haven: Yale University Press, 1999), pp. 165, 108–113; and Alicia H. Munnell, "Reforming Social Security: The Case Against Individual Accounts," *National Tax Journal*, vol. 52, no. 4 (December 1999), pp. 803–818.

5. U.S. Census Bureau, Population Division, Population Projections Branch, "National Population Projections: Total Population by Age, Sex, Race, and Hispanic Origin," www.census.gov/population/www/projections/natsum-T3.html (accessed 05/14/03).

6. Social Security Trustees, *The 2004 Annual Report of the Board of Trustees of the Federal Old-Age and Survivors Insurance and Disability Insurance Trust Funds* (Washington, D.C.: Government Printing Office, 2004), pp. 46–49.

7. U.S. Census Bureau, *Historical Statistics of the United States: Colonial Times to 1970, Part 1* (Washington, D.C.: Government Printing Office, 1976), table B107–115,

p. 55; U.S. Census Bureau, Population Division, Population Projections Branch, "Summary of Fertility, Mortality, and Migration Assumptions by Race and Hispanic Origin: Lowest, Middle, and Highest Series, 1999 to 2100," www.census .gov/population/www/projections/natsum-T7.html (accessed 05/14/03), mortality tables: "If present trends continue those who are twenty today can expect to spend up to a third of their lives in retirement"—years that must be financed; Dora Costa, *The Evolution of Retirement: An American Economic History, 1880–1990* (Chicago: University of Chicago Press, 1998), p. 6; and Teresa Ghilarducci, *Labor's Capital: The Economics and Politics of Private Pensions* (Cambridge, Mass.: M.I.T. Press, 1992).

8. Social Security Trustees, *The 2004 Annual Report of the Board of Trustees of the Federal Old-Age and Survivors Insurance and Disability Insurance Trust Funds* (Washington, D.C.: Government Printing Office, 2004), pp. 57–60, 63; and Sylvester J. Scheiber and John B. Shoven, *The Real Deal: The History and Future of Social Security* (New Haven: Yale University Press, 1999), p. 210. Social Security estimates the present value of Social Security's lifetime unfunded liability to be $10.4 trillion. The seventy-five-year financing gap ($3.7 trillion) is equal to 1.89 percent of taxable payroll over the projection period—an immediate payroll tax increase of 1.92 percentage points (i.e., a 15 percent increase of the current tax) would be needed to cover the expected shortfall.

9. Baker, "The Assumptions Are Too Pessimistic," pp. 31–32.

10. Several polls have demonstrated public resistance to benefit cuts or to an increase in the payroll tax rate. In 2000, 72 percent of respondents in a *Newsweek* poll stated that maintaining current benefit levels should be the president's "top" priority. A national Kaiser Family Foundation poll found that 90 percent oppose reducing benefits (including 73 percent who "strongly oppose") and almost half—47 percent—said they would vote against their member of Congress if he or she acted to reduce benefits. A national 1998 poll by the Employee Benefit Research Institute found that 71 percent opposed increasing the payroll tax (45 percent strongly). *Newsweek* poll, October 28, 2000; Kaiser Family Foundation, May 20, 1999; and Employee Benefit Research Institute, 1998; all accessed via Polling the Nation. On the political difficulties facing standard reform options, see also Susan Page, "Why Social Security Reform Is Dead, For Now," *USA Today*, December 4, 2001, p. 1A.

11. This figure includes both the employer and employee share of payroll taxes. Of households that paid either payroll or income taxes, 45.2 percent paid more in employee-share payroll taxes than income taxes. Congressional Budget Office, "Effective Federal Tax Rates, 1997 to 2000" (Washington, D.C.: Government Printing Office, August 2003), www.cbo.gov/ftpdoc.cfm?index=4514&type=1 (accessed 10/06/03).

12. Office of Management and Budget, *Budget of the United States 2005: Historical Tables* (Washington, D.C.: Government Printing Office, 2004), w3.access.gpo .gov/usbudget/, tables 2.2, 2.4.

13. "Strengthening Social Security and Creating Personal Wealth for All Americans," *Report of the President's Commission to Strengthen Social Security*, December 21, 2001.

14. Dean Baker, *The Full Returns from Social Security*, Century Foundation/Economic Policy Institute Report (1998).

15. Ted Halstead, "The Big Tax Bite You Don't Even Think About," *Washington Post*, April 23, 2000, p. B5.

16. Halstead hopes to replace the revenue lost through "increases in the capital gains tax rate; auctions of new segments of the electromagnetic spectrum; claiming a share of the revenue from the commercial applications of government research and development; instituting an array of pollution fees; or closing various corporate and individual tax loopholes." Halstead, "The Big Tax Bite You Don't Even Think About," *Washington Post*, April 23, 2000, p. B5.

17. Gene Sperling, "Who Lost the Surplus?" *Blueprint Magazine*, Democratic Leadership Council, March 25, 2002.

18. Paul Krugman, "Fabricating a Crisis," *New York Times*, August 21, 2001, p. A17; Richard Kogan, Robert Greenstein, and Peter Orszag, "Social Security and the Tax Cut: The 75-year Cost of the Tax Cut Is More Than Twice as Large as the Long-Term Deficit in Social Security," Center on Budget and Policy Priorities, April 11, 2002; and William H. Gates Sr. and Chuck Collins, "Tax the Wealthy," *The American Prospect*, vol. 13, no. 11 (June 17, 2002).

19. Leon Friedman, "A Better Kind of Wealth Tax," *The American Prospect*, vol. 11, no. 23 (November 6, 2000). For a discussion of the constitutionality of wealth taxes see chapter 17, note 17 in this book.

20. Although Social Security benefits are generally small (only 10.7 percent of beneficiaries receive a monthly payment of $1,300 or more), they make up a substantial portion of elderly income. In 2001 Social Security made up 39 percent of the total income of the population sixty-five or older, followed by earnings (24 percent), pensions (18 percent), and asset income (16 percent). Social Security accounts for 75 percent or more of total income for 44 percent of persons sixty-five or older living alone and 24 percent for those living in families. Supplemental Security Income (SSI) is an additional source of income for the elderly, blind, and disabled. In 2001 nearly 2 million persons sixty-five or older received SSI, with an average monthly payment of $316.55. Social Security Administration, *Annual Statistical Supplement to the Social Security Bulletin, 2001* (Social Security Administration, 2001), tables 3.E6, 5.B6, 7.A1; and Social Security Administration, *Income of the Aged Chartbook, 2001*, p. 11.

21. Employee Benefit Research Institute, "U.S. Retirement Income System," EBRI Fact Sheet, December 1998, www.ebri.org/facts/index.htm (accessed 01/16/03); and Bureau of Labor Statistics, "Employee Benefits in Private Industry, March 2003," www.bls.gov/news.release/ebs2.toc.htm (accessed 10/06/03), table 1.

22. Employee Benefit Research Institute, "U.S. Retirement Income System," EBRI Fact Sheet, December 1998, www.ebri.org/facts/index.htm (accessed 01/16/03); and Bureau of Labor Statistics, "Employee Benefits in Private Industry, March 2003," www.bls.gov/news.release/ebs2.toc.htm (accessed 10/06/03), table 1; www.bls.gov/news.release/ebs2.toc.htm (accessed 05/02/03), table 1.

23. Employee Benefit Research Institute, "401(k) Plan Account Balances, Asset Allocation, and Loan Activity Plan Year 2000," EBRI Fact Sheet, January 2002, www.ebri.org/facts/index.htm (accessed 01/16/03); and Elena Gouskova and Frank Stafford, "Trends in Household Wealth Dynamics, 1999–2001," Institute for Social Research, University of Michigan, September 2002, www.psidonline.isr.umich.edu/Publications/Papers/TrendsIndynamics1999–2001.pdf (accessed 10/06/03). The median value of retirement accounts—401(k)-type accounts and IRAs—according to the Federal Reserve, for forty-five to fifty-four year-olds was $48,000 and $55,000 for fifty-five to sixty-four year-olds in 2001. Ana M. Aizcorbe, Arthur B. Kennickell, and Kevin B. Moore, "Recent Changes in U.S. Family Finances: Evidence from the 1998 and 2001

Survey of Consumer Finances," *Federal Reserve Bulletin,* January 2003, p. 13, table 5.B.

24. Bureau of Labor Statistics, "Employee Benefits in Private Industry, March 2003," www.bls.gov/news.release/ebs2.toc.htm (accessed 10/06/03), table 1. In 2000, 55 percent of those age sixty-five and older had *no* pension income (which, as noted, also brings average pension income down—to $4,000 per year). Social Security Administration, "Income of the Population, 55 and Older, 2000," p. 95 (table 5.C10, all); and "Income of the Elderly, 2000," Employee Benefits Research Institute, June 2002. The poverty rate for retirees without pension income in 1998 was 21 percent, compared to 10.5 percent for the elderly population and 12.7 percent overall; see General Accounting Office, "Pension Plans: Characteristics of Persons in the Labor Force without Pension Coverage," GAO/HEHS-00-131, August 2000; and U.S. Census Bureau, "Historical Poverty Tables," www.census.gov/hhes/poverty/histpov/perindex.html, (accessed 05/13/03), tables 2, 3.

25. Bureau of Economic Analysis, "Personal Saving Rate," www.bea.gov/briefrm/saving.htm, (accessed 06/05/04); Bureau of Economic Analysis, "Personal Income and its Disposition," NIPA, table 2.9; Social Security Administration, "Income of the Population, 55 and Older," 2000, p. 98, table 5.d1; and "Income of the Elderly, 2000," Employee Benefits Research Institute, June 2002. For all households, between 1983 and 1998, the share of households with zero or negative net worth increased from 15.5 percent to 18 percent. The share of households with zero or negative financial (i.e., excluding home-ownership) worth is roughly 26 percent. (These figures, based on information available through 1998, are likely to worsen when new data that include stock market declines since 1998 are fully analyzed). Edward Wolff, "Recent Trends in Wealth Ownership, 1983–1998," in *Assets for the Poor,* eds. Edward Wolff and Thomas Shapiro, (New York: Russell Sage Foundation, 2001), p. 38. The journal *Pensions and Investments* observes: "401(k) savings simply have replaced other personal savings." "Tottering Stool," *Pensions and Investments,* vol. 30, no. 6 (March 18, 2002), p. 10. Economist Edward Wolff estimated in 1998 that fully 42.5 percent of those who were currently in the forty-seven to sixty-four "pre-retirement" age bracket could expect to retire with income less than half their current income. Almost one in six (15.5 percent) could not expect to replace even 25 percent of their income—a figure that had doubled from 7.7 percent two decades earlier. The estimates were made before stock market declines lowered the value of IRAs, 401(k) plans, and other retirement assets and are also clearly conservative. Edward Wolff, *Retirement Insecurity: The Income Shortfalls Awaiting the Soon-to-Retire* (Washington, D.C.: Economic Policy Institute, 2002), pp. 12, 49.

26. W. Andrew Achenbaum, *Social Security: Visions and Revisions* (Cambridge: Cambridge University Press, 1987); Edward Berkowtiz, "The First Advisory Council and the 1939 Amendments," in *Social Security After Fifty,* ed. Edward Berkowitz (New York: Greenwood Press, 1987); and Sheryl Tynes, *Turning Points in Social Security: From "Cruel Hoax" to "Sacred Entitlement"* (Stanford, Calif.: Stanford University Press, 1996), pp. 87–88. The original Social Security fund was invested entirely in government instruments.

27. Robert Ball, Edith U. Fierst, Gloria T. Johnson, Thomas W. Jones, George Kourpias, and Gerald M. Shea, "Social Security for the 21st Century: A Strategy to Maintain Benefits and Strengthen America's Family Protection Plan,"

Report of the 1994–1996 Advisory Council on Social Security, Vol. 1: Findings and Recommendations (Washington, D.C.: Social Security Administration, 1997).

28. Amy Goldstein and George Hager, "President Ties Social Security's Future to Stocks," *Washington Post*, January 20, 1999, p. A1. The proposal was shot down by, among others, Federal Reserve Chairman Alan Greenspan. Greenspan argued the Clinton plan would not increase overall national savings (and that any investment gains might be offset by interest rate increases in the private market resulting from a diversion of investment funds). He also feared government interference in the private economy through stock ownership. Others, such as Teresa Ghilarducci, point out that state, local, and federal retirement plans (including that of the Federal Reserve Board) offer precedent and experience that establish the basis for a viable federal plan. The level of interest rates—as current experience (as of this writing) with very large deficits and very low rates suggests—clearly is not wholly dependent on changes in federal investment strategies. On the other hand, it is possible that investment gains for Social Security might not be as large as a static analysis might suggest. Alan Greenspan, "On Investing the Social Security Trust Fund in Equities," testimony before the Subcommittee on Finance and Hazardous Materials, Committee on Commerce, U.S. House of Representatives, March 3, 1999; Teresa Ghilarducci, "Public Fund Investments in the Stock Market: Chairman Greenspan's Irrational Pessimism," *FOMC Alert*, vol. 3, no. 2 (March 30, 1999); Wilshire Associates, "Private versus Public Pension Fund Investment Performance," February 4, 1999, www.calpers.ca.gov/whatshap/hottopic/w-study.htm (accessed 06/04/03); and Cost Effectiveness Management, "Do Public Funds Underperform Corporate Pension Funds?" February 5, 1999, www.calpers.ca.gov/whatshap/hottopic/cem-study.htm (accessed 06/04/03). A modest move in the same general direction has also been proposed by *Newsweek* columnist Allan Sloan. Sloan points out that under existing law the Social Security Trust Fund could even now invest in assets other than U.S. Treasury securities, such as government-guaranteed securities offered by the Government National Mortgage Association ("Ginnie Maes"). Allan Sloan, "A Ginnie Mae Solution for Social Security," *Washington Post*, August 7, 2001, p. E3.

29. Henry Aaron and Robert Reischauer, "Should We Retire Social Security: Grading the Reform Plans," *Brookings Review* (Winter 1999), pp. 6–11; Alicia Munnell and R. Kent Weaver, "How to Privatize Social Security," *Washington Post*, July 9, 2001, p. A17; and Flan Fry, "Canada Moves Toward Fuller Funding for Its Pension Plan," *Social Security Bulletin*, vol. 61, no. 1 (1998), pp. 63–64. The Canada Pension Plan is moving from a pay-as-you-go system to a partially funded one that will hold assets equal to 25 percent of liabilities. See CPP Investment Board, "Annual Report, 2002," and www.cppib.ca/invest/results/index.html (accessed 05/05/03).

30. Thomas Michl, "Why We Should Fund Social Security Permanently," *Challenge*, vol. 44, no. 6 (November–December, 2001), pp. 78–92; and Thomas Michl, "Prefunding Is Still the Answer," *Challenge*, vol. 45, no. 3 (May–June 2002), pp. 112–116.

31. Robert William Fogel, *The Fourth Great Awakening and the Future of Egalitarianism* (Chicago: University of Chicago Press, 2000), pp. 184–201, 238. On the issue of time in retirement, see also Teresa Ghilarducci, *The Attack on Retirement* (Princeton: Princeton University Press, forthcoming). See Chapter 17 in this book for further discussion of time-related issues.

32. Robin Blackburn, *Banking on Death, Or, Investing in Life: The History and Future of Pensions* (London and New York: Verso, 2002). A related effort by President Carter's 1979 Commission on Pension Policy (whose primary report was "Coming of Age: Toward a National Retirement Income Policy") proposed a mandatory universal pension system (MUPS), which would have required all employers to contribute 3 percent of payroll for all employees twenty-five or older with at least one year of service with the company, instituted instant vesting of pension rights, and enhanced pension portability. See Spencer Rich, "All Employers Are Asked to Set Up Pension Plans," *Washington Post,* February 27, 1981, p. D1. Also, see page 22 in this book for Clinton's related USA accounts proposal.

33. Blackburn, *Banking on Death,* pp. 469–471. For the original Swedish Meidner Plan, see Rudolf Meidner, *Employee Investment Funds: An Approach to Collective Capital Formation* (Boston: Allen & Unwin, 1978). A detailed account of the evolution and implementation of the Meidner Plan in all its various drafts can be found in Jonas Pontusson, *The Limits to Social Democracy: Investment Politics in Sweden* (Ithaca, N.Y.: Cornell University Press, 1992). For other historical and political accounts see Donald Sassoon, *One Hundred Years of Socialism: The West European Left in the Twentieth Century* (New York: The New Press, 1996); and Robert L. Heilbroner, "The Swedish Promise," *New York Review of Books,* vol. 27, no.19 (December 4, 1980). Blackburn, a former editor of *New Left Review,* has offered an interesting defense of his approach (and, implicitly, of similar strategies involving mixes of ownership) against critics on the left; see Blackburn, *Banking on Death,* p. 524.

34. U.S. Census Bureau, *Statistical Abstract of the United States, 2002,* table 112; Bureau of Economic Analysis, Gross Domestic Product, www.bea.gov/bea/dn/ nipaweb/index.asp, table 1.1; Center for Medicare and Medicaid Services, "National Health Care Expenditure Projections: 2002–2012," www.cms.hhs .gov/statistics/nhe/projections-2002/proj2002.pdf; Graham T. T. Molitor, "Millennial Perspectives on Employee Benefit Changes: The Impact on the Financial Modernization Act," *Vital Speeches of the Day,* vol. 66, no. 15 (May 15, 2000), pp. 457–471; and Stephen Heffler, Sheila Smith, Sean Keehan, M. Kent Clemens, Mark Zezza, and Christopher Truffer, "Health Spending Projections Through 2013," *Health Affairs,* Health Tracking Trends Web Exclusive, February 11, 2004, content.healthaffairs.org/cgi/content/full/hlthaff.w4.79v1/DC1 (accessed 03/30/04).

35. Robert J. Mills and Shailesh Bhandari, "Health Insurance Coverage in the United States: 2002," U.S. Census Bureau, September 2003, www.census.gov/ prod/2003pubs/p60-223.pdf (accessed 10/06/03). For Medicare estimates, see irm.wharton.upenn.edu/WP-Fiscal-Smetters.pdf (accessed 07/05/04).

36. Victor R. Fuchs, "Provide, Provide: The Economics of Aging," NBER Working Paper No. 6642, July 1998; Victor R. Fuchs, "The Future of Health Economics," NBER Working Paper No. 7379, October, 1999; and U.S. Census Bureau, Population Division, Population Projections Branch, "National Population Projections: Total Population by Age, Sex, Race, and Hispanic Origin," www .census.gov/population/www/projections/natsum-T3.html (accessed 05/14/03).

37. Cover the Uninsured, cochaired by former presidents Gerald Ford and Jimmy Carter, is sponsored by, among others, the U.S. Chamber of Commerce, the AFL-CIO and affiliated unions SEIU and AFSCME, Healthcare Leadership Council, the American Medical Association, Health Insurance Association of

America, Families USA, Blue Cross and Blue Shield Association, Catholic Health Association of the United States, AARP, United Way of America, and the Robert Wood Johnson Foundation, www.coveringtheuninsured.org (accessed 05/06/03); Milt Freudenheim, "Businesses Begin to Consider the Cost for the Uninsured," *New York Times*, March 6, 2003. Various states have attempted different approaches to extending health care. The early to mid-1990s generated efforts, through the Medicare and Medicaid waiver programs, to extend health care in such states as Vermont, Oregon, Hawaii, and Tennessee, among others. More far-reaching efforts in California, Massachusetts, and Maine (each of which has bills pending) would set up single-payer health care plans within the state: *Health Policy Reform in America: Innovations from the States*, ed. Howard M. Leichter (Armonk, N.Y.: M.E. Sharpe, 1997); and "Summaries of Universal Health Care Legislation in the States," Universal Health Care Action Network, www.uhcan.org/files/states/UHC_reformplans.html (accessed 06/04/04). Related to this, the Maine Rx program, approved in 2003 by the Supreme Court, is among the more far-reaching state prescription drug efforts. It allows the state to use its role in Medicaid to bargain for lower drug prices for all low-income citizens. The National Conference of State Legislatures maintains an extensive database of state health care and prescription drug programs. See "State Pharmaceutical Assistance Programs," National Conference of State Legislatures, www.ncsl.org/programs/health/drugaid.htm (accessed 05/29/03).

38. Tom Hamburger, "Big Business Upset with Bush Health Reforms," *Star Tribune* (Minneapolis), February 7, 1992, p. D1. Statistics from the U.S. Bureau of Economic Analysis support this dramatic rise. Total employer contributions for employee group health care rose over 3,000 percent, from $5.9 million in 1965 to $192.8 million in 1991, a period in which pretax corporate profits quadrupled (before adjusting for inflation). Bureau of Economic Analysis, tables 6.11, 6.17, www.bea.gov/bea/dn/nipaweb/index.asp (accessed 05/25/04).

39. Kathleen Day, "Corporate America at Odds Over Curing Health Care System," *Washington Post*, April 13, 1993, p. D1. Jane Baird, "Reformers' Ad Blitz Rips Health Insurers; All Sides Intensifying Their Lobbying," *Houston Chronicle*, January 25, 1994, p. 1; and Bennett Roth, "2 Business Groups Differ on Key Health Plan Mandate," *Houston Chronicle*, April 15, 1994, p. 5.

40. John B. Judis, "Abandoned Surgery," *The American Prospect*, vol. 6, no. 21 (March 21, 1995).

41. Robin Toner and Sheryl Gay Stolberg, "Decade After Health Care Crisis, Soaring Costs Bring New Strains," *New York Times*, August 11, 2002, p. A1; Ceci Connolly and Amy Goldstein, "Health Insurance Back as Key Issue," *Washington Post*, March 16, 2003, p. A5; and Gerard F. Anderson, Uwe E. Reinhardt, Peter S. Hussey, and Varduhi Petrosyan, "It's the Prices, Stupid: Why the United States Is So Different from Other Countries," *Health Affairs*, vol. 22, no. 3 (May–June 2003) pp. 89–103.

42. For estimates of savings that a single-payer system may offer over present plans, see, among others, Edie Rasell, "Universal Coverage: How Do We Pay for It?" Economic Policy Institute, June 1998, michuhcan.tripod.com/finance.htm (accessed 05/06/03). See also the review of recent research by Professor Michael McCally of the Oregon Health and Sciences University—and his conclusion that "a combination of single-payer and universal national health insurance is the only reform option that can provide high quality healthcare for all without increasing overall healthcare spending." Michael McCally,

"Single-Payer National Health Insurance," *Oregon's Future* (Fall 2002), www.willamette.edu/publicpolicy/OregonsFuture/PDFvol3no2/F2Mccally20.pdf (accessed 04/30/03), pp. 20–23.

17. A TWENTY-FIVE-HOUR WEEK?

1. Joseph S. Zeisel, "The Workweek in American Industry, 1850–1956," *Monthly Labor Review*, vol. 81, no. 1 (January 1958), pp. 23–29; and Benjamin Kline Hunnicutt, *Work Without End: Abandoning Shorter Hours for the Right to Work* (Philadelphia: Temple University Press, 1988), p. 1.

2. Data on the average American workweek from Bureau of Labor Statistics, "Characteristics of the Employed from the Current Population Survey," table 19, ftp://ftp.bls.gov/pub/special.requests/lf/aa2000/AAT19.TXT (accessed 11/03/03). Share of workers working forty or more hours a week from OECD, "Labour Force Statistics 1982–2002, 2003 Edition," www.oecd.org/scripts/cde/members/lfsdataauthenticate.asp (accessed 11/03/03). In 2000 the average American worker worked 126 more hours than the average British worker, 334 more hours than the French, and 371 hours more than the German. See OECD, "Labour Force Statistics 1982–2002, 2003 Edition," www.oecd.org/scripts/cde/members/lfsdataauthenticate.asp (accessed 11/03/03). In large part because of different data collection methods, there has been debate over the precise number of annual hours worked in different countries. However, the overall trends are not in doubt. For a useful overview, see *Working Time in Comparative Perspective, Vol. I: Patterns, Trends, and the Policy Implications for Earnings Inequality and Unemployment*, eds. Ging Wong and Garnett Picot (Kalamazoo, Mich.: W. E. Upjohn Institute for Employment Research, 2001); and *Working Time: International Trends, Theory and Policy Perspectives*, eds. Lonnie Golden and Deborah M. Figart (New York: Routledge, 2000).

3. For the average U.S. vacation, see Bureau of Labor Statistics, Employment Benefits Survey, table 4, "Average paid holidays and days of paid vacation and paid sick leave, full-time employees, 1997," www.bls.gov/news.release/ebs3.t04.htm (accessed 11/03/03); for European vacation requirements, see International Labor Law Committee, *International Labor and Employment Laws*, 2 vols. (Washington, D.C.: Bureau of National Affairs, 1997), 2002 supplements. The OECD estimates, used here in order to achieve comparability with other countries, utilize a specific methodology that makes it appear that average annual hours in the United States fell by four hours between 1979 and 2000. However, direct estimates of the change in work hours indicate a very significant increase in U.S. hours worked. (See chapter 15 and related endnotes in this book.) In England OECD estimates indicate annual work-time declined relative to American worktime by 103 hours. Despite continued American stereotypes of the workaholic Japanese, average annual work hours in Japan declined by 305 hours from 1979 to 2000 and are currently lower than U.S. annual work hours. See also Steven Greenhouse, "Americans' International Lead in Hours Worked Grew in 90's, Report Shows," *New York Times*, September 1, 2001, p. A8.

4. James T. Bond, Ellen Galinsky, and Jennifer E. Swanberg, *The 1997 National Study of the Changing Workforce* (New York: Families and Work Institute, 1998), Executive Summary, p. 8, www.familiesandwork.org/summary/nscw.pdf (accessed 11/15/02).

5. I have chosen the extremely cautious "sixfold" growth estimate because of well-known deficiencies in data in the early years of the twentieth century. Official statistics suggest that per capita growth in the twentieth century may well have been sevenfold. This, projected forward, would yield $250,000 per capita or $1 million for families or groups of four by century's end. 1900 GNP per capita (in 2003 dollars) was estimated to be $5,214 (GDP per capita was slightly lower); in 2000 it was $36,732 (in 2003 dollars). For the earlier figure, see *Historical Statistics of the United States, Colonial Times to 1970, Part 1* (Washington, D.C.: U.S. Department of Commerce, 1975), p. 224, table F1-5. For the current figure, see Bureau of Economic Analysis, National Income and Product Accounts tables 1.1.5, 2.1, www.bea.gov/bea/dn/nipaweb/index.asp, (accessed 05/20/04). Projecting similar growth in per capita GDP over the twenty-first century using Census intermediate projections of population growth implies a 2.7 percent annual growth in GDP. The Social Security Trustees Report makes conservative projections of GDP. Projecting their assumptions forward to 2100 yields an annual average GDP growth estimate of 1.94 percent and annual average population growth of 0.7 percent (using the "low cost" estimates of population growth, which are closer to the Census intermediate projections of population growth). See also Angus Maddison's estimate that GDP per capita increased by a factor of 6.8 between 1894 and 1994. Angus Maddison, *Monitoring the World Economy, 1820–1992* (Paris: Development Centre of the Organization for Economic Co-Operation and Development, 1995), pp. 196–197. For more on per capita output growth see Richard Du Boff, *Accumulation and Power: An Economic History of the United States* (Armonk, N.Y.: M. E. Sharpe, 1989), p. 196. See also Social Security Administration, 2004, "The 2004 Annual Report of the Board of Trustees of the Federal Old-Age and Survivors Insurance and Disability Insurance Trust Funds," Washington, D.C.: Social Security Administration, tables V.A2 and V.B2, www.ssa.gov/OACT/TR/TR04/ (accessed 05/25/04).

6. European Industrial Relations Observatory, "2002 Annual Review for France" (European Foundation for the Improvement of Living and Working Conditions, March 2003), www.eiro.eurofound.ie/2003/01/Feature/FR0301108F.html (accessed 07/23/03); "French Slash Work Hours," *Labour Research*, vol. 90, no. 5 (May 1, 2001), pp. 20–22; Anders Hayden, "The Price of Time," *New Internationalist*, no. 307 (November 1998), p. 16, www.newint.org/issue307/contents. html (accessed 04/28/03); European Industrial Relations Observatory, "IG Metall Discusses Working Time Policy" (European Foundation for the Improvement of Living and Working Conditions, November 2002), www.eiro.eurofound.ie/2002/11/feature/DE0211204F.html (accessed 10/06/03); European Industrial Relations Observatory, "IG Metall Suffers Defeat Over 35-hour Week in East German Metalworking" (European Foundation for the Improvement of Living and Working Conditions, July 2003), www.eiro.eurofound.ie/2003/07/Feature/DE0307204F.html (accessed 10/06/03); and European Industrial Relations Observatory, "Working Time Developments—2002" (European Foundation for the Improvement of Living and Working Conditions, March 2003), www.eiro.eurofound.ie/about/2003/03/update/TN0303103U.html (accessed 09/24/03).

7. Juliet B. Schor, *The Overworked American: The Unexpected Decline of Leisure* (New York: Basic Books, 1992), p. 147.

8. Robert William Fogel, *The Fourth Great Awakening and the Future of Egalitarianism* (Chicago: University of Chicago Press, 2000), pp. 183–188, 194–201, 238.

9. Labor leaders have been appropriately worried about proposals that trade time reductions for greater "flexibility," since often these involve forced imposition of uncertainty about working time, and are tailored to enhance employer responsiveness to the business cycle with little regard to the individual preferences of the employee. In Europe such proposals also have been viewed as a Trojan horse aimed at rolling back previous union gains over shop floor working practices. The issue surfaced in the United States in a 2003 congressional battle over a bill allowing employers to offer compensatory time as an alternative to overtime pay for work beyond forty hours a week. As of this writing, the Bush legislation is stalled in Congress. See Helen Dewar, "Senate Rebuffs Bush, Blocks New Rules on Overtime Pay," *Washington Post*, May 5, 2004, p. A4. For labor's resistance to time-flexibility trade-offs, see Karl Hinrichs, William Roche, and Carmen Sirianni, "From Standardization to Flexibility: Changes in the Political Economy of Working Time," and Carmen Sirianni, "The Self-Management of Time in Postindustrial Society," both in *Working Time in Transition: The Political Economy of Working Hours in Industrial Nations,* eds. Karl Hinrichs, William Roche, and Carmen Sirianni (Philadelphia: Temple University Press, 1991); and Kim Moody, *Workers in a Lean World* (New York: Verso, 1997). For the U.S. comp time battle see Steven Greenhouse, "Bill Offers Option of Compensatory Time," *New York Times*, May 10, 2003, p. A15.

10. Schor, *The Overworked American,* pp. 146–147.

11. "Employment Options for the Future: Actual and Preferred Working Hours, National Report on Austria" (Dublin: European Foundation for the Improvement of Living and Working Conditions, 2000), www.eurofound.ie/working/options/austria.doc (accessed 12/11/02); and Marco Biaggi et al., "Employment Options of the Future: Actual and Preferred Working Hours, Italian Report—First Draft" (Dublin: European Foundation for the Improvement of Living and Working Conditions, 2000), www.eurofound.ie/working/options/italy.doc (accessed 12/11/02). Italian law provides for incentives aimed at the reduction and reorganization of working time to increase employment. The incentives—subsidies to employers, social security contribution credits, and/or phased retirement subsidies—are primarily directed to situations where reduced work-time favors new hiring and where full-time contracts are transformed into part-time in order to avoid layoffs—including *contratti di solidarietà,* special collective bargaining agreements signed at the plant level.

12. As of March 2003, eleven states and the District of Columbia offered a refundable tax credit based on a percentage of the federal Earned Income Tax Credit, ranging from 5 percent and 6 percent of the federal EITC in Oklahoma and Indiana, respectively, to 32 percent in Vermont. The Wisconsin and Minnesota laws adjust for the number of children and/or income and provide refunds worth over 40 percent of the federal EITC for some families. (Five additional states offer nonrefundable tax credits. Montgomery County, Maryland, and Denver, Colorado, also have established local tax credit programs in recent years.) Nicholas Johnson, Joseph Llobrera, and Bob Zahradnik, "A Hand Up: How State Earned Income Tax Credits Help Working Families Escape Poverty in 2003," Summary (Washington, D.C.: Center for Budget and Policy Priorities, March 3, 2003), www.cbpp.org/3-3-03sfp.htm (accessed 02/17/03); and Jerome M. Segal, *Graceful Simplicity: Toward a Philosophy and Politics of Simple Living* (New York: Henry Holt, 1999), pp. 92–95. Segal also proposes addi-

tional legislation that would require "three-day weekends, reduced daily hours, and guaranteed extended vacations" (pp. 86–87).

13. Corporate leaders are concerned not only with costs but also with management prerogatives. Although additional funding is likely to be of very substantial importance, clearly long-term efforts to achieve greater free time ultimately will have to resolve many difficult issues concerning how the flexibility of free time is determined.

14. Sirianni notes a number of other possible reforms that would also "favor voluntary time-income tradeoffs"—including increasing tax "progressivity, reducing the tax incentives for other fringe benefits relative to extra free time, and raising or removing earnings ceilings for the unemployment insurance and Social Security contributions of employers, which encourage them to hire fewer workers for longer hours in order to maximize nontaxable hours of work." Other policies include support for sabbaticals, social service activities, and leisure time. A very ambitious proposal—originally offered by Swedish economist Gösta Rehn—would involve government-mandated individual funds that could be drawn on to finance leisure time throughout life (including retirement). Carmen Sirianni, "The Self-Management of Time in Postindustrial Society," and Hinrichs, Roche, and Sirianni, "From Standardization to Flexibility," pp. 8, 265, respectively. Many aspects of the system now operating in the Netherlands involve individual choice; see Peter Berg, Eileen Applebaum, Tom Bailey, and Arne L. Kalleberg, "Contesting Time: International Comparisons of Employee Control of Working Time," www.cww.rutgers.edu/dataPages/CT.pdf (accessed 11/04/03).

15. Ackerman and Alstott, *The Stakeholder Society;* Michl, "Prefunding Is Still the Answer," *Challenge,* vol. 45, no. 3 (May–June 2002), pp. 112–116; Leon Friedman, "A Better Kind of Wealth Tax," *The American Prospect* (November 6, 2000); Phillips, *Wealth and Democracy,* p. 422; Gates, *The Ownership Solution,* p. 217; Robert Kuttner, "Bully for Trump," *The Boston Globe,* November 14, 1999, p. D7; David Cay Johnston, "Dozens of Rich Americans Join in Fight to Retain the Estate Tax," *New York Times,* February 14, 2001, p. 1; Gates and Collins, *Wealth and Our Commonwealth;* and Leon Friedman, "Trump's Wealth Tax," *The Nation,* vol. 269, no. 19 (December 6, 1999), pp. 4–5.

16. Edward N. Wolff, *Top Heavy,* revised ed. (New York: The New Press, 2002), pp. 42–48, 72.

17. Some have objected that this might reduce investment. The experience of other countries, however, suggests there is no clear connection between wealth taxes and savings rates. Other OECD countries, for example, have significant wealth taxes and a savings rate commonly higher than the United States. "Household Saving Rates" (OECD Economic Outlook: Paris, June 2003), annex table 24. In addition, of course, using the proceeds of the wealth tax to encourage low-income savings would add to the funds available for investment. See Wolff, *Top Heavy,* pp. 42–74. There is debate over the constitutionality of a wealth tax or variant based on wealth-related principles. Peter Barnes and Leon Friedman, for instance, hold that such a tax would require a constitutional amendment. See Peter Barnes, "Fair Shares," *New Republic,* available online at www.progress.org/archive/barnes25.htm (accessed 06/16/03); and Leon Friedman, "A Snare-The-Wealth Tax," *The Nation,* vol. 264, no. 1 (January 6, 1997), pp. 23–24. Others disagree: Ackerman and Alstott—in *The Stakeholder Society,* pp. 121–122, 124—argue on the basis of historical precedent that "if stakeholding wins political support, the courts will readily recognize its legitimacy," and that "[t]here is every

reason, then, to suppose that the Court will respond to our taxation initiatives as courts have traditionally responded through the centuries—by upholding the federal government's power to use the tools of taxation to further the majority's vision of social justice." Jeff Gates holds a similar position, though he believes that in practice, amending the Constitution may become politically necessary; see *Democracy at Risk* (Cambridge, Mass.: Perseus, 2000), p. 317. Ackerman has also offered a fully developed legal argument suggesting that the tax is already constitutional and would likely be deemed so; see Bruce Ackerman, "Taxation and the Constitution," *Columbia Law Review*, vol. 99, no. 1 (January 1999), pp. 1–58. Robin Blackburn's proposal of a "share levy" (similar to a wealth tax in that it dilutes existing financial wealth) either might be deemed constitutional already or could probably be configured so as to be constitutional—possibly, for instance, by taxing a certain percentage of corporate profits and either requiring that this be paid in new stock, or providing incentives to do so, or simply collecting the taxes and using the funds to purchase the stock. See Blackburn, *Banking on Death;* and Robin Blackburn, "The Great Pension Crunch," *The Nation*, vol. 276, no. 6 (February 17, 2003), pp. 24–26.

18. Paul Krugman, "America the Polarized," *New York Times*, January 4, 2002, p. A21.
19. Paul Krugman, "Plutocracy and Politics," *New York Times*, June 14, 2002, p. A37; Paul Krugman, "Into the Wilderness," *New York Times*, November 8, 2002, p. A31; Phillips, *Wealth and Democracy*, p. xv; and Robert H. Frank, *Luxury Fever: Why Money Fails to Satisfy in an Era of Excess* (New York: Free Press, 1999), pp. 2, 9, 16–35.
20. Curt Anderson, "Govt. Expands Charges Against Enron Execs," *Washington Post*, May 1, 2003, www.washingtonpost.com/wp-dyn/articles/A64929–2003May1.html (accessed 05/01/03); Joseph Weber, "CFOs on the Hot Seat," *Business Week*, No. 3824 (March 17, 2003), p. 67, via Lexis Nexis; Laura Sullivan, "Ex-Enron Official Accused of Fraud," *Baltimore Sun*, October 3, 2002, p. A1, via Lexis Nexis; Mark Gimein, "The Greedy Bunch: You Bought. They Sold," *Fortune*, September 2, 2002, www.fortune.com (accessed 11/11/02); and Barnaby J. Feder, "Turmoil at WorldCom," *New York Times*, June 28, 2002, p. C6.
21. For the wealthiest 1 percent see "Changes in Household Wealth in the 1980s and 1990s in the U.S.," in *International Perspectives on Household Wealth*, ed. Edward N. Wolfe (Elgar Publishing Ltd., forthcoming), p. 12 of 46 unnumbered pages, table 6. Unpublished estimate of 67.6 percent of financial wealth for the top 5 percent for 2001 provided to the author by Edward Wolff. This was virtually unchanged from the 1998 figure in Edward Wolff, *Recent Trends in Wealth Ownership, 1983–1998*, Jerome Levy Economics Institute Working Paper No. 300, April 2000, table 2, www.levy.org/docs/wrkpap/papers/300.html (accessed 04/05/04). Wolff's definition of financial wealth refers to net marketable wealth less net equity in owner-occupied housing. A Federal Reserve Board paper reached a similar conclusion: the top 5 percent of households ranked by total net worth earned 65 percent of net worth less net equity in primary residence. See Arthur Kennickell, *A Rolling Tide: Changes in the Distribution of Wealth in the U.S., 1989–2001*, Federal Reserve Board, March 2003, www.federalreserve.gov/pubs/oss/oss2/papers/concentration.2001.9.pdf (accessed 04/05/04). See also Edward Wolff, *Recent Trends in Wealth Ownership, 1983–1998; Assets for the Poor: The Benefits of Spreading Asset Ownership*, ed. Thomas Shapiro and Edward Wolff (New York: Russell Sage Foundation, 2001), pp. 34–73, table 2.2; Internal Revenue Service, "Sales of Capital Assets Reported on Individual

Income Tax Returns, 1998 and 1997," IRS Statistics of Income Bulletin, Summer 2002, table 2B; Internal Revenue Service, "Sales of Capital Assets Reported on Individual Income Tax Returns, 1999," IRS Statistics of Income Bulletin, Summer 2003, table 2B. In 1999, of the 127,667,890 tax returns filed, only 204,491 had adjusted gross incomes of $1 million or more. These tax returns made up just over 50 percent of long-term capital gains minus long-term capital loss. (Data analysis provided by Jeff Chapman.)

22. Paul Krugman, "For Richer," *New York Times,* October 20, 2002, Section 6, p. 62. Alan Wolfe quoted in Rick Lyman, "Every Four Years, Blue Bloods Put on a Blue Collar," *New York Times,* October 5, 2003, p. D14.

23. For a general discussion, see Ann B. Barnet and Richard J. Barnet, *The Youngest Minds: Parenting and Genes in the Development of Intellect and Emotion* (New York: Simon & Schuster, 1998); for the significance of early care, see Rima Shore, *Rethinking the Brain: New Insights into Early Development* (New York: Families and Work Institute, 1997); NICHD Early Child Care Research Network, "Mother-Child Interaction and Cognitive Outcomes Associated with Early Child Care: Results of the NICHD Study," Poster Symposium presented at the Biennial Meeting of the Society for Research in Child Development, Washington, D.C., April 1997; Jennifer Ehrle, Gina Adams, and Kathryn Tout, "Who's Caring for Our Youngest Children? Child Care Patterns of Infants and Toddlers," Occasional Paper No. 42 (Washington, D.C.: The Urban Institute, 2001); and Carnegie Task Force on Meeting the Needs of Young Children, *Starting Points: Meeting the Needs of Our Youngest Children* (New York: Carnegie Corporation, 1994).

24. Linda Giannarelli and James Barsimantov, "Child Care Expenses of America's Families" (Washington, D.C.: Urban Institute, December 2000), www.urban.org/url.cfm?ID=310028 (accessed 05/01/03); Natasha Lifton, "Child Care Is a Labor Issue," *Social Policy,* vol. 31, no. 3 (Spring 2001), pp. 4–10; and Karen Schulman, *Issue Brief: The High Cost of Child Care Puts Quality Care Out of Reach for Many Families* (Washington, D.C.: Children's Defense Fund, 2000), p. 1, www.childrensdefense.org/pdf/highcost.pdf (accessed 10/06/03). See also Nancy Folbre, "Universal Childcare: It's Time," *The Nation,* vol. 271, no. 1 (July 3, 2000), pp. 21–23.

25. Arlie Hochschild, *The Second Shift* (New York: Avon Books, 1989), p. 8.

26. Ann Crittenden, *The Price of Motherhood: Why the Most Important Job in the World Is Still the Least Valued* (New York: Metropolitan Books, 2001), p. 22. Juliet Schor calculates that employed mothers now average sixty-five hours of work a week—adding, however, that a Boston study and two nationwide studies of white, married couples estimated women's average workweek at from seventy-six to eighty-nine hours. Schor, *The Overworked American,* p. 21.

27. The Bureau of Labor statistics found that, as a rule, women earned 77 cents for every dollar earned by men in 1999. Stephanie Boraas and William M. Rogers III, "How Does Gender Play a Role in the Earnings Gap? An Update," *Monthly Labor Review,* vol. 126, no. 3 (March 2003), pp. 9–15. This had narrowed very slightly—to 77.5 cents on the dollar, the smallest gap on record—in 2002. Women's pay is still lower than men's across practically all sectors. David Leonhardt, "Gap Between Pay of Men and Women Smallest on Record," *New York Times,* February 17, 2003, p. A1.

28. Crittenden, *The Price of Motherhood,* p. 89. See also Joan Williams, "Why Moms Stay Home," *Washington Post,* Thursday, July 17, 2003, p. A21.

29. Multiple job-holding declines as income increases, but only slightly; from 6.4 percent in the bottom income quintile (in 1995) to 5.9 percent in the highest. Peter Coy, "Who's Working Two Jobs?" *Business Week* (August 28, 1997), www.businessweek.com/1997/36/b3543050.htm (accessed 05/01/03). In 2001 there were 3.6 million women with multiple jobs (47 percent of the total number of workers with multiple jobs, compared to 20 percent in 1973). AFL-CIO, "Facts About Working Women," www.aflcio.org/yourjobeconomy/women/factsaboutworkingwomen.cfm (accessed 05/01/03). For number of earners per household see U.S. Census Bureau, "Historical Income Tables—Households," table H-12, www.census.gov/hhes/income/histinc/h12.html (accessed 05/01/03).

30. Suzanne W. Helburn and Barbara R. Bergmann, *America's Child Care Problem: The Way Out* (New York: St. Martin's Press, 2002), pp. 11, 216; Nancy Folbre, "Universal Childcare: It's Time," *The Nation,* vol. 271, no. 1 (July 3, 2000), p. 23; and Barbara R. Bergmann, "Decent Child Care at Decent Wages," *The American Prospect,* vol. 12, no. 1 (January 1–January 15, 2001). Anne Alstott has suggested a system of "caretaker resource accounts" that would provide $5,000 a year to all parents (at an estimated cost of $100 billion annually) and that could be used for child care, further self-education, or to otherwise partially offset the economic burdens imposed by child-rearing (particularly the adverse effects on women's career development). See Anne L. Alstott, *No Exit: What Parents Owe Their Children—And What Society Owes Parents* (New York: Oxford University Press, 2004).

31. Philip Green, *Retrieving Democracy: In Search of Civic Equality* (Totowa, N.J.: Rowman & Allanheld Publishers, 1985), p. 99.

32. Though wealth-related strategies have yet to be discussed by most feminists, Joan Williams, in particular, has begun to define some of the critical linkages: "Instead of defining equality as allowing women into market work on the terms traditionally available to men, we need to redefine equality as changing the relationship of market and family work so that all adults—men as well as women—can meet both family and work ideals. This new strategy holds far greater potential for raising support for feminism by building effective coalitions between women and men, as well as with unions, the 'time movement,' and children's rights advocates." Joan Williams, *Unbending Gender: Why Family and Work Conflict, and What to Do About It* (Oxford: Oxford University Press, 2000), p. 41.

33. Linda Martin and Kerry Segrave, *The Servant Problem: Domestic Workers in North America* (Jefferson, N.C.: McFarland & Company, 1985), pp. 32–33. An insightful study of the sociology of race and class in domestic work is Mary Romero, *Maid in the U.S.A.* (New York: Routledge, 1992).

34. Dolores Hayden, "What Would A Non-Sexist City Be Like?", p. 173.

18. BEYOND SUPER-ELITES AND CONSPICUOUS CONSUMPTION: REAL ECOLOGICAL SUSTAINABILITY IN THE TWENTY-FIRST CENTURY

1. Peter M. Vitousek et al., "Human Alterations of the Global Nitrogen Cycle: Sources and Consequences," *Ecological Applications,* vol. 7, no. 3 (August 1997), pp. 737–750; Elena Bennett and Steve R. Carpenter, "P Soup," *World-Watch* magazine, vol. 15, no. 2 (March–April 2002), pp. 24–32.

2. *World Resources 2000–2001: People and Ecosystems: The Fraying Web of Life* (Washington, D.C.: World Resources Institute, 2000), p. 27; The Worldwatch Institute, *Vital Signs 2002* (New York: W.W. Norton, 2002), pp. 28, 38, 52; and Ralph C. Kirby and Andrew S. Prokoprovitsh, "Technological Insurance Against Shortages in Minerals and Metals," *Science*, vol. 191, no. 4227 (February 20, 1976), pp. 713–719.

3. Kenneth Boulding quoted in John S. Dryzek, *Rational Ecology* (Oxford, U.K.: Basil Blackwell, 1987), p. 73.

4. Ed Ayres, *God's Last Offer: Negotiating for a Sustainable Future* (New York: Four Walls Eight Windows, 1999), p. 34.

5. Thorstein Veblen, *The Theory of the Leisure Class* (New York: Macmillan, 1912).

6. Juliet B. Schor, *The Overspent American: Upscaling, Downshifting, and the New Consumer* (New York: Basic Books, 1998), p. 15; and U.S. Census Bureau, "Families by Median and Mean Income: 1947 to 2001," table F-5, www.census.org/hhes/income/histinc/fo5.html (accessed 06/18/03).

7. Richard Easterlin, "Will Raising the Incomes of All Increase the Happiness of All?" *Journal of Economic Behavior and Organization*, vol. 27, no. 1 (1995), pp. 35–47; and Alan Thein Durning, "Are We Happy Yet?" in *Ecopsychology*, eds. Theodore Roszak, Mary E. Gomes, and Allen D. Kanner (San Francisco: Sierra Club Books, 1995), pp. 70–76, esp. 71, citing National Opinion Research Center surveys. See also Richard Layard, "Happiness: Has Social Science a Clue?" Lionel Robbins Memorial Lectures 2002/3, delivered on March 3–5, 2003, London School of Economics, cep.lse.ac.uk (accessed 04/28/03); and Robert Edwards Lane, *The Loss of Happiness in Market Democracies* (New Haven: Yale University Press, 2000).

8. Juliet B. Schor, "What's Wrong with Consumer Society? Competitive Spending and the 'New Consumerism'," in *Consuming Desires*, ed. Roger Rosenblatt (Washington, D.C.: Island Press, 1999), pp. 37–50, esp. 46.

9. Recent studies have begun to give more precision to our understanding of the impact of growing inequality on measures of happiness and welfare as defined in economic and other theory. See Richard Layard, "Happiness: Has Social Science a Clue?" Lionel Robbins Memorial Lectures 2002/3, delivered on March 3–5, 2003, London School of Economics, cep.lse.ac.uk (accessed 04/28/03); and Robert Edwards Lane, *The Loss of Happiness in Market Democracies* (New Haven: Yale University Press, 2000).

10. Robert H. Frank, "The Victimless Income Gap?" *New York Times*, April 12, 1999, p. A25. See also Frank, *Luxury Fever*.

11. Paul Krugman, "Plutocracy and Politics," *New York Times*, June 14, 2002, p. A37; Krugman's data drawn from Phillips, *Wealth and Democracy*, pp. 151–153.

12. Schor, *The Overspent American*, pp. 164–165; and Americans for Tax Reform, "McCain Declares War on the Internet," www.atr.org/pressreleases/2000/021500pr-2.html (accessed 04/28/03).

13. The luxury pen market has grown over 20 percent in recent years. Simon Brooke, "The Pen Is Mightier," *Financial Times* (London), January 4, 2003, p. 8, via Lexis Nexis. Montblanc has introduced a new line of styluses for personal digital assistants (the pointers with which one taps the screen)—ranging from a mere $1,465 for a stainless steel model to the all-platinum version for $3,910. "We All Live in a Private Submarine," *Too Much*, vol. 8, no. 3 (Winter 2003), p. 5; Joann S. Lublin, "Fountain-Pen Fashion: Try 5,072 Diamonds Or Abe Lincoln's DNA," *Wall Street Journal*, August 24, 2002, p. A1; Mark Levine,

"The $19,450 Phone," *New York Times Magazine,* December 1, 2002; Guy Tre-
bay, "Faster Than Croesus: A Formula One for Success," *New York Times,* April
7, 2002; and Warren Brown, "Exotic, Exclusive—and Expensive," *Washington
Post,* November 10, 2002, p. N1. The uncertain economy has not dampened
luxury sales; see Tracie Rozhon, "A Rebound for U.S. Luxury Goods," *New York
Times,* October 14, 2003, p. C1.

14. Frank, *Luxury Fever,* pp. 214–215.

15. Salary costs over $1 million are not deductible under current law. Rep. Martin
Sabo, "The Income Equity Act of 2001 (H.R. 2691)," www.house.gov/sabo/
IEPage107th.htm (accessed 12/10/02).

16. Other strategies might build upon wage supplement programs like those urged
by Edmund Phelps. See Edmund S. Phelps, *Rewarding Work: How to Restore Participation and Self-Support to Free Enterprise* (Cambridge, Mass.: Harvard University Press, 1997).

17. Office of Management and Budget, *Budget of the United States 2005: Historical
Tables* (Washington, D.C.: Government Printing Office, 2004), w3.access.gpo
.gov/usbudget/fy2004/pdf/hist.pdf (accessed 08/22/03), pp. 31–32, table 2.2. For
2003 numbers see Congress of the United States, Joint Economic Committee,
"U.S. Corporate Taxes are Very Low from Both an Historical and International
Perspective," November 6, 2003, jec.senate.gov/democrats/Documents/Releases/
dc6nov2003.pdf (accessed 05/25/04); and Laura Mansnerus, "Corporate Tax
Deal Ends Trenton Budget Standoff," *New York Times,* July 3, 2002.

18. David Bollier, *Public Assets, Private Profits: Reclaiming the American Commons in
an Age of Market Enclosure* (Washington, D.C.: New America Foundation,
2001), pp. 60, 79.

19. Bollier, *Public Assets, Private Profits,* p. 41.

20. Peter Barnes, *Who Owns the Sky? Our Common Assets and the Future of Capitalism*
(Washington, D.C.: Island Press, 2001), pp. 71, 119. The Climate Stewardship
Act of 2003, introduced by Senators Lieberman and McCain, is in part based on
the concepts described in the Sky Trust. For a discussion see www.usskytrust.org.

21. If achieved, slower growth might alter these replacement rates. On the other
hand, implementation of strategies important to ecological sustainability in
general, and in particular to renewable energy and perhaps a hydrogen-based
economy, might require even greater investment. Based on Bureau of Economic Analysis estimates of service life, "BEA Depreciation Rates, Service
Lives, and Declining-Balances Rates," www.bea.doc.gov/bea/an/0597niw/
tableA.htm (accessed 12/10/02).

22. Tim Kasser and Richard M. Ryan, "A Dark Side of the American Dream: Cor-
relates of Financial Success as a Central Life Aspiration," *Journal of Personality
and Social Psychology,* vol. 65, no. 2 (1993), p. 420; Paul L. Wachtel, *The Poverty
of Affluence: A Psychological Portrait of the American Way of Life* (New York: The
Free Press, 1983), p. 65. See also Aric Rindfleisch and James E. Burroughs,
"Materialism and Childhood Satisfaction: A Social-Structural Analysis,"
Advances in Consumer Research, vol. 26 (1999), pp. 519–526; Raymond De
Young, "Expanding and Evaluating Motives for Environmentally Responsible
Behavior," *Journal of Social Issues,* vol. 56, no. 3 (Fall 2000), pp. 509–526; James
B. Allen and Jennifer L. Ferrand, "Environmental Locus of Control, Sympathy,
and Proenvironmental Behavior," *Environment and Behavior,* vol. 31, no. 3
(May 1999), pp. 338–353; Stephen Kaplan, "Human Nature and Environ-
mentally Responsible Behavior," *Journal of Social Issues,* vol. 56, no. 3 (Fall

2000), pp. 491–508; and Tim Kasser, *The High Price of Materialism* (Cambridge, Mass.: M.I.T. Press, 2002).

23. Thomas Michael Power, "The Pursuit of Quality," *Orion* (Summer 1993), pp. 30–35, esp. p. 34.

24. Barry Feig, *Marketing Straight to the Heart* (New York: American Management Association, 1997), pp. 9, 23–39.

25. See also Carmen Sirianni, who urges support for activities like those discussed in chapter 3 in this book that in a regime of greater free time facilitate "individual and community self-help and service, ecologically sound cooperative and craft production, as well as athletic and leisure pursuits . . . [and] for community activities that reinforce local solidarities and *gemeinschaftliche* relationships, and . . . the provision of service and care in less bureaucratic ways." Sirianni, "The Self-Management of Time in Postindustrial Society," pp. 259–260. See also Andre Gorz, *Reclaiming Work: Beyond the Wage-Based Society*, trans. Chris Turner (Cambridge, U.K.: Polity Press, 1999).

26. For information on the Army Corps of Engineers, see Public Employees for Environmental Responsibility, "Army Corps Wetlands Report Card," www.peer.org/corps/Report02.html (accessed 12/13/02); and Gary Cartwright, "Eerie Canal," *Texas Monthly*, vol. 24, no. 7 (July 1996), pp. 82–93. On the more general problem see David Armstrong, "The Nation's Dirty, Big Secret," *Boston Globe*, November 14, 1999, p. A1; and H. Basic and A. Kung, "America's Worst Polluter," *Rolling Stone*, no. 577 (May 3, 1990), p. 47. On the Soviet record see Murray Feshbach and Alfred Friendly, Jr., *Ecocide in the USSR* (New York: Basic Books, 1992). See pages 96–97 in this book for information on public utilities.

19. CODA: TWENTY-FIRST-CENTURY POPULISM

1. Lawrence Goodwyn, *Democratic Promise: A Populist Moment in America* (New York: Oxford University Press, 1976), p. 614. For a general history of populism in America, see Michael Kazin, *The Populist Persuasion: An American History* (Ithaca, N.Y.: Cornell University Press, 1998). See also Harry C. Boyte, *Everyday Politics* (September 2004).

PART V: TOWARD A MORALLY COHERENT POLITICS

1. Douglass C. North, *The Economic Growth of the United States, 1790–1860* (New York: W.W. Norton, 1966), p. 17; U.S. Census Bureau, *Rank by Population of the 100 Largest Urban Places, Listed Alphabetically by State: 1790–1990;* and U.S. Census Bureau, *Population of the 24 Urban Places: 1790,* both at www.census.gov/population/documentation/twps0027/tab02.txt (accessed 11/22/02).

2. Alexander Keyssar, *The Right to Vote: The Contested History of Democracy in the United States* (New York: Basic Books, 2000), p. 7; and U.S. Census Bureau, *Historical Statistics of the United States: Colonial Times to 1970, Part 2* (Washington, D.C.: Government Printing Office, 1976), p. 1104.

3. U.S. Census Bureau, *Statistical Abstract of the United States: 2002*, pp. 30, 31, tables 28, 29.

4. The first U.S. edition of Adam Smith's *Wealth of Nations* appeared in 1789: see Daniel J. Boorstin, "Foreword," in *The Timetables of History: A Horizontal Linkage of People and Events,* 3rd ed., ed. Bernard Grun (New York: Simon & Schuster, 1991). For Adam Smith's strictures on corporations, see Scott R. Bowman,

The Modern Corporation and American Political Thought (University Park, Penn.: Pennsylvania University Press, 1996), pp. 320–321, note 64.

5. Data for the early period are obviously limited. One of the most useful estimates, that of historian Edwin Perkins of the University of Southern California, is that per capita income in the colonies in the 1770s (for the free population) was equivalent to $1,805 (2002 dollars). Actual income per capita in 2002 was $31,034. The 1770s figure is roughly 6 percent of the modern figure. Edward Perkins, *The Economy of Colonial America* (New York: Columbia University Press, 1988), p. 212; Thomas Weiss and Donald Schaefer, "Introduction," *American Economic Development in Historical Perspective*, eds. Thomas Weiss and Donald Schaefer (Stanford, Calif.: Stanford University Press, 1994), p. 2; and Bureau of Economic Analysis, "National Income and Product Accounts Tables," table 1.9, www.bea.gov/bea/dn/nipaweb/index.asp (accessed 04/28/03).

6. See James Burke, "Inventors and Inventions—Accidents Plus Luck: The Sum of Innovation Is Greater Than Its Parts," *Time*, vol. 156, no. 22 (December 4, 2000).

CONCLUSION: THE CHALLENGE OF THE ERA OF TECHNOLOGICAL ABUNDANCE

1. For an earlier formulation of some of these themes see Gar Alperovitz, "Distributing Our Technological Inheritance," *Technology Review*, vol. 97, no. 9 (October 1994), pp. 31–36.

2. An important illustration of the relationship of norms to public policy involves accepted child labor laws that regularly challenge free-market doctrine. For a discussion see Dani Rodrik, *Has Globalization Gone Too Far?* (Washington, D.C.: Institute for International Economics, 1997).

3. For a forceful statement of the argument that there is "surging discontent just below the surface" of the U.S. political system, see Walter Dean Burnham, "Whole Lotta Shakin' Goin' On: A Political Realignment Is on the Way," *The Nation*, vol. 270, no. 15 (April 17, 2000), pp. 11–15.

4. William J. Baumol, "Rapid Economic Growth, Equitable Income Distribution, and the Optimal Range of Innovation Spillovers," in *Economic Events, Ideas, and Policies: The 1960s and After*, eds. George L. Perry and James Tobin (Washington, D.C.: Brookings Institution Press, 2000), p. 27.

5. Robert M. Solow, Nobel Prize Lecture, December 8, 1987, www.nobel.se/economics/laureates/1987/solow-lecture.html (accessed 05/13/03); Barry Bluestone and Bennett Harrison, *Growing Prosperity: The Battle for Growth with Equity in the Twenty-first Century* (Berkeley: University of California Press, 2000), pp. 105–106; Edward F. Denison, *Accounting for United States Economic Growth 1929–1969* (Washington, D.C.: The Brookings Institution, 1974), p. 79; and Edward F. Denison, *Trends in American Economic Growth, 1929–1982* (Washington, D.C.: The Brookings Institution, 1985), p. 28.

6. Joel Mokyr, *The Lever of Riches: Technological Creativity and Economic Progress* (New York: Oxford University Press, 1990), p. 3.

7. Seth Shulman, *Owning the Future* (Boston: Houghton Mifflin, 1999), p. 155.

8. Bob Thompson, "Sharing the Wealth?" *Washington Post*, April 13, 2003, p. W8; and Gates and Collins, *Wealth and Our Commonwealth*.

9. Letter from Herbert A. Simon, reproduced as "Herbert Simon, the Flat Tax and Our Common Patrimony," *Basic Income*, no. 29, Newsletter of the Basic Income

European Network (Spring 1998), www.bien.be/Files/Newsletter/BINews29. pdf (accessed 01/06/03). In fact, per capita GDP was $31,830 in 1998.

10. As previously noted, Edward Perkins estimates that per capita income in the colonies in the 1770s (for the free population) was roughly equivalent to $1,805 (2002 dollars). See the Introduction to Part V, note 5 in this book. Actual income per capita in 2002 was $31,034. The 1770s figure is approximately 6 percent of the modern figure. If, on a rough assumption, individuals worked as hard in both periods, the extraordinary seventeen-fold increase is a rough measure of the contribution of inherited technology and capital accumulation in the United States over this time period. And—given the longer hours commonly worked in the earlier period—there is every reason to believe that this is a conservative estimate. Edward Perkins, *The Economy of Colonial America* (New York: Columbia University Press, 1988), p. 212; Thomas Weiss and Donald Schaefer, "Introduction," in *American Economic Development in Historical Perspective*, eds. Thomas Weiss and Donald Schaefer (Stanford, Calif.: Stanford University Press, 1994), p. 2; and Bureau of Economic Analysis, "National Income and Product Accounts Tables," table 1.9, www.bea.gov/bea/dn/nipaweb/index.asp (accessed 04/28/03). See also Moses Abramovitz and Paul David, "American Macroeconomic Growth in the Era of Knowledge-Based Progress: The Long Run Perspective," *The Cambridge Economic History of the United States*, Vol. III, *The Twentieth Century*, eds. Stanley Engerman and Robert Gallman (Cambridge: Cambridge University Press, 2000), pp. 1–92; and Joseph Stiglitz, "Public Policy for a Knowledge Economy," address delivered to the Department for Trade and Industry and Center for Economic Policy Research, London (January 17, 1999), p. 1.

Index